Contemporary States and the Crisis of the Western Order

STUDIES IN EUROPEAN INTEGRATION, STATE AND SOCIETY

Edited by Magdalena Góra, Zdzisław Mach and Katarzyna Zielińska

VOLUME 7

PETER LANG

Marek Aleksander Cichocki (ed.)

Contemporary States and the Crisis of the Western Order

PETER LANG

Bibliographic Information published by the Deutsche Nationalbibliothek
The Deutsche Nationalbibliothek lists this publication in the Deutsche Nationalbibliografie; detailed bibliographic data is available online at http://dnb.d-nb.de.

Library of Congress Cataloging-in-Publication Data
A CIP catalog record for this book has been applied for at the Library of Congress.

The texts in this publication are synthesis of the research conducted by the Natolin European Centre in 2017-2019 as a part of the "Dialog" programme financed by the Ministry of Science and Higher Education (Poland). The decision number: 0104/DLG/2017/10.

DIALOG

NATOLIN EUROPEAN CENTRE

Printed by CPI books GmbH, Leck.
ISSN 2193-2352
ISBN 978-3-631-80390-5 (Print)
E-ISBN 978-3-631-80951-8 (E-PDF)
E-ISBN 978-3-631-80952-5 (EPUB)
E-ISBN 978-3-631-80953-2 (MOBI)
DOI 10.3726/b16460

Peter Lang – Berlin · Bern · Bruxelles · New York · Oxford · Warszawa · Wien

This publication has been peer reviewed.

www.peterlang.com

Contents

Marek Cichocki

Introduction

This book is the result of a project carried out in 2017–2019 at the Natolin European Centre Foundation by a team of Polish scholars.[1] The main objectives of this project encompassed an analysis of attitudes and behaviours adopted by contemporary European countries, including Poland, in response to the crisis of the existing international order, which emerged in Europe and in the world after the end of the Cold War in 1989.

The research problem framed in this way was aimed at contributing – after the required analyses were carried out – to finding answers to two underlying questions:

- What is a state in the contemporary world, and are we still dealing with a specifically European model of the state, different from models functioning in other parts of the world?
- How to properly define the nature and scope of the current crisis of the Western (liberal) concept of international order with its unique element – European integration?

There is little doubt that the current crisis can be boiled down to the issue of geopolitics in modern international relations, the rivalry between old and new powers and challenging the liberal concept of globalisation. This is also not the case of a purely structural crisis, evidenced by the insufficiency and failings of the increasingly inefficient and overburdened institutions and mechanisms tasked with maintaining the existing order. It is also a crisis of a certain model and ideas of order, which – above all, as a result of the financial and migration crisis in Europe – were invalidated by reality and must be reconsidered.

What is the behaviour of European countries in this context? Do they serve as a factor reinforcing the crisis of the current order, or are they rather a necessary starting point for creating an opportunity to resolve the crisis and re-emerge

1 Research project "Resources of the humanities for building and improving the integrated state management model in the light of the dynamics of crises and threats. The dialogue between the humanities and the administration, and the challenges facing Poland", financed under the "Dialog" programme, carried out in 2017–2019 by the Ministry of Science and Higher Education. Decision of the Ministry of Science and Higher Education no. 0104/DLG/2017/10.

again? An important starting point for finding an answer to these questions may be the statement by G. John Ikenberry, who believed that it was the conviction that we managed to build a lasting accord revolving around the balance in relations between state sovereignty, the area of international order and the ever-growing interdependence of nations was one of the foundations of post-war, liberal international order and its stability.

From this point of view, the case of European integration was of key importance, along with the effects and outcomes of the process of economic and political transition in Central and Eastern Europe, as well as the vision of a broader, worldwide transition, inscribed in the liberal vision of globalisation. This is why the crisis of faith in the existence of such a balance seems to be one of the most crucial aspects of the ongoing crisis, which should point our attention towards the role of the state as a key factor, and – by extension – the state-formatted, modern electoral democracy.

The issue of finding the main source of the current crisis in the Western world is also not without its significance. Does it stem primarily from the political crisis of the internal, national models of social and economic development or in other words from challenging the existing post-war social and political contract? Or perhaps it is rather a result of an international liberal model of order and development, created at the behest of the West? If both of these phenomena are what is *de facto* taking place, it is definitely worthwhile to consider the relationship and interdependence between them. This issue has been the subject of new discussions and debates for a decade now, which is reflected in the expansive subject literature, and which also served as a starting point for our research project and this publication.[2]

---

2 P. Blokker (2010): *Multiple Democracies in Europe*, London: Routledge; D. Bohle, B. Greskovits (2012): *Capitalist Diversity on Europe's Periphery*, Cornell University Press; G. Dale (2011): *First the Transition, then the Crash. Eastern Europe in the 2000's*, Pluto Press; R. Eatwell, M. Goodwin (2018): *National Populism. The Revolt Against Liberal Democracy*, Penguin Random House; B. Emmott (2018): *The Fate of the West*, The Economist Books; G. Evans, A. Menon (2017): *Brexit and British Politics*, Polity; F. Furedi (2018): *Populism and the European Culture Wars*, London: Routledge; Ch. Guilluy (2019): *Twilight of the Elites*, Yale University Press; J. Kirchick (2017): *The End of Europe*, Yale University Press; I. Krastev (2017): *After Europe*, University of Pennsylvania Press; Ch. von Marschall (2018): *Wir verstehen die Welt nicht mehr*, Herder; L. van Middelaar (2019): *Alarums and Excursions. Improvising Politics on the European Stage*, Agenda Publishing; Y. Mounk (2018): *The People vs. Democracy*, Harvard University Press; C. Offe (2015): *Europe Entrapped*, Polity; D. Rodrik (2012): *The Globalisation Paradox*, Norton & Company; S. Shields (2012): *The International Political Economy*

One of the most important aspects of this book is a closer look at the issue of the role of contemporary European countries and the crisis of the Western, liberal international order from the perspective of the experience of Central and Eastern Europe and from the point of view of Poland, as the largest country in the region. After all, the economic and political transition of the entire region, later combined with the process of extension of European integration, was an element of a broader liberal design of post–Cold War order, regardless of the contradictions or conflicts, which emerged between Europe and the United States, particularly in 2003–2009.

That is why the first chapter of the book features essays that constitute an attempt at diagnosing the causes and the nature of the ongoing crisis of the liberal and Western international order, as well as presenting the perception of this issue from the point of view of Poland and the Central and Eastern Europe region. Looking at this crisis from this exact point of view seems important, because the "peripheral" nature of the transition process, we make note of some aspects of the crisis which could have been unnoticed from the standpoint of the "centre." We also pose the question of how the crisis of the liberal order is perceived by those, who have become its biggest beneficiaries, perhaps only second to Germany, over the course of the last three decades. This issue is particularly interesting and worth reflecting upon.

The second part of the book covers three case studies: France, Germany and the United Kingdom, juxtaposed with Poland in the context of the consequences of the migration crisis. These three examples are, of course, hardly exhaustive for the entire, increasingly complex spectrum of the European Union or Europe as a whole. They are, however, symptomatic from the point of view of the issue of the actions of a contemporary state in the face of a crisis, as well as crucial for the process of European integration. From the standpoint of Poland and the entire Central and Eastern Europe region, they are certainly authoritative and robust, serving as the main economic and political benchmark for comparison with Western Europe after 1989.

These examples serve as a good illustration of the overarching European tendency for states, particularly the large ones, to seek their own national strategies to respond to the European and global crisis, as well as to look for new international and supranational solutions.

---

of Transition, Routledge; W. Streeck (2013): *Gekaufte Zeit. Die vertagte Krise des demokratischen Kapitalismus*, Suhrkampf; H.A. Winkler (2017): *Zerbricht der Westen?*, C. H. Beck; J. Zielonka (2018): *Counter-Revolution. Liberal Europe in Retreat*, Oxford University Press.

The third part consists of essays devoted exclusively to Poland. It comprises analyses of the Polish political scene, the structures of Polish strategic thought, as well as examples referring to the migration policy and the conflict with the EU regarding the rule of law.

In the summary of this part, we attempt to answer the question to what extent Poland – a post-transition country, currently at a specific and difficult stage of its political evolution – can respond to the crisis of the existing international order without closing down paths towards future development and growth, and while opening new ones instead.

The objective of this publication is not only to present the way of thinking of Polish scholars on the ongoing crisis of the liberal West. It is, first and foremost, intended to help the reader better understand how contemporary European states attempt to be active actors, responding to the crisis of the international order, in different and sometimes contradictory ways. This phenomenon inevitably leads to the undermining of many existing cooperation mechanisms, but on the other hand, it also reveals the limitations in terms of the state actions.

This is why this crisis is not only forcing us to rethink the model of international cooperation, but it will also eventually considerably impact our understanding of the role of the contemporary state in Europe. One thing seems to be certain – it will be difficult to rebuild mutual trust without creating a new type of balance between the dimension of national sovereignty and the structures of international governance in Europe and the broadly understood Western world.

Part I Sources of the Crisis of Liberal Order

Marek Cichocki

The crisis of liberalism vs. the future of the global order

Abstract: In order to understand the current crisis of the liberal Western order, one should first look at its genesis and structure. The author begins this by reflecting on liberal internationalism in a historical context, and then presents the identity of the West and liberalism itself. Based on these observations, he analyzes three areas of liberal international order: security order, economic order and order of values. The current crisis of liberalism has external causes in the form of growing ambitions of such countries as China or Russia, but also the internal ones – growing divisions and contradictions within the West. Up to the present time, Poland has not experienced directly the manifestations of the crisis of liberal order; however, there is a growing uncertainty and external threats as well as national divisions related to the normative and cultural aspects.

Keywords: liberalism, liberal order, liberal institutionalism, security order, economic order, order of values, crisis

Do we live in the moment of change of world orders that must be understood as a deep crisis of the international system existing so far? One of the most popular topics in modern political science and in political journalism in European countries and the USA is the question about the condition of the postwar Western liberal order. At the same time, the current debate focuses strongly on the threats that cast doubt on the likelihood of further dominance of the liberal order around the world or even allow us to assume the possibility of its collapse and ultimate end. Brexit, Donald Trump's victory in the presidential election and the rising populist movements in Europe that challenge the *status quo* on the wave of consequences of the economic and social crisis in the Western world stimulate fears of this kind and sometimes lead to completely apocalyptic visions. However, if we want to avoid the situation in which the crisis of the existing liberal order would lead us to total cultural and political defeatism, as a result of which we would still be able to recognise the nature of ongoing transformations, we must first ask the question about the essence and ingredients of this endangered global liberal order. This text is aimed mainly at answering this question through the reconstruction of fundamentals of the Western liberal order prevailing in the world after the end of the Cold War. We also want to show that the current crisis of this order is not only a consequence of the growing pressure from non-liberal states gaining the status of powers in global politics, as in the case of China, but also reflects deep internal splits and disagreements. Because of the globalisation of internal liberalism, hidden internal splits begin to result in increasingly stronger tensions and conflicts in deep crisis situations. The concept of Western liberalism as a foundation for a new type of internationalism has never been as cohesive and homogeneous as we commonly think. Thus, the future of the liberal order will be decided not only in confrontation with the rising competitive powers; it will also depend on whether it produces new forms of effective management of growing internal diversity. Finally, we also want to consider how the crisis of liberal internationalism, both in view of the pressure of external factors and internal disagreements, may influence the position of Poland in Europe and in international relations.

Liberal internationalism in a historical perspective

An apparently simple question involves a complex answer. John Ikenberry assumes that it is possible to identify at least five basic principles due to which he regards the Western liberal order as a cohesive and functional concept. It is, firstly, openness manifesting itself in free trade, exchange and mutual relations; secondly, attachment to a certain set of common rules determining the relations and behaviours of actors that support multilateral co-operation between them; thirdly, actions aimed at reinforcing international security (for example, by resigning from the use of means of violence); fourthly, conviction of the possible progress occurring in international politics thanks to the ability to improve it and to draw conclusions from earlier errors and catastrophes; fifthly, the belief that compliance with all of these rules will bring advantages to all states and will contribute to the dissemination of the benefits of liberal democracy and global capitalism.[1] However, the sense of obviousness that often accompanies the concept of the Western liberal order in the world in political or academic debates conceals actual deep ambiguity. We can also see clearly that the current situation of crisis and uncertainty in the West enforces a new reflection on this concept and leads to attempts to present new precise definitions of Western liberalism in its actual sense and of the world order built on it.[2] In this context, however, we

---

1 J.G. Ikenberry (2018): The end of liberal international order?, *International Affairs*, 94/1, p. 11.

2 G. Allison (2018): The Myth of the Liberal Order, *Foreign Affairs*, vol. 97, Iss. 4; J. Ikenberry (2018): The End of Liberal International Order?, *International Affairs*, 94/2018; H. Kundnani (2017): What is the Liberal International Order?, GMF Policy Essay, no. 17/2017; P. Porter (2018): A World Imagined. Nostalgia and Liberal Order,

cannot avoid asking additional questions, mainly about the way of understanding the West and liberalism and about their mutual relationship, which involves also the coherence and nature of the concept of the Western liberal order; whether we actually deal here with the coherent idea of such an order, a homogeneous and valid concept and its concrete expression in various dimensions of politics, or we rather employ a certain idea or myth that arouses sentiment and longing in some people and anger and impatience in others. It is worth reflecting on all of these things, particularly because, from a historical viewpoint, the concepts of the West, liberalism or the Western liberal order are dynamic and have been subject to serious evolution.

World War II is obviously the turning point for the materialisation of structures of the Western liberal order around America's leadership. Nevertheless, the roots of this process date back to an earlier period and concern mainly changes in the functioning of international politics brought on by World War I. This refers to the very idea of liberal internationalism expressed in Woodrow Wilson's doctrine[3] that is based on the mechanism of growing interdependence and mutual and equal relationships that functions in international relations through the promotion of liberal political rules of the state, the free market and liberal values, such as respect for minorities and human rights. As a new organising principle of the international order around the United States and their allies, this idea replaced the 19th-century order of the balance of European powers, European colonialism and American isolationism. Historically speaking, liberal internationalism appeared even earlier, at the turn of the 19th century, as an idea of international order built around the principles of liberal utilitarianism founded by Jeremy Bentham.[4] In 19th-century European politics, liberal internationalism was connected mainly with Great Britain and Richard Cobden, who supported free trade as the basis of international co-operation and peace, but also the right of nations to decide about their fate. This early form of liberal internationalism was in conflict with the traditional internationalism symbolised by the Holy Alliance and Metternich's policy that prevailed on the Continent since the Vienna Congress in 1915. As a result of the idea of brotherhood of

---

Cato Institute Political Analysis, no. 843/2018; P. Staniland (2018): Misreading the "Liberal Order": Why We Need New Thinking in American Foreign Policy, Lawfare Blog.

3 L. Ehrlich (2018): The War and Political Theory, *California Law Review*, vol. 6 (Sept. 1918) and vol. 7 (Nov. 1918).

4 P. Wandycz (1993): Liberal Internationalism: The Quest for a "Polish Variant", *Polish Western Affairs*, no. 2, p. 17.

nations (Giuseppe Mazzini, Jules Michelet) and growing pressure from workers' movements and emerging Marxist internationalism, liberalism has been shifting towards interventionism in international politics in favour of the promotion of its values since the middle of the 19th century, which culminates in Wilson's policy but is also strongly connected with the change that makes Great Britain lose the role of the main liberal ruler to the United States.[5]

The concept of the Western liberal order as a transatlantic system[6] appears as a result of World War II and the ideological conflict with fascism and Nazism in Europe and then becomes strengthened in confrontation with communist Russia. The Atlantic Charter of 1941 can be regarded as the first coherent communication of the rules of the new postwar system led by two Anglo-Saxon states: the United States and Great Britain. But the USA became the main architect and promoter of the new world order after the war as the only power capable of designing a system of institutions, norms, practices and interdependencies forming the basis for the transatlantic order. In view of the new Cold War conflict, in opposition to communism and world aspirations of the USSR, it became mainly the Western order.[7] Thanks to postwar institutions, organisations and international agreements, such as the UN, Bretton Woods, World Bank, IMF, GATT or subsequently OSCE, the Western liberal order based on the superpower position of the United States could have a global impact in spite of the bipolar division of the world persisting because of the Cold War. Only after the end of the Cold War did the Western liberal world become fully global. The belief that the fall of Communism and the USSR opens the way to the inevitable globalisation of the Western liberal order and that the transformation and unification of Europe is the starting point for this huge process can be found in the text of the Charter of Paris for a New Europe (1990) and in texts of influential authors such as Francis Fukuyama or subsequently Robert Cooper.[8] Thus, what

---

5 Cf. M. Mazower (2012): *Governing the World. The History of an Idea*, London: Penguin Books; C. Holbraad (2003): *Internationalism and Nationalism in European Political Thought*, New York: Palgrave.

6 In 1950, following the trail of Eric Fischer and his 1943 book *The Passing of European Age – A Study of the Transfer of Western Civilisation and Its Renewal on Other Continents*, Oskar Halecki put forward an idea that World War II marks the essential end of the European history, which is replaced with the transatlantic era in the history of the West, *Historia Europy – jej granice i podziały* [*The History of Europe – Its Borders and Divisions*], Lublin: Instytut Europy Środkowo-Wschodniej, p. 66.

7 J.L. Gaddis (2005): *The Cold War: A New History*, New York: The Penguin Press.

8 F. Fukuyama (1992): *The End of History and the Last Man*, New York: Free Press; R. Cooper (2003): *The Breaking of Nations*, New York: Grove Press.

is today often described as a crisis, threat or the possibility of disintegration, refers to the globalised form of the earlier concept of the Western liberal order formed a result of World War II and based on the political, economic, technological and military supremacy of the United States with an important supplementary role of united Europe and the European Union – the role that is the subject of an ongoing strategic dialogue or occasional crises within the scope of the transatlantic co-operation.

Today the crisis and future of liberal internationalism is the subject of important debates concerning primarily the evolution of American politics. There is also a frequently prevailing opinion that Donald Trump is essentially responsible for breaking with the rules of liberal internationalism in American foreign policy, but the gradual abandonment of these rules by the political establishment of Washington has been indicated at least since the Iraq War during George W. Bush's presidency. In its more radical form, this argument claims that, under the pressure of the influential group of neo-conservatives after 11 September attacks, the policy of Bush's administration has completely abandoned the traditional assumptions of American foreign policy that effectively formatted the unity of the West since World War II, submitting to a specific kind of war and unilateral aberration in its strategic decisions and rhetorics.[9] In its milder form, this argument states that Bush's policy was a symptom rather than the cause of the collapse of the existing *modus vivendi* of American politics supported both by Democrats and Republicans, and the projection of American strength was combined with the projection of the co-operation with transatlantic allies, which essentially guaranteed the stability and unity of the Western order.[10] However, not everyone shared this critical point of view – at least until the election of Donald Trump as president of the USA. Some commentators and analysts thought that Barack Obama's presidency is a proof of the fact that the period of political aberration of Bush's administration was followed by the return to Washington's consensus around liberal internationalism in the USA's foreign policy.[11] But there were also critical opinions on that subject according to which Obama not only

---

9 F. Fukuyama (2006): *America at the Crossroads: Democracy, Power, and the Neoconservative Legacy*, New Haven: Yale University Press; G.J. Ikenberry (2004): The End of the Neo-Conservative Moment, *Survival*, vol. 46, no. 1 (Spring 2004), pp. 7–22.

10 Ch.A. Kupchan, P.L. Trubowitz (2007): Dead Center. Demise of Liberal Internationalism in the United States, *International Security*, vol. 32, no. 2/2007, pp. 7–44.

11 S. Chaudoin, H. Milner, D. Tingley (2010): The Center still Holds. Liberal Internationalism Survives, *International Security*, vol. 35, no. 1 (Summer 2010), pp. 75–94.

failed to rebuild a political consensus around liberal internationalism with his policy,[12] but even escalated the abandonment of the traditional policy dominating since World War II.[13] Only against the background of these earlier debates can we consider the current discussion regarding Trump and his policy, where two main opinions clearly collide: one opinion asserting that the system of liberal internationalism created over the decades is so strong that its rules cannot be destroyed by any kind of political voluntarism of the presidential administration in Washington limited by its term of office, which also applies to Trump,[14] and the other opinion claiming that the political consensus around American politics has irretrievably collapsed during the last two decades and even if Trump is not the cause of the current change, he is its symptom announcing the transition to a new situation in international relations, which would mean in practice the end of the previous order based on the rules of liberal internationalism and the unconditional dominance of the USA as its guarantor.[15]

Today the discussion on the crisis of the existing order in international relations as a crisis of liberal internationalism concerns essentially the question about the place of the USA in the security system and mutual dependence. Will the United States make a real decision to withdraw from the role of the guarantor of the western order that they have continued to fulfil since World War II? Fears in this respect have been fuelled, particularly recently, by Trump's numerous declarations, his strategy "America first!", the actual withdrawal of Washington from some international agreements and organisations, the criticism of the NATO and the EU, or the focus on economic patriotism (nationalism) and on cultural sovereignty in international relations.[16] The discussion about whether and to what extent America still wants to act as the protector of the liberal international order has been going on for a long time, at least since George W. Bush's administration, and has not disappeared during the presidency

---

12 Ch.A. Kupchan, P.L. Trubowitz (2010): The Illusion of Liberal Internationalism's Revival, *International Security*, vol. 35, no. 1 (Summer 2010), pp. 95–109.

13 N. Ferguson (2016): Barack Obama's Revolution in Foreign Policy, *The National Business Review*, 10 May 2016.

14 S. Chaudoin, H. Milner, D. Tingley (2011): Roundtable. Is Liberal Internationalism Still Alive?, *H-Diplo/ISSF Roundtable Reviews*, vol. II, no. 4 (2011), p. 2.

15 H. Kissinger, an interview to Edward Luce for "Financial Times", *We are in a very, very grave period*, 20 July 2018.

16 Trump's speech in the UN: https://www.whitehouse.gov/briefings-statements/remarks-president-trump-73rd-session-united-nations-general-assembly-new-york-ny/, [Access: 11.02.2019].

of Barack Obama, whose attitude to America's presence in Europe was strongly hesitant, among others, because of his Asiatic pivot policy. Thus, the question whether contemporary American politics follows the path of withdrawal from the existing transatlantic model and whether Europe becomes increasingly dependent on itself has been present for a long time and emerged before Trump's presidency.[17]

The identity of the West and liberalism

When we want to define clearly the concept of the Western liberal order, we come across serious difficulties also because of the ambiguity of the concept of the West and the concept of liberalism as well as their mutual relationship. Of course, looking from the perspective of the rules of liberal internationalism, the answer seems simple: the core of the world order globalised after the Cold War that is based on these rules is the liberal West understood as transatlantic unity with the dominant position of the United States. However, the problem is that, on the one hand, such a picture of the world order is actually not consistent with real attitudes and aspirations of the main world actors, the United States, (partly) Europe, Russia, China or other Asiatic powers any more, and, on the other hand, it ignores the diversity of traditions referring to the West itself as a historical and geopolitical concept and simplifies the relationship between the West and liberalism. With regard to the issue of the crisis of the Western liberal order, apart from the question about the further role of the United States in the protection of liberal internationalism and about the policies of their biggest global competitors, we also deal with the more strongly emphasised problem of the internal unity of the West, which is primarily a European problem. In order to illustrate this problem, we will refer to one example: In his book *Qu'est-ce que l'Occident?*,[18] Philippe Nemo begins his reflections on that subject with an obvious statement that the term "West" needs to be specified in detail. Why? Because it has stood for very different things in its diverse historical forms. In history, the West meant Christian Europe opposed to countries of the Levant, the Arabian-Muslim Orient and the Indian and Chinese Far East; it could also mean the Western hemisphere, i.e., the New World, America, which was opposed to reactionary, non-democratic, fossilised Europe, for example, thanks to Monroe's doctrine; or the Roman world or the Anglo-Saxon world rejected in the first case by Luther's Reformation and in the second case by German nationalism; finally,

17 J. Shapiro, N. Witney (2009): Towards a Post-American Europe, ECFR 2009.
18 Ph. Nemo (2006): *What is the West*?, Duquesne University Press.

it could be identified with the Latin world, which was regarded as a deadly enemy by Holy Rus and Russian Slavophiles. During the Cold War, the West became yet another thing – the bloc of countries of freedom, states of Western Europe and America connected by the fact of fighting against the East, the world of communism. This ambiguity does not make it easy to give a clear answer to the question what we mean exactly by the concept of the West today. For this reason, at the end of this enumeration of various historical incarnations of the West that might be presumably even further, Nemo reaches his essential conclusion: how to understand the West in modern times; since, as he states, the collapse of the Berlin Wall brings about a new world order, the term "West" regains … its geopolitical value.[19] Therefore, the analysis of the profound cultural content behind it is an even more urgent issue. For the author of searches of an answer to the question of his book: *What is the West?*, it is obvious that, when regaining its geopolitical value after the fall of the Cold War and communism, the West should rely mainly on the foundations of postwar liberalism, the world of rules and values consisting of intellectual liberalism; in the sphere of culture, science, public affairs and politics, the latter means primarily the superiority of neutral critical pluralism, and in the political sense, it consists of liberal democracy and economic liberalism. Thus, belonging to the Western world means for him mainly the ability to adopt institutional solutions concerning liberal democracy, the pluralism of civil society and the free market. Writing his book *What is the West?* in 2004, Nemo thought that it was the 15 member states of the EU before its expansion with Central and Eastern Europe that achieved the state of deepest integration among those liberal institutions and mechanisms, presenting them as the modern expression of the West along with the United States. In this perspective, the West is entirely identical with liberalism – both as a historical process[20] and as its final shape that appears in the form of neo-liberalism in the 1970s and the 1980s as a challenge towards the alternative of communism on the one hand and an answer to the internal crisis of the postwar model of a welfare state on the other hand. The triumph of neo-liberalism over both the external

19 *Ibid.*, pp. 13–15.

20 According to Ikenberry, in a long-term historical perspective, the global dominance of the West should be perceived as a phenomenon encompassing the entire era of two hundred years of liberal modernity. "Beginning with the Enlightenment and running through the industrial revolution and the rise of the West, world-historical change seemed to be unfolding according to a deep developmental logic. It was a progressive movement driven by reason, science, discovery, innovation, technology, learning, constitutionalism and institutional adaptation", The End of Liberal…, *op. cit.*, p. 8.

and internal alternative fuses it with the concept of the modern West, which vividly resembles the principles adopted by Francis Fukuyama at the beginning of the 1990s at the time of formulating his loud idea of the end of history. Also, it is not accidental that, when specifying the term "West" in this way, Nemo strongly relies on a very specific interpretation of liberalism borrowed directly from Friedrich Hayek.[21]

Such a reduction of the West to liberalism or even neo-liberalism of the 1970s and 1980s, as well as the strict association of liberal internationalism with the will of the United States to use its power advantage in the world for the promotion and protection of its rules, are essential elements of the concept of the Western liberal order in the world after the end of the Cold War. The supporters of this concept admit that this order is a kind of "artefact"[22] – a structure that makes it possible to shape the policy of the West towards the world in a more or less successful way. Today, however, this structure is subject to the increasing pressure of external factors and internal inconsistencies that have been ignored so far (anyway, the ignorance of these inconsistencies determined the ideological strength of the structure of the liberal order to a certain moment). The West itself is not so unequivocally liberal, let alone the rest of the world; the politics of the United States is not so unconditionally and eternally connected with the assumptions of liberal internationalism, either. Therefore, some commentators will think that the conviction of the emergence of a permanent and globalised Western liberal order in the world that prevailed after the end of the Cold War was either only a reflection of a specific historical moment, or simply a certain myth, a set of beliefs that were not confirmed by reality in the perspective of a few decades.[23]

Three areas of the liberal international order

Thus, the Western liberal world order is not a coherent and unequivocal concept, and its basic assumptions arouse strong protest and criticism today. At the same

21 It is worth mentioning that, apart from this "market" approach to liberalism, we also deal with the perception of liberalism in terms of the cultural revolution and the post-modernity project as a reflection of the revolution of the 1960s, to which Nemo has a critical attitude in his book.

22 Referring to R. Kagan's book *The world America made*, Ikenberry says openly that "Liberal internationalism is essentially 'an artefact' of the rapidly receding Anglo-American era", The End of Liberal…, *op. cit.*, p. 8.

23 G. Allison, P. Porter, P. Staniland, *op. cit.*

time, it is based on the belief that after World War II the United States imposed a system of common rules, institutions and values binding democratic and free market states into one common system of co-operation and security that brings us peace, stability and development.[24] There are many different typologies of such liberal international order. Hans Kundnani suggests considering this order primarily in terms of three essential dimensions: as a security order, as an economic order and, finally, as an order of human rights.[25] For the needs of this analysis, we will use this categorisation, modifying it slightly to the dimension of international security, the dimension of a political-economic model and the dimension of values. We will consider them separately, however, bearing in mind that they are interconnected and form a certain whole.

Security order

Referring to the concept of the Western liberal world order, we mean primarily the security order that is a common structure based on the central dominant role of the United States as a liberal world power and on Europe and the European Union as their strategic ally and actual supplement. As the strategic centre being created by the Atlantic community (the key importance of the NATO), from the Atlantic Charter and co-operation during the Cold War to the Paris Charter, the West gradually built the structure of common institutions, rules, alliances and international law that, through mechanisms of integration and internationalisation, made it possible to achieve the level of co-operation and interdependence on an unprecedented global scale. Based essentially on the promotion of liberal principles, the co-operation turned out to be the most effective method of putting international relations in order and solving potential conflicts. Thus, it was assumed that this kind of security order was the most desirable one and would become common and universal in the course of time, making it possible to overcome old traditional mechanisms of international politics based mainly on territorial wars, exclusive impact zones or the balancing of competing blocs. However, because of various security crises, such as the annexation of the Crimea by Russia and the war with the Ukraine, the Syrian War and the crisis in the Middle East or strategic challenges from China in the South China Sea, the belief in the further reinforcement of the liberal security order in this sense

24 J. Suri (2017): How Trump's Executive Orders Could Set America Back 70 Years, *Atlantic*, January 27, 2017.

25 H. Kundnani (2017): What is the Liberal International Order?, *GMF Policy Essay*, no. 17, Liberal International Order Project.

was seriously undermined. But the question is whether the liberal security order is confronted with new crises and new aggressively operating rivals today, or maybe it is a kind of auto-mystification that has simply become more visible due to new events and new actors.

The historian Patrick Porter states simply that the concept of the liberal world order is an ahistorical idea based on certain illusion; in any case, it certainly must be essentially corrected in confrontation with historical facts.[26] In his opinion, the security order built around the transatlantic core after World War II till modern times was not as liberal, consensual and homogeneous as we would tend to present it today. He also draws our attention to a very important aspect of the postwar security system that, in the case of the Western liberal order, was based not only on the rules of integration and internationalisation around common institutions, rules and values, but its keystone was the United States' imperial policy of force as the leader of the system. Thus, the prometheism of the postwar liberal order could not be possible without American imperialism – a policy that was not based only on common rules and institutions, consensus, co-operation and integration, but it also frequently involved the use of force, compulsion, blackmail, "law of the jungle" or dirty agreements. In times of the Cold War, in the context of rivalry with the Soviet Union, the negative features of the imperial policy of the USA (but also other actors of the Western liberal order) were easier to accept according to the logic of the "lesser evil", but they became much more visible and controversial after the transformation in 1989. Porter reminds us that since the beginning of existence of postwar liberal internationalism, the USA's security policy assumed co-operation with totalitarian regimes in the UN's Security Council (Russia under Stalin and China under Mao); that Truman's internationalism of the 1940s encompassed not only actions aimed at creating the UN and the Charter of the United Nations, but also the decision to use an atom bomb against Japan; that Washington could also openly act against its traditional European allies, as in the case of the Suez Crisis, and that it often supported not only non-liberal governments in various parts of the world or overthrew democratically elected governments, but also agreed to the membership of authoritarian states in the NATO, as in the case of Portugal or Greece at the beginning of the 1970s. In this way, Porter wants to show that what we call the liberal world order is not only a result of the dissemination of common shared rules and institutions, but also – maybe even to a larger extent – a consequence of the imperial position of the USA in the system.

---

26 P. Porter, *op. cit.*, p. 3.

Porter's argument corresponds with the text of another author, Graham T. Allison, for whom the primary element of the influential myth about the dominance of the liberal order in the world after the Cold War is the conviction that the political elites of the United States and the American public opinion decided that the basic strategic goal of American politics is to export the rules of political and economic liberalism in the world and to protect them instead of taking care mainly of the continuity and development of its own liberal and economic model. In Allison's opinion, this belief that the United States will take care of the world on a global scale at the cost of its own internal situation is absurd and results from the assumption that the role played by the USA in global politics since World War II is the only proper one for it. This belief was reinforced and has become a sort of ideology thanks to the ideas of the end of history that were popular in the 1990s, where the end of history was understood as the common global victory of the liberal rules of the free market, free trade and democracy. According to the assumptions of the best-known representative of this vision – Fukuyama, the end of the Cold War was not the end of a stage in postwar history, but the end of history as such, a turning point in the ideological history of humanity and the moment in which Western liberal political and economic values were to bring about a universal and final form of government in the world.[27] In such an end of history, the United States would assume the role of the common guarantor. However, Allison states that the conviction about this role of the USA resulted from the wrong assumption that the United States, which actually engaged in the construction of the global security system as a strategy of protection of its own interests after the Great Crisis and World War II, would undoubtedly continue such a policy as the essence of its own raison d'etat. In fact, as the author claims, instead of engagement in the maintenance of the world order, the essence of American policies has always been the protection of its own political freedoms, the institutional foundations of the American political system and primary American values determining the uniqueness of the specific American lifestyle.[28] In short, American global policy have never been liberal to such an extent, which Porter proves by indicating its elements of imperial power, or so Promethean and idealistic, which is proved by Allison in turn.

27 J.L. Gaddis (1991): Toward the Post-Cold War World, *Foreign Affairs*, 1991/70/2.
28 G. Allison, *op. cit.*, p. 5.

Economic order

The economic dimension is one of the key elements of the liberal world order. Its essence is openness, which manifests itself mainly in open free trade and in globalised market capital. This order is expressed mainly by the WTO, and the accession of states like China (2001) or Russia (2012) to it reinforced faith in the global and common character of the liberal order in the world. The supporters of the global economic order based on liberal rules that came to voice with particular strength at the turn of the 1980s in the form of a neo-liberal revolution (Thatcher, Reagan) think that the liquidation of "artificial borders", the minimisation of the role of states and their protectionist policies and the free flow of capital, labour, services, ideas, information and people serves as the basic flywheel of global development and international order. Therefore, the protection of this order, its further liberalisation (advancing), compliance with its rules and the recognition of its institutions are regarded as most favourable for everyone. Big transcontinental trade agreements, such as the Transatlantic Trade and Investment Partnership (TTIP) and the Trans-Pacific Partnership (TPP), have been an important element of the advancing and extension of the economic dimension of the liberal world order in recent times.

The belief in the commonly beneficial results of the economic globalisation and the resulting consolidation of the general dominance of liberal economic rules of the free market have been undermined primarily by the great financial and economic crisis at the beginning of the 21st century. Openness – the key value of liberalism – has been questioned and is no longer associated with development, security and justice; in social reception, it means increasingly often growing inequalities[29] or the import of threats from the outside. Because of the overlapping of the consequences of two great crises: the financial crisis and the migrant crisis, openness and many liberal values, such as the independence of self-regulating markets, multiculturalism or globalisation, have been under the spotlight.[30]

Dani Rodrik noted that the great optimism that accompanied the deepening of the global dimension of the economic liberal order at the end of the 20th century concealed the existence of fundamental internal inconsistencies that may lead to its inevitable fragmentation in the long term. Its fundamental argument is: the belief in the effectiveness and favourable results of the economic

---

29 T. Piketty (2014): *Capital in the Twenty-First Century*, Cambridge: Harvard University Press.

30 I. Krastev (2017): *After Europe*, University of Pennsylvania Press.

dimension of the global liberal order that emerged primarily after the fall of communism and the end of the Cold War was based on the right assumption that the globalising world needs the existence of certain common rules and institutions and some kind of global management of world economy, but at the same time it failed to bring any deeper reflection on the negative consequences and potential inconsistencies resulting from the profound globalisation. The liberal internationalism that initially contributed to the formation of a common framework for the Western economic and financial order in the form of Bretton Woods and GATT after World War II, which was described in terms of "embedded capitalism",[31] entered the phase of hyperglobalisation without deeper reflection on its results after the Cold War, under the influence of the new ideology of neoliberalism and, last but not least, as a result of changes caused by the third industrial revolution (digitisation and the Internet). The inconsistencies revealed by the financial and economic crisis of the last decade were described by Rodrik in the form of a theory about the paradox of globalisation. According to this theory, it is impossible to open up to the rules of profound globalisation completely while maintaining the sovereignty of the state and the rules of democratic society, i.e., participation of citizens in the government. The profound globalisation forces democratic states and societies to make a frequently irresolvable choice: either we have to resign from the national forms of democracy in favour of the supranational democracy that would theoretically serve as a counterbalance for the "unrestrained" globalisation, or the government of the state decides to introduce globalisation solutions in its policies, but at the expense of interests of citizens electing it, or, in the name of reinforcement of internal democracy, states decide to adopt policies restricting the impacts of the globalisation. In any case, Rodrik thinks it is not possible to have a profound globalisation, a state and democracy at the same time and this problem was essentially ignored by the supporters of the advancement of the economic dimension of the liberal world order until the outbreak of the great economic and financial crisis.

Thus, what is collectively called populism today and what describes social and political forces acting against the economic dimension of the profound liberal globalisation from the position of economic nationalism or protectionism, cannot be treated as a dangerous political deviation, but as a consequence of

31 J. Ruggie (1982): International Regimes, Transactions, and Change: Embedded Liberalism in the Postwar Economic Order, *International Organisation*, vol. 36, no. 2, pp. 379–415.

the emergence of internal inconsistencies within the liberal world order that demand a political and economic response.

Order of values

When speaking of the liberal world order, we often mean also a certain order of values. In the dimension of international politics, it is usually a question of human rights and rights of minorities (this includes increasingly often not only national minorities, but also all kinds of discriminated groups). In the economic dimension, we often deal with the value of the rule of law or the theological value of economic growth; the issue of social justice emerges to a lesser extent. Essentially, however, the issue of values goes beyond individual dimensions of the liberal world order and is connected with the evolution of the postwar liberalism that started to become an increasingly dominant ideology in the Western world after the 1960s (the key role of the cultural revolution in 1968), determining the conditions in which politics, economy and culture should function. Nevertheless, this evolution changes essentially the content of liberal values by shifting the liberal axiology from the classic traditional 19th-century liberalism towards postmodern liberalism and adding new senses to the modern Western liberalism as a cultural and civilisational project. According to the theory of the end of history that was popular after the end of the Cold War, this project should mark the final moment for the entire ideological evolution of humanity, being in symbiosis with the supremacy of the global free market economy. According to Mark Lilla, it is mainly the New Left movement of the 1960s and 1970s that caused an essential change of liberal values referring to the understanding of the public sphere and political culture of the West.[32] In the first place, it changed the traditional liberal understanding of civil society dating back to Locke or Hegel by turning it into a network of movements of various social groups acting for the purpose of solving or protecting certain issues, such as consumer rights, animal rights or rights of sexual minorities. It also influenced the key factor of liberalism – the way of understanding the status and rights of an individual – by defining the latter primarily in respect of his/her individual identity, psyche, emotions, experiences and beliefs, according to the theory that politics is a question of personal beliefs and feelings, which has become, mainly in the USA, the basis for formulating the term "identity politics" and taking actions against all kinds of discrimination. Consequently, however, this modified way

32 M. Lilla (2017): *The Once and Future Liberal. After Identity Politics*, New York: HarperCollins Publisher.

of understanding liberal values made postmodern liberalism unable to embrace further such community terms as citizenship, state, society as a whole, or collective (political or cultural) identity.

The emergence of postmodern liberalism as a consequence of the changes occurring since the 1960s and the adoption of its dominant axiological position as the determining factor of the final ideological change after the end of the Cold War essentially contributed to the formulation of the concept of liberal democracy as the only acceptable and proper form of government.[33] Not only did it defeat communism, which was its biggest postwar rival during many decades of the Cold War, but it also overshadowed any other alternative conceptions, such as social democracy or Christian democracy, which were still quite popular in the early 1990s, and made them quite relevant. Becoming the leading ideology in this way, liberal democracy assumed a symbiosis with the neo-liberal concept of economy and with globalisation and was based on certain fundamental principles, such as the rule of law, the separation of powers or the free and fair election, and on the protection of fundamental rights, such as the right of assembly, the freedom of speech, the freedom of religion and rights of minorities. In the course of time, however, it focused more and more strongly on cultural values formulated as obvious rights in a positive sense, such as multiculturalism, secularisation, transnationality, or the equal status of different identities. Liberal democracy often meant also the redefinition of the traditional understanding of democracy in accordance with the new concept of monitored democracy.[34] While the traditional form of representative democracy was connected primarily with the state and the community of citizens and was based mainly on the public opinion and a system of political parties, which was a convenient method of choosing the parliamentary majority by election and establishing a government, monitored democracy is based on the functioning of the entire network mechanism of non-parliamentary and non-state government control centres (international agencies, institutions and organisations, civil societies, the media, courts and tribunals) acting for the purpose of protecting international standards, public interest and responsibility. Actually, however, monitored democracy changes importantly the sense of sovereignty of democratic society and the practice of representation, democratic control and public participation and connects citizens' majority decisions with non-parliamentary and non-state monitoring institutions as unelected representatives. Generally, liberal democracy should be

33 F. Zakaria (1997): The Rise of Illiberal Democracy, *Foreign Affairs*, Nov/Dec, 76/6.
34 J. Keane (2009): *The Life and Death of Democracy*, New York: Norton & Company.

open to connections of this kind and support them in accordance with the general conviction about the increasingly interconnected nature of the postmodern world[35] and the emergence of a new kind of global ethics.[36]

The liberal world order as a global projection of normative power in the world (alongside military power and economic power), which means the power of a certain community of cultural values of postmodernism, has recently been under the strong pressure of alternative opposing cultural and civilisational concepts represented by increasingly stronger and ambitious international actors, such as China, Russia or Islamic societies. Such a scenario has already been foreseen to a certain extent in earlier concepts of the conflict of civilisations, which pointed out the fact of cultural and religious diversity of the world globalising on the economic and communication level, with particular regard to the irreconcilable differences between the values of the liberal West and the world of Islam. The collapse of the normative power of the liberal world order has also a very important internal aspect that has become visible particularly due to consequences of various crises: the financial crisis, the social inequality crisis, the migrant crisis, the European integration crisis, or the crisis of liberal internationalism (the role of the United States). Thus, apart from the external dimension of growing opposition between the vision of the liberal West and the non-liberal rest of the world with regard to recognised values, there is also an aspect of the internal "culture war" within the West, which is expressed mainly by challenging the dominance of the paradigm of liberal democracy that was previously unquestionable since the end of the Cold War.[37] Here I mean the multidimensional dispute with postmodernism that is taking place in Europe between the liberal and conservative-national form of populism in the name of the restoration of the value of modernity: the dispute between tradition as an irremovable element of each social order and the will to overcome this tradition entirely as a condition of full emancipation, between historical continuity as the basis of identity and connection with the past and the necessity to break it, the national culture within the sovereignty of the state and the concept of floating identities without permanent borders, between attachment to one's own national state and subordination to the network of transnational institutions and mechanisms, between the solidarity of the community and dispersed diversity, politics based on the democratic civil election and the power of meritocracy and experts.

---

35 A.-M. Slaughter (2004): *A New World Order*, Princeton: Princeton University Press.

36 P. Singer (2002): *One World. The Ethics of Globalization*, New Haven: Yale University Press.

37 F. Furedi (2018): *Populism and the European Culture Wars*, London, New York: Routledge.

Thus, the axiological fundamentals of the liberal order are subject today to clear fragmentation both in the external global dimension towards the West and the internal dimension by revealing ideological splits within the borders of the West, which also proved not fully postmodern.

Can this crisis be waited out?

How deep is the crisis of the American liberal world order and how should we identify its causes? The crisis itself is largely connected with the awareness of external limitations encountered by the liberal order in the world as a result of the new balance of power, and with gradually emerging internal inconsistencies and splits that could be ignored so far. Therefore, the future of the liberal Western order will depend on the ability to find an innovative answer to both kinds of challenges rather than on persistent adherence to current values and their defence. The West and liberalism must be reconsidered and reinvented to a certain extent. John Ikenberry has a strongly dark vision of the current crisis of the American liberal world order, forecasting a completely new situation of the end of global supremacy of America and the West and the collapse of the liberal modernisation process that he considers to have taken place for two centuries. It is actually an apocalyptic picture resulting from the author's conviction that the crisis of the liberal order is rooted in its unexpected success after the end of the Cold War. In his opinion, as a result of the globalisation of the Western order, its fundamentals have become subject to the pressure of the growing diversity of states becoming a part of the Western liberal community. The previously elaborated mechanisms and institutions have become overburdened due to the growing diversity, leading both to the crisis of authority and a decrease of effectiveness of the entire system. At the same time, because of its globalisation, the liberal order could fulfil primary expectations to a decreasing extent with regard to its capacity to operate as a functional security community. Thus, in Ikenberry's view, "current problems may be perceived as a typical example of crisis according to Karl Polanyi – the growing chaos and destabilisation as the result of the rapid mobilisation and dissemination of global capitalism, market society and comprehensive interdependence, which … leads to the overburdening of political foundations of the system that previously supported its emergence and evolution".[38] In his analysis of the negligences of modern liberalism, Patrick Deneen turns the argument about the sources of the crisis of the liberal order that lie in

38 The end of liberal…, *op. cit.*, p. 10.

its astonishing success after the Cold War in a completely different direction.[39] In his opinion, the error is not a typical tactical trap encountered by liberalism and resulting in the overburdening of the system as a result of the excessively advanced globalisation, as Ikenberry thinks, but it results from the emergence of certain negative phenomena within the scope of liberalism on which no deeper reflection has been made. In Deneen's view, the current crisis is caused mainly by the internal failure of liberalism.

It is difficult to imagine the complete disintegration of the liberal international order that emerged after World War II and became largely reinforced and globalised after the end of the Cold War. The global anarchy or the state of nature used as threats by Trump's critics today are actually impossible. However, the liberal order will certainly be subject to serious transformation as a result of internal and external forces. Some form of global structure of order (common institutions and rules), still combined with the principles according to which the postwar world has functioned so far, is absolutely necessary.

The transformation process that is already taking place will not only concern the new balance of power and influences between the biggest political actors (such as the United States, China, Russia or India) that attempt to define their own interests in a new way in mutual relations, primarily in areas of global economy and security policy. Therefore, the character of this transformation will not be limited only to the strategic rivalry between powers that must result in the fundamental diversification of the liberal understanding of globalisation that has prevailed so far. As Hans Kundnani aptly notices, this means that if the world order changing under the influence of the strategic rivalry is to persist, it probably has to be less liberal; or, according to Robin Niblett, it has to be a less ambitious project that, while sticking to the primary liberal free market rules of global economy, will also be more "tolerant" towards various states and their different political systems.[40] This assumes that the world order would have to be released, to some extent, from the rules of political liberalism and from liberalism as a cultural choice. The transformation of the Western liberal order occurs also because of the growing internal changes resulting from the emergence of significant internal differences within the territory of the West. These differences have been ignored so far according to the paradigm of the full victorious identity of liberalism and the West adopted in compliance with the idea of the end of history. Also because of the character of the currently rising conflict

39 P.J. Deneen (2018): *Why liberalism failed*, New Haven: Yale University Press.
40 R. Niblett (2017): Liberalism in retreat, *Foreign Affairs*, January/February.

between the West and non-liberal powers, such as China and Russia, the importance of internal differences between countries of the West is perceived as deformation or a sign of weakness that must be fought. The external adversaries of the West and its global order are rightly perceived as revisionist forces that not only resort to means of military or economic rivalry, but also, using the state-of-the-art technologies, try to undermine the belief of Western societies in their own values that constitute the foundation of the West. In fact, however, important differences within the identity of the West have existed before – now they were only identified and used against the West by its external adversaries. Ignoring their existence, the liberal West has built a political culture that is often unable to cope with its own axiological diversity. Thus, it is necessary to supplement liberalism today with elements of conservative-national, Christian and social-democratic tradition that constitute the axiological fundamentals of the West to an equal extent.

The supporters of the current order will think that one of its greatest achievements making it possible to maintain peace and promote co-operation was the resolution of the old conflictogenic dilemma between the sovereignty of national states and international interdependence. In her book about the new world order as a network, Anne-Marie Slaughter shows how one-sided this solution is today. The increasingly profound interdependence as the basis of liberal global governance leads to the gradual erosion of traditional state sovereignty and the promotion of a new type of structured and institutionalised forms of transnational connections between national centres of regulation, legislation, administration, justice or non-governmental organisations.[41] This leads to the blurring of the border between what determines the internal and external policy of states, between what is national and what results from international interdependence, from globalisation, and between what determines the democratic responsibility of national governments and what is the driving force of mechanisms of global international governance. The phenomenon that is described today, often very critically, as the populism of[42] European and American societies is connected directly with the consequences of this process as an increasingly open refusal to accept this phenomenon: refusal to accept the lack of political responsibility, the escape of democratically elected representatives from making decisions, the fragmentation of the state and democratic society, the blurring of borders between what is the essence of the commitment to one's own political and

41 A.M. Slaughter, *op. cit.*, pp. 8–10.

42 J.W. Müller (2016): *What is Populism?*, University of Pennsylvania Press.

cultural identity and what is a consequence of opening up to a free exchange and the development of interdependencies. The disturbance of the balance between both of these sides is undoubtedly one of the fundamental reasons for the loss of trust by Western societies in the positive results of liberal internationalism as the basis of functioning of the world order.

Poland in view of the crisis of liberal internationalism

Finally, we want to ask a question how the crisis of the liberal Western world order affects the situation of Poland in Europe and around the world? Is Poland subject to this crisis at all? There is no doubt that Poland and the entire region of Central Europe became the beneficiaries of the expansion of liberal internationalism after the fall of the Soviet Union after 1989. Thus, the end of the Cold War and the triumph of the liberal order are an important historical turning point for Poles. Ilya Prizel notices that, like after 1918, Polish foreign policy and security policy has been strongly determined by the sense of geopolitical dilemma of a big Central European country situated between the forces of the West and the East since the beginning of the period after 1989; however, in the context of the end of the Cold War, the West aroused enchantment and admiration (which was sometimes too naive – Sztompka[43]), whereas the East inspired fear … Hence the axiom of leaving the grey zone of post-Cold War geopolitics and defining clearly the place of Poland in the new order.[44] This axiom resulted in the accession of Poland to two most important structures on which postwar Western internationalism was based: the NATO and the EU.

Thus, after the transformation in 1989, Poland was a beneficiary of post-Cold War liberal internationalism in the sense that it helped to neutralise fundamentally two most important geopolitical threats for Central Europe. The unification of Germany took place in the atmosphere of certain concern about the future of Europe in some Western European states (France, Great Britain), but in full accordance with the assumptions of American security policy towards Europe adopted by George Bush and his administration, which was subsequently reinforced by Clinton's policy towards united Germany under the strategy of partnership for leadership in Europe. Within this policy, Germany played the role of America's strategic partner in the establishment of the guarantee of development

43 P. Sztompka (1993): Civilisation Incompetence. The Trap of Post-Communist Societies, *Zeitschrift fur Soziologie*, Jg. 22. Heft 2, April 1993, pp. 85–95.

44 I. Prizel, A. Michta (1995): *Polish Foreign Policy Reconsidered*, New York: St. Martin's Press, p. 158.

of the liberal European order. Also with regard to transformation processes in Russia and in the post-Soviet territory, liberal internationalism played an important role in the neutralisation of the potential risk of resurrection of threats from the East due to its openness towards Moscow, strategic concessions and the development of new forms of co-operation. The results of this policy coincided with the objective weakening of Russia as the former superpower after the collapse of the Soviet Union. Thus, in the 1990s, both Germany and Russia were compatible, each in its own way, with post–Cold War assumptions of the liberal order in Europe, which had a favourable impact on the security of Central Europe. This solution made it possible to avoid the situation from the interwar period, when two revisionist forces towards the Versailles order – Germany and Russia – eventually brought about its collapse and a new war.[45]

However, the impact of the liberal order on Poland was not only a geopolitical factor. Equally important was the economic and systemic transformation being carried out in accordance with the then-prevailing neo-liberal paradigm and with the assistance of the main international organisations. The aim of the process was to integrate Poland as a country recovering from communism with the economic, institutional and political system of the liberal order and to adapt the functioning of the state and society to liberal practices and norms. The author's intention is not to evaluate this transformation process, but it must be noticed that, in spite of various achievements, it has met with increasing internal criticism referring to social costs, inequalities, the lack of participation in the process, weak transparency and democratic control, or excessive interference in issues concerning identity, culture and traditional norms.[46] Thus, while geopolitical consequences of Poland's integration in the structures of the liberal order did not cause serious controversy, its economic and social or normative results gradually aroused intense fears and criticism. The call for openness and liquidation of borders that was a characteristic factor of liberal internationalism and the European integration and related practices were undoubtedly revealing both their positive and negative consequences.

From the viewpoint of the current crisis of liberal internationalism, Poland is still a country that has not experienced directly any of its concrete symptoms. Unlike Baltic states or Hungary, Poland did not suffer substantially the consequences of the financial crisis after 2009. It was not affected directly by the migrant crisis after 2015, either. Even the Ukrainian crisis caused by Russia and

45 *Ibid.*, p. 159.

46 Cf. T. Kowalik (2009): www.Polskatransformacja.pl, Warsaw: Muza.

the annexation of the Crimea in 2014 affects the security of Poland only to an indirect extent. Apart from producing certain tensions and a sense of insecurity, Brexit or the serious change of American policy towards Europe under Donald Trump's administration have not brought existential threats from the perspective of Poland's interests so far. In this sense, Poland is not subject to the crisis of the liberal order and does not suffer its consequences directly, which does not mean that the crisis has no impact on the intellectual and political atmosphere in and around Poland or that the change of the situation in Europe and around the world do not result in processes that will have a fundamental impact on circumstances for Poland in the next few years. The prospect of a trade war, the pressure towards protectionism in Europe, the change of American security policy, particularly towards Europe, growing internal conflicts in the EU that increasingly often become normative and ideological – all of these factors create potentially serious challenges for Poland. In one aspect, however, Poland has already become clearly subject to the crisis of the liberal West. It is a question of the normative aspect, the order of values and the culture war. The liberal vs. non-liberal opposition has become a clear sign of the crisis of the perception of the West as a community fostering liberal values and the main line of conflict within Europe. The placement of current Polish policies on the "non-liberal" side, regardless of how we evaluate its reasons, leads to real consequences, such as the undermining of Poland's position in Western countries and conflicts with European institutions, but on the other hand, it also moves Poland clearly towards those that make attempts to understand the West in a more differentiated manner without identifying it with liberalism on a full scale. Thus, being a beneficiary of the post–Cold War Western liberal order after 1989, modern Poland is facing the potential consequences of its crisis today. Also the attitude to liberal internationalism increasingly often becomes a part of the internal political dispute in Poland.

References

Allison G. (2018): The Myth of the Liberal Order, *Foreign Affairs*, vol. 97, Issue 4.

Chaudoin S., Milner H., Tingley D. (2010): The Center still Holds. Liberal Internationalism Survives, *International Security*, vol. 35, no. 1, pp. 75–94.

Chaudoin S., Milner H., Tingley D. (2011): Roundtable. Is Liberal Internationalism Still Alive?, *H-Diplo/ISSF Roundtable Reviews*, vol. II, no. 4 (2011) 2.

Cooper R. (2003): *The Breaking of Nations*, New York: Grove Press.

Deneen P.J. (2018): *Why liberalism failed*, New Haven: Yale University Press.

Ehrlich L. (1918): The War and Political Theory, *California Law Review*, vol. 6 (Sept. 1918) and vol. 7 (Nov. 1918).

Ferguson N. (2016): Barack Obama's Revolution in Foreign Policy, *The National Business Review*.

Fukuyama F. (1992): *The End of History and the Last Man*, New York: Free Press.

Fukuyama F. (2006): *America at the Crossroads: Democracy, Power, and the Neoconservative Legacy*, New Haven: Yale University Press.

Furedi F. (2018): *Populism and the European Culture Wars*, London, New York: Routledge.

Gaddis J.L. (1991): Toward the Post-Cold War World, *Foreign Affairs*, vol. 70, no. 2.

Gaddis J.L. (2005): *The Cold War: A New History*, New York: The Penguin Press.

Halecki O. (2000): Historia Europy – jej granice i podziały [The History of Europe – Its Borders and Divisions], Lublin: Instytut Europy Środkowo-Wschodniej.

Holbraad C. (2003): *Internationalism and Nationalism in European Political Thought*, New York: Palgrave.

Ikenberry G.J. (2004): The End of the Neo-Conservative Moment, *Survival*, vol. 46, no. 1, pp. 7–22.

Ikenberry J.G. (2018): The end of liberal international order?, *International Affairs*, 94/1.

Keane J. (2009): *The Life and Death of Democracy*, New York: W. W. Norton & Company.

Kissinger H. (2018): We are in a very, very grave period, Financial Times, 20 July 2018.

Kowalik T. (2009): *www.Polskatransformacja.pl*, Warsaw: Muza.

Krastev I. (2017): *After Europe*, Philadelphia: University of Pennsylvania Press.

Kundnani H. (2017): What is the Liberal International Order?, GMF Policy Essay, no. 17/2017.

Kupchan Ch.A., Trubowitz P.L. (2007): Dead Center. Demise of Liberal Internationalism in the United States, *International Security*, vol. 32, no. 2, pp. 7–44.

Kupchan Ch.A., Trubowitz P.L. (2010): The Illusion of Liberal Internationalism's Revival, *International Security*, vol. 35, no. 1 (Summer 2010), pp. 95–109.

Lilla M. (2017): *The Once and Future Liberal. After Identity Politics*, New York: HarperCollins Publisher.

Mazower M. (2012): *Governing the World. The History of an Idea*, London: Penguin Books.

Müller J.W. (2016): *What is Populism?*, Philadelphia: University of Pennsylvania Press.

Nemo Ph. (2006): *What is the West?*, Pittsburgh: Duquesne University Press.

Niblett R. (2017): Liberalism in retreat, *Foreign Affairs*, January/February 2017.

Piketty T. (2014): *Capital in the Twenty-First Century*, Cambridge: Harvard University Press.

Porter P. (2018): A World Imagined. Nostalgia and Liberal Order, Cato Institute Political Analysis, no. 843/2018.

Prizel I., Michta A. (1995): *Polish Foreign Policy Reconsidered*, New York: St. Martin's Press.

Ruggie J. (1982): International Regimes, Transactions, and Change: Embedded Liberalism in the Postwar Economic Order, *International Organisation*, vol. 36, no. 2, pp. 379–415.

Shapiro J., Witney N. (2009): Towards a Post-American Europe, ECFR.

Singer P. (2002): *One World. The Ethics of Globalization*, New Haven: Yale University Press.

Slaughter A.-M. (2004): *A New World Order*, Princeton: Princeton University Press.

Staniland P. (2018): Misreading the "Liberal Order": Why We Need New Thinking in American Foreign Policy, Lawfare Blog.

Suri J. (2017): How Trump's Executive Orders Could Set America Back 70 Years, "Atlantic", January 27, 2017.

Sztompka P. (1993): Civilisation Incompetence. The Trap of Post-Communist Societies, *Zeitschrift fur Soziologie*, Jg. 22. Heft 2, April 1993, pp. 85–95.

Trump's speech in the UN: https://www.whitehouse.gov/briefings-statements/remarks-president-trump-73rd-session-united-nations-general-assembly-new-york-ny/, [Access: 11.02.2019].

Wandycz P. (1993): Liberal Internationalism: The Quest for a "Polish Variant", *Polish Western Affairs*, no. 2.

Zakaria F. (1997): The Rise of Illiberal Democracy, *Foreign Affairs*, Nov/Dec 1997, 76/6.

Olaf Osica

Crisis and adjustment. The liberal order in Europe from the perspective of Poland

Abstract: The author presents the basic models of international order organization, and then discusses the concept of liberal order and its functioning in post Cold War Europe. On this basis, he formulates the thesis that the current crisis is the result of the simultaneous overlap and persistence of many other crises that have been strengthened as a result of the technological revolution in the information culture. Not only did countries lose a significant part of their ability to communicate and influence social attitudes but they also proved vulnerable in the face of the speed of socio-political processes. However, the crisis has forced a correction that creates opportunities for the liberal order to continue functioning in Europe but at the price of lowered global ambitions and focus on internal socio-economic problems. Finally, the context of Poland is presented below as a state which is a beneficiary of the liberal order. However, further development dilemmas require greater compatibility with Western countries.

Keywords: world order, liberal order, crisis

It is not accidental that discussions on global governance – its essence, structure and goal – have always characterised turning points in which the rules of global politics change significantly. This turning point may be sometimes the end of the war or sometimes the belief that growing problems cannot be solved effectively within the current system of international co-operation. The modern Western world, particularly Europe, is facing such a turning point nowadays.

The constantly smouldering economic and political crisis in Europe, the growing popularity of political groups questioning not only the rules of functioning of Western institutions, but primarily their democratic legitimacy, the rise of China's power and the partially resulting attack on free trade as a pillar of modern global economic governance – all of these processes seem to destroy the liberal principles of international politics irreversibly.

Because of the fragmentariness of the analysis, the insufficient interpenetration of political, economic, social and technological perspectives, the excessively small time distance and the diversity of national and social experiences, it is difficult to adopt one coherent definition of the phenomenon that is usually labelled as the crisis of the Western community.

For some people, the factor of key importance is the crisis of American leadership resulting from the rebellion against the USA as the "liberal Leviathan" after 1945 and the growing objection against globalisation and free trade flow.[1] For others, civilisational elements are decisive: they think that liberal ideas have led to the self-destruction of Western identity, which has become diluted in the world of universalistic ideas and has lost the ability to defend its own narration and, consequently, interests.[2] According to Tony Judt, the problem lies in the crisis of the middle class in Western Europe, which has been deprived of state support as a result of the disintegration of public services.[3] The reasons for the crisis from the perspective of political economy were analysed by Dani Rodrik, who depicted mutual controversies between globalisation, democracy and sovereignty, as a result of which states cannot attempt to fulfil all of these three conceptions at the same time.[4]

The list of authors analysing the reasons for the Western crisis could be much longer.[5] However, the aim is not to prove the generality of beliefs concerning the Western crisis, but to stress that the visible process of weakening of the liberal global governance is mainly a consequence of the internal problems of Western politics. The economic crisis, the growing importance of movements undermining the social order and rules of political game in Europe and the sense of endangered security seem to foreshadow the end of the liberal empire. However, as this paper shows, the conviction that the world has suddenly become an unwelcoming place for liberal ideas is illusory to a large extent. Actually, it has always been such a place, but the opponents were weak and the Western world was aware of its own limitations and errors. It is not accidental that the 1990s were defined as the time of chaos by contemporary observers, but this was not quite true, either.[6]

---

1 G.J. Ikenberry (2011): *Liberal Leviathan. The Origins, Crisis, and Transformation of the American World Order*, Princeton: Princeton University Press, p. 10, I. Krastev (2016): The Specter Haunting Europe: The Unravelling of the Post-1989 Order, Journal of Democracy, 27 (7), p. 5.

2 A. Michta (2017): The Deconstruction of the West, *The American Interest*, 12 April 2017, https://www.the-american-interest.com/2017/04/12/the-deconstruction-of-the-west/.

3 T. Judt (2011): *Źle ma się kraj. Rozprawa o naszych współczesnych bolączkach*, Wołowiec: Wydawnictwo Czarne.

4 D. Rodrik (2007): The inescapable trilemma of the world economy, 27 June 2007, https://rodrik.typepad.com/dani_rodriks_weblog/2007/06/the-inescapable.html.

5 See the anthology of texts Foreign Affairs 2017.

6 See S. Hoffmann (2000): *World Disorders. Troubled Peace in the Post-Cold War Era*, Rowman & Littlefield Publishers.

So, does the problem lie in the exhaustion of the model, or are we witnessing the crisis of confidence in liberal ideas or the crisis of the liberal force that is unable to defend its own governance against its enemies?

In order to take a step towards the answer, this essay will present primary models of organisation of global governance. Later, the concept of liberal governance and its functioning in post–Cold War Europe will be discussed. On this basis, the author will put forward the thesis that the current crisis is a result of the simultaneous overlapping and permanence of many other crises that have been reinforced as a result of the technological revolution in the information culture. States not only have lost an essential part of their ability to communicate and influence social attitudes, but have also proved defenceless in view of the speed of social-political processes. However, the crisis enforced an adjustment that creates an opportunity for the further existence of liberal governance in Europe, but at the expense of lower global ambitions and concentration on internal social-political issues.

Three models of the "logic of hierarchies"

In political debates concerning the crisis or, according to some opinions, the end of the liberal global governance, we can observe very often the disregard of the concept of "global governance", which is not an obvious phenomenon in itself. In the classical theory of international relations, according to which the world is governed by the logic of anarchy, the rivalry between sovereign states tends to encourage them to enter into temporary alliances aimed at the maximisation of their own strength. The aims of state policy are to multiply resources and gain advantage over others, not to build permanent foundations of co-operation. From this perspective, global governance is only a description of the multi-level rivalry between states in the permanently unstable environment.

Thus, governance understood as an international order assumes hierarchisation that is an essential part of each organisation and structure. This means that it is a consequence of states' actions rather than a reflection of the natural state of affairs, which is always closer to anarchy. The form of global architecture resulting from state attempts differs with regard to ways of organisation of strength, power and institutions.

Global governance can be created and maintained in one of the three fundamental ways: by balancing the interests of states, the rule (dominance) of some states over others, or as a result of agreement between states.

Global governance based on the mutual balancing of states is maintained by using the balance of powers between them. Therefore, the order is a result of the stalemate in which players cannot make a movement because no one can dominate and control others. From this perspective, governance is maintained by means of alliances, or by hindering the growth of others' strength or blackmailing them with actions targeted at others' interests. The Concert of Powers or the Cold War functioned within the order understood in this way.

The second model approach to global governance assumes the dominance of one state that organises and enforces order. States are organised vertically and their position in the hierarchy is determined according to the top-down principle. The method of enforcement of order is similar: force is used towards some states and negotiations towards others. Everything depends on how the leader defined the place and role of each state in the hierarchy. Examples of international imperial orders are countless: from the Roman Empire and the British Empire to the Soviet Union. The common feature of imperial governance is the economic exploitation of states by the leader and the imposition of the legal order and the dominant culture upon them. In other words, imperial governance is based on the formal inequality of states towards the creator of the system, which is manifested by the obligation to participate, the lack of possibility of forming legal principles and institutions and the absence of any strategical autonomy. The aim of such governance is only to fulfil the leader's interests.

The third type of global governance is the order based on rules and institutions agreed upon and accepted by participants in governance that regulate the rights and obligations of states. Common institutions determine also the limits of strength of states. Consensual global governance does not imply the political equality of states, which is reflected by differences in the voting power of states in institutions, both in the formal sense (e.g., the number of votes) and the actual sense (the advantage of strength in terms of bigger economic or political strength). Nevertheless, no state can impose its rules on others straightforwardly. It must negotiate them and persuade others to adopt them within the scope of applicable rules. Also the pressure that is an essential element of political activity must fall within the canon of rules acceptable by the parties. This model of governance is the closest to the understanding of the liberal order built around the USA in the form of the North Atlantic Alliance or around France and Germany in the form of the European Union (more about this below), but is characterises many systemic solutions that sought stability in the creation of the order based on common rules and the formal equality of states.

It depends mainly on the intentions of states whether orders based on rules prove effective or become only a curtain for the unrestrained will of states. If joining an international institution is motivated not by compliance with rules, but by the use of membership only for extending the field of political manoeuvres, such an institution will never fulfil its goals. Examples of this include the United Nations System or its copy – the concept of building European safety on the basis of the Organisation for Security and Co-operation in Europe. Both orders proved unable to secure global governance for real due to the divergence of states' interests, i.e., the readiness to comply with the rules that they formally accepted. The same is happening to the World Trade Organisation today. The only modern example of consensual governance existing on a global scale is still the International Monetary Fund, which results from the conviction of states that there is no real alternative to obtaining financial aid on a large scale that is not followed by the dependence occurring in bilateral agreements between borrowers and creditors.

In various moments of history, international order has been organised according to one of the aforementioned rules or has been a combination of them. Differences in the evaluation and perception of governance obviously depend on the position of the evaluating party. The perspective of political beneficiaries of governance differs from the perspective of those on whom this governance is imposed. In times of the Cold War, Pax Americana ensured the safety of Europe, but on the other hand, it was a curse for nations of Latin America that experienced military interventions and sponsored revolutions. The experience of Soviet policy in Eastern Europe and Latin America is also different.

Another important factor is time. Each governance becomes the object of contesting or irredentism, when, as a result of a change in the balance of powers between states – the weakening of some states and the increase of others' strength – it becomes a way of petrification of former rules than a form of arrangement of contemporary relations between states. This is one of the reasons for which Poland's opinion on the role of the USA in transatlantic relations differs from the opinion of France or Germany, which have a longer experience in this area.

Liberal governance: from Pax Britannica to Pax Americana

"The liberal international order is not just a collection of liberal democratic states but an international mutual-aid society – a sort of global political club that provides members with tools for economic and political advancement".[7] The entire century had to pass before such a definition of the liberal order could start

7 G.J. Ikenberry (2011): The Future of the Liberal World Order, *Foreign Affairs*, May/June.

its career – first in Western Europe after World War II and then in the whole Europe and the world after the end of the Cold War.

The concept of the liberal international order evolved in the course of time. It is historically attributed to the birth of British power, which promoted the stability and openness of the international system on the basis of free trade in the 19th century. The British conception of the liberal order was, on the one hand, a reflection of internal processes in England, primarily the Industrial and Democratic Revolution that formed the foundations of state power; however, in the strategical sense, Pax Britannica was considerably different from the modern understanding of liberal governance. It was based on the imperial attitude to other nations, particularly those being conquered in Africa and Asia, which manifests itself in the stress on the primacy of the white man, the economic exploitation of colonies and the imposition of one's own rules of law and culture.

In the 20th century, the construction of the liberal order became the goal of American policy. This process had three stages. The first one occurred in the interwar period (1918–1939), when U.S. President Woodrow Wilson promoted the project of the League of Nations and the self-determination of states; however, he kept the United States far from direct involvement in European affairs. However, this ended in a rapid crisis and led to the collapse of the governance, which never achieved critical political mass, becoming a conception under construction rather than the foundation of real politics.

The second stage concerned the victory of the Allies over Nazi Germany and the decision to leave American troops in Europe in view of the expansion of the Soviet Union. The Cold War was a clash of two hierarchically built international orders: the American order based on the promotion of the open political and economic model that brought an increase of strength and position to Europe, Japan and South Korea, and the Soviet order based on the imperial logic assuming the full subordination and exploitation of the allied states. In Europe, the driving force for the new order was both the North Atlantic Alliance and the subsequent European Economic Community. Both institutions complemented each other, laying the foundations for the Atlantic security community acting on the basis of consensus in spite of obvious differences in the potential and strength of states and divergent interests.

And the final stage of the American concept of the liberal world order took place after the end of the Cold War. In Europe, its essence was the inclusion of Central European states in the joint institutions of the Western world, particularly the NATO and the EU, and the enlargement of the impact of Western political and socio-economic ideas and concepts with the post-Soviet territory, including Russia. In the global dimension, global governance after the Cold War was symbolised by the dominance of Western political and economic thought in the global discussion on sources of development. Free trade in goods and services, the unrestrained flow of capital and ideas, and market economy based on the minimum intervention of the state formed the creed of liberal governance.

In international security matters, the sovereignty of the state was subjected to restrictions. The liberal international society reserved not only the right to intervene in situations when governments violate the rights of citizens of states. Established in the mid-1990s, the conception of co-operative security included also the restriction of conventional armaments, mutual access to inspections of military infrastructure or co-operation in military missions as well as political and economic aspects, such as the recognition of the international position, participation in decisions on the rules of co-operation and access to markets and capital. Moreover, it created a series of incentives in the form of broadly understood access to resources and institutions, i.e., participation in politics, in return for the adoption of liberal solutions in internal policy.

The juxtaposition of possible constellations of global governance based on the balance of powers, dominance or consensus with the sketchy history of development of the liberal conception allows us to identify the characteristics that constitute the liberal world order as a separate type of governance.[8]

Firstly, the concept of liberal governance is characterised by its regulatory openness, which allows institutions to act as a place where agreement is reached and, at the same time, to guarantee the flexibility of the system as such. In the ideal world of liberal governance, there is no balancing of interests or need to dominate, because states are in the permanent process of negotiation based on entering into agreements in consideration of mutual interests. The rules of law and procedures of institutions replace the need for the policy of strength and physical constraint.

Secondly, the concept of liberal governance does not assume in advance any specific hierarchy, rigid principles of ruling or certain fixed relations between states. Thus, changes in hierarchy can occur within the scope of the system without destroying it, which is impossible in orders based on rigidly assigned places and roles of states. The attractiveness of the liberal world order for small and weak states manifests itself in the fact that they can compensate their strategic weaknesses with a strong economic position as areas of strong growth, with a strong political position as effective negotiators or with a strong regional position as important liaisons and leaders. A unique characteristic of the liberal order

8 G.J. Ikenberry (2011): *Liberal…, op. cit.*, pp. 18–20.

is the co-existence of institutions with a global reach and regional institutions, as well as the possibility of overlapping of competences of organisations that compete with each other.

Thirdly, it is often forgotten that the liberal world order is based on states as dominant actors and modern institutions serving as frameworks for the management and, consequently, restraining of powers. In this sense, the liberal international order results from the realistic perception of the reality in which the strength and interests of states is a key concept. However, it forms the reality in a manner that makes it impossible to amortise and restrain the selfish intentions of states.

From a historical perspective, liberal global governance reflected the interests of its main promoters – Great Britain and subsequently the United States, which fulfilled their global domination through co-operation, negotiations and openness – the foundations on which their internal development was based. This also explains why the permanence of liberal governance enforces the convergence of political and social foundations of states in the long term.

The crisis, adjustment or exhaustion of the model?

In the introductory part of the Munich Security Report opening the 2017 Munich Security Conference – one of the oldest conferences devoted to European and global safety that is attended by a few hundred leaders of governments and international organisations and influential experts, we can read that the world is facing an illiberal moment.

> Across the West and beyond, illiberal forces are gaining ground. From within, Western societies are troubled by the emergence of populist movements that oppose critical elements of the liberal-democratic status quo. From outside, Western societies are challenged by illiberal regimes trying to cast doubt on liberal democracy and weaken the international order. And Western states themselves seem both unwilling and unable to effectively tackle the biggest security crises – with Syria as the prime example.[9]

The above diagnosis contains many elements that seem familiar, even though their scale may be really surprising. Thus, when analysing the reasons for problems that led to the crisis of liberal governance built after the Cold War, it is necessary to separate the political reality from the political myth, because the political reality of the post–Cold War era has never been idyllic.

9 Munich Security Report 2017 – Munich Security Conference 2017.

Firstly, the order built around European integration and Atlantic co-operation resulted in the economic boom of Central Europe and the unprecedented sense of stability in the region troubled by the rivalry between superpowers. However, it failed to cover everyone to an equal extent.

In spite of compromises and openness regarding arms control, co-operation with the North Atlantic Alliance and resignation from the deployment of military infrastructure and forces in territories of new NATO members, Russia chose to remain outside the Western system, retaining only channels of co-operation. The goal of Russia was to carry out its own idea for the organisation of order in Europe, which was based on the separation of the political zones of influence and loose economic co-operation, mainly with regard to deliveries of energy resources. This idea was symbolised by Russian attempts to turn the Organisation for Security and Co-operation in Europe into the main institution managing Europe's security, with the European Security Council as the body of superpowers. Russia tried to force a similar idea in co-operation with the European Union when attempting to transform bilateral summits into a place of making key decisions concerning the rules of functioning of the unified market, as well as the economic activity of the EU in the East.

The Balkans, Eastern Europe and Caucasus found themselves on the margin of the system, though not entirely of their own choice. In spite of the intentions of these regions to join the EU and the NATO, they were not able to generate a strong impulse for modernisation or had a dissuasive scale of problems. The Balkan Civil War, the frozen conflicts in Transnistria and the Nagorno-Karabakh and the strong influence of Russia created a hybrid zone of influence around the enlarged EU, in which European hopes and ambitions of societies clashed with the tough political reality of governments balancing on the border of Russian pressure and European requirements.

The second departure from the conviction that the past was a streak of successes, whereas the present proves the collapse of the liberal order, was caused by the dimension of security. The wars around Europe did not cease along with the end of the Cold War era. On the contrary, they continued to break out in many areas: from the Balkans and North Caucasus to Georgia. If those events did not signify the crisis of the governance, why would Ukrainian and Syrian wars indicate it? The same goes for the breakdown of the political map of North Africa and the Middle East. At the time of the outbreak of the Arab Spring, this process was fuelled on the social level by disagreement with the regional order based on brutal persecutions of societies by governments and permanent social underdevelopment resulting from endemic corruption. This order functioned with the consent and participation of creators of liberal governance in Europe. Also wars in Iraq and Afghanistan resulted from the will to enlarge the liberal sphere of life of states and societies. Today the Arab Spring and both interventions are quoted as errors that contributed to the erosion of the liberal order. In reality, they were an unsuccessful attempt to spread this order onto the neighbouring regions of Europe.

Thirdly, the dominance of the Western conception of global governance resulted from the lack of other real conceptions. Both the EU and the NATO were strong not only due to their own resources and abilities, but also due to the weakness of their competitors. Neither Russia nor China had the sufficient strength and conviction that they could win a dispute about the form of governance. They were economically weak states focusing on their own problems and lacking an interesting political offer for other states. Russia demanded being recognised and invited to "take a seat at the table" as the successor of the Soviet Union. Focusing on economic transformations, China was not interested in building independently an alternative to the system that opened for them the way to global trade expansion without the requirement of "internal liberalisation".

The accession of new states to the North Atlantic Alliance and the European Union was possible not only due to the good economic situation in the West and the activity of Western companies in entering the markets of Central Europe, but also the lack of alternative conceptions of the organisation of governance backed up by relevant political and financial resources. Similarly, the NATO's interventions in Bosnia and in Kosovo would not have been possible if Russia would have had real retaliatory measures.

In such a context, the crisis of American leadership and disputes with Europe did not seem as threatening as today, but, after all, they have gone hand in hand with the transatlantic co-operation since its beginning. Europe experienced them both during the Cold War (the Suez Crisis in 1956, the policy of Ronald Reagan's administration towards the USSR) and after it. It is sufficient to recall Bill Clinton's policy in the first years of the Balkan War or the dispute about Iraq with George W. Bush's administration. These moments provided political fuel to the followers of European autonomy, but the conviction of one's comfortable situation and the lack of agreement with regard to the scope and definition of autonomy did not lead to real redefinitions. The creation of institutions devoid of real resources and support was the result of crises. The current dispute concerning the policy of Donald Trump's administration is potentially more significant. The blow was aimed not at European strategic ambitions, but at the very heart.

The belief in the power of the liberal organisation of institutions of the Western world brought about the tendency to turn a blind eye to the shortcomings of the process of building strong democratic institutions in candidate countries intending to join the EU and the NATO. A leading example of this was the fact that none of the new member states of the alliance reformed their military education system or elaborated a civil army control system; all they did was nominate a civil politician as head of the ministry of defence. Also in the European Union enlargement process, many weaknesses concerning the functioning of public institutions – from the health care sector and the higher education system to courts, prosecutors, the police and the media – were omitted in the conviction that the power of impact of European institutions combined with economic growth will ensure adjustment and making up for deficits.

Therefore, looking back (*post factum*), we can put forward the thesis that the idea of the golden age of safety and development built on the basis of liberal institutions and ideas has always been strongly marked by hypocrisy or naivety. Thus, it was an expression of unusual courage in the modelling of the world according to liberal standards rather than the price for belief in the "end of history". However, for all contemporary challenges, the balance-sheet of gains and losses is still positive. However, the current crisis of the West caused a radical change of perspectives.

Western politics looks at the world no longer as a place to be conquered, but as a place that produces only threats. Revolutions in North Africa, the Syrian War, terror attacks in Europe, the aggression of Russia against Ukraine and the wave of migrations put an end to the belief in the opportunity to build a stable and prosperous neighbourhood around Europe according to the order based on the liberal conception of co-operation. The Western world experienced not only a structural economic crisis, but also war.

All fears of the West were presented to the fullest extent by Ivan Krastev.[10] In his opinion, the post–Cold War order is disintegrating in three ways. Firstly, the West is losing strength and influence in the international system, as reflected in the rising position of China and Russia, and a proliferating number of armed conflicts. Secondly, the Western model of market democracy is losing its universal appeal, as we can see from the widespread backlash now taking place against globalisation and the free movement of goods, capital, people and ideas. Thirdly, the West's own liberal-democratic regime model is facing pressure from populist forces and governments. In Krastev's view, all of this is leading to the full or partial disintegration of the European Union, Turkey's exit from the NATO,

10 I. Krastev (2016), *op. cit.*

the breakup of Belgium and Spain and the return of Central Europe to authoritarian regime models known from the 1930s.

The ideas of Krastev and many other authors have a weakness: they focus on the symptoms of the problem rather than on its sources. The essence of the problem seems to be the situation defined by Dani Rodrik as a conflict between the democratic system of the state, the advanced integration of its economy with global economy and sovereignty in the economic and social policy of states.[11] Just as free competition is able to create conditions for the monopolisation of economy sectors as a result of the takeover of weaker players by stronger players in the course of time, the liberal idea of global governance created conditions for the emergence of mutually exclusive trends. Rodrik's trilemma assumes that we can have at the same time only two out of the three values of liberal governance: democracy, sovereignty and integration. Democracy goes hand in hand with sovereignty, but not with globalisation. The latter can co-exist with the democratic idea, but at the cost of sovereignty of states, and globalisation impeded by the sovereign government requires the restriction of democratic rights.

Rodrik suggests that what is called the end of liberal governance, is actually the result of two processes: the weakening of Western power, which does not allow the West to impose its sovereignty on others, and the rebellion of citizens who demand the protection of their cultural and social identities, at the same time wanting to enjoy the benefits arising from the openness of the world.

In political practice, it is not possible to go back to the good old times when globalisation was only a source of Western advantages. The trilemma drawn by Rodrik is obviously unsolvable. The answer can be only the adjustment of the system.

It seems that the fundamental reason for errors underlying the current condition of liberal governance was the prevailing conviction of the absence of enemies. Thus, a different perception and the adoption of the assumption that liberal governance in the world and Europe has an enemy change much, if not everything. It is the beginning of deep adjustment and the beginning of the end of the crisis of this order. This can be seen on all levels: from withdrawal from an active role in international conflicts in order not to disperse strength, the recognition of Russia as the sponsor of the information war and the maintenance of sanctions towards it, to a change of the approach to the rules of free trade and the protection of the European market from Chinese investments

11 D. Rodrik (2012), *op. cit.*

in strategic sectors. In particular, a change of attitude to China seems to be a breakthrough.

For the period of the 1990s and 2000s, the increase of the economic position of China was regarded as a factor that stabilises global governance. China was entering global game not through an increase of armaments, the creation of conflicts and the demolition of global governance, but as a humble pupil of the liberal world exploiting the freedom of seas and oceans, the openness of markets and free competition. Today, the same China is treated as a player that only wants to have rights – access to other markets, infrastructure and technology, but refuses to assume obligations – opening its own market or building stable governance around itself.

The second error that has contributed to today's condition of liberal ideas of global governance was the overlooking of the moment in which its rules began to strike at the societies that were to make use of it. An example of this is the rebellion against successive free trade agreements that, by opening the wealthy markets of the West to competition from emerging economies, brought about an increase of trade turnover and economic growth, but at the expense of impoverishment of local societies.

The problem lies in the fact that governments have ignored a simple principle: the real competition takes place when its essence is better organisation, work efficiency or the intellectual advantage. However, if the competitive edge results from actions that are treated in Western states and societies (the destruction of the environment and slave labour), it has nothing in common with real competition. Therefore, the demand for free trade assumes the form of fair trade today.

It is too early to prejudge how the adjustment of the system will translate to the political hierarchy, rules and institutions and whether it succeeds. However, on the level of both the North Atlantic Alliance, the European Union and individual states, we deal with the consolidation of liberal governance based on abandoning universalistic areas and closing off from others on the geographical and regulatory level. The aim is to rebuild resources and abilities that will make it possible to restore influence in the future.

Crisis or Polish incompatibility?

From the Polish viewpoint, the adjustment of Polish governance in Europe entails a number of challenges and risks that require not only the consideration of one's place and role in the new reality, but also a change of the political strategy. In unfavourable circumstances, the Polish reaction to changes in the Western system may become a source of strategic misunderstanding.

Firstly, from the perspective of the Polish political strategy towards the Western world, the value of liberal governance is reduced primarily to the presence of the leader and the guardian of the order and only secondarily to the rules of functioning of the system: the role of rules, institutions and principles of co-operation between states. This approach departs from the Polish historical experience, in which the conception and durability of liberal governance was a guarantee of Polish sovereignty and development in 1918 and of support for the fight against communism in the 1970s and 1980s, and after 1989. In other words, Polish sovereignty is a product of the liberal conception of the international order, not only American politics. Other forms of organisation of global governance brought the end of independence, functioning with the colonial status, or the lack of interest in the Polish cause. Being America's ally in the liberal world order and in the world based on the "traditional" balance of powers are two diametrically different perspectives. In the first case, Poland can act as a partner; in the second case, it can only be a client. Such is the historical experience, too.

The period of the best relations between Poland and the United States, when Poland's international position was really on the increase, occurred during the rule of presidents who wanted to promote the liberal ideas of world organisation: Woodrow Wilson, Jimmy Carter, Ronald Reagan, Bill Clinton and George W. Bush. Both terms of office of Barrack Obama and the current presidency of Donald Trump prove how much America's closing off from the problems of the world and the departure from the gendarme's role to the function of an active observer results in the narrowing of the room for manoeuvre of Polish politics in the transatlantic model.

Secondly, as mentioned above, the liberal order of the Western world contains many Hobbesian elements, not only Kantian ones. It was built on the basis of culturally similar national states in the conviction that the law and institutions would not eliminate the problem of force in politics, but they would hinder and restrain it. Thus, the real hierarchy of influences in the Western world is always the product of the strength of states, not a question of treaties. The formal balance in institutions created on the basis of the potential (population, economic index, defence expenses, etc.) is aimed at stabilising the system, but it does not grant the right to question the hierarchy on the basis of legal provisions. In other words, liberal governance inscribed in the DNA of the North Atlantic Alliance or the UE boosts the confidence of the weak, but any change of the hierarchy occurs on the basis of a real increase of the state's strength, which is not tantamount to the increase of its potential.

Therefore, speaking about the dominance of big states and institutions shows the lack of understanding of the essence of the liberal order, the superior value of which is not the actual equality of states, but the possibility of improving one's own position thanks to access to resources of other partners.

Thus, the absence of the adjective "liberal" in governance is not a question of semantics, but of transition to an open system absorbing various institutional hierarchies and actively reducing the strength of the biggest players towards a system of limited co-operation of states, with the maintenance of real differences in their strength and actual imbalances resulting from the different potential. Such would be the consequence of transferring the consensus-based model of decision-making in the NATO to the European Union on the basis of the Council of Europe and eliminating the Commission and the Parliament as bodies having prerogatives to create law and conduct policy.

Thus, the crisis of the liberal world order does not create any opportunity for Polish politics to benefit from being an immanent part of the Western system while maintaining distance towards it, regaining formal sovereignty and increasing the field of political manoeuvre. On the other hand, assigning a more real dimension (based on the power of states at the expense of institutions and standards) to current institutions will result in Poland's drop in the hierarchy of the system due to the lack of possibility of borrowing "strength" from other institutions.

In this situation, Poland's reasonable response to the crisis of liberal governance would be to act resolutely for the purpose of its renewal by looking for methods and ways of reinforcing institutions and increasing the real influence of the West on political processes. Contesting the rules, reviewing the crisis or looking for alternative solutions within the scope of current governance seems to be a perspective affecting primarily the interests of Poland.

Polish incompatibilities: sovereignty, power and security

The inclusion of Poland in the process of repair of liberal institutions calls for the redefinition of the concept of sovereignty and strength and going beyond the simple scheme of war and peace in the approach to security. Polish political, development and security dilemmas result mainly from the incompatibility of the aforementioned concepts and, consequently, the dysfunctional organisation of the state.

Firstly, this refers to the way in which sovereignty is understood. Globalisation and the growing importance of intangible resources – capital, knowledge, services, information – is still a challenge for the coherence of the Western world and the ability to defend it against the unfavourable consequences of the open socio-economic model. It is a much bigger challenge than facing traditional threats that are physically recognisable.

The strongest Western states have various models in this respect. They are always connected with mature work culture (i.e., based on mutual respect or trust) on the political and clerical level, the co-ordination of processes and the sharing of information. On the legislative level, it is mainly high legislative culture, which can work out effective legal solutions that sometimes precede Community acts and become a reference point for other states and institutions. Economic sovereignty is connected with the skill of defining technical (sanitary and related) standards for the purpose of protecting the market against low-quality goods and services that replace innovative goods. In the field of public security, sovereignty requires the monopoly of the state to provide critical digital services (e.g., the authentication of identity) and, therefore, the ability to conduct the independent production of digital components.

In such a context, the real sovereignty of the state manifests itself in the ability to negotiate the scope of interference of other states, institutions and private entities rather than blocking the very fact of interference. Therefore, the level of the state's sovereignty is derived from the ability to negotiate, to create intelligent legislation and to enforce regulations effectively. An example of such a situation is the amendment of Polish banking law in July 2011 that managed to block the possibility of draining Polish branches of foreign banks that are struggling with financial difficulties. Many Polish branches had a better solvency index than their mother companies in the West.

The inconsistent undertaking of efforts by Poland in the creation of the "resource of sovereignty" consisting of the above elements may lead to the formation of imbalance and pressures both in the field of European policy (the impact on legislation) and Atlantic policy (the purchase of arms).

The second challenge is a different look at the concept of strength. The classic concept of strength reduces it to the potential of the state: the abundance of raw materials, the size and strength of the army, the size of the population and territory. The development of technology and economy based on knowledge at the turn of the 21st century proves that information technologies, the digitalisation of economy, the Internet, nanotechnology and biotechnology or the energy industry based on renewable energy sources is an important resource of the state's strength today. These are the resources that do not only allow states to build the economic and political advantage in areas that have not been connected with the concept of state strength so far, but they also decrease their exposure to the impact and blackmail of other states.

The growing significance of the club of "green" states that chose to focus on the development of renewable energy technologies is an example of this. Here, alongside China, the leading states are Germany and Denmark – the countries that do not sit in the Security Council and do not have atomic weapons. Russia and the USA are lagging behind, even though the technological race in the field of energy is an equivalent of the arms race from the Cold War period. "Green energy" is a promise of higher resistance to external energy blackmail, which means the enlargement of the strategic autonomy of the state. This leads to a change of the configuration of alliances with states where the only economic resource is the sale of energy products. For example, the pressure on electromobility in road transport has both a technological and strategic dimension: it reduces the importance of possessing petroleum in Europe's relations with Russia and Middle Eastern states.

Knowledge and science as modern critical resources of state strength are necessary to build the aforementioned modern sovereignty. The potential of economy and the army is not a strength in itself if its aggregation deviates from the ability to mobilise complex structures of state institutions, including allied institutions. Innovative thinking that is capable of searching and finding unconventional answers to development and security challenges calls for a profound change of the culture of education. Innovativeness is a state of mind, not a new way of communication of old problems. A systemic proof of this is the Israeli start-up market, whose culture is founded both on the permanent state of national threat (innovativeness in thinking about the conflict) and the army training system based on the need to make key decisions quickly by "bottom-level" commanders.

The third element is the real ability to go beyond the simple scheme of war and peace in the approach to state security. The abundance of threats and potential scenarios of deterioration of security in the territories around Poland makes it necessary to go beyond thinking about security narrowly in terms of GNP expenses on national defence and the purchase of arms. Strategic documents may only capture trends; they will never enable states to be prepared for all scenarios. The acquisition of new defence systems takes years, and their purchase is only the beginning – institutions and people still have to learn them. Because of the huge military advantage of Russia, including its possession of nuclear weapon, Poland should develop the abilities to deliver a point blow to the enemy that are described in the Strategic Defence Review 2017 and thus gain some time for the reaction of the allies. Equally important is the ability to protect the economic interests of the state, which require the ability to react outside the borders of the North Atlantic Alliance due to the growing export rate that has reached 50 % of the Polish GNP, investments beyond Europe and the strategic significance of transport routes for deliveries of raw products. Other necessary abilities include the protection of citizens (building a civil defence system from scratch in the event of catastrophes or terror attacks) and the mobilisation of civil structures of the state.

As a result of the migration crisis that swept throughout Western Europe and terror attacks, many states carried out a profound audit of police and military resources and the accompanying infrastructure. The security of Western Europe and its ability to anticipate threats seems to be improving, even though the outlays for military purposes have not increased.

Summary

The Polish experience of functioning in the post–Cold War world of the liberal conception and global governance is unique. On the one hand, Poland is the political product of this order; on the other hand, its accession to Euro-Atlantic institutions was a proof of their strength and vitality.

From the perspective of socio-economic growth, the situation is equally special. Poland did not cease to be the beneficiary of the liberal conception even at the time of crisis. This refers both to economic growth stimulated by transfers from the EU and the improvement of security as a result of the deployment of American troops in Poland. Thus, we can say that the crisis of Western liberal governance is still unfamiliar to the Polish experience.

This paradoxical situation in the history of Poland should be used for the second integrative leap. The first leap concerned the accession to a Western institution. The second one should consist in becoming an immanent part of the process of formation of rules governing the emerging new West.

The redefinition of the approach to the essence of sovereignty and the concept of strength and the practical enlargement of the concept of state security should increase the compatibility of Poland with other participants of liberal governance in Europe. Higher compatibility means the improvement of communication and co-operation and, therefore, helps to decrease Poland's development dilemmas related to the crisis and subsequent adjustment of the Western liberal system.

References

Foreign Affairs (2017): What Was the Liberal Order? The world we may be losing, available at: https://www.foreignaffairs.com/anthologies/2017-02-23/what-was-liberal-order on 27th November 2017.

Hoffmann S. (2000): *World Disorders. Troubled Peace in the Post-Cold War Era*, Lanham: Rowman & Littlefield Publishers.

Ikenberry G.J. (2011a): *Liberal Leviathan. The Origins, Crisis, and Transformation of the American World Order*, Princeton: Princeton University Press (Princeton Studies in International History and Politics).

Ikenberry G.J. (2011b): The Future of the Liberal World Order, *Foreign Affairs*, May/June 2011.

Judt T. (2011): *Źle ma się kraj. Rozprawa o naszych współczesnych bolączkach* (Polish translation), Wołowiec: Wydawnictwo Czarne.

Krastev I. (2016): The Specter Haunting Europe: The Unraveling of the Post-1989 Order, *Journal of Democracy*, 27 (7), pp. 5–15, https://www.journalofdemocracy.org/article/specter-haunting-europe-unraveling-post-1989-order, 22nd November 2017.

Michta A. (2017): The Deconstruction of the West, *The American Interest*, available at: https://www.the-american-interest.com/2017/04/12/the-deconstruction-of-the-west/ on 26th November 2017.

Munich Security Report 2017 – Munich Security Conference (2017), available at: https://www.securityconference.de/en/discussion/munich-security-report/munich-security-report-2017/, last update: 27th November 2017.

Rodrik D. (2007): The inescapable trilemma of the world economy, http://rodrik.typepad.com/dani_rodriks_weblog/2007/06/the-inescapable.html, 26th November 2017.

Rodrik D. (2012): *The Globalization Paradox. Democracy and the future of the world economy*, New York: W. W. Norton & Company.

Tomasz Grzegorz Grosse

The crisis of the West in the light of Arnold Toynbee's conception

Abstract: The conception of Arnold Toynbee assumes that the disintegration does not depend on the crises and their frequency, but rather on the deeper social and political phenomena that prevent development or even just the continuance of a given civilisation. The purpose of this chapter is to try to capture these phenomena of disintegration, as well as reflect upon whether similar phenomena can be identified in the US and during the European crises at the beginning of the twenty-first century.

Keywords: US, European Union, crisis of the West, Toynbee

Introduction

Arnold Toynbee's historiosophical conception is an attempt to analyse the rise and collapse of various civilisations. It can be a source of inspirations for scientists dealing with the "decline of the West". In this chapter, it is understood mainly with regard to the USA and the EU; at the same time, the declining tendency is reflected by the crises that have affected America and the European integration. These crises reached their height at the time of the Great Recession in the years 2008–2010, although many structural problems had emerged in the West much earlier. Toynbee's vision is pessimistic. It assumes that, since increase and development processes become exhausted at some point, the occurrence of disintegration processes that lead to the collapse of a given civilisation is inevitable, too. The scientist refers to the earlier famous work of Oswald Spengler, who dealt with the diagnosis of the decline of the West.[1] He also interpreted the Western (European and American) civilisation as resembling a living being that is born, grows up, then gets old and finally dies. Just like Spengler, Toynbee assesses various systemic phenomena that, in his opinion, signify the disintegration processes, although he does this in a more structured manner. In Toynbee's opinion, they occur within a large historical perspective, but they become more

1 O. Spengler (2001): *Zmierzch Zachodu. Zarys morfologii historii uniwersalnej*, Warsaw. English version (1991): *The Decline of the West* (Oxford Paperbacks), Oxford University Press; 1 edition, Oxford.

intense in crisis situations. And the attempt to indicate these phenomena seems to be the greatest achievement of his work.[2]

The last success preceding the decline of the civilisation is the establishment of a universal state. It is an attempt to overcome internal pressures and disintegrational tendencies and to save the ruling elites from the loss of power. Actually, however, the universal state is merely the last stage leading to the inevitable end. The USA's efforts aimed at creating a universal global order based on liberal economic and political value and on the military strength of the biggest Western power fit into this conception. The culmination point of this universalistic project was the end of the Cold War, when the global hegemony of America seemed unquestionable. Shortly afterwards, however, the ambitions of the USA turned out to be excessive, and the American power began to shake along with an increase of international importance of other powers, particularly from Asia. Another example of Toynbee's conception may be the establishment of the European Union, which has many characteristics of a universal state. After the period of unshakeable faith in the progress of integration, the EU also started to encounter huge structural problems, and successive crises in Europe were only sharp manifestations of these issues.[3]

Obviously, it is difficult to predict whether the civilisation of the West is facing the inevitable end according to Toynbee's theory. Critics of this civilisation stress the end of a certain era when the old order is dying and the new one cannot emerge yet.[4] For Zbigniew Brzeziński, the "fading of the West" involves primarily the internal structural problems of the USA that diminish its potential and capacity to adopt an optimal strategy in international relations.[5] According to Emmanuel Todd, the inevitable decline of the international role of the United States manifests itself in the militarism of this power.[6] For Wolfgang Streeck, the collapse of the West results mainly from the crisis of liberal capitalism, which has entered the period of self-destruction – self-propelling mechanisms that lead

2 A. Toynbee (1972): *A Study of History*, London.

3 Comp. T.G. Grosse (2018b): The Crisis of European Integration in the Light of the Theories of Arnold Toynbee, Western Review, *Journal of the Institute for Western Affairs in Poznań*, 2018, Special Issue 1, pp. 7–22.

4 Cf. as an example of such position: A. Gramsci (1971): *Selections from the Prison Notebooks*, London.

5 Z. Brzeziński (2013): *Strategiczna wizja. Ameryka a kryzys globalnej potęgi*, Kraków 2013. English version (2012): *Strategic Vision: America and the Crisis of Global Power*, Basic Books; 1 edition, London.

6 E. Todd (2003): *After the Empire. The Breakdown of the American Order*, New York, p. 7.

to the disintegration of the Western model of capitalism.[7] According to another similar opinion, the European Union as an integrational project has reached the end of its road, or at least has exhausted its potential for development.[8] At the same time, many researchers perceive rising powers as an alternative to the Western civilisation. On the one hand, they occupy an increasingly stronger position in the declining Western order and, to some extent, gain control of the processes and institutions of this order; on the other hand, they organise their own institutions of international order with increasing vigour.[9]

In his historiosophical conception, Toynbee incorporated the most important phenomena that indicate the disintegration and collapse process. This also applies to American hegemony, which is becoming weaker on the economic, geopolitical and ideological level. Toynbee's thought creates also an opportunity to elaborate the assumptions of the theory of regional disintegration that can be applied to the current situation in Europe.[10] In his conception, disintegration depends most strongly not on crises and their frequency, but rather on more profound social and political phenomena that prevent the development or even duration of the civilisation. In this chapter, the author attempts to capture these disintegrational phenomena and to consider whether similar ones can be identified with regard to the crisis of the West at the beginning of the 21st century.

The phenomenon of *hybris*

The universalism of the civilisation involves mainly strong expansionism, which is often undertaken through military measures. In the case of the European Union, the universal tendency refers to legal norms and values that should serve as a standard not only for the EU and its member states, but also on an international scale. The basic weapon of the EU is economic strength, which turns it into a specific geoeconomic power. Although the EU utilises economic instruments for its own benefit, they tend to be economically important for individual companies or EU states, but they represent mutual goals and geopolitical benefits to

7 W. Streeck (2016): *How Will Capitalism End? Essays on Failing System*, London – New York 2016, pp. 12–13, 16–36.

8 L. Tsoukalis (2016): *In Defence of Europe. Can the European Project Be Saved?* Oxford – New York, pp. 150, 175, 206.

9 G. Allison (2017): *Destined for War. Can America and China Escape Thucydides's Trap?* Boston – New York.

10 T.G. Grosse (2016a): Assumptions of the theory of regional disintegration: suggestions for further research, *Przegląd Europejski*, 4 (42), 2016, pp. 11–22.

a lesser extent.[11] The USA also strives to promote its values and standards in the universal international environment, but military and economic resources are the main weapon here.[12] At the same time, America's goals are geoeconomic – they assume both economic and political expansion.

Toynbee attaches much importance to the phenomenon of *hybris* – i.e., excessive ambitions (or even arrogance) that are inadequate to the actual capabilities of the universal state. Excessive expansionism generates a series of costs, particularly on the military level. Sooner or later, it also proves unadjusted to the internal potential or capacity of organisational and political structures. Thus, exaggerated ambitions resulting from universalistic attempts cannot be actually satisfied; instead, they multiply costs and, consequently, accelerate the collapse.

The United States are a good example of the aforementioned processes. According to Andrew Bacevich, America is an example of a historical empire that fulfils its hegemony and expansionism, e.g., with military means. At the same time, the American authorities create an illusion that the goals of successive wars waged by them are freedom, democracy and the defence of the liberal order based on values.[13] The military dominance of the USA towards other powers created a sense of triumphalism and the will to use military tools for intensifying economic and political influences. The American military expansion did not result in attempts to build a colony; it was rather aimed at changing governments and led to the creation of clientelistic states in various parts of the globe.[14]

The political economy of American hegemony is based on very high military expenses; their average level has reached 6 % of GDP per annum since the 1950s. These are not only the biggest expenses on a global scale – they are also the most important item of the federal budget in the USA. According to scientists, such a budget is a result of the very strong political position of the "security community", i.e., various interest groups connected with the army and the defence industry.[15] It is these groups that try to justify such high expenses by

---

11 T.G. Grosse (2014b): *W poszukiwaniu geoekonomii w Europie* [*In search of geoeconomy in Europe*], Warszawa.

12 E. Todd, *op. cit.*, p. 3.

13 A.J. Bacevich (2002): *American Empire. The Realities and Consequences of U.S. Diplomacy*, Cambridge – London, pp. 243–244.

14 M. Mann (2013): *The sources of social Power. Globalizations, 1945–2011*, Cambridge, pp. 273–275.

15 This interest group is also called a "military & industrial complex". Cf. P.W. Singer (2003): *Corporate Warriors. The Rise of the Privatized Military Industry*, Ithaca – London.

looking for an external enemy and provoking further armed conflicts.[16] Because of the resistance of electorate and political & economic elites, costs of militarism are transferred outside, which results from the internationalisation of the dollar as the main currency in global economic trade. Instead of increasing taxes, American authorities increase the amount of external debt. It grows every time the USA wages a war or increases arms expenditure. This occurred, e.g., during the Vietnam War, during the Cold War (particularly in the 1980s) and at the beginning of the 21st century as a result of the war against terror. In each case, this contributed to financial imbalance around the world and led to crises. In this way, militarism combined with the internationalisation of the dollar and liberal financial markets brought cyclic destabilisation on a global scale.[17]

Although costs of American militarism are at least partly transferred abroad (i.e., to financial investors as well as allied states and rivals of the USA), they continue to affect America itself. Even though the increase of military expenses contributes to the flourishing of development research and innovativeness of the USA and even improves consumption and reduces unemployment in the short term, it is usually followed, as a result of the influx of capital (mainly for the financing of arms expenditure) to the United States, by the appreciation of the dollar and, consequently, the weaker competitiveness of economy and export from the USA. This leads to an increase of import and the trade deficit of this state. It is worth noting that the American power has had a trade deficit since the 1970s; its average level has reached 45 billion USD in the last few years.[18] This results in a decrease of the employment level, which has an adverse impact on the tax base of the state.[19] Many scientists indicate that the final outcome of militarism is unfavourable for American economy, e.g., due to the reduction of investments.[20] Because of the concentration of federal expenses on the army,

---

16 S. Reich, R.N. Lebow (2014): *Good-Bye Hegemony! Power and Influence in the Global System*, Princeton, p. 138.

17 T. Oatley (2015): *Political Economy of American Hegemony. Buildups, Booms, and Busts*, Cambridge, pp. 4–13, 16.

18 U.S. Census Bureau, https://www.census.gov [access: 27.10.2017].

19 T. Oatley, *op. cit.*, pp. 85–106, 159.

20 D. Calleo (1982): *The Imperious Economy*, Cambridge; D. Calleo (1992): *The Bankrupting of America*, New York, 1992; R. Gilpin (1981): *War and Change in World Politics*, Cambridge; P. Kennedy (1987): *The Rise and Fall of Great Powers,* New York; Ch. Layne (2012): The Times It's Real: The End of Unipolarity and Pax Americana, *International Studies Quarterly*, No. 1 (56), pp. 203–213; K. Narizny (2007): *The Political Economy of Grand Strategy*, Ithaca; P. Trubowitz (2011): *Politics and Strategy: Partisan Ambition and American Statecraft*, Princeton.

there are fewer possibilities of financing other areas of public affairs that are indirectly or directly connected with economic growth – for example, with regard to education or public infrastructure. Both the external debt and the trade deficit signify the phenomenon of de-accumulation of capital, which proves the loss of wealth necessary to conduct an ambitious global policy in the long term.[21] It is also a proof of imperial overstretch, which characterises all empires in the history of the world and precedes their collapse.[22]

We should also take into account the geopolitical costs of the USA's militarism. Practice shows that American interventions are not always successful and do not always stabilise the situation of the region. They often lead to the escalation of conflicts between various groups or global and regional powers, political chaos and successive economic, humanitarian, migrant and other crises. American (and international) interventions are sometimes prolonged without time limitations.[23] This generates not only further financial costs, but also geopolitical costs – among others, by undermining the USA's authority in the international community and the legitimacy of this power to lead others. This harms the USA's image and international reliability, particularly with regard to values being promoted. It is also increasingly difficult to convince allies to engage in further interventions. For this reason, Brzeziński regarded wars in Iraq and Afghanistan as strategic failures of the USA.[24]

As I have mentioned, the USA's militarism is one of the reasons for the crisis of the American state. It affects many spheres of social life, which has an adverse impact on economic, social and political growth. Streeck writes about the collapse of state and democratic structures in the USA and about the big capital preying on political institutions.[25] Brzeziński indicates a series of the USA's weaknesses that not only reduce structurally the American potential, but also – as the USA is the leader of the trans-Atlantic community – have an adverse impact on the whole West. Among America's weaknesses, he mentions the undercapitalisation of the infrastructure, the shortcomings of the educational system and the growing ignorance of the Americans, the lack of effective

21 W. Streeck, *op. cit.*, p. 18; Ch. Layne, *op. cit.*, p. 204.

22 P. Kennedy, *op. cit.*, p. 158; M. Mann, *The sources of social Power*, *op. cit.*, p. 318.

23 R. Pape (2009): Empire Falls, *National Interest*, no. 22, January 2009, p. 158; S. Reich, R.N. Lebow, *op. cit.*, pp. 1, 137; E. Todd, *op. cit.*, pp. 2, 21; M. Mann (2003): *Incoherent Empire*, London – New York, pp. 13–15, 253–260; M. Mann, *The sources of social Power*, *op. cit.*, pp. 319–320.

24 Z. Brzeziński, *op. cit.*

25 W. Streeck, *op. cit.*, p. 15.

regulations of economy, particularly capital markets, and the paralysis of the political system, which is increasingly often unable to conduct a strategic and effective foreign policy.[26] It is difficult not to regard this as a sign of the imperial *hybris*.

In Europe, we can also observe exaggerated ambitions and attempts that are disproportionate towards the structural potential, particularly its organisational and financial aspects. The European *hybris* has no reference to militarism yet, but it clearly goes hand in hand with institutional, political and administrative weaknesses, which also characterises the American crisis of state structures. The reason of these weaknesses is simple: the European Union itself is not a state – it is based to a large extent on the potential of member states, which are often weakened by the integration.

It is not a coincidence that the promoters of European integration treated the EU as a project aimed at continuous development and the successive intensification of co-operation, which cannot be reversed and, therefore, leaves no possibility of disintegration. The discrepancy of these ambitions with reality during successive crises prevents further expansion, or even may contribute to an internal collapse. In the UE, the introduction of the common currency was an example of excessive ambitions that were not backed up by relevant institutional activities. This project was aimed not only at cementing the internal market, but also at opening the possibility of competing with the American dollar as an international currency and, therefore, ensuring economic and geopolitical benefits to Europe on a global scale. Last but not least, it was to pave the way to a political union – a future European federation. However, it turned out that the currency union was not properly institutionalised in case of a serious crisis, which brought this project to the brink of bankruptcy in 2012, and a number of problems have not been solved since then.[27] According to Streeck, since it is impossible to reform the Eurozone, this idea would have to be abandoned because it entails too high costs for the integration process and for democracy in Europe.[28]

The eastern expansion of the EU (i.e. 2004–2007 enlargement) is regarded as another proof of European expansionism going beyond its institutional

---

26 Z. Brzeziński, *op. cit.*, pp. 67–79.

27 H. Zimmermann (2016): The euro trilemma, or: how the Eurozone fell into a neofunctionalist legitimacy trap, *Journal of European Integration*, vol. 38, no. 4, 2016, pp. 425–439.

28 W. Streeck, *op. cit.*, p. 182.

capacity.[29] Here, the biggest problem was the maladjustment of the organisation to such large expansion, particularly refraining from the introduction of bold reforms improving management mechanisms and increasing the funding of the Community. New members from Central Europe were treated patronisingly, if not neo-colonially. They were mainly to import EU institutions, regulations or values, and adapt to the expectations of the leading EU members. Integration problems started when, to the surprise of Western Europe, new members began assertive to Brussels's demands, expected agentship and equal participation in decision-making processes.[30] Supposed to build a friendly Europeanised regional environment, the EU's neighbourhood policy was also conducted in a cautious manner, without a relevant scale of funding and a bold geopolitical strategy. When further crises emerged, including the Ukrainian conflict on the eastern borders of the EU (started in 2014) and the destabilisation of North Africa as a result of the Arabian Spring (2010–2014) and the related great migrant crisis, the EU was not prepared to react to them effectively. The earlier policy proved insufficient in view of rising crisis tendencies and even contributed indirectly to destabilisation in both regions. An example of this is the support of the abolition of Mu'ammar al-Kaddafi's regime (2011) by some EU states, which became a source of destabilisation of Libya that Europe could not cope with subsequently. European ambitions with regard to the promotion of Europe's own regulations and institutions may be sometimes regarded as a sign of hypocrisy, particularly when promoted norms and values are treated in an instrumental manner.[31] In this perspective, integration is a sort of illusion that must be out of touch with tough reality. This is exactly the way in which Toynbee perceives the universal state.[32]

The conception of a universal state

Although the American empire has some universal characteristics, it is not a universal state. However, Toynbee's conception can be applied also towards the

---

29 W. Münchau (2015): Enlargement and the euro are two big mistakes that ruined Europe, *Financial Times*, 1 November 2015, p. 9; L. Tsoukalis, *op. cit.*, p. 148.

30 T.G. Grosse (2014a): The golden straitjacket of Poland's membership in the EU, *Yearbook of Polish European Studies*, vol. 17/2014, pp. 117–138.

31 Cf. S.T. Hansen, N. Marsh (2015): Normative power and organized hypocrisy: European Union member states' arms export to Libya, *European Security*, vol. 24, no. 2, pp. 264–286.

32 A. Toynbee, *op. cit.*, p. 266.

USA, particularly towards the international order at the turn of the 21st century. The term "American empire" refers to the entire area of the USA's political influence, including a number of international institutions co-created by the Americans, such as the NATO, the International Currency Fund, the World Bank, the World Trade Organisation, etc., as well as the allied or clientelistic states influenced by the USA and regional organisations supported by the biggest power, the most important example of which is the EU. There are three elements that give a common aspect to this system. These are: (1) universal human rights and other standards of international law, (2) neo-liberal economic rules promoted on a global scale, (3) the protection of peace, freedom and democracy around the world with the help of the USA's military force, which is sometimes called Pax Americana.

The formation of common standards of human rights and the promotion of other values, including democracy and the free movement of people, ideas, goods and capital on a global scale is rooted in the presidency of Woodrow Wilson and then Franklin Delano Roosevelt. But the aforementioned policy gained momentum in the 1970s. Scientists indicate the messianic role of the USA and the conviction of its indispensability to the good of the world and humanity.[33] According to Mark Mazower, America used the United Nations (UN) for the promotion of universal values, e.g., for the purpose of rebuilding trust in Third World countries. This was also an ideological weapon against the USSR[34] during the Cold War; its aim was to discredit the enemy and to reinforce the USA's legitimacy to lead the free world. That was significant for the consolidation of the West under American leadership and the expansion of influences in various regions of the globe. This shows that the promotion of human rights and liberal values was very important from a geopolitical perspective from the beginning and was often used in an instrumental manner. For example, the Central Intelligence Agency supported financially over a hundred non-governmental organisations in various parts of the world, including Central Europe, in order to promote human rights and democracy and, at the same time, weaken political regimes opposed to the USA.[35] In this way, standards of international law and liberal values became a pretext for interventions in internal affairs of geopolitical rivals and for the development of international support for activities of this kind. Other ideas, e.g., regarding economic freedoms or fight against corruption, were used

---

33 S. Reich, R.N. Lebow, *op. cit.*, pp. 134–136; A.J. Bacevich, *op. cit.*, p. 1.

34 The Union of Soviet Socialist Republics.

35 M. Mazower (2013): *Governing the World. The History of an Idea*, London – New York, pp. 320–323.

for the promotion of American (and, more broadly, Western) investors, which means that they were supposed to support particular interests of corporations or financial institutions.[36]

The instrumental use of universal values and human rights provoked a series of accusations concerning the hypocrisy of American authorities[37] and the frequent practice of using double standards, for example, the support of authoritarian regimes having friendly relations with the USA or the avoidance of the introduction of internationally promoted standards of law by the Americans in their own land. For example, the USA refused to submit to the jurisdiction of the International Criminal Court, which would mean putting American citizens to trial with regard to universal human rights.[38] All of this made it difficult for the Americans to authenticate their own leadership and decreased their legitimacy in the international community.[39]

The universal approach of the Americans to globalisation is most evident with regard to the promotion of economic freedoms and the neo-liberal economic doctrine. The outcome of this international regime is unequivocal. On the one hand, it ensured the growth of Western economies, particularly after World War II, and has been very favourable for the emerging markets in recent years. On the other hand, it brought frequent crises, destabilisation and costs to many countries – both from the West and other parts of the world. The problem still lay in poorly regulated financial markets and in the rising debt that reached the enormous amount of 135 trillion dollars only in G20 states in 2017.[40] The Great Recession was overcome after 2010 largely due to the active monetary policy of Western central banks, which led to an increase of private and public debt but did not translate significantly into the stimulation of investments in real economy. Moreover, the aforementioned regime brought increasingly fewer benefits to the West. At the beginning of the 21st century, its economic growth was meagre; for its geoeconomic rivals, particularly China, it was much more favourable.[41] Over the years, the USA incurred increasingly higher costs of globalisation, which was reflected by the weakening industrial base, the low average employment level, the chronic trade deficit or the rising foreign debt. Even if the aforementioned debt was a method of transferring costs of American policy outside, it created a

---

36 M. Mazower, *op. cit.*, p. 393; A.J. Bacevich, *op. cit.*, p. 92.
37 A.J. Bacevich, *op. cit.*, pp. 94–95.
38 M. Mazower, *op. cit.*, p. 398.
39 M. Mann, *Incoherent Empire*, *op. cit.*, p. 9.
40 IMF warns of $135tn debt threat to recovery, *Financial Times*, 11.10.2017, p. 2.
41 M. Mann, *The sources of social Power*, *op. cit.*, p. 356.

risk for the entire international economic order. The global currency on which economic exchange was based at the beginning of the 21st century belonged to the biggest debtor on a global scale. In addition, this was happening at the expense of huge influence gained by financial markets (and biggest bankers) on the policy of American authorities and on all other Western countries, as well as many other governments around the world. The USA was gradually losing its impact on the functioning of international institutions, too. It was increasingly difficult for the Americans to seek their own interests while successfully blocking the increase of benefits of their biggest geoeconomic rivals.

This brought a series of attempts to modify the rules of functioning of global economy and international economic institutions; however, they failed to reverse the trends that had an unfavourable impact on the West. Consequently, the distance of America towards multilateral institutions, including those established on the USA's initiative years ago, increased. The most striking examples of this tendency were actions of President Donald Trump; within a short period after his election, he resigned from the TPP,[42] suspended talks with the EU regarding TTIP,[43] withdrew from the Paris climate agreement (supplementing the framework convention of the United Nations regarding climate changes) and undertook the renegotiation of the NAFTA.[44] These decisions were commonly interpreted as the return to protectionist tendencies in the USA. The decisions of Trump, who rebelled against liberal globalisation and wanted to restore benefits for American interests according to the slogan "America First", were signs of the earlier tendency. In the past, American politicians also withdrew from their "own" global order institutions when they brought them smaller benefits (or even growing costs) in relation to other powers. Such was the case of the Bretton Wood regime, whose collapse was brought by the USA's unilateral decision to cease the exchange of dollars for gold.[45] Thus, Trump's actions were another stage of the policy of destruction of international institutions that had been established by the USA beforehand and that had proved unfavourable for it over the years.

42 Trans-Pacific Partnership – a multilateral agreement regulating the rules of trade, concluded between 12 countries from the Asia and Pacific region on 5 October 2015.
43 Transatlantic Trade and Investment Partnership – a trade agreement negotiated since 2013, aimed primarily at creating a free trade zone between the USA and the EU.
44 North American Free Trade Agreement – an agreement concluded between the USA, Canada and Mexico that established a free trade zone between those states; negotiated in 1992, it entered into force in 1994.
45 T.G. Grosse (2017a): Bretton Woods jako reżim geoekonomiczny [Bretton Woods as a geoeconomic regime], *Stosunki Międzynarodowe – International Relations*, pp. 65–82.

According to some opinions,[46] the United States was becoming dependent on its own empire – the international order created by it. The external world was the emanation of American hegemony and the necessary area for its military expansion. In economy, it was necessary for financial institutions forming the most influential sector of American economic elites. At the same time, global financial markets were the key method of financing federal expenses, including those that fuelled militarism. The American internal policy was largely dependent on globalisation, too. In the economic and social model adopted in the USA, relatively cheap import fuelled domestic consumption and ensured peace to the poorest social strata and the middle class, which is subject to pauperisation. At the same time, active foreign policy provided an alibi for growing idleness in domestic policy and was even an attempt to solve some internal problems, e.g., in energy policy.[47]

In the course of time, America's control of the external world was becoming weaker. This brought a surprising phenomenon of the USA's growing distance towards universal rules and institutions of economic, political and military order. Already in the 1970s, the Americans applied the policy of withdrawing from their own initiatives, e.g. those undertaken under the aegis of the United Nations, which resulted in the weakening of this organisation.[48] In 2017, President Trump withdrew the USA from the UNESCO.[49] The same may affect the biggest military pact – the NATO, which was harshly criticised both by prominent American and European politicians. At the same time, American militarism began to endanger peace around the world and, consequently, the international Western order called Pax Americana.[50]

Another example of building a universal state can be the European integration process, particularly after the adoption of the Maastricht Treaty (1992) that established the European Union and the Economic and Monetary Union. According to Toynbee, each universal state is characterised by the expansion of the communication network,[51] which is illustrated by investments of the cohesion policy. Moreover, official languages are determined in a universal state, although one of

46 E. Todd, *op. cit.*, pp. 15–21.

47 The military intervention in Iraq was partly motivated by the will to increase energy security and to ensure access to energy resources of that state. Cf. M. Mann, *Incoherent Empire*, *op. cit.*, pp. 206–250.

48 M. Mazower, *op. cit.*, p. 308–311.

49 UNESCO: United Nations Educational, Scientific and Cultural Organization.

50 E. Todd, *op. cit.*, p. 21; W. Streeck, *op. cit.*, p. 15.

51 A. Toynbee, *op. cit.*, pp. 288–318.

them strongly dominates. Both in the American empire and in the EU, English is such a *lingua franca*. A state has one or several political & administrative capitals; in the EU, such a role is played by Brussels and, to a lesser extent, by Strasbourg. Finally, a universal state builds its own administration and civil service, examples of which can also be found in the EU (the corps of clerks of Brussels institutions and the European External Action Service). A universal state ensures peace. Such was the case in Europe, which has actually[52] been free of wars since the end of World War II, even though military forces of European states and the EU participated in local external conflicts. In this way, a universal state favours economic growth and pacifistic moods.

A universal state is an attempt to build a political structure above existing divisions, in the entire area of impact of the given civilisation. The centre of the European civilisation developed in Western Europe, where European Communities were initially built after 1957. Subsequently, the European Union was expanded with Central Europe, which involved the characteristic features of this project: territorial expansion and the attempt to expand the impact of its own institutions, laws and values. According to Toynbee, all of these features characterise a universal state with ambitions of territorial expansion and the promotion of its own standards and values, which are treated as universal for the external environment. In the case of the EU, its "normative power" is often mentioned, which is supposed to mean that its means of international impact are based mainly on the export of norms and ideas rather than economic or military pressure.[53]

The aforementioned phenomena are signified by universalism. European values and law were not only supposed to integrate European Communities from the inside; they were to promote them as the best standards on an international scale. In a similar way, a universal state opens up to the outside, becoming a home for all nations (coming both from its territory and from external areas).[54] In the EU, this tendency manifested itself in the focus on universal human rights, which constitute the basis of massive acceptance of refugees and immigrants from outside Europe.

A universal state is a response to crises and "cracks" in the civilisation that have led directly to its destruction until now. It is also the reaction of elites, which would otherwise reckon with the loss of power and international importance.[55]

52 Excluding the Balkan War following the split of Yugoslavia in the years 1992–1995.
53 I. Manners (2002): Normative Power Europe: A Contradiction in Terms?, *Journal of Common Market Studies*, vol. 40, no. 2, 2002, pp. 235–258.
54 *Ibidem*, p. 267.
55 A. Toynbee, *op. cit.*, pp. 255–276.

This is how European integration is interpreted by Alan Milward,[56] according to whom it was a rescue for elites in national states exhausted by bloody armed conflicts and anxious of economic challenges in the second half of the 20th century. It seems that European Communities were a response to the nightmare of both world wars, which can be regarded as the culmination of the destruction of the Western civilisation. According to Fernand Braudel, this civilisation is based on the tradition of the national state as the supreme formula of political order. At the same time, two tendencies could be seen in history. The first one was the maximisation of power by the biggest European states – in certain historical periods, it was tantamount to the attempt to establish hegemony on a continental scale. The state that expressed such ambitions most frequently was Germany – big enough to have such aspirations and too small to put them into practice effectively.[57] The second tendency characterising the European civilisation was, according to Braudel, the curbing of the state claiming hegemony by other powers, which is also called a strive for the "balance of power".[58]

Braudel thinks that peaceful attempts to ensure unity on the continent have always been weak and unsuccessful. The success of the integration in the second half of the 20th century was enforced by the United States of America, which was an external hegemon for Europe weakened by the wars.[59] At the same time, the external threat from the USSR was a stimulating factor. The Cold War order served as a binder for the integration. However, after its end (1989–1990), we saw the revival of internal European tendencies to maximise the power of the biggest states on the one hand and to curb these powers on the other hand. The frameworks of the EU not only ceased to suppress these tendencies, but actually became instruments in this game. As a result of crisis, many social groups protested against the non-democratic power of Brussels and the growing power of Berlin in the EU or against the "new concert of powers", mainly the dominance of the French-German tandem in European politics.[60] If the project of a universal state in Europe was supposed to counteract the cataclysms of nationalisms and rivalry between the biggest states, the resurrection of these tendencies may signify the end of this project. German Chancellor Angela Merkel became famous

56 A. Milward (1992): *The European Rescue of the Nation State*, New York.

57 Cf. B. Simms (2013): Europe: The Struggle for Supremacy, from 1453 to the Present, New York.

58 F. Braudel (1994): *A History of Civilizations*, London, pp. 416–421.

59 *Ibidem*, p. 422.

60 More details in: T.G. Grosse (2016b): Overcoming the crisis in the Economic and Monetary Union, *Przegląd Europejski*, no. 1, pp. 28–50.

for her support of the "Union method", which she believed would concentrate power in European politics in the hands of member states, thereby weakening the role of supranational institutions, such as the European Commission or the European Parliament.[61] Experts emphasise the increase of the intergovernmental factor in European politics as a result of the crisis in the Eurozone.[62]

Toynbee notices also another problem of universal states.[63] Historically speaking, each of these states attempted to create moral power with a universal dimension that would serve as a binder for such an organism and, at the same time, the highest instance for the mitigation of internal disputes. One of such examples is the papacy during the period of the Holy Roman Empire. The problem emerged when this moral institution became a political actor which either aspired to be the supreme political power within a universal state or turned into an instrument in the game between other entities. This accelerated internal divisions and became the leaven of disintegrational phenomena. The same problem affects modern Europe. Previously, the European Commission was an institution having moral authority and mitigating disputes between member states, but it became gradually politicised during crises at the beginning of the 21st century.[64] According to the head of the Commission, its politicisation was to be a method of improving management during crises and adapting its actions flexibly to the current political situation.[65] However, this led to the arbitrariness of decisions of the EU executive and destroyed its authority as an impartial institution acting mainly according to legal standards. In this way, the Commission lost also its autonomy towards the most powerful states, almost taking part in the

---

61 Speech by Federal Chancellor Angela Merkel at the opening ceremony of the 61st academic year of the College of Europe, Bruges, 2 November 2010, http://www.bruessel.diplo.de/contentblob/2959854/Daten/ [access: 27.12.2016].

62 S. Fabbrini (2015a): The Euro Crisis and Its Constitutional Implications, in: S. Champeau, C. Closa, D. Innerarity, M. Poiares Maduro (ed.), *The Future of Europe. Democracy, Legitimacy and Justice After the Euro Crisis*, London, pp. 19–36; S. Fabbrini (2015b): *Which European Union. Europe After the Euro Crisis*, Cambridge; V.A. Schmidt (2015): *The Forgotten Problem of Democratic Legitimacy*, in: M. Matthijs, M. Blyth (ed.), *The Future of the Euro*, Oxford – New York, pp. 91, 111; M. Brunnermeier, H. James, J.-P. Landau (2016): The Euro and the Battle of Ideas, Princeton.

63 A. Toynbee, *op. cit.*, pp. 199–201.

64 See discussion on that subject: T.G. Grosse (2017b): Introduction, in: T. G. Grosse (ed.), *European Union Policies at a Time of Crisis*, Scholar Publishing House, Warsaw, pp. 9–32.

65 Juncker elected: promises more social EU, more political commission, *EUobserver*, Brussels, 15. July 2014, https://euobserver.com/political/124980 [access: 29.12.2016].

rivalry between them. This contributed to the revival of the intergovernmental tendency: the dominance of national governments in EU policy, as well as the use of the "policy of force" by the biggest states towards weaker entities. In this way, in the days of crisis, Europe saw the revival of historical processes that had almost brought the European civilisation to a disaster many years ago. These processes include national particularisms, the rivalry of powers and the strive for the "balance of power".

The universal project in Europe could be formed thanks to support from the USA and under the military umbrella of this power during the Cold War. However, along with geopolitical changes at the end of the 20th century, Western Europe made increasingly strong attempts to achieve strategical autonomy towards the USA. During the presidency of Donald Trump, when the United States was withdrawing from many institutions of universal global order, the EU even had the ambition to take over leadership from the Americans within the scope of this liberal order and to extend the norms of a European universal state to a global scale. This was one of many signs of excessive ambitions of Europeans that did not match the real potential and capabilities of the EU.

The lack of creativity

According to Toynbee, one of the most important traits of the disintegration of the given civilisation is the weakness of elites, which manifests itself mainly in the lack of creativity and intellectual laziness.[66] It is often accompanied by a sense of complacency in spite of obvious signs of collapse of the order prevailing so far. This results in the mimesis of old institutions without taking the changing circumstances and new challenges into account. The elites make fruitless attempts to restore the former *status quo*, which is usually treated as a period of excellence. The atrophy of creativity is particularly dangerous in conditions of an expansive universal state whose existence entails the requirement to meet the challenges resulting from the expansion of the scale of functioning.[67] In this situation, the phenomenon of *nemesis*, understood as inevitable historical justice, is unavoidable. Wrong management and the shortage of institutional creativity must lead to problems that intensify disintegration.

The phenomena described above were visible in the American empire. The militarism of the USA was a kind of trap for this superpower. On the one hand, the erosion of international influences led to an increase of the tendency to

66 A. Toynbee, *op. cit.*, pp. 141, 161–166.
67 *Ibidem*, p. 170.

solve the emerging problems by means of military methods.[68] This narrowed the field of strategic choices and caused controversies even among the USA's allies, let alone among opponents of Western dominance. On the other hand, the increase of the role of the "security community" in internal policy weakened American democracy and diminished the efficiency of the economic model existing so far. At the same time, it was difficult to notice the forces that would allow for a creative change of these processes.

Also the superior doctrine in economic policy, which also shaped the liberal dimension of globalisation, started to become increasingly costly for America over the years. However, even the Great Recession at the beginning of the 21st century failed to bring about essential improvement. The regulation of financial markets was not increased sufficiently, and the government's policy regarding the support of real economy was not reformed, particularly in terms of reconstruction of the industry and stimulation of export. The decision-makers lacked creativity, and influential interest groups connected with financial circles prevailed. As a result of this, most members of American elites were influenced by liberal mythology and were unable to remodel their approach to national economy and globalisation. In this situation, the attempt to correct the USA's policy undertaken by President Trump since 2017 should be regarded as the chaotic and slightly emotional rebellion of this leader rather than the innovative strategy of the federal government.

The lack of creativity of elites was visible also during European crises, particularly at the time of difficulties in the Eurozone. Some scientists accuse EU decision-makers of excessive attachment to previous ideas and models of behaviour, mainly German ordoliberal thought.[69] Therefore, solving a crisis was based mainly on forcing fiscal savings in states that were most heavily indebted and affected by the crisis. This method was very difficult to implement, involved high social and political costs and solved the essential problems of the common currency system only to a small extent. Other scientists add that the aim of the anti-crisis policy was to reconstruct the previous *status quo*: stabilisation on foreign markets with the maintenance of trade imbalances existing so far.[70] They were favourable primarily for the biggest economy in this zone – German economy, which had very significant export surpluses in comparison to other

68 E. Todd, *op. cit.*, p. 21.

69 M. Matthijs (2016): Powerful rules governing the euro: the perverse logic of German ideas, *Journal of European Public Policy*, vol. 23, no. 3, pp. 375–391.

70 H.J. Bieling, J. Jäger, M. Ryner (2016): Regulation Theory and the Political Economy of the European Union, *Journal of Common Market Studies*, vol. 54, no. 1, pp. 53–69.

member states, particularly those least competitive from the south of the continent. As a result of anti-crisis actions, this fundamental economic imbalance in the zone did not change – attempts were only made to reduce the debt level of some countries and help them regain financial balance. According to Lawrence Summers, the European problem – just like a broader problem regarding the West – lay in decreasing investments and productivity, which consequently led to weaker internal demand, low increase and long-term employment (Summers refers to this as "secular stagnation").[71] In such a situation, increasing fiscal savings could not be an effective solution. According to economists, it is impossible to restore growth in depressed economies only on the basis of monetary policy interventions.[72] In this way, the passiveness of elites brought social dissatisfaction and a number of political problems in the EU.

The problem of particularism and individualism

According to Toynbee, an important sign of the disintegration of a civilisation is the process of increasing individualisation along with the weakening community approach, which means that it takes place at the expense of care about the community as a whole. The aforementioned phenomenon seems to occur both in the USA and in the EU. In both cases, it derives from the neo-liberal conception of economy, society and the state, although the United States is the primary example of the aforementioned phenomena. According to Streeck, the crisis of Western capitalism manifests itself not only in the destabilisation of markets, but also in deepening individualisation, rising social inequalities and the weakening of states. We can observe the concentration of wealth and power in the hands of the financial elite, which poses an increasing threat to democracy. With regard to the USA, Streeck recalls the conception of an "authoritarian state" coined by Carl Schmitt. Such a state protects capital against the excessive influence of electorate, including redistributional and compensatory tendencies, at the same time leaving almost full freedom to market players.[73] In Streeck's opinion, a state of this kind is subordinated to big capital (or is almost appropriated by it) and, on the other hand, oppressive towards the rest of the society. Thus, it serves particular

---

71 L.H. Summers (2016): The Age of Secular Stagnation. What It Is and What to Do About It, *Foreign Affairs*, March/April, pp. 2–9.

72 Cf. the opinion of the main strategist of JP Morgan Asset Management for European markets: S. Flanders (2017): Tear up the rule book to secure Europe's future, *Financial Times*, 9 January 2017, p. 9.

73 W. Streeck, *op. cit.*, pp. 151–152.

interests of elites while ignoring the interests of the entire society or even the state itself. At the same time, it is weak and limited, particularly in internal policy. Other scholars also indicate that the source of weakness of the American state lies in the excessive particularism of the political system, which – on the one hand – favours the fulfilment of partial interests of local groups of electors or wealthy financial institutions and – on the other hand – leads to the paralysis of the decision-making process of political structures, which are unable to overcome fractional interests.[74] It also harms the strategy in foreign policy, which is very strongly affected by particular interests of the "security community".[75]

According to Robert Putnam, the result of growing individualism was the collapse of social bonds or social capital in America.[76] This posed a threat to the quality of American democracy. Other scientists indicated the weakening sense of citizenship among the Americans, which was understood as diminishing involvement in public, social and political activity.[77] Citizens became reduced to the role of consumers necessary to maintain the increase of demand. It is the degradation of lofty ideas of individualism to instrumentalised masses of consumers.

Another phenomenon described by Toynbee is the "schism of soul", which means rising pessimism and apathy understood both in a social sense (as the lack of faith in a universal state) and from an individual perspective (as a sense of loss of lifetime chances[78]). It seems that the aforementioned phenomenon can be noticed in modern Europe. The crises have brought not only the deterioration of the welfare of European societies, but also the rising sense of the loss of lifetime chances. According to research,[79] almost 70 % of households in 25 highly developed Western states had the same or worse level of income in 2014 as compared to income in 2005. For example, almost the entire society of Italy (exactly 97 % of households) faced stagnation or lower income. Before the crisis, the suspension or decrease of social income had covered only 2 % of the population. The level of unemployment among young people in the Eurozone was very high.[80] All of

74 A.J. Bacevich, *op. cit.*, pp. 95–96.

75 M. Mann, *Incoherent Empire*, *op. cit.*, p. 9.

76 R. Putnam (2000): *Bowling Alone*, New York, pp. 247–276.

77 Ch. Lasch (1995): *The Revolt of the Elites and the Betrayal of Democracy*, New York, pp. 3–22.

78 A. Toynbee, *op. cit.*, pp. 241–254.

79 Poorer than their parents? Flat or falling incomes in advanced economies, McKinsey & Company, London 2016.

80 According to the Eurostat data, the level of unemployment among young people since the outbreak of crisis in the Eurozone exceeds 20 %; according to the data for

this created pessimistic moods and lowered the evaluation of individual lifetime chances, particularly among the young generation.

Scholars analysing the crisis in the Eurozone stress the dominance of national particularisms over thinking in terms of the common good, i.e., taking care of the long-term prosperity of the entire currency union.[81] This refers particularly to German decision-makers who transferred costs of macroeconomic adaptations to the periphery of the Eurozone, which was a very strong burden for their societies (although slowed down the growth rate in Germany).[82] The resulting phenomenon is called by me "asymmetry of rationality", where the rationality (and interests) of dominating political leaders prevailed over the rationality of the stable and long-term development of the entire Eurozone.[83]

Moreover, scholars stress the fact that European societies addressed requests for help to their own governments and gathered around national political communities in conditions of prolonged crisis, particularly the low effectiveness of European institutions. This reinforced domestic democratic structures as a tool of influence on political decision-makers to conduct a policy meeting the expectations of electorate.[84] If the elites favouring integration did not fulfil such expectations, voters were inclined to support less experienced Eurosceptic politicians. This increased the temperature of political disputes and created conditions favouring disintegration. In literature, we can find the explanation why anti-system movements, even if they had initially referred to cosmopolitan ideas, often assumed the form of nationalism in Europe.[85] Firstly, because national identifications have always been stronger than universal or cosmopolitan identifications. Secondly, revolutionists needed the state apparatus to implement their postulates effectively. This is why anti-system movements addressed against the political system functioning within the scope of integrating Europe

the year 2016, it exceeded 21 %. Cf. http://www.tradingeconomics.com/euro-area/unemployment-rate [access: 29.12.2016].

81 G. Falkner (2016): The EU's problem-solving capacity and legitimacy in a crisis context: a virtuous or vicious circle?, *West European Politics*, vol. 39, no. 5, pp. 953–970.

82 M. Matthijs, *op. cit*., pp. 378, 384–387.

83 T.G. Grosse (2016c): The Eurozone crisis, in: *The aspects of a crisis. An analysis of crisis management from an economic and political perspective*, ed. M.A. Cichocki & T.G. Grosse, Natolin European Centre, Warsaw 2016, pp. 11–56.

84 H. Zimmermann, *op. cit.*

85 Cf. G. Arrighi, T.K. Hopkins, I. Wallerstein (1989): *Antisystemic Movements*, London – New York, pp. 27–31.

referred to national patriotisms and democracy in member states as primary mechanisms of implementation of the political will of societies.[86]

The aforementioned phenomena favoured the stimulation of national identifications and dampened European identity, which had already been superficial anyway. According to sociological research, the sense of identity with Europe has always been relatively weak. In 2005, less than 3 % of the EU's population regarded it as their own primary identification, whereas it only supplemented national identifications in a majority of other inhabitants. During the crises after 2008, these tendencies clearly became more intense. The European identification, particularly if treated as a supplement to national identifications, declined. At the same time, we could observe an explicit increase of the number of exclusively national identifications (i.e., those that are not associated with European identity, even if perceived as secondary). Within the entire EU, there were already almost 50 % of such persons.[87] Moreover, research showed that an increasing number of inhabitants did not want further European integration, or even expected at least the partial renationalisation of the EU's competencies.[88] The same research proved that the dislike for the EU resulted primarily from the ineffective management of the Eurozone crisis and the migrant crisis.

It is worth noting two more general phenomena being the reason for the weakness of the European community. The first one is a specific structure of values and historical tradition, which served as a basis for European identity promoted within the EU. The second reason is the growing influence of individualism on the European culture.

With regard to the first issue, we must say that European decision-makers rejected a large part of Europe's historical heritage, including the tradition referring to Christianity that dated back to the times of ancient Rome, as inconsistent with the idea of secularity of public authorities in the EU. Already at the end

---

86 Cf. T.G. Grosse (2015): A Potential for Revolution in Europe?, in: B.J. Góralczyk (ed.), *European Union on The Global Scene: United or Irrelevant*? Warsaw, pp. 203–223.

87 A. Polyakova, N. Fligstein (2016): Is European integration causing Europe to become more nationalist? Evidence from the 2007–9 financial crisis, *Journal of European Public Policy*, vol. 23, no. 1, 2016, pp. 60–83; A.M. Messina (2014): Introduction: Identifyi ng with Europe?, in: A.C. Gould, A.M. Messina (ed.), *Europe's Contending Identities. Supranationalism, Ethnoregionalism, Religion, and New Nationalism*, Cambridge, p. 11.

88 Among inhabitants of 10 member states accounting for 80 % of the EU's population, 42 % of respondents thought that power should be handed over from EU institutions to national governments, whereas only 19 % spoke in favour of further integration. Cf. *Euroscepticism Beyond Brexit*, Pew Research Center, June 2016, p. 2.

of the 18th century, such an approach initiated by Enlightenment thinkers was criticised.[89] It was believed to deprive Europe of civilisational contents and the cultural base being a necessary binder for societies. According to this opinion, the respect for human rights and human dignity, as well as the preservation of social morality and mutual trust, would only be a propaganda slogan without Christianity. Acting in favour of European identification, the EU decision-makers avoided also references to the centuries-long history of national states, because they might reinforce national identities instead of European identity. If anything, the negative consequences of rivalry between states for Europeans were indicated. Finally, the shameful part of the colonial history, within which the strength of powers was built on the basis of the conquest and exploitation of non-European territories, was rejected. Instead of this, European decision-makers tried to build European identification and sense of community around Enlightenment values, including the secularity of public authority, human rights, the rule of law and the strive for material prosperity and economic growth.[90]

This kind of cultural base proved relatively superficial, because it rejected a huge part of the common past of Europeans and treated the rest in a selective manner. Moreover, it adopted many values whose geographical and cultural references clearly went beyond the borders of Europe.[91] This applied in particular to the principles of multiculturalism, which assumed an open attitude to non-European traditions. Such an approach resulted from the will to respect international human rights. However, universal values cannot become a foundation for the primary mechanism creating a strong identity, i.e., the discrimination between "others" and "us", i.e., members of the local community. That was one of the reasons for the weakness of the EU's citizenship and low identification with the EU and the clarification of much stronger national sentiments and identification with one's own nation in Europe.[92] As one of the researchers said, European identification turned out to be an abstract concept and does not cause such social emotions as national identifications do.[93] Moreover, since the strive for welfare was one of the primary values supposed to build a sense of attachment to the EU, European identification vanished almost immediately in conditions of

89 E. Burke (1867): *Reflections on the Revolution in France*, https://sourcebooks.fordham.edu/mod/1791burke.asp, access: 12.04.2019.

90 M. Guibernau (2011): *The Identity of Nations*, Cambridge, pp. 115–116.

91 *Ibidem*, p. 115.

92 C. Colliot-Thélène (2016): What Europe does to citizenship, in: D. Chalmers, M. Jachtenfuchs, C. Joerges (ed.), *The End of the Eurocrats' Dream*, Cambridge, p. 129.

93 M. Guibernau, *op. cit.*, p. 118.

prolonged crises. For the same reasons, economic immigrants arriving in the EU became disappointed with Europe and its inhabitants if they failed to fulfil their aspirations regarding the improvement of their material status.

As I have mentioned, European culture became more and more individualised, which affected the sense of responsibility for the common good. This indirectly weakened the possibility of building a strong community on the European level. Individualism derives from the philosophy of English liberalism, but it was also largely promoted by the French Enlightenment. In the second case, it is combined with the 18th-century approach to the individual and the world of politics, which should become free of religious limitations and of previous values regarded as natural.[94] The focus on individual rights contributed to economic growth and the development of democracy in Western Europe, but it promoted increasingly often the self-fulfilment of the individual rather than the care of the social good. Within the scope of European integration, this tendency was additionally reinforced by laying emphasis on universal human rights, trying to weaken attachment to national communities and making unsuccessful attempts to build a sense of relationship with the community among all Europeans.

Divisions as a sign of decomposition

According to Toynbee, growing divisions or the loss of harmony between individual elements of the social and political system are an important element of the decomposition of a civilisation. For the weakening West, the growing divisions between the USA and some states of Western Europe were the biggest problem. They covered both economic issues (e.g., the trade surplus of Germany in relations with the USA) and geopolitical challenges (e.g., the issue of the military intervention in Iraq, the attitude to Russia and the Ukrainian conflict). They resulted, on the one hand, from American militarism and, on the other hand, from searching for strategical autonomy among European states. Germany, France and Italy perceived the threat from Russia in a different way than the USA did, even after its annexation of the Crimea in 2014; at the same time, they became increasingly bigger rivals of Americans on the economic level.

According to Toynbee, the alienation of elites (i.e., the dominating minority) from the internal and external proletariat is highly important for the processes of disintegration of a given civilisation.[95] One of the signs of this tendency is the

94 Cf. T. Sowell (2007): *A Conflict of Visions. Ideological Origins of Political Struggles*, New York 2007.

95 A. Toynbee, *op. cit.*, pp. 211–240.

"detachment" of elites from real problems faced by the rest of the society, i.e., the lack of understanding of these problems and the decreasing sense of responsibility for solving them. Instead of this, elites tend to take care of their own interests. On the other hand, the internal proletariat – i.e., native inhabitants of the universal state – have a sense of growing pauperisation, because successive crises are methodically shifted mainly on them. Therefore, they gradually turn away from political ideas and narrations promoted by elites towards anti-system views, which results in rebellions and other political turbulences. Another element of Toynbee's conception is the external proletariat – the migrant population from outside the borders of the universal state. This population is attracted both by the wealth of the state, relative stability, peace and cultural attractiveness. However, immigrants are subject to strongest exploitation and pauperisation in times of crises. Because of this, they start to reject the dominant culture in the course of time and have a hostile attitude to their values, becoming one of the direct reasons of the disintegration of the civilisation.

The aforementioned processes of internal decomposition are visible both in the USA and in the EU. Neo-liberal capitalism leads to social inequalities and divisions, promotes particularly the concentration of wealth and political power in the hands of financial elites and leads to the corruption of democracy.[96] The most meaningful examples of these tendencies can be observed in the United States. According to economists, a strong concentration of income in the hands of 1 % of the wealthiest Americans occurred between 1981 and 2014. At the end of this period, they earned 81 times more than the half of the society representing the low-income group. On the other hand, these 50 % of inhabitants from the low-income group never increased their remuneration during more than 30 years.[97] This means their actual pauperisation. A similar phenomenon affected the middle class – the foundation on which democracy had been based so far – to a growing extent. This led to the increase of the wealth gap between the elite and the rest of the society (i.e., the proletariat in Toynbee's terminology). According to Peter Temin, the model of dual economy formed

96 M. Mann, *The sources of social Power. Globalizations*, *op. cit.*, p. 356; W. Streeck, *op. cit.*, p. 30; J.C. Ott (2011): *When Wall Street Met Main Street: The Quest for an Investors' Democracy*, Cambridge; A.Z. Kamiński, B. Kamiński (2004): *Korupcja rządów* [*The Corruption of Governments*], Warszawa 2004.

97 T. Piketty, E. Saez, G. Zucman (2016): Distributional National Accounts: Methods and Estimates for the United States, *NBER Working Paper* 22945, December.

in the USA as a result of this.[98] It required, on the one hand, high competences and offered very high remunerations; on the other hand, low-skilled employees received low remuneration and often worked illegally. According to Temin, the increasing social division in terms of income largely overlaps with racial criteria. In the poorest and lowest-skilled social strata, there is the largest group of Afro-Americans and Latinos. Among them, there is the highest per cent of unemployed persons and criminals. This means that racial categories were important not only for cultural reasons in the USA – they also referred to the wealth status, lifetime chances resulting from education and, finally, political attitudes.[99] Among ethnic minorities, the largest group consisted of inactive persons who did not take part in elections and did not engage in American democracy in any other way.[100]

Noticing the growing divisions within the scope of the political community, some scientists think that one of the reasons is the idea of multiculturalism and the excessively liberal approach to all cultures, values and traditions in the USA. According to Bacevich, the rejection of the tradition of white Anglo-Saxon Protestants from Europe as a cultural foundation was a critical mistake. It weakened the American nation and democracy.[101] Thus, the divisions can be largely attributed to economic and political ideas rooted in liberal values. In Bacevich's opinion, these ideas were responsible for primary economic process in the USA and for the state policy. They shaped the policy towards immigrants (or opening up to the external proletariat) as a cheap workforce, particularly for the underpaid segment of American economy. They also had an impact on the indifference of public authorities towards the issue of growing social inequalities, i.e., towards the internal proletariat that is gradually left to its own fate.

Temin indicates the dual policy of the state. On the one hand, the state is very generous for the wealthiest, e.g., due to tax exemptions. On the other hand, it treats harshly the poorer strata. An example of this is the educational and academic policy; in the scientist's opinion, it reinforces the gap between the lifetime chances of elites and the remaining part of the population. It is also worth mentioning high expenses for the judicial, police and prison system, which are means

---

98 P. Temin (2017): *The Vanishing Middle Class. Prejudice and Power in a Dual Economy*, Cambridge 2017, pp. IX, 5–40.

99 P. Temin, *op. cit.*, pp. 49–60, 104.

100 M. Gilens (2012): *Affluence and Influence: Economic Inequality and Political Power In America*, Princeton, pp. 235–239.

101 A.J. Bacevich, *op. cit.*, p. 83.

of repression aimed at ensuring social peace.[102] This is confirmed by other studies. According to Martin Gilens, political preferences of 90 % of less wealthy persons in the USA are considered by decision-makers less frequently than those of 10 % of the wealthiest. This goes particularly for the conflict between the interests of both sides. The wealthier an inhabitant of America is, the statistically higher chances he has to exert an effective impact on the policy of the government. It turns out that all American congressmen were among 10 % of the best-earning people at the beginning of the 21st century, and nearly 50 % of members of the Congress were multimillionaires.[103] The wealthiest government in the history of the USA was the one created by the anti-establishment President Donald Trump; apart from him, it included three billionaires.[104] At the same time, one of the key actions of President Trump in internal policy was to attempt to decrease taxes for enterprises, to loosen regulations for financial institutions and to dismantle the public health insurance funding system (benefits are restricted mainly to elder and less wealthy persons). President Trump announced also a considerable increase of military expenses.

According to Temin, politics is determined not by values prevailing in America, but rather by the increasing influence of financial spheres and big enterprises on the federal government.[105] In Gilens's opinion, the political system of this country is closer to plutocracy than democracy. Streeck notices the phenomenon of elites turning away from the society in the USA and Europe[106] – a sort of alienation of elites towards the proletariat that was described by Toynbee. This often results in the pursuit of policy regardless of election results and changes between political groups,[107] and brings first the decreasing electoral turnout and the dislike of increasingly larger social groups for politics and then an increase of popularity of extreme and anti-system politicians on both sides of the Atlantic.[108]

Many intellectuals accuse the Western civilisation of excessive elitism. The Enlightenment, whose ideas were among the foundations of European integration, was a particular breakthrough period here. According to researchers[109] the Enlightenment and the French Revolution made attempts to

102 P. Temin, *op. cit.*, pp. 105–114.
103 M. Gilens, *op. cit.*, pp. 1–2, 5–10, 77, 82–83, 235–241.
104 Trump's wealthy cabinet choices hark back to Gilded Age, *Financial Times*, 2 December 2016, p. 3.
105 P. Temin, *op. cit.*, pp. 61–64.
106 W. Streeck, *op. cit.*, p. 73.
107 P. Temin, *op. cit.*, p. 64; E. Todd, *op. cit.*, p. 18.
108 W. Streeck, *op. cit.*, p. 21.
109 D. Outram (2013): *The Enlightenment*, Cambridge, pp. 114–115.

diminish the role of Christianity and the Church, at the same time assigning the responsibility for the control of society and individuals to the state apparatus. The rule of a modern state over the society in Europe is called "pastoral" by Foucault, because it took over the former rights of parish priests, but was implemented on a nationwide scale. He also uses the term "total and manipulative rule", because it was supposed to shape the thoughts of individuals and the public opinion as a whole by subordinating them to the policy of the ruling elite. Foucault ascertains that after the French Revolution the secular power created a "new man" and "new society" that was controlled and manipulated much more strongly than in previous historical periods.[110] Burke is of the same opinion, but he adds that this "new man" was to be adjusted to slavery and to a new form of government that he usually calls oligarchy.[111] Sowell also states,[112] that the vision of politics unrestricted by earlier religious and moral norms that was formed in the Enlightenment is an intrinsically elitist and accumulates power in the hands of the enlightened avant garde leading the masses and forming them in accordance with new secular rules.

Let us look at the European Union in this context. This project has often been criticised for being excessively elitist and for engaging larger social groups only to a superficial and relatively instrumental extent.[113] Some thought that it serves economic elites at the expense of poorer social groups.[114] The EU's political management system favours the interests of big enterprises, at the same time limiting the influence of national democracies, which leads to the smaller significance of employees' interests and poorer social groups. In the democratic government system, poorer voters should have a certain impact on the protection of their own interests towards other social groups that are wealthier, better educated and usually have a stronger impact on the media. It is worth noticing that a similar criticism of the Western civilisation was formulated by Spengler at the beginning of the 20th century. In his opinion, the Europe and USA of that time was ruled by plutocracy, the media and politicians promoting their own interests and, at the same time, manipulating the masses for the purpose of maintaining social

---

110 M. Foucault (2000), *Power*, New York, pp. 332–334.

111 E. Burke, *op. cit.*, pp. 103, 139, 208.

112 T. Sowell, *op. cit.*

113 One of many examples: J. Habermas (2013): *The Crisis of the European Union*, Cambridge, pp. VII–XII.

114 B. Van Apeldoorn (2002): *Transnational Capitalism and the Struggle Over European Integration*, Abingdon; C. Crouch (2011): *The Strange Non-Death of Neoliberalism*, Cambridge.

peace.[115] During crises after 2008, pro-European elites were criticised for their increasing "alienation" from the masses, particularly by mitigating the results of economic problems for some societies to an insufficient extent.[116] Another criticised aspect was the tendency to shift costs of macroeconomic adjustments in an economic crisis to societies affected most seriously by problems.[117] Research indicated an increase of economic and social inequalities between the wealthiest states and the poorer states of the EU,[118] as well as "winners" and "losers" of European integration.[119] The latter included mainly the middle class and poorer social strata in South European countries. Other studies also show that the integration even before the outbreak of crises promoted the development of inequalities in member states, mainly by supporting elites at the expense of other social groups.[120]

On the grounds of universal human rights, the European Union equalled a large part of privileges resulting from the EU citizenship (i.e., the prerogatives of the internal proletariat, using Toynbee's terminology) with rights of immigrants and refugees (i.e., the external proletariat).[121] As I have already mentioned, this action deprived the EU citizenship of distinctness and content. It prevented the building of social emotions around it in connection with the creation of strong European identification. According to specialists,[122] the EU citizenship has become devoid of substance and is reduced to technical functions.

This kind of opening up to the outside was to serve partly as compensation towards descendants of inhabitants of former European colonies. Thus, European integration was supposed to help "redeem" old sins, but also to "conceal" them

115 O. Spengler, *op. cit.*, pp. 404, 416–425.

116 J.E. Stiglitz (2016): *The Euro and its Threat to the Future of Europe*, New York.

117 W. Streeck, *op. cit.*, pp. 176–177.

118 W. Streeck, L. Elsässer (2016): Monetary disunion: the domestic politics of Euroland, *Journal of European Public Policy*, vol. 23, no. 1, pp. 1–24.

119 L. Tsoukalis, *op. cit.*, p. 152.

120 In the years 1999–2010, inequalities became deepest in Spain, Portugal, Ireland, Great Britain, Greece and Italy. Cf. M.R. Busemeyer, T. Tober (2015): European integration and the political economy of inequality, *European Union Politics*, vol. 16, no. 4, 2015, pp. 536–557.

121 For more details, see: H. Ballin (2014): *Citizens' Rights and the Right to Be a Citizen*, Leiden.

122 K. Krūma (2014): EU *Citizenship, Nationality and Migrant Status. An Ongoing Challenge*, Leiden, p. 418.

by introducing a new formula of political organisation in Europe.[123] Moreover, the policy of openness to immigration was to enable European economy to fill in the gap on the labour market. In practice, it allowed for the further exploitation of the non-European population. These people were most often engaged for works not requiring skills that native inhabitants did not want to perform and against relatively lower remuneration. Opening up to the outside has also become an example of the growing discrepancy between ideas promoted by European elites and expectations of the growing part of societies. The influx of millions of immigrants to Europe that had begun as early as the 1960s eventually led to the dissatisfaction of the native population, particularly in the context of welfare expenses limited by crisis and growing difficulties on the labour market. This was one of the reasons of the dislike for immigrants, but also for political elites that defended universal human rights and the principle of multiculturalism in accordance with the prevailing rules of political correctness. After some time, this stimulated part of European societies to support anti-system movements questioning the prevailing liberal values and the ruling elites.[124]

The external proletariat – immigrants from outside the EU – was attracted with the vision of prosperity by former colonial metropolises.[125] Unfortunately, their assimilation in the spirit of European values was not fully successful.[126] Just like in the USA, the liberal conception of multiculturalism opened Europe up to other traditions even when they negated some values of the EU. At the same time, the European tradition rooted in Christianity etc. was devalued.[127] The policy of multiculturalism has failed, which was admitted, e.g., by the leading politicians of Western Europe.[128] For example, the population with Islamic roots

123 E. Buetter (2016): *Europe after Empire. Decolonization, Society, and Culture*, Cambridge, pp. 13, 502.

124 T.G. Grosse (2015): A Potential for Revolution in Europe?, in: B.J. Góralczyk (ed.), *European Union on The Global Scene: United or Irrelevant*? Warsaw, pp. 203–223; B. Góralczyk (2017): Powrót Historii, czyli rewolucja antyliberalna [The return of history: anti-liberal revolution], *Studia Europejskie*, 1 (81), pp. 9–31.

125 E. Buetter, *op. cit.*

126 A.M. Messina, *op. cit.*, pp. 15–16; M.L. Fernando (2014): *The Republic Unsettled: Muslim French and the Contradictions of Secularism*, Durham 2014; T. Huizinga (2016): *The New Totalitarian Temptation. Global Governance and the Crisis of Democracy in Europe*, New York – London, pp. 175–177.

127 D. Murray (2017): *The Strange Death of Europe. Immigration, Identity, Islam*, London – Oxford, pp. 3, 94–122.

128 D. Murray, *op. cit.*, pp. 96–97; C.L. Adida, D.D. Laitin, M.-A. Valfort (2016): *Why Muslim Integration Fails in Christian-Heritage Societies*, Cambridge, pp. 177–179.

rejects to a large extent the principle of secularity of the state and the division between the public sphere and the religious sphere even in the second generation after its arrival on the Old Continent.[129] According to scientists,[130] the Muslims living in Europe find it harder to accept liberalism, secularism and democracy – i.e., a majority of values on which the EU was built. They accept women's rights and rights of sexual minorities to a much smaller extent than the rest of the population does. They find it more difficult to cope on the labour market. They live in districts resembling ghettos, where unemployment and crime rates are much higher than elsewhere.

According to some opinions, the attitude of the Europeans to immigrants is ambivalent.[131] On the one hand, part of the EU's citizens has a sense of guilt for the colonial past and shows an open attitude to other cultures. On the other hand, a large part of Western societies, even with a liberal approach, has a sense of superiority and wants to maintain the old hierarchy and economic dependencies. Apart from that, the group of persons having a hostile attitude to migrants from outside the EU is increasing.[132] In such a situation, many immigrants feel alienated and left on the margin in a material sense. They develop a feeling of hostility towards Europe and its inhabitants and the will to adopt other than European values that would become a source of self-esteem.[133] Some of them turn towards ethnicity or religion, e.g., Islam. According to research,[134] the

---

129 C.L. Adida, D.D. Laitin, M.-A. Valfort, *op. cit.*, pp. 79–92. According to research done in 2016, almost 30 % of French Muslims reject the principle of the secular state and consider Sharia law to be more important for them than the law of the French Republic. Cf. French secular laws rejected by three in 10 Muslims, *Financial Times*, 18 September 2016, p. 3.

130 S. Sayyid (2014): *Recalling the caliphate: decolonization and world order*, London.

131 C. Kinnvall (2016): The Postcolonial Has Moved into Europe: Bordering, Security and Ethno-Cultural Belonging, *Journal of Common Market Studies*, vol. 54, no. 1, pp. 152–168.

132 Most of Europe's inhabitants are afraid of the influx of refugees, thinking that this means a higher terror threat, more limited public services and fewer vacant jobs. Cf. Europeans Fear Wave of Refugees Will Mean More Terrorism, Fewer Jobs, Pew Research Center, July 2016.

133 E. Buetter, *op. cit.*, p. 498; J. Kurth (2003): Who Will Do the Dirty Work?, in: A.J. Bacevich (ed.), *The Imperial Tense. Prospects and Problems of American Empire*, Chicago, pp. 251–252.

134 L. Berger (2016): Local, National and Global Islam: Religious Guidance and European Muslim Public Opinion on Political Radicalism and Social Conservatism, *West European Politics*, vol. 39, no. 2, 2016, pp. 205–228.

radicalism of European Muslims is strictly connected with their piousness (religious practice) and pauperisation. At the same time, we can see the bilaterally growing mechanism of mutual dislike and radicalisation, both on the part of the native population and immigrants. It is a source of serious social cracks and political problems that destabilise European integration.

Summary

The European Union has much in common with Arnold Toynbee's conception of a universal state. According to this conception, it is an attempt to build a state organism – a political structure above existing divisions, in the entire area of impact of the given civilisation. In Toynbee's view, universal states are usually an attempt to respond to crises and "cracks" of the civilisation that have led to its destruction so far. In the case of European Communities and then the European Union, this project was aimed at saving the old continent after war disasters by protecting it against the disastrous influence of nationalisms and the rivalry between European powers. It was also supposed to be an opportunity for local elites, particularly economic ones, to stabilise the political situation and reconstruct economy.

Toynbee assumed that the goals of a universal state are utopian, cannot be put into practice and are increasingly inconsistent with social expectations.[135] He thought that, even though attempts to establish such a state are praiseworthy and aimed at saving the civilisation, there is a number of factors preventing the fulfilment of these plans and bringing the results that are different from expectations in the course of time. These factors include, e.g., excessive ambitions, including actions aimed at external expansion, that are not adequate to the actual capabilities of a universal state. In the case of the European Union, this kind of expansion happened, e.g., through expansion to the East, which was carried out without the proper adjustment of the formula of management or funds towards the scale of the entire project. Therefore, as a result of crises, part of Western European elites made intense attempts to return to a smaller formula

---

135 A. Toynbee, *op. cit.*, pp. 245–249. About the utopian character of the European project: K. Szczerski (2017): *Utopia europejska. Kryzys integracji i polska inicjatywa naprawy* [*A European Utopia. The Crisis of Integration and the Polish Reform Initiative*], Kraków; T.G. Grosse (2018a): Federacja w Europie, czyli dążenie do utopii? [The federation in Europe: striving for utopia?], in: *Integracja europejska – polska perspektywa [European Integration – The Polish Perspective]*, Z. Czachór, T.G. Grosse, W. Paruch (ed.), Wydawnictwo Sejmowe, Warsaw, pp. 79–106.

of integration concentrated in the south-western part of the continent. Another example of ambitious actions that were not adequately backed up by institutional reforms and secured by financial instruments was the creation of the common currency. The crisis exposed these deficiencies, but did not lead to an essential reform in the monetary union. This resembles the phenomenon of *hybris* that, according to Toynbee, characterises the decline of a universal state. It brings inevitable crises and internal shocks because of the excessively large discrepancy between undertaken expansionistic actions and the reality of available resources and management methods.

Both the EU and the American empire were built on universal liberal values, including those referring to economy, politics and society. However, while Europe focused on the peaceful dissemination of these values, the USA supported the Western order in a military sense. Moreover, it promoted intensely the neo-liberal economic doctrine, and its currency and American financial institutions made economic exchange possible on a global scale. At the same time, economic globalisation and militarism became a sort of trap for the USA. In both of these spheres, the American incurred rising costs and were increasingly often responsible for the destabilisation of the international order. Both spheres are also an example of the phenomenon of *hybris*, which means the ambition to reinforce global hegemony with the weakening internal potential and the growing resistance of both rivals and allied, clientelistic or satellite states. It is worth noting that the American empire is another phase of evolution of the Western civilisation after the period of self-destruction of Western Europe in both world wars. The USA's strong pursuit of military and geoeconomic expansion refers to primary characteristics of imperialism practised by European powers, at least in the modern era. Thus, American imperialism was a continuation of the European tradition based historically on military and economic dominance. After World War II, under the American military umbrella, the mutated formula of European imperialism based on economic and regulatory expansion and the promotion of liberal values came into being.[136] Both forms of imperialism – the American one and the new European formula – were affected by the problem of *hybris*: exaggerated ambitions towards one's own potential and management methods.

State, social and political structures were too weak both in the USA and in the EU at the beginning of the 21st century. Europe failed to build a strong state or democracy on the EU level, whereas in the USA we could see the erosion of the

136 J. Zielonka (2006): *Europe as Empire: The Nature of the Enlarged European Union*, Oxford – New York: Oxford University Press.

state and democracy at that time. In both cases, public structures were carriers of elites' interests rather than community interests, which harmed social coherence and democracy. In both parts of the Western civilisation, society was an increasingly weaker foundation, not only due to demographic processes, but primarily due to numerous internal divisions, income inequalities, the weakening social capital and the decreasing activity of citizens in favour of the common good. The political community was the problem. In the EU, the European nation did not emerge; by contrast, nationalism and political polarisation became more intense in individual countries at the time of crisis. In the USA, the political community was becoming weaker and divided.

Toynbee points out all elements of decadence of a universal state, such as the loss of creativity of elites, the growing dominance of particularisms over the community approach and, finally, the deepening internal divisions. The limitation of creativity in the EU was most strikingly visible during successive crises and in the use of very conservative methods of overcoming them by elites. Therefore, crises brought huge social and political costs: for example, they intensified particularistic actions, stirred nationalisms and deepened divisions within the UE. The integration process has been marked by particularism or a weak sense of community almost since the beginning, and crises only reinforced this tendency. It is not a coincidence that many observers criticised Europe for the growing decline of solidarity during that period.[137] There was a shortage of relevant political institutions binding societies with the government on the EU level in a permanent and profound manner. Another type of problem was the construction of European values on the basis of universal human rights and with a very selective approach to historical heritage. This type of construction weakened the sense of the EU citizenship and made it difficult to build a strong European identity and, consequently, the awareness of the political community on a supranational level. Similar phenomena were visible in the USA. For example, the conception of multiculturalism accompanied by the deprecation of the tradition of white Anglo-Saxon Protestants was supposed to reinforce the weakening cohesion of the American society. The will to build a political community based on universal values was, however, put to a serious test in view of the liberal conception of the market and the marginalisation of citizens to the role of consumers and

137 T.G. Grosse, J. Hetnarowicz (2016): The discourse of Solidarity and the European Migrant Crisis, *Yearbook of Polish European Studies*, Centre for Europe, University of Warsaw, vol. 19/2016, pp. 35–62.

within the scope of the liberal state that has withdrawn from many compensatory policies.

Finally, divisions in the West were numerous and increasingly visible. This refers both to disputes between the USA and some EU states and inside the Union. The period of crises released old demons from which European integration was supposed to save people. There was a shift towards national egoisms, the rivalry of powers and the political hierarchy putting strong states over weak ones. That was an attempt to "return to the past" (which meant a form of archaism in Toynbee's terminology). In both analysed areas of the Western civilisation, we could also see divisions similar to Toynbee's conception: between elites and the proletariat, as well as between the internal proletariat and the external proletariat.

Do the tendencies described above signify the decline of the Western civilisation? Over the centuries, this civilisation has had many ups and downs, but it has resurrected in further political forms, often drawing upon previous experiences and cultural models. For example, the rise of the USA's importance after World War II allowed Western Europe and the entire Western civilisation to revive. Although the assumptions of Toynbee's historiosophical conception were pessimistic, it should be treated primarily as one of the intellectual tools useful for the analysis of Western crises. Nevertheless, it foreshadows profound changes in the USA and in Europe in the further years of the 21st century.

References

Adida C.L., Laitin D.D., Valfort M.-A. (2016): Why Muslim Integration Fails in Christian-Heritage Societies, Cambridge.

Allison G. (2017): Destined for War. Can America and China Escape Thucydides's Trap? Boston – New York: Houghton Mifflin Harcourt.

Arrighi G., Hopkins T.K., Wallerstein I. (1989): Antisystemic Movements, London – New York: Verso.

Bacevich A.J. (2002): American Empire. The Realities and Consequences of U.S. Diplomacy, Cambridge – London: Harvard University Press.

Ballin H. (2014): Citizens' Rights and the Right to Be a Citizen, Leiden: Brill - Nijhoff.

Berger L. (2016): Local, national and global Islam: religious guidance and European Muslim public opinion on political radicalism and social conservatism, *West European Politics*, vol. 39, no. 2, pp. 205–228.

Bieling H.J., Jäger J., Ryner M. (2016): Regulation theory and the political economy of the European Union, *Journal of Common Market Studies*, vol. 54, no. 1, pp. 53–69.

Braudel F. (1994): A History of Civilizations, London: Penguin Books.

Brunnermeier M., James H., Landau J.-P. (2016): The Euro and the Battle of Ideas, Princeton: Princeton University Press.

Brzeziński Z. (2012): Strategic Vision: America and the Crisis of Global Power, London: Basic Books.

Buetter E. (2016): Europe after Empire. Decolonization, Society, and Culture, Cambridge: Cambridge University Press.

Burke E. (1867): Works, Reflections on the Revolution in France, London, https://sourcebooks.fordham.edu/mod/1791burke.asp, access: 12.04.2019.

Busemeyer M.R., Tober T. (2015): European integration and the political economy of inequality, *European Union Politics*, vol. 16, no. 4, pp. 536–557.

Calleo D. (1982): The Imperious Economy, Cambridge: Harvard University Press.

Calleo D. (1992): The Bankrupting of America, New York: Avon Books.

Colliot-Thélène C. (2016): What Europe Does to Citizenship, in: D. Chalmers, M. Jachtenfuchs, C. Joerges (ed.), The End of the Eurocrats' Dream, Cambridge: Cambridge University Press.

Crouch C. (2011): The Strange Non-Death of Neoliberalism, Cambridge: Polity.

EUobserver, Brussels, 15 July 2014, https://euobserver.com/political/124980 [access: 29.12.2016].

Europeans Fear Wave of Refugees Will Mean More Terrorism, Fewer Jobs, Pew Research Center, July 2016.

Euroscepticism Beyond Brexit, Pew Research Center, June 2016, p. 2.

Fabbrini S. (2015a): The Euro Crisis and Its Constitutional Implications, in: S. Champeau, C. Closa, D. Innerarity, M. Poiares Maduro (ed.), The Future of Europe. Democracy, Legitimacy and Justice after the Euro Crisis, London: Rowman & Littlefield International, pp. 19–36.

Fabbrini S. (2015b): Which European Union. Europe after the Euro Crisis, Cambridge: Cambridge University Press.

Falkner G. (2016): The EU's problem-solving capacity and legitimacy in a crisis context: a virtuous or vicious circle?, *West European Politics*, vol. 39, no. 5, pp. 953–970.

Fernando M.L. (2014): The Republic Unsettled: Muslim French and the Contradictions of Secularism, Durham: Duke University Press.

Flanders S. (2017): Tear up the rule book to secure Europe's future, *Financial Times*, 9 January 2017, p. 9.

Foucault M. (2000): Power, New York.

French secular laws rejected by three in 10 Muslims, *Financial Times*, 18 September 2016.

Gilens M. (2012): Affluence and Influence: Economic Inequality and Political Power in America, Princeton: Princeton University Press.

Gilpin R. (1981): War and Change in World Politics, Cambridge: Cambridge University Press.

Góralczyk B. (2017): Powrót Historii, czyli rewolucja antyliberalna [The return of history: anti-liberal revolution], *Studia Europejskie*, vol. 1, no. 81, pp. 9–31.

Gramsci A. (1971): Selections from the Prison Notebooks, London: International Publishers Co.

Grosse T.G. (2014a): The golden straitjacket of Poland's membership in the EU, *Yearbook of Polish European Studies*, vol. 17/2014, pp. 117–138.

Grosse T.G. (2014b): W poszukiwaniu geoekonomii w Europie [In Search of Geoeconomy in Europe], Warsaw: ISP PAN.

Grosse T.G. (2015): A Potential for Revolution in Europe? in: B.J. Góralczyk (ed.), European Union on the Global Scene: United or Irrelevant?, Warsaw: CE UW, pp. 203–223.

Grosse T.G. (2016a): Assumptions of the theory of regional disintegration: suggestions for further research, *Przegląd Europejski*, vol. 4, no. 42, pp. 11–22.

Grosse T.G. (2016b): Overcoming the crisis in the Economic and Monetary Union, *Przegląd Europejski*, no. 1, pp. 28–50.

Grosse T.G. (2016c): The Eurozone Crisis, in: M.A. Cichocki & T.G. Grosse (ed.), The Aspects of a Crisis. An Analysis of Crisis Management from an Economic and Political Perspective, Natolin European Centre, Warsaw, pp. 11–56.

Grosse T.G. (2017a): Bretton Woods jako reżim geoekonomiczny [Bretton Woods as a geoeconomic regime], *Stosunki Międzynarodowe – International Relations*, pp. 65–82.

Grosse T.G. (2017b): Introduction, in: T.G. Grosse (ed.), European Union Policies at a Time of Crisis, Warsaw: Scholar Publishing House, pp. 9–32.

Grosse T.G. (2018a): Federacja w Europie, czyli dążenie do utopii? [The federation in Europe: striving for utopia?], in: Z. Czachór, T.G. Grosse, W. Paruch (ed.), Integracja europejska – polska perspektywa [European Integration – The Polish Perspective], Warsaw: Wydawnictwo Sejmowe, pp. 79–106.

Grosse T.G. (2018b): The crisis of European integration in the light of the theories of Arnold Toynbee, *Western Review, Journal of the Institute for Western Affairs in Poznań*, Special Issue 1, pp. 7–22.

Grosse T.G., Hetnarowicz J. (2016): The Discourse of Solidarity and the European Migrant Crisis, *Yearbook of Polish European Studies*, Centre for Europe, University of Warsaw, vol. 19/2016, pp. 35–62.

Guibernau M. (2011): The Identity of Nations, Cambridge: Polity.

Habermas J. (2013): The Crisis of the European Union, Cambridge: Polity, pp. VII–XII.

Hansen S.T., Marsh N. (2015): Normative power and organized hypocrisy: European Union member states' arms export to Libya, *European Security*, vol. 24, no. 2, pp. 264–286.

Huizinga T. (2016): The New Totalitarian Temptation. Global Governance and the Crisis of Democracy in Europe, New York – London: Encounter Books.

IMF warns of $135tn debt threat to recovery, *Financial Times*, 11.10.2017.

Kamiński A.Z., Kamiński B. (2004): Korupcja rządów [The Corruption of Governments], Warsaw: ISP PAN.

Kennedy P. (1987): The Rise and Fall of Great Powers, New York: Random House.

Kinnvall C. (2016): The postcolonial has moved into Europe: bordering, security and ethno-cultural belonging, *Journal of Common Market Studies*, vol. 54, no. 1, pp. 152–168.

Krūma K. (2014): EU Citizenship, Nationality and Migrant Status. An Ongoing Challenge, Leiden: Martinus Nijhoff.

Kurth J. (2003): Who Will Do the Dirty Work? in: A.J. Bacevich (ed.), The Imperial Tense. Prospects and Problems of American Empire, Chicago: Ivan R. Dee.

Lasch Ch. (1995): The Revolt of the Elites and the Betrayal of Democracy, New York: W. W. Norton & Company.

Layne Ch. (2012): The times it's real: the end of unipolarity and Pax Americana, *International Studies Quarterly*, vol. 1 (56), pp. 203–213.

Mann M. (2003): Incoherent Empire, London – New York: Verso.

Mann M. (2013): The Sources of Social Power. Globalizations, 1945–2011, Cambridge: Cambridge University Press.

Manners I. (2002): Normative Power Europe: A Contradiction in Terms?, *Journal of Common Market Studies*, vol. 40, no. 2, pp. 235–258.

Matthijs M. (2016): Powerful rules governing the euro: the perverse logic of German ideas, *Journal of European Public Policy*, vol. 23, no. 3, pp. 375–391.

Mazower M. (2013): Governing the World. The History of an Idea, London – New York: Penguin Books.

Messina A.M. (2014): Introduction: Identifying with Europe? in: A.C. Gould, A.M. Messina (ed.), Europe's Contending Identities. Supranationalism, Ethnoregionalism, Religion, and New Nationalism, Cambridge: Cambridge University Press.

Milward A. (1992): The European Rescue of the Nation State, New York: Routledge.

Münchau W. (2015): Enlargement and the euro are two big mistakes that ruined Europe, *Financial Times*, 1 November 2015.

Murray D. (2017): The Strange Death of Europe. Immigration, Identity, Islam, London – Oxford: Bloomsbury Continuum.

Narizny K. (2007): The Political Economy of Grand Strategy, Ithaca: Cornell University Press.

Oatley T. (2015): Political Economy of American Hegemony. Buildups, Booms, and Busts, Cambridge: Cambridge University Press.

Ott J.C. (2011): When Wall Street Met Main Street: The Quest for an Investors' Democracy, Cambridge: Harvard University Press.

Outram D. (2013): The Enlightenment, Cambridge: Cambridge University Press.

Pape R. (2009): Empire Falls, *National Interest*, no. 22, January 2009, p. 158.

Piketty T., Saez E., Zucman G. (2016): Distributional National Accounts: Methods and Estimates for the United States, *NBER Working Paper* 22945, December 2016.

Polyakova A., Fligstein N. (2016): Is European integration causing Europe to become more nationalist? Evidence from the 2007–9 financial crisis, *Journal of European Public Policy*, vol. 23, no. 1, pp. 60–83.

Dobbs R. et al., Poorer than their parents? Flat or falling incomes in advanced economies, McKinsey & Company, London 2016.

Putnam R. (2000): Bowling Alone, New York: Touchstone Books.

Reich S., Lebow R.N. (2014): Good-Bye Hegemony! Power and Influence in the Global System, Princeton: Princeton University Press.

Sayyid S. (2014): Recalling the Caliphate: Decolonization and World Order, London: Hurst.

Schmidt V.A. (2015): The Forgotten Problem of Democratic Legitimacy, in: M. Matthijs, M. Blyth (ed.), The Future of the Euro, Oxford – New York: Oxford University Press.

Simms B. (2013): Europe: The Struggle for Supremacy, from 1453 to the Present, New York: Basic Books.

Singer P.W. (2003): Corporate Warriors. The Rise of the Privatized Military Industry, Ithaca – London: Cornell University Press.

Sowell T. (2007): A Conflict of Visions. Ideological Origins of Political Struggles, New York: Basic Books.

Speech by Federal Chancellor Angela Merkel at the opening ceremony of the 61st academic year of the College of Europe, Bruges, 2 November 2010, http://www.bruessel.diplo.de/contentblob/2959854/Daten/ [access: 27.12.2016].

Spengler O. (1991): Zmierzch Zachodu. Zarys morfologii historii uniwersalnej, Warszawa 2001. English version: The Decline of the West (Oxford Paperbacks), Oxford University Press; 1 edition, Oxford.

Stiglitz J.E. (2016): The Euro and its Threat to the Future of Europe, New York: Allen Lane.

Streeck W. (2016): How Will Capitalism End? Essays on Failing System, London – New York: Verso.

Streeck W., Elsässer L. (2016): Monetary disunion: the domestic politics of Euroland, *Journal of European Public Policy*, vol. 23, no. 1, pp. 1–24.

Summers L.H. (2016): The age of secular stagnation. What it is and what to do about it, *Foreign Affairs*, March/April 2016, pp. 2–9.

Szczerski K. (2017): Utopia europejska. Kryzys integracji i polska inicjatywa naprawy [A European Utopia. The Crisis of Integration and the Polish Reform Initiative], Kraków: Biały Kruk.

Temin P. (2017): The Vanishing Middle Class. Prejudice and Power in a Dual Economy, Cambridge: The MIT Press, pp. IX, 5–40.

Todd E. (2003): After the Empire. The Breakdown of the American Order, New York: Columbia University Press.

Toynbee A. (1972): A Study of History, London: Oxford University Press.

Trubowitz P. (2011): Politics and Strategy: Partisan Ambition and American Statecraft, Princeton: Princeton University Press.

Trump's wealthy cabinet choices hark back to Gilded Age, *Financial Times*, 2 December 2016, p. 3.

Tsoukalis L. (2016): In Defence of Europe. Can the European Project Be Saved?, Oxford – New York: Oxford University Press.

U.S. Census Bureau, https://www.census.gov [access: 27.10.2017].

Van Apeldoorn B. (2002): Transnational Capitalism and the Struggle over European Integration, Abingdon: Routledge.

Zielonka J. (2006): Europe as Empire: The Nature of the Enlarged European Union, Oxford: Oxford University Press.

Zimmermann H. (2016): The euro trilemma, or: how the Eurozone fell into a neofunctionalist legitimacy trap, *Journal of European Integration*, vol. 38, no. 4, pp. 425–439.

Part II Crisis of the Liberal Order – Different Case Studies

Ryszarda Formuszewicz

Germany and the decade of the crisis – 2008–2017

Abstract: The author attempts to characterize the German response to the crisis phenomena growing from 2008 to 2018. The text is a presentation of the analysis of budget debates in the Bundestag from the period in question. The adoption of such a research approach is motivated by the fact that since the state, through the budget, pursues a policy aimed at achieving political, economic and social goals, parliamentary discussion of income and expenditure may provide meaningful indicators as to the strategy and actions of the government in relation to individual crises.Comparison of the process and content of debates allows the author to make an attempt to formulate comparative conclusions regarding particular crises by indicating their specificity and common elements of the German state's reaction.

Keywords: budget debate, Bundestag, crisis, public policies, Germany

This paper looks at the reaction of Germany to the crisis phenomena that have been emerging since 2008. This attempt to characterise the German response has been made on the basis of the analysis of budget debates in the Bundestag from the period in question.

The adoption of such a research approach was motivated by the assumption that since the state uses budget to implement budgetary policies aimed at achieving political, economic and social objectives, parliamentary discussion on revenues and expenditures can provide meaningful indicators of government strategies and actions in relation to individual crises. The comparison of the course and content of the debates enables formulating comparative conclusions regarding individual crises by indicating their specificity as well as common elements of the German state's reaction.

The scope of the analysis was limited to the debates devoted to the budget of the Chancellery (*Einzelplan 04*) – the so-called general debates (*Generaldebatte*). Formally, they concern a budget with a relatively small volume; however, they are a culmination point of parliamentary budget debates, taking on the character of a discussion on government policy with evaluation elements. Their aim is to present and consider the priorities of the ruling coalition, identify key challenges for German politics and work out responses to these challenges. By linking them to decisions on the management of public resources, they provide a picture of the real options for the actions of the state.

The format of a debate reflects the key role of the Chancellery as the main centre of power and the key actor in formulating a political reaction to the crisis. The Chancellor, heads of parliamentary groups and other relevant politicians are all actively involved in these. The debate is mostly devoted to issues denoted as *Chefsache*– the domain of the head of the government, which includes crisis management. The fact of Angela Merkel's continued leadership in changing coalitions, which is something unique in Europe, serves as an additional justification for narrowing down the area of analysis to debates on the Chancellery's budget.

Focusing the analysis on sources that are a part of the debate on the German budget also causes some limitations. The content of the general debates is influenced by the coincidence in time with other events – for example the proximity to European Council meetings is conducive to references to EU policies; however, it can be assumed that the main line of communication on crisis management is maintained. This paper also takes into consideration the cases of adapting the message within the framework of communication policy, namely the possibility of concealing certain aspects of the crisis as part of the strategy. A characteristic feature is communication focused on highlighting one's own strengths by the representatives of particular political groups, as well as party competition, mostly between the government and the opposition, with lesser intensity in the conditions of a grand coalition.

The analysis covers 18 budget debates – two from the 16th, eight from the 17th and eight from the 18th term of the Bundestag.[1] The two analysed debates of 2008 (first and second reading of the draft budget) reflect the still late phase of the first grand coalition under the leadership of Chancellor Angela Merkel. The subsequent ones concern the period of the centre-right coalition of Christian Democrats and the Free Democratic Party (FDP) and the next instalment of the grand coalition after the 2013 elections.

The aim of the analysis was to answer the following questions:

- What was the role of the crisis in justifying decisions on the state's budgetary policy regarding mobilising its resources?
- How was the crisis diagnosed and what conclusions were drawn regarding the state's actions based on this diagnosis?

1 The list of analysed debates can be found at the end of the paper.

- What was the relationship between national measures and crisis management activities within the EU?
- How was the strategy towards the crisis shaped in terms of finding the solution, alleviating its symptoms and preventing the occurrence of a similar crisis in the future?

The combination of these components is aimed at formulating comparative conclusions for each crisis as well as at determining which elements of the German response were permanent and which were modified in relation to subsequent crises. This approach also implies restraint in assessing the effectiveness and appropriateness of the measures taken by Germany.

Financial and economic crisis

The beginning of the financial crisis in Germany was marked by the practical bankruptcy of IKB Deutsche Industriebank AG on the 30th of July 2007, the bailout of which cost the German taxpayer 9.6 billion euro.[2] The destabilisation of the US financial sector hit the country hard after the bankruptcy of Lehman Brothers on the 15th of September 2008. During the week-long budget debates in the Bundestag, which were just starting at the time, the Minister of Finance had to address the situation at hand. Chancellor Angela Merkel also touched upon various forecasts concerning the situation, while considering the prospects for economic development in Germany. The government was aware of the possible consequences for domestic companies resulting from the openness of the economy, which has been benefiting "more than any other" from globalisation. Evaluating the prospects for the dynamics of the world economy, the Chancellor pointed out the development of alternative growth centres in Asia, Latin America and the EU as a positive aspect. She also highlighted better availability of credit for enterprises, compared to other countries, as an important factor (A. Merkel, BT 2008–175, p. 18639).

Considering possible responses to adverse developments in the global economy, Angela Merkel declared that Germany – largely prosperous on world markets – would remain an open country. Giving up isolationism entailed a commitment to active policies aimed at increasing opportunities and reducing possible risks: *Politik muss gestalten* (A. Merkel, BT 2008–175, p. 18639). The

---

2 M. Hellwig (2017): Deutschland und die Finanzkrise(n), *Wirtschaftsdienst* 97. Jahrgang, Heft 9 s. 606–607, https://archiv.wirtschaftsdienst.eu/jahr/2017/9/deutschland-und-die-finanzkrisen/.

Chancellor specified this imperative as follows: "The importance of politics in the times of globalisation is not diminishing – it is growing and it requires new insights from all of us. (…) The social market economy has always required activity, but right now it is all about developing its international dimension" (A. Merkel, BT 2008–175, p. 18641). The social market economy was also indicated as a German response to the challenges and crisis (H.-P. Friedrich (CDU/CSU), BT 2010–15, p. 1286).

Before the second reading of the 2009 draft budget, the crisis caused by the disruption of the US financial system had spread, bringing about serious repercussions for other countries. On Sunday, the 5th of October 2008, Chancellor Angela Merkel and Minister of Finance Peer Steinbrück issued a joint statement on deposit protection to prevent a loss of public confidence in the banking system.[3] The statement was followed by a protective mechanism for banks, as well as measures to protect employment in order to stop the destabilisation of the financial market.

The breakdown of financial market impacted traditional sectors of the economy and the labour market. The effects of the crisis, in terms of both scope and impact, required a state response at the executive and legislation level.[4] A detailed list of actions at the state level, comprising two economic stimulus packages of November 2008 and January 2009, was supposed to mitigate the effects of the crisis and maintain production capacity throughout the recession. The CDU/CSU-FDP coalition introduced some complementary corrections conducive to growth, in the form of a law on stimulating growth. Particular attention was paid to the difficult situation of the automotive industry, particularly ensuring the availability of credit for entrepreneurs (A. Merkel, BT 2008–189, p. 20336). Crisis management was based on the principle of helping people to help themselves, as well as an assumption that the provided instruments would be temporary in nature (A. Merkel, BT 2008–189, p. 20336).

The German government believed that the crisis was caused by the availability of too cheap money in the United States (A. Merkel, BT 2008–189, p. 20339), as well as insufficient regulation of financial markets (A. Merkel, BT 2012–207, p. 25234). The nature of disruption in the functioning of world

---

3 Detailed information: P. Steinbrück (2011): Unterm Strich, *dtv München*, erweiterte Ausgabe 2011, p. 209 et seq.

4 See: W. Małachowski (2010): Skutki kryzyski i działania antykryzysowe w gospodarce Niemiec, in: *Państwa narodowe wobec kryzysu ekonomicznego*, ed. Joachim Osiński, Warsaw: SGH.

markets was also defined as an export crisis (L. Stiegler (SPD), BT 2008–189, p. 20363). The opposition interpreted the situation at hand as a crisis of the economic and social order caused by neo-liberalism (O. Lafontaine (Linke), BT 2008–189, p. 20342) and called for taking a broader perspective on the crisis phenomena, taking into account the global food, climate and financial crisis (R. Künast (Bündnis 90/Die Grünen), BT 2008–189, p. 20353). The interpretation of the crisis as an exogenous phenomenon was conducive to the rapid emergence of the question of responsibility: "When the big players in global competition do not follow the rules, everyone has to suffer the consequences" (A. Merkel, BT 2010–15, p. 1257).

The debates on the Chancellery's draft budgets show the reflection on the role of the state in the context of economic turmoil, caused by the financial crisis. Peter Struck (SPD) pointed to the ongoing renaissance of the state on a global scale, since, as he pointed out, "a strong, capable state is more important than ever in the times of global and open markets of the 21st century." In line with social needs, it needs to provide an ethical and legal framework for the market (BT 2008–189, p. 20350). Given the insufficient disciplinary effect of the market, the state was responsible for establishing and enforcing the rules (L. Stiegler (SPD), BT 2008–189, p. 20364). The Chairman of the CDU/CSU parliamentary group, Volker Kauder, explained: "Our motto is: As a state, we are taking measures to protect jobs and to emerge stronger from the crisis" (BT 2008–189, p. 20355). Even the FDP has spoken about the need for a strong state that establishes the necessary laws and ensures their enforcement (B. Homburger (FDP), BT 2010–15, p. 1270). It was believed that the crisis showed that the state had responsibilities (A. Merkel, BT 2010–15, p. 1259).

Regarding the financial sector, a decisive state intervention was deemed necessary in the event of a threat to the entire national economy and the social sphere of the state (A. Merkel, BT 2008–189, p. 20336). Financial services were deemed a public good of existential importance for international economy, which served as a justification for a rapid and comprehensive mobilisation of public resources with as short a decision-making process as possible. This fact was criticised by the pro-interventionist Linke party. Gregor Gysi pointed out that the government needed just one week to make a decision to earmark nearly 480 billion euro for guarantees and recapitalisation aid, while reaching an agreement on a budget of 320 billion euro takes several months to reach. He also criticised the establishment of a parliamentary committee with limited informational powers that deliberated in camera as unconstitutional disenfranchisement of the Bundestag (BT 2010–58, p. 6049). In addition, some alleged that that the ruling coalition had a wrong approach to saving financial institutions, as it did not envision taking over their shares, and pointed out the failure to reflect the awarded guarantees in the budget (BT 2008–175, p. 18645).[5]

The crisis has been defined as an emergency situation, justifying the use of exceptional measures, in particular in the context of the experience of the 1930s. (A. Merkel, BT 2008–189, p. 20335, BT 2010–15, p. 1251, BT 2010–30, p. 2711). These exceptional measures encompassed a bailout package for banks, followed by a turnaround in budgetary policy. In September 2007, Peer Steinbrück presented the prospect of giving up new debt. During the first reading of the 2009 draft budget, this goal was still considered to be reachable as early as in 2011. Meanwhile, as a result of the crisis, the 2010 budget envisioned a record net borrowing exceeding 85 billion euro, with public debt rising to 83.2 % of GDP in 2010, while budget deficit shot up to 5 % of GDP.

Despite the abandonment of conservative budgetary policies in the time of crisis, budget consolidation was to remain a priority (A. Merkel, BT 2010–74, p. 8057), and the German culture of stability was supposed to serve as a role model for Europe (A. Merkel, BT 2010–58, p. 6039). A step towards achieving these goals was the adoption of the so-called debt brake in 2009, which at that time meant that the authority of the parliament over budget was effectively limited (H.P. Friedrich (CDU/CSU), BT 2010–74, p. 8084). Debt and interest were seen as a limitation of the state's ability to act (T. Oppermann (SPD) BT 2014–29, p. 2334).

In 2011, Chancellor Angela Merkel announced the fulfilment of her main electoral promise that Germany would emerge stronger from the crisis. She admitted that the difficulties were overcome partially thanks to tax money, and she stressed the importance of reducing the debt accumulated over the years in the context of problems in the euro area (A. Merkel, BT 2011–123, p. 14470). The return to pre-crisis levels was faster than expected, with economic growth already at 3.7 % in 2010. In the government narrative, Germany became the " growth locomotive" in Europe (A. Merkel, BT 2010–58, p. 6039, BT 2011–123, p. 6039).

German politicians were convinced that it was the good condition of Germany at the time of the crisis, which helped them to achieve the objectives of crisis management (A. Merkel, BT 2010–15, p. 1253; H.-P. Friedrich (CDU/CSU), BT 2010–15, p. 1285, BT 2010–58, p. 6067). The list of success factors mentioned

5 Summary of costs of rescuing banks and domestic banks: Bilanz der Bankenrettung in Deutschland, Drucksache 19/4243, Bilanz der Landesbankenrettung in Deutschland Drucksache 19/4242.

by the politicians included the consolidated state finances, the position of "the growth locomotive" in the European Union (P. Struck (SPD), BT 2008–175, p. 18650), maintaining and modernisation of the industrial base, contrary to general trends (H. Heil, (SPD) BT 2008–175, p. 18678; V. Kauder (CDU/CSU), BT 2014–29, p. 2338, T. Oppermann (SPD), BT 2014–29, p. 2334). The forecasts assumed that the economy would return to its pre-crisis level in 2013 (A. Merkel, BT 2010–15, p. 1251). German politicians noted the relatively good situation of Germany in comparison to other European countries with satisfaction. The fact that Germany became one of the main actors in the fight against the crisis, unlike during the Great Recession in the 1930s, was seen as an opportunity (L. Stiegler, (SPD) BT 2008–189, p. 20362).

Regulation of the financial sector was seen as the key measure to prevent a similar crisis in the future. This action was postulated by Germany as part of the G7 since the beginning of 2007, as well as at the G20 Forum. The principle that every product, every actor and every financial market participant must be regulated was derived from the social market economy (A. Merkel, BT 2010–30, p. 6041). Faced with difficulties in developing solutions within multilateral frameworks, some instruments were introduced by legislation at the national level. These included bank tax, supervision, restriction of short selling, as well as a law on bank restructuring. It was hoped that the German solutions would be followed shortly by European regulations. Difficulties in forcing restrictions at the international level have sometimes also served as an excuse for abandoning specific regulations at a national level. Due to the lack of broader support for financial transaction tax, Germany has attempted to introduce it within the formula of enhanced EU cooperation (A. Merkel, BT 2012–207, p. 25234).

The awareness that not all global trends could be tackled using national measures highlighted the importance of cooperation at European level and justified the three-level approach – national, European and global. (A. Merkel, BT 2008–189, p. 20338). The opposition criticised Merkel's aloof and reserved attitude towards crisis management at EU level ("Madame Non"), while the coalition believed it to be appropriate in view of German interests (P. Ramsauer, (CDU/CSU) BT 2008–189, p. 20365), as well as doubts regarding the commitment of German funds (P. Struck (SPD), BT 2008–189, p. 20349). The combination of national and European measures aimed at counteracting the crisis was considered to be the appropriate course of action; however, the limited possibilities of copying these solutions by other Member States due to different circumstances were also pointed out (P. Struck (SPD), BT 2008–189, p. 20349). Recalling contradictory recommendations from various international institutions, Angela

Merkel opted for moderate solutions tailored to the situation in Germany (A. Merkel, BT 2008–189, p. 20337).

Numerous reservations were related to the proposal to establish an economic government at European level, which left German politicians afraid of curbing the competitiveness of the country's economy, having to abandon their own strengths, as well as taking weaker actors as a benchmark, instead of focusing on "the fastest and best" (A. Merkel, BT 2010–30, p. 2715) and of arbitrary imposition of economic structures typical of other systems to the detriment of small and medium-sized enterprises (H.P. Friedrich, (CDU/CSU) BT 2010–30. p. 2741). The criticism of the EU 2020 Strategy ("*Gleichmacherei*") was similar in its tone. H-P Friedrich, referring to the discussion about the causes of the public debt crisis, argued: "The whole of Europe will not be more competitive, it will not be in better shape if the strongest – Germans – are told that we can no longer be diligent or economical" (BT 2010–30, p. 2742). The head of CDU/CSU parliamentary group, Volker Kauder, deplored the possibility that the European Commission might threaten the German economic power (BT 2014–29, p. 2338, similarly to R. Brüderle (FDP), BT 2011–123, p. 25244; R. Kruse (CDU/CSU), BT 2012–207, p. 25257).

The attacks on the German export-based economic model were resisted. Angela Merkel emphasised the relationship between remaining a strong "export power" and maintaining prosperity (BT 2010–15, p. 1254). She considered it necessary to develop and strengthen industries believed to be German assets – including chemical and automotive industries, medical technology and transport technology.

She also voiced her objections towards Brussels regarding the perceived threat to the interests of the automotive industry, which was intensively supported at the national level at the time, seen in the climate policy negotiations (A. Merkel, BT 2008–189, p. 20337). She also expected that the European Commission would at least temporarily relax the regulations on subsidies for small and medium-sized enterprises (A. Merkel, BT 2008–189, p. 20338).

Characteristics of the response to the crisis

The German response to the crisis took on the form of a manifestation of the state's agency, including communication – as it was the case of the joint statement by the Chancellor and the Minister of Finance on deposit guarantees.

The state's involvement in crisis management was subject to a consensus. The differences in the stances of the various political groups represented in the Bundestag concerned the degree of intensity of state intervention, with dominant views referring to the ordoliberal principles. The overarching objective of the policy in Germany was to ensure competitiveness in order to maintain the German export-based economic model.

Tax-funded measures taken at national level played a vital role in the crisis management strategy. The list of measures aimed at mitigating the effects of economic turmoil was quickly specified and implemented in a relatively smooth manner.

The global crisis was considered an emergency, justifying in particular the deviation from the stated strategic objective of fiscal consolidation and the imposition of the cost of banking sector overhaul on taxpayers.

The relatively rapid return to growth was interpreted as a confirmation of validity of the assumed crisis management strategy and, at the same time, as a successful verification of the social market economy model. This was conducive to reinforcing the belief that the German approach to budgetary and economic policy, including its focus on export, is the right choice. In addition, overcoming the crisis in a quick manner ensured public support for the measures taken and their costs.

Here, one should also highlight the perception of the European Union as an actor whose actions may undermine the effectiveness of national measures. During the financial and economic crisis, Germany called for a relaxation or greater flexibility in enforcement of EU rules.

Despite the awareness of the depth of economic ties due to globalisation, German politics were not immediately aware of the scale of the potential threat to the economy as a result of the destabilisation initiated by the collapse of the American financial sector.

Crisis in the euro area

In 2009, Germany – absorbed by their own political calendar (Bundestag elections on the 27th of September, establishing a new coalition and the inauguration of a new government on the 28th of October), as well as focused on tackling the economic crisis – did not immediately recognise the full extent of the risk associated with the release of amended budget deficit figures by the Greek Prime Minister. The severity of the situation was properly assessed only when the problems spread to other euro area members: Ireland, Portugal and Spain. As a result, aid programmes were prepared for countries affected by the crisis. At the same time, a joint European crisis management and stabilisation mechanism for the EFSF was established. It was only in autumn of 2011 that Germany decided to try and formulate a comprehensive response to the crisis in cooperation with France. Summer of 2012 brought the shift in Germany's position in favour of maintaining the integrity of the euro area in its current shape, as well as establishing aid mechanisms.[6]

The difficult situation in Greece and the resulting challenges for the euro area were raised for the first time at a budgetary debate during the second reading of the 2010 draft budget. The long-running violations of the Stability and Growth Pact were pointed out as the cause of the problems, later exacerbated by financial market speculation. (A. Merkel, BT 2010–30, p. 1718). During the next debate, the Chancellor also raised the issue of imbalances, as well as uneven distribution of sound budgets and growth in the EU, which were revealed by the crisis (BT 2010–58, p. 6040). A full diagnosis of the crisis was presented in 2011, identifying high debt levels in many countries of the euro area as the main cause, while pointing out that it was not a result of supporting the economic growth during the international financial and economic crisis, but the result of decades of following the wrong philosophy of achieving growth no matter the cost (A. Merkel, BT 2011–123, p. 14470). Defining the situation as a public debt crisis, the origins of which were older than the recent economic crisis, confirmed the attribution of responsibility to the affected countries.[7] At a later time, Angela Merkel also characterised the crisis from the standpoint of a deficit in financial markets' confidence, which was lost as a result of long-running violations of the Stability and Growth Pact (BT 2011–142, p. 16915). Opposition parties, however, directly linked this "deepest existential crisis of the European Union" with the consequences of the ongoing financial crisis (F.W. Steinmeier (SPD), BT 2011–123, p. 14464). Ireland's difficulties were also attributed to "unreasonable neo-liberal economic policies" and tax dumping (R. Künast (Bündnis 90/Die Grünen), BT 2010–74, p. 8074; J. Poß (SPD) BT 2010–74, p. 8083). The Left Party criticised the lack of understanding of the nature of a single currency and defined the situation as a "systemic crisis of democracy" caused by the "dictatorship" of the financial markets, followed by stabilisation of the financial sector throughout the crisis at the expense of taxpayers (G. Gysi (Linke), BT 2011–123, p. 14474, BT 2012–191, p. 22992). FDP, which was a part of the ruling coalition, referred to the situation at hand as "euro crisis/euro area crisis" (*Euro-Krise*) (B. Homburger

---

6 See: D. Schwarzer (2013): Germany's Role and Strategy in the Euro Area – Determining Factors and Scenarios, *The Polish Quarterly of International Affairs*, no. 2/2013 s. 62 et seq.

7 Cf. K.H.F. Dyson (2014): *States, debt, and power: 'saints' and 'sinners' in European history and integration*, Oxford University Press.

(FDP), BT 2010–58, p. 6052), which diverged from the way Christian democratic parties saw it (V. Kauder (CDU/CSU), BT 2011–123, p. 14488).

In terms of internal politics, throughout the entire 17th term of office, the ruling coalition blamed the crisis on the previous government of SPD and the Greens, accusing them of weakening the Stability and Growth Pact and agreeing to the adoption of single currency by Greece. However, the incomplete architecture of the euro area was not criticised, since that would shift the responsibility onto Christian Democrats (cf. V. Kauder (CDU/CSU), BT 2011–123, p. 14488).

The German crisis management strategy was based on the assumptions of the German culture of stability, presented as "growth-oriented consolidation," which was justified, among others, by the good condition in which the country emerged from the crisis: "Germany remains the anchor of stability and the driving force for growth in the euro area and in the European Union as a whole" (A. Merkel, BT 2014–42, p. 3691). Germany's monetary and fiscal policy were presented as role models.[8] All aid to the countries affected by crisis was based on strict conditions.

One of the most important elements of the German struggle with the euro area crisis were the challenges pertaining to the legitimacy. The issue of Bundestag's budget powers resounded most strongly during the first reading of the 2012 draft budget on the day the judgement of the Federal Constitutional Court on measures supporting Greece and the EFSF was announced,[9] followed by the first reading of the 2013 draft budget in connection with the conditional approval of the ESM by the Federal Constitutional Court.[10] In addition, the lack of the democratic legitimacy as a result of the ECB's takeover of the crisis management was also heavily criticised (F.W. Steinmeier (SPD), BT 2011–123, p. 14464; G. Gysi BT 2011–123, p. 14476). Some members of the Bundestag voiced their doubts as to whether there is any point of conducting any budget debates before clarifying the scope of further euro stabilisation commitments (K. Kipping (Linke), BT 2012–207, p. 25237, P. Steinbrück (SPD), BT 2012–207, p. 25227). The question of the relationship between legitimacy provided by national parliaments and legitimacy at the European level with regard to the Economic and Monetary

8 See: L. Bonatti, A. Fracasso, The German Model and the European Crisis, *Journal of Common Market Studies*, 51(6), p. 10023–1039.

9 BVerfG, Urteil des Zweiten Senats vom 07. September 2011- 2 BvR 987/10 – Rn. (1–142), http://www.bverfg.de/e/rs20110907_2bvr098710.html.

10 BVerfG, Urteil des Zweiten Senats vom 12. September 2012- 2 BvR 1390/12 – Rn. (1–215), http://www.bverfg.de/e/rs20120912_2bvr139012.html.

Union, which was crucial for ensuring public acceptance, remained open (A. Merkel, BT 2012–191, p. 22987).

In the subsequent years of the crisis, the legitimacy of measures taken during the crisis of the euro area was often referred to by their output – the diligent recording of all signs of improvement in the situation in countries struggling with problems.

The controversies surrounding the management of the euro area crisis, the extent of the risk for the budget and the economy and the fear of lack of public acceptance imposed a particular obligation on politicians to justify their decisions. Thus, one of the main themes of general debates was presentation of the motives behind the course of action taken to manage the crisis at hand. The speakers mostly presented the benefits of the single currency for Germany (V. Kauder (CDU/CSU), BT 2011–123 p 14488; G. Hasselfeldt (CDU/CSU), BT 2011–123, p. 14497; G. Gysi (Linke), BT 2012–191, p. 22993), in particular the role of the euro in overcoming the financial and economic crisis (A. Merkel, BT 2010–58, p. 6040; G. Hasselfeldt (CDU/CSU), BT 2011–123, p. 14497; M. Roth (SPD), BT 2012–191, p. 23012). In a broader context, they also pointed out the connection between the prosperity of Germany and that of Europe, as well as the political dimension of monetary integration as a guarantee of peace and the process of European integration (A. Merkel, BT 2011–123, p. 14470, BT 2012–191, p. 22992, BT 2014–29, p. 2327, BT 2014–42, p. 3691; V. Kauder (CDU/CSU), BT 2014–42, p. 3706). The Chancellor prioritised the goal of strengthening Europe throughout the crisis as the "key task of the current term of office," convinced that a strong Europe was in Germany's best interest (BT 2011–123, p. 14470). "A strong and capable Europe" was presented as a condition for Germany to maintain a competitive edge compared to other regions of the world (V. Kauder (CDU/CSU), BT 2011–123, p. 14491, BT 2011–142, p. 16932).

The ruling coalition also justified its actions with having to maintain the stability of the single currency, which was both in the interest of the economy, as well as individual deposit holders – a kind of a "silent social policy," aimed at protecting the poor (H.-P. Friedrich (CDU/CSU), BT 2010–74, p. 8085; R. Brüderle (FDP), BT 2012–191, p. 22999). It was also pointed out that euro was in fact more stable than the German mark (G. Hasselfeldt (CDU/CSU), BT 2011–123, p. 14497). Some deputies recalled that maintaining stability was promised as one of the key aspects of introduction of the single currency (A. Merkel, BT 2011–123, p. 14470; R. Brüderle (FDP), BT 2011–142, p. 16926, BT 2012–191, p. 22999) and highlighted the importance of social trust: "People also have confidence in this country and in this state, because they trust in the stability of our currency" (H.-P. Friedrich (CDU/CSU), BT 2010–30, p. 2742). The stability of the currency was elevated to the level of a *Magna Carta* of the social market economy (R. Brüderle (FDP), BT 2012–191, p. 22999). Politicians also recalled the negative historical experience of extreme inflation and two currency reforms: "Fear of hyperinflation is inscribed in German DNA, while Americans fear deflation" (R. Brüderle (FDP), BT 2011–142, p. 16926).

The debates also brought up the issue of the communitarisation of responsibility for the debts of euro area member states in numerous contexts. The opposition accused the government of misleading the public by allowing the EFSF to buy bonds on the secondary market as a result of its own failure to act (F.W. Steinmeier (SPD), BT 2011–123, p. 14463), just like it happened with the ECB (F.W. Steinmeier (SPD), BT 2011–123, p. 14463, BT 2012–191, p. 22983; C. Schneider (SPD), BT 2014–42, p. 3709; P. Steinbrück (SPD), BT 2012–207, p. 25228).

The coalition rejected Eurobonds in any shape or form (e.g. A. Merkel, BT 2011–123, p. 14471; R. Brüderle (FDP), BT 2011–123, p. 14483; V. Kauder (CDU/CSU), BT 2011–142, p. 16932). On the other hand, the SPD was willing to accept them, under the proviso that they enabled interfering with the expenditures of the beneficiary countries (F.W. Steinmeier (SPD), BT 2011–123, p. 14463). The government was accused of introducing "Merkel-Bonds" through the back door, due to the activity of the ECB (S. Gabriel (SPD), BT 2011–142, p. 16912).

Some politicians praised the positive role of interest rate differences between euro area member states, which serves as a bonus for good governance and a means of exerting pressure to maintain budgetary discipline and implement structural reforms (A. Merkel, BT 2011–123, p. 14471; G. Hasselfeldt (CDU/CSU), BT 2011–123, p. 14498; R. Brüderle (FDP), BT 2012–191, p. 23001).

Similarly, the coalition had a critical attitude towards the fund's proposal to old debt repayment (*Schuldentilgungsfonds*) (G. Hasselfeldt (CDU/CSU), BT 2012–191, p. 23014; H.O. Solms (FDP), BT 2012–191, p. 23011). The key argument against any form of communitarisation of debts and obligations was the inability to interfere in the budgets of other Member States (A. Merkel, BT 2011–123, p. 14471).

In addition to the concept of the "Union of Stability," which was key to the German strategy, in the debates, the politicians used negative terms that synthetically express concepts considered to be a threat to German interests: "transfer union" (e.g. H.-P. Friedrich (CDU/CSU), BT 2010–74, p. 8085; B. Homburger (FDP), BT 2010–74, p. 8071), "debt union" (A. Merkel, BT 2011–123, p. 14471; G. Hasselfeldt (CDU/CSU), BT 2012–191, p. 23014) "interest socialism" and "inflation union" (R. Brüderle, BT 2011–123, p. 14483, BT 2012–191, p. 23000).

Another aspect highlighted in the budget debates was the issue of cost incurred by Germany as a result of the crisis itself, as well as – as opposition parties claimed – as a result of the errors in crisis management, made by the ruling coalition, which had difficulty in presenting a consistent agenda to the outside world. The ruling coalition believed that questioning the official position was an act of turning away from German interests (A. Merkel, BT 2010–58, p. 6040). Hans-Peter Friedrich (CSU) was pleased to note that the current government had more influence on Europe than the Red-Green coalition has had under its rule. "Contemporary Europe is led by Germany and the German Chancellor" (BT 2010–74, p. 8084). The opposition accused the government of hiding the need to bear the costs of managing the crisis and the scale of incurred debt from the general public (F.W. Steinmeier (SPD), BT 2011–123, p. 14463; P. Steinbrück (SPD), BT 2012–207, p. 25228; J. Trittin (Bündnis 90/Die Grünen), BT 2012–207, p. 25245). According to the opposition, the ruling coalition is detrimental to taxpayers (S. Gabriel (SPD), BT 2010–58, p. 6032, BT 2011–142, p. 16911; G. Gysi (Linke), BT 2014–50, p. 4552; J. Trittin (Bündnis 90/Die Grünen), BT 2012–207, p. 25245; R. Künast (Bündnis 90/Die Grünen), BT 2011–142, p. 16929; F.W. Steinmeier (SPD), BT 2012–191, p. 22983), while the ruling coalition itself believed otherwise (H.O. Solms (FDP), BT 2011–123, p. 14495).

In the context of crisis management, the general debates rarely addressed the relationship between the euro area and the EU as a whole. The role of the EU internal market was also marginalised.

Characteristics of the response to the crisis

The management of the crisis in the euro area was dominated by the desire to transfer German ideas and concepts regarding budgetary stability to the European level. This was the second attempt to do so, after the negotiations accompanying the preparations for the introduction of the single currency. German solutions were presented as a role model and a condition for maintaining competitive edge of the EU in the global market.

Contrary to its own previous conviction, when dealing with the financial and economic crisis, Germany preferred a solution based on the "one size fits all" principle for the euro area crisis, ordering its European partners to adopt a financial consolidation policy.

Another difference in crisis management concerned a lack of certainty as to the proper choice of instruments, reactive modification of the country's stance and delaying the initiation of next steps.

A new element, which did not emerge during the financial and economic crisis, was the multifaceted legitimacy challenges. The government's options were determined, on the one hand, by the national constitutional constraints, regarding traditional powers of parliament and the control of the European integration process, and on the other hand by the division of competencies in the euro area, with the budgetary authority preserved by the Member States.

The lack of consensus on crisis management tactics within the ruling coalition resulted in difficulties in presenting a coherent agenda. At the same time, the scale of debt incurred to stabilise the single currency required a convincing justification presented to the general public. The difficulty of this task grew with the emergence of subsequent manifestations of the worsening crisis.

Efficient crisis management was stunted by the long-running belief of the ruling coalition that the problem only concerns peripheral economies, especially Greece, and not the "core" Member States.

Germany's credibility as a promoter of conservative fiscal policy was undermined by the recent fight against the economic crisis by increasing public debt. The persuasive power of the German model was also reduced by the exceptionally favourable conditions for implementing budgetary policy.

Security crisis

The third government led by Angela Merkel was inaugurated on the 17th of December 2013, straddled with debts of unresolved problems of the euro area and, at the same time, with the prospect of problems in the EU's eastern neighbourhood. The protests, which sparked in Maidan Nezalezhnosti in Kiev on the 21st of November after the withdrawal of the Ukrainian authorities from signing an association agreement with the EU, which was supposed to take place at the Eastern Partnership Summit in Vilnius on the 28th and 29th of November 2013, were already taking place at that time. The subsequent annexation of the Crimea and the conflict in Eastern Ukraine, followed by the destabilisation of the Middle East and the terrorist threat in Europe have extended the government's crisis agenda to include external and internal security.

Contrary to the earlier economic turmoil, the German government's response to the worsening European security was not purely reactive in nature, but also served as implementation of the adopted principles of the government's programme. The demand for greater involvement of Germany in the international arena, including crisis management, was expressed by President Joachim Gauck at the opening of the 50th Munich Security Conference, and supported by similar statements by foreign and defence ministers.[11] According to Frank-Walter Steinmeier, "Germany must be ready to engage at an earlier stage and in a more decisive manner."[12] This declared level of ambition (referred to as the Munich Consensus[13]) was quickly – perhaps even too quickly, taking the German perspective into consideration – put into test as a result of Russian Federation's aggression against Ukraine and the subsequent expansion of the so-called Islamic State (IS). What is more, the deteriorating security environment in the neighbouring countries soon began to have an impact on internal security, first due to the threat of international terrorism in Germany and then through the increasing number of refugees entering the European Union.

Since the beginning of the 18th term of office of the Bundestag, the new component of general uncertainty was reflected in the Chancellery budget debates. The first of these debates took place on the 9th of April 2014, after President Viktor Yanukovych was ousted and after Crimea was annexed by Russian Federation. During the debate, the topic of response to the Russian-Ukrainian conflict was regularly brought up. Afterwards, the issue of involvement in the Southern Neighbourhood was addressed and, following the attacks in Paris in November 2015, more attention was paid to internal security issues. At the same time, the issue of refugees and prevention of the causes of mass migration have become increasingly important (A. Merkel, BT 2015–120, p. 11613; V. Kauder (CDU/CSU), BT 2015–120, p. 11622). The final budget debate during this term of office took place on the 23td of November 2016, in the wake of Donald Trump's victory in the US presidential elections, which was the second shock for the German political class after the bad outcome of the Brexit referendum in the United Kingdom on the 23rd of June 2016.

In 2014 Angela Merkel concluded her speech at the budget debate with: "After several years of serious economic crises, which had serious social consequences, this year we are confronted in particular with security and humanitarian policy

---

11 The speeches are available on the Conference website: https://www.securityconference.de/aktivitaeten/munich-security-conference/munich-security-conference/msc-2014/reden/.

12 Rede von Außenminister Frank-Walter Steinmeier anlässlich der 50. Münchner Sicherheitskonferenz, 01.02.2014, https://www.auswaertiges-amt.de/de/newsroom/140201-bm-muesiko/259554.

13 See: B. Giegerich, M. Terhalle (2017): The Munich Consensus and the Purpose of German Power, in: James Bindenagel/Matthias Herdegen/Karl Kaiser (eds.), *International Security in the 21st Century: Germany's International Responsibility*, Göttingen, p. 241 et seq.

crises that pose a threat and result in deaths, while bringing countries to the brink of collapse. Once again, we feel the need for policy, for taking responsibility for our values and interests, for shaping a humanitarian world order, for promoting peace and freedom. The federal government is aware of this responsibility towards the people of our country and towards our partners in Europe" (BT 2014–69, p. 6507).

During the second reading of the 2017 draft budget, Chancellor Angela Merkel argued: "We are living in a time of rapid global change. We have the possibility of gradually shaping these changes in a human way (*schrittweise menschlich zu gestalten*). This, in turn, requires openness. I believe that openness will bring us more security than isolationism ever would – more security in terms of economic situation, more security in terms of social situation and more security in terms of peace and freedom" (BT 2016–202, p. 20172). Even during the previous term of office, the Chancellor argued that given the circumstances of globalisation, no state is able to maintain its own prosperity and ensure its own security alone (BT 2010–15, p. 1251).

Apart from the condition of the world economy, the context of the "geopolitical circumstances" was also used to justify the government's budgetary policy (A. Merkel, BT 2014–69, p. 6504; V. Kauder (CDU/CSU), BT 2014–50, p. 4573; G. Hasselfeldt (CDU/CSU), BT 2014–69, p. 6525).

The German response to the European security crisis encompassed increased diplomatic activity, taking over the leadership role in shaping the EU's policy regarding the Russian-Ukrainian conflict and greater involvement of crisis management in the Southern Neighbourhood.

Angela Merkel based the German authorities' approach to the Russian-Ukrainian conflict on four principles – dismissing a military solution, coordination within the EU and with the United States, no acceptance for violation of territorial integrity and destabilisation of Ukraine, expressed in economic sanctions, as well as efforts to resolve the conflict by way of diplomacy (BT 2014–50, p. 4558). At the same time, Germany also responded to the crisis by supporting Ukraine politically and economically, both within the EU and through the International Monetary Fund. The Chancellor deemed Russia's actions as undermining the European peace and violating international law and declared: "Our objective is a sovereign and territorially integral Ukraine, which can decide its own future – no more and no less" (BT 2014–69, p. 6503).

The activity of Germany focused on diplomacy and negotiations carried out in the minilateral Normandy Format. In the multilateral dimension, the role of the OSCE was highlighted, particularly in the context of the German Presidency in 2016 (A. Merkel, BT 2014–50, p. 4558, BT 2015–120, p. 11611).

The EU economic sanctions, which were regularly brought up by the ruling coalition and the Greens in the budget debates were presented as a necessary element of the response to the violation of international law and the destabilisation of Eastern Ukraine. The pro-Russian Left criticised these sanctions as a manifestation of an erroneous political course resulting in a "senseless economic war," harmful to German society and economy, especially in the eastern states of the federation. (G. Gysi, BT 2014–42, p. 3688, BT 2014–50, p 4558, BT 2015–120, p. 11606; S. Wagenknecht, BT 2014–69, p. 6501).

On the other hand, the Greens saw inconsistencies in the crisis response, by allowing deepening of Russian-German cooperation in the field of energy, which is why they highlighted the risk of growing dependence on Russia (K. Göring-Eckardt (Bündnis 90/Die Grünen), BT 2014–50, p. 4560). In the subsequent debate, the Chancellor informed about the efforts to ensure the security of gas supplies, undertaken as part of all negotiations (BT 2014–69, p. 6503).

Tensions within the ruling coalition, which emerged between the supporters of a decisive course or normalisation of relations with Russia, could be noted in the second reading of the 2015 draft budget, particularly in the reaction of SPD politicians to the accusation that Foreign Minister Frank-Walter Steinmeier conducted a "parallel foreign policy," which was perceived as too pro-Russian, in relation to the Chancellery agenda, expressed not long before by the CSU chairman Horst Seehofer in *Der SPIEGEL* weekly (in particular by R. Mützenich, BT 2014–69, p. 6523). In general, during budget debates the coalition presented a difficult compromise, while the clash of positions was clearly visible in the case of the normative argumentation of the Greens and the pro-Russian narrative of Die Linke.

The differences between the ruling coalition and the opposition emerged in the case of the involvement in crisis management in the Southern Neighbourhood.[14] The Greens criticised the focus on the military action, neglecting prevention and the limited participation of German police force in UN missions (A. Hofreiter (Bündnis 90/Die Grünen), BT 2014–42, p. 3700–3701).

Germany's ambitions for greater involvement were confirmed by the decision to support the armed forces of the Kurdish regional authorities with the consent of the central government in Baghdad and in close cooperation with international partners. These reasons were strongly highlighted in particular (A. Merkel

---

14 See more in: A. Rinke (2017): Deutschlands neue Nachbarn. Die Bundesregierung weitet ihren Blick auf den Krisenbogen um die EU, *Internationale Politik* 4, Juli-August 2017, pp. 42–48.

BT 2014–50, p. 4559). By providing training and weapons to the Peshmerga, Germany joined the open armed conflict. In relation to the fight against the IS terrorist organisation, the German authorities believed that a military response is necessary, while declaring their support for political solutions that guarantee stabilisation of the region. The so-called IS was explicitly recognised as a threat to Germany's security (A. Merkel, BT 2014–69, p. 6504). France's call for assistance under the Article 42(7) of the EU Treaty was followed by a decision to increase German involvement in Mali and to extend the military presence in Afghanistan.

Both the support for Kurdish units and the Bundeswehr's involvement against the IS after the Paris bombings were criticised by Die Linke, which – regardless of their generally negative stance towards military involvement – criticised the coalition framework and the lack of a UN mandate. As an alternative, it postulated an embargo on the export of arms to the areas embroiled in crisis, as well as a restriction on the possibility of financing terrorist organisations (G. Gysi, BT 2014–50, p. 4547, BT 2014–69, p. 11604; D. Bartsch, BT 2015–139, p. 13606).

In the wake of the migration crisis, diplomatic and military engagement in the Southern Neighbourhood has already been presented since 2015 as an element of a broader response and a way to address the root causes of migration, alongside cooperation aimed at development. In retrospect, Angela Merkel admitted: "… we did not understand it clearly enough at the time that what was happening in Aleppo and Mosul could be relevant to Essen or Stuttgart. We have to deal with that. This will bring a change in our policy in favour of foreign policy and cooperation based on development, because we will have to keep asking the questions about the significance of individual actions for us here" (BT 2015–139, p. 13611).

Interestingly enough, the general debates did not see much controversy over the budget of the Ministry of Defence. At the same time, the effects of underinvestment in the Bundeswehr, which has been affected by budget cuts for many years, were pointed out not only by experts, but also increasingly in the media.

The NATO strategic adaptation was mentioned in Angela Merkel's speech at the first reading of the 2015 draft budget on the 10th of September 2014, after the NATO summit in Wales at the beginning of the month. Germany's contribution to increasing the ability to defend the Alliance, in particular by strengthening the Multinational Corps Northeast in Szczecin, was justified by its solidarity within the alliance – the Baltics and Eastern European partners. At the same time, the Chancellor highlighted the importance of maintaining restrictions on NATO military presence on the eastern flank derived from the NATO-Russia Founding Act (BT 2014--50, p. 4559). Similarly, Thomas Oppermann (SPD) argued against permanent stationing of NATO forces in Eastern Europe and said that the sanctions were a sufficient response to Vladimir Putin's violation of the spirit of this agreement (BT 2014–50, p. 4565). Referring to President Bronisław Komorowski's speech in the Bundestag on the same day, he argued: "For decades, others took the responsibility for us – Germans, for our security. Now it should be clear, that we should also take responsibility for others" (BT 2014–50, p. 4565).

The opposition criticised the decisions made at the Newport Summit by the NATO, in particular the leader of Die Linke, Gregor Gysi, who estimated the cost of achieving the benchmark target of 2 % of GDP earmarked on defence spending to be 24 billion euro, and thus was opposed to further arming of Germany, the NATO and the USA (BT 2014–50, p. 4549). K. Göring-Eckardt, co-head of the Greens, also opposed the increase of military spending (BT 2014–50, p. 4560).

The unpopular issue of the defence budget was not raised again until the last budget debate of the 18th term of office. Referring to the example of smaller European countries that have increased their spending in line with their commitments, the Chancellor admitted that Germany was still far from meeting the expectations of the allies. She spoke in favour of maintaining the direction in line with the promise made jointly by the Christian Democrats and Social Democrats within NATO (BT 2016–202, p. 20167).

During the same budget debate, the Chancellor also spoke in favour of strengthening cooperation in defence policy in the EU in the form of permanent structural cooperation, arguing that the solution promoted by Defence Minister Ursula von der Leyen will not harm cooperation within NATO (BT 2016–202, p. 20167).

The issue of internal security was raised for the first time in connection with the issue of fighters of the IS from the EU (more than 500 people), some of whom were returning home at the time. Volker Kauder, head of the Christian Democratic parliamentary group, stressed the scale of the organisational effort for the observation of potentially dangerous persons (*Gefährder*) and advocated for the reduction of recruitment opportunities (BT 2014–69, p. 6520). In the wake of the Paris attacks in November 2015, the response to the threat of Islamic terrorism in the country has already been formulated, in line with public expectations. It encompassed a declaration of political support for the security authorities, as well as reinforcement of their human and technical resources, which was promptly reflected in the budget. The Federal Police have gained 1,000 new posts, with plans to expand that number to 3,000 by 2018, and the government also announced that new units, trained and properly equipped to respond to terrorist threats, would be embedded in its structures, to complement the capabilities of national police and special forces. Further reinforcement of human and technical resources of intelligence services has also been ensured

(BT 2015–139, p. 13611). Due to the terrorist threat, some postulated facilitating the exchange of information between authorities and services (T. Oppermann (SPD), BT 2016–186, p. 18425). Germany also modified its stance on uniform border control and uniform registers of entry and exit into the Schengen area (A. Merkel, BT 2016–202, p. 20167). In addition to new posts in the Federal Police and nearly 1,000 additional posts in the federal security services, which were supposed to materialise by 2018, it was expected that modern technology and equipment would be financed and a new cyber-security strategy would be adopted by 2020. (A. Merkel, BT 2016–186, p. 18414).

Characteristics of the response to the crisis

The increased diplomatic activity and involvement in crisis management were first and foremost an attempt to transpose Berlin's strengthened position as a result of the crisis in the euro area, to the level of international policy. As the European security deteriorated, the motivational significance of the direct implications for Germany kept growing, with preference for actions undertaken within mini- and multilateral frameworks.

The German response to the security crisis was limited mostly by its internal circumstances, in a way similar to the measures taken to deal with the crisis in the euro area. Despite the "Munich consensus," the international use of the full spectrum of instruments was hampered by sceptical public opinion.[15] Internal dispute in the coalition over fulfilment of the commitment to increase the defence budget to 2 % of the country's GDP undermined Germany's credibility within NATO and translated into the real capabilities of the German armed forces.[16] On the other hand, Germany's involvement in strengthening the NATO eastern flank confirmed the solidarity with its allies.

The political dispute over the correct approach to Russia in response to the violation of international law and disturbing the order of European security was impacted not only by differences in the assessment of interests, but also by tensions between the traditional role of mediator and the new leading position

15 Cf. Pew Research Center, NATO Public Opinion: Wary of Russia, Leery of Action on Ukraine, 10 June 2015, http://www.pewresearch.org/wp-content/uploads/sites/2/2015/06/Pew-Research-Center-Russia-Ukraine-Report-FINAL-June-10-2015.pdf.

16 Cf. H. Maull (2015): Deutsche Außenpolitik – Verantwortung und Macht, *Zeitschrift für Außen- und Sicherheitspolitik*, Vol. 8, p. 213–237, quoted p. 227.

in formulating EU's response to the crisis in terms of external relations, with limited willingness and readiness to accept the costs associated with this role.

The communication policy on security spending differs in relation to the internal and external dimensions. The detailed presentations of data on police and security reinforcements, tailored to the electorate's preferences, clearly contrasted with the rather reserved approach regarding the size of the defence budget and the spending on the equipment of the armed forces.

Migration crisis

In the case of the German response to the migration crisis, the main starting point is 4–5 September 2015 – accepting the refugees from Hungary and derogation from the rules set forth in the Dublin Regulation.[17] The earlier phase of the crisis was reflected in the budget debates in 2014, during which the representatives noted a growing migration problems worldwide and in Germany itself in connection with the war in Syria (T. Oppermann (SPD), BT 2014–42, p. 3703). The Greens criticised the insufficient activity of the government in the face of this challenge (K. Göring-Eckardt (Bündnis 90/Die Grünen), BT 2014–50, p. 4564). The Chancellor addressed the migration and asylum policy in the context of the upcoming European Council agenda (A. Merkel, BT 2014–42, p. 3696).

First reading of the 2016 draft budget on the 9th of September 2015 was dominated by the subject of migration and used by the Chancellor to present a seven-point crisis response agenda (BT 2015–120, p. 11612 et seq.). Angela Merkel gained political support for her actions and at the same time the opposition demanded a greater involvement in the refugee crisis.

The response to the crisis was again based on the rejection of isolation and the declared readiness to get involved – based on the experience of social market economy – in shaping globalisation within the framework of international cooperation (A. Merkel, BT 2015–139, p. 13616, BT 2016–186, p. 18414, BT 2016–202, p. 20166). Germany's approach to refugee issues was also justified by a commitment based on a historical argument (A. Merkel, BT 2014–50, p. 4555; K. Göring-Eckardt (Bündnis 90/Die Grünen), BT 2016–186, p. 18422). The

17 Detailed reconstruction of the events of 4–5 September: Georg Blume, Marc Brost, Tina Hildebrandt, Alexej Hock, Sybille Klormann, Angela Köckritz, Matthias Krupa, Mariam Lau, Gero von Randow, Merlind Theile, Michael Thumann, Heinrich Wefing, Grenzöffnung für Flüchtlinge: Was geschah wirklich?, *DIE ZEIT*, no. 35/2016, 18. August 2016; R. Alexander (2017): *Die Getriebenen – Merkel und die Flüchtlingspolitik: Report aus dem Innern der Macht*, Siedler Verlag.

issue of responding to the growing number of refugees was defined as not only a matter of national or European importance, but also a global one (A. Merkel, BT 2015–139, p. 13611).

German politicians realistically assessed the long-term perspective of dealing with the migration crisis and the scale of the challenge (A. Merkel, BT 2015–120, p. 11613; V. Kauder (CDU/CSU), BT 2015–120, p. 11624; K. Göring-Eckardt (Bündnis 90/Die Grünen) BT 2015–120, p. 11618). Like in the case of the previous crises, they pointed to the strength of Germany as the main proof of its ability to successfully face the challenge (A. Merkel, BT 2015–120, p. 11613; V. Kauder (CDU/CSU), BT 2015–120, p. 11624; K. Göring-Eckardt (Bündnis 90/Die Grünen), BT 2015–120, p. 11614; T. Oppermann (SPD), BT 2015–120, p. 11619; R. Kruse (SPD), BT 2015–139, p. 13632).

A new element in the migration crisis was the emphasis on the strength of the state resulting from the widespread social involvement: "In the Greek crisis, we learned about the significance of a functioning statehood (*Staatswesen*). In the case of the refugee crisis, we can now clearly see how invaluable an empathic, active and well-organised civil society really is" (T. Oppermann (SPD), BT 2015–120, p. 11619; see also A. Merkel, BT 2015–139, p. 13611; K. Göring-Eckardt (Bündnis 90/Die Grünen), BT 2015–120, p. 11614 and others).

The difficulties resulting from the federal state structure were also a new systemic factor in terms of crisis management. The actual costs of implementing the federally regulated asylum law were borne by the Länder and by municipalities, which also affected the diversity of reception and support standards. Recognising these circumstances, in June 2015, the migration challenge was defined as a national task to be carried out in a "community of responsibility."[18]

The problem of the burden on the Länder and municipalities was first highlighted by opposition during a general debate (K. Göring-Eckardt (Bündnis 90/Die Grünen), 2014–29, p. 2332, BT 2014–50, p. 4564; T. Oppermann (SPD), BT 2014–69, p. 6517). The Chancellor addressed the logistical challenge in the second half of 2014. (BT 2014–50, p. 4555, BT 2014–69, p. 13615) and announced the mobilisation of material resources. In particular, the fact that the Federation took responsibility for the crisis was manifested by a law on benefits for asylum seekers (A. Merkel, BT 2015–139, p. 13614). Regarding the support for municipalities, the emphasis was first placed on the logistical issues related

18 Pressekonferenz der Bundeskanzlerin und der Regierungschefinnen und Regierungschefs der Bundesländer, 18. Juni 2015, https://www.bundesregierung.de/breg-de/aktuelles/pressekonferenz-der-bundeskanzlerin-und-der-regierungschefinnen-und-regierungschefs-der-bundeslaender-846066.

to accommodation, followed by integration. Dialogue with the Länder took the form of special conferences with the prime ministers of the federal states. An important motive for supporting municipalities was the fear of the impact on social order, should their resources be overstretched (T. Oppermann (SPD), BT 2015–120, p. 11619).

The systemic conditions of the federal state were used by the Greens, who were in favour of the most liberal approach to mass migration. They criticised expanding the list of countries considered to be safe in terms of the laws on granting asylum (Western Balkans and Northern Africa), as well as the limitation of family reunification in case of subsidiary protection and the subsequent suspension of this possibility. They have also criticised benefits in kind. Using the balance of power in the Bundesrat, they blocked government initiatives aimed at making the asylum law stricter, which was repeatedly raised by representatives of the coalition during general debates.

The involvement of the federation was also necessary for the return procedure in case of migrants without right of residence and without documents (A. Merkel, BT 2015–139, p. 13614).

With regard to the functioning of the state apparatus, during the budget debate the Greens pointed out various disfunctions in the functioning of the government centre caused by competition between the coordinator for refugees in the Chancellery and the Minister of Interior (A. Hofreiter (Bündnis 90/Die Grünen), BT 2015–139, p. 13619).

The unprecedented scale of the logistical, integration and political challenge has been reflected in the management of budgetary resources (A. Merkel, BT 2015–139, p. 13614, p. 13633). At the same time, Germany's ability to mobilise financial resources in the face of unforeseen challenges was used to justify the fiscal consolidation course (A. Merkel, BT 2015–120, p. 11609, BT 2015–139, p. 13615).

The increased budget outlays also reflected the appreciation of the importance of integration policies, also expressed in the adoption of the federal Integration Act (A. Merkel, BT 2015–120, p. 11612, BT 2015–139, p. 13614, BT 2016–186, p. 18414; K. Göring-Eckardt (Bündnis 90/Die Grünen), BT 2015–120, p. 11616, BT 2016–186, p. 18419; B. Hagedorn (SPD), BT 2016–186, p. 18438). Counteracting the emergence of parallel communities was also taken into consideration in terms of internal security (T. Oppermann (SPD), BT 2015–139, p. 13622). However, the course of the budget debates indicates a limited scope of discussions on security in the context of the migration crisis. The events in Cologne were only signalled once ("*es gab Köln*" – K. Göring-Eckardt (Bündnis 90/Die Grünen), BT 2016–186, p. 18419), the attacks in Ansbach and Würzburg were also pointed out (A. Merkel, BT 2016–186, p. 18414). There was a clear fear of arousing resentment towards refugees, and the weakening sense of security was counteracted by specific measures aimed at strengthening the police and other security structures (A. Merkel, BT 2016–186, p. 18414, BT 2016–202, p. 20171; T. Oppermann (SPD), BT 2015–139, p. 13622).

While considering the final shape of the budget, the politicians also pointed out the risk of strengthening the extreme right wing in the case of political polarisation regarding the issue of migration, as well as the need to ensure social acceptance for refugees (V. Kauder (CDU/CSU), BT 2014–42, p. 3706; T Oppermann (SPD), BT 2014–42, p. 3703, BT 2014–50, p. 4569, BT 2014–69, p. 6517; G. Hasselfeldt (CDU/CSU), BT 2015–120, p. 11629; J. Kahrs (SPD), BT 2015–139, p. 13630). It was considered important to counteract the impression that state resources were earmarked for satisfying the needs of migrants, while neglecting the needs of citizens (G. Gysi (Linke) BT 2015–120, p. 11605; B. Hagedorn (SPD), BT 2016–186, p. 18438; K. Göring-Eckardt (Bündnis 90/ Die Grünen), BT 2015–120, p. 11614; T. Oppermann (SPD), BT 2015–139, p. 13624). This led to the recommendations to adjust the budget in this respect while maintaining its balanced structure (J. Kahrs (SPD), BT 2015–139, p. 13628).

In addition to providing funds for crisis management, the main component of Germany's activities was reduction of the number of asylum seekers in Germany, which was justified by the need to provide assistance to people who were genuinely in need (mainly Syrians) and their efficient integration (T. Oppermann (SPD), BT 2014–42, p. 37043; G. Hasselfeldt (CDU/CSU), BT 2016–202, p. 20185). Some also recommended taking into account the views of the society regarding the limit on accepting and integration capacity (G. Hasselfeldt (CDU/ CSU), BT 2015–139, p. 13632).

At the national level, this objective was achieved by modifying the existing regulations in the form of the so-called two asylum packages. The ruling coalition tried to expand the list of countries treated as safe countries of origin within the meaning of asylum regulations, first regarding the Western Balkans, followed by Northern Africa. Some pointed out the need to differentiate between economic migrants and refugees (T. Oppermann (SPD), BT 2016–202, p. 20177; G. Hasselfeldt (CDU/CSU), BT 2015–139, p. 13631). Christian Democrats also highlighted the need to reduce or eliminate inappropriate systemic incentives for migrants (such as social security benefits paid out in cash). The general debates also covered the issue of introducing the so-called *Obergrenze*, i.e. the upper limit for the number of accepted refugees (criticised by T. Oppermann (SPD), BT 2015–139, p. 13623) and transit zones.

Counteracting the widespread perception that the government had lost control, debates focused on the problem of law enforcement with regard to the deportation (A. Merkel, BT 2015–120, p. 11612). The Chancellor explicitly referred to the issue of social perception of persons without the right to stay remaining in the country and she stressed the need to ensure "order and management" in Germany, particularly in the situation where law is broken at the external border of the EU (BT 2015–139, p. 13614, BT 2016–186, p. 18414). Ensuring the functioning of the rule of law regarding asylum was referred to as "a legitimate expectation of citizens" (BT 2016–202, p. 20171, cf. J. Kahrs (SPD), BT, p. 13629). CSU called for consistent registration and documentation of the refugees (G. Hasselfeldt (CDU/CSU), BT 2015–139, p. 13631).

As announced in the coalition agreement, the Federal Office for Migration and Refugees was expanded by 300 employees in 2014 in order to improve the asylum process efficiency. As the crisis unfolded, the pressure was mounting to speed up the process, which resulted in particular in the decision to entrust the management of the Office to the head of the Federal Labour Agency, also motivated by the desire to facilitate integration into the labour market.

In the eyes of politicians, "flexibility" has become an important attribute of the state in the context of the migration crisis. The unique nature of the situation was to require a rethinking of the existing regulations, and even a temporary suspension of some of them (A. Merkel, BT 2015–120, p. 11612), or diminishing some administrative standards (V. Kauder (CDU/CSU), BT 2015–120, p. 11622).

The number of refugees was also to be lowered thanks to support provided directly in conflict areas, reflected in an increase of resources available to the Ministry of Foreign Affairs and Ministry for Economic Cooperation and Development earmarked to crisis prevention and humanitarian aid (A. Merkel, BT 2014–42, p. 3696, BT 2016–186, p. 18415, BT 2016–202, p. 20171; T. Oppermann (SPD), BT 2014–69 p 6517, BT 2015–120, p. 11619; G. Hasselfeldt (CDU/CSU) BT 2016–202, p. 20184). Aid to the residents of refugee camps has been identified as the potentially fastest-acting measure (G. Hasselfeldt (CDU/CSU), BT 2015–139, p. 13632). The opposition considered the budget increase in this respect to be insufficient – the value of development aid still did not meet the benchmark of 0.7 % of Germany's GDP (A. Hofreiter (Bündnis 90/Die Grünen), BT 2014–42, p. 3701; D. Bartsch (Linke), BT 2015–139, p. 13608). Some also pointed out the government's support for political resolutions to conflicts in the Middle East (A. Merkel, BT 2014–42, p. 3696; T. Oppermann (SPD), BT 2015–139, p. 13622). Another component of activities aimed at addressing the root cause of migration was also German involvement in the fight against the IS in Syria and Iraq, as well as the mission to Afghanistan (A. Merkel, BT 2014–69, p. 6517).

In response to the migration challenge, the significance of Africa in German policy has increased.[19] Germany promoted the deepening of cooperation for the improvement of living conditions and the opening of legal migration channels within the European Union, in a minilateral and multilateral formula, which included the G20 Presidency (A. Merkel, BT 2015–120, p. 11612, BT 2015–139, p. 13615, BT 2016–202, p. 20171, BT 2016–186, p. 18415).

The reduction of the number of migrants arriving in Germany was also to be achieved by regaining control of the EU's external borders (G. Hasselfeldt (CDU/CSU), BT 2015–139, p. 13632; J. Kahrs (SPD), BT 2015–139, p. 13629; B. Hagedorn (SPD), BT 2016–202, p. 20187). Apart from ensuring security and stabilising the situation at hand, the intention was to stop the process of renationalisation of border control within the Schengen area (V. Kauder (CDU/CSU), BT 2015–139, p. 13626; T. Oppermann (SPD), BT 2015–139, p. 13622), all while Germany also made use of the possibility to reinstate border control. Restoration of regulated border relations was also connected with reinforcing the Frontex (A. Merkel, BT 2016–186, p. 18414).

Turkey played a key role in the German crisis strategy (A. Merkel, BT 2015–120, p. 11612; BT 2015–139, p. 13612). The controversial concept of delegating the protection of the EU's external border to the Turkish authorities was also reflected in the disputes taking place as part of the general debate. Despite the awareness of financial and political costs, the supporters of this option were convinced of the validity of, or even a lack of any alternative for an agreement with Ankara (A. Merkel, BT 2015–139, p. 13612, BT 2016–186, p. 18415;J. Kahrs (SPD), BT 2015–139, p. 13630; T. Oppermann (SPD), BT 2015–139, p. 13622, BT 2016–186, p. 18423). This stance was linked to a conviction that Greece was unable to ensure border control. It was expected that the number of migrants would be reduced, smuggling would be curbed and the number of victims among migrants trying to cross the EU border would go down. The agreement with Turkey was treated as a model for regulating cooperation with EU's neighbours in the area of maritime border control (A. Merkel, BT 2016–186, p. 18414). Germany also got involved in the Operation EUNAVFOR MED Sophia in the

19 See more in: A. Rinke (2016): Migration, Sicherheit, Wirtschaft. Afrika wird zu einer Priorität der deutschen und europäischen Politik, *Internationale Politik*, 6, November/Dezember 2016, p. 8–16.

Mediterranean Sea and NATO operations in the Aegean Sea.[20] During the budget debate, the representative of CSU (G. Hasselfeldt (CDU/CSU), BT 2016–202, p. 20186) appreciated the positive impact of closing the Balkan route.

The central component of the German approach to the migration crisis constituted the striving for "European solution" (A. Merkel, BT 2015–120, p. 11613, BT 2015–139, p. 13613, BT 2016–202, p. 20170), including a "fair" mechanism for relocating asylum seekers to other Member States (T. Oppermann (SPD), BT 2015–139, p. 13622, BT 2014–50, p. 4569; G. Hasselfeldt (CDU/CSU), BT 2015–120, p. 11629; A. Özoğuz (SPD), BT 2014–50, p. 4575). The mandatory nature of this distribution mechanism was supposed to ensure the participation of all Member States in counteracting the causes for the migration crisis and international conflicts (A. Merkel, BT 2015–120, p. 11613), as well as to ensure co-operative attitude of countries managing the EU's external borders (A. Merkel, BT 2015–139, p. 13613).

The initial normative justification for the refugee quotas (A. Merkel, BT 2015–120, p. 11613; G. Hasselfeldt (CDU/CSU), BT 2015–120, p. 11629; T. Oppermann (SPD), BT 2015–120, p. 11619; D. Bartsch (Linke), BT 2015–139, p. 13608) has been reinforced over time with the argument of maintaining open borders in the EU being dependent on obligatory quotas (T. Oppermann (SPD), BT 2015–120, p. 11619). Angela Merkel highlighted the analogous nature of structural deficits in the case of single currency and in the second pillar of European integration. When the Schengen area was initially established, political agreement regarding solidarity, competence and relocation in the event of increased pressure on the external borders was not reached, as in the case of the Economic and Monetary Union, either. The system, therefore, needs to be complemented, like the euro: "Therefore, the relocation of refugees based on solidarity – according to economic strength and circumstances, with the required readiness for a permanent distribution mechanism is noting small. It is a matter of being able to maintain the Schengen area in the long term" (BT 2015–139, p. 13613).

The development of a "European solution" was linked to the long-term survival of the EU (V. Kauder (CDU/CSU), BT 2015–139, p. 13627), while some demanded structural funds cuts for Eastern and Southern European countries contesting the centralised model of asylum policy (V. Kauder (CDU/CSU) BT 2015–139, p. 13627; G. Gysi (Linke), BT 2015–120, p. 11605).

---

20 For more information about the role of Germany in launching the operation, see: R. Alexander, *op. cit.* p. 239 et seq.

Characteristics of the response to the crisis

In the case of the German response to the migration crisis, the key priority was to reduce the number of asylum seekers by making it more difficult to get to Germany, as well as by increasing the efficiency of procedures and tightening asylum regulations. In the acute phase of the migration crisis in autumn of 2015, logistical challenges related to ensuring the necessary supplies for the immigrants played a central role.

The mobilisation of the financial resources at the disposal of the state was presented as an important element of the crisis response mechanism. State expenditure was both internal – with the objective of relieving the burden on municipalities and the Länder –like in the case of the financial and economic crisis, as well as external, aimed at counteracting the root causes of migration, in a way similar to controlling the turmoil concerning the single currency. The government's active communication policy with regard to budget outlays on migration challenges differed – *toutes proportions gardées* – from the policy adopted in the euro area crisis management, where the politicians avoided disclosing the scale of Germany's financial liabilities.

The direct impact of the migration crisis on Germany was decisive due to the mounting pressure, urging the government to act quickly, which was reflected in the action at the EU level. Unlike the case of the euro area crisis, this time Germany was in favour of rapid action, even in the event of a lack of consensus among Member States.

Another difference compared to the management of the euro area crisis, is the fact that the constitutional tension between the executive and the legislation regarding parliamentary budget powers was replaced by the problems caused by the distribution of competences and burdens in the federal system. The balance of power allowed the opposition to use Bundesrat as an institutional barrier to the implementation of the government's plans. The regional differences in the efficiency of administrative structures also became apparent.

In the case of a migration crisis, difficulties in reaching a consensus regarding the response to the crisis within the framework of the coalition of Christian Democrats and Liberals were superseded by disfunctions in the relations between the Chancellery (coordinator for refugees) and the Ministry of the Interior, which were both in the hands of CDU. The modifications in the functioning of the government as part of the crisis management contributed to marginalisation of the issues of security in the context of mass migration.

The migration crisis also caused the emergence of doubts as to the state's ability to perform its key tasks. As a consequence, some of the activities within the scope of crisis management were aimed at counteracting the perception of state structure inefficiencies.

Conclusions

The issue of crises played an important role in budget debates – it was used both in order to justify the actions taken by the government, as well as to highlight the positive outcomes (in the case of the ruling coalition), as well as criticising neglect and inaction (in the case of opposition). From 2015 onwards, the migration challenges were becoming more and more prevalent in these debates.

It is worth noting that German politicians underlined the overarching value of openness of the economy and society both in the case of the financial crisis, as well as the migration one, which also required awareness of the risk of negative impact of the external turmoil. The conviction about the benefits of globalisation was reflected both in the careful linking of crisis phenomena with its progress, as well as in the preference for multilateralism as an opportunity to exert successful impact on international politics.

The postulate of the shaping role of the policy in the case of the financial crisis was derived from the concept of social market economy, which, in the one hand, was appreciated for effective protection against crisis phenomena, and on the other hand for creating a framework conducive to efficient adaptation to changing conditions and circumstances resulting from the crisis. However, it should be noted that the conviction regarding the stability of the German economy and efficient functioning of the state was detrimental to proper identification of the negative potential of crisis phenomena at an early stage, particularly in terms of economy, and contributed to the delay in responding to challenges at the national level and within the EU.

Undoubtedly, the decisive stimulus to adopt a proactive approach to crisis phenomena was their direct impact on Germany. The severe impact of the economic downturn following the global financial crisis in the first place, followed a couple of years later by the accumulation of logistical, social, integration and internal security problems within Germany as a result of mass migration, resulted in an ad hoc mobilisation of state resources to alleviate the symptoms of the crisis. This approach differs from the reaction to the euro area turmoil, which was not felt directly by German society for a long time. In the case of the euro area crisis, the German stance was based on assurance, resisting the pressure to act quickly.

The relatively quick and efficient management of the impact of the financial crisis and its consequences for the real economy strengthened Germany's positive evaluation of its own solutions, which started to be promoted as model at the

European level, including the public debt brake – *Schuldenbremse*. The growing role of Germany in the formulation of the response to the EU crisis was accompanied by the narrative placing the country as the "growth locomotive" and an "anchor of stability" for the single currency. At the same time, the communication strategy, which highlighted the better condition of Germany could have contributed to the deterioration of solidarity within the euro area.

Other noteworthy aspects include recognising the financial crisis as an emergency situation in order to justify the exceptional measures taken by a state, including dropping the strategic objective of balancing the budget. Within the deep framework of euro area integration, this argument was already of limited use. The emphasis on legitimacy requirements narrowed down Germany's ability and readiness to use the instruments proposed in the debate on various ways of overcoming the crisis. This situation was reversed during the migration crisis, when the extensive solutions forced by Germany met with opposition referring to the powers of Member States.

List of budget debates used in the above analysis

1. Erste Beratung des von der Bundesregierung eingebrachten Entwurfs eines Gesetzes über die Feststellung des Bundeshaushaltsplans für das Haushaltsjahr 2009 (Haushaltsgesetz 2009); Unterrichtung durch die Bundesregierung: Finanzplan des Bundes 2008 bis 2012, Deutscher Bundestag, Stenografischer Bericht, 175. Sitzung, 17. September 2008, Plenarprotokoll 16/175 (cited as BT 2008–175);
2. Zweite Beratung des von der Bundesregierung eingebrachten Entwurfs eines Gesetzes über die Feststellung des Bundeshaushaltsplans für das Haushaltsjahr 2009 (Haushaltsgesetz 2009); Beschlussempfehlung des Haushaltsausschusses zu der Unterrichtung durch die Bundesregierung: Finanzplan des Bundes 2008 bis 2012, Deutscher Bundestag, Stenografischer Bericht, 189. Sitzung, 26. November 2008, Plenarprotokoll 16/189 (cited as BT 2008–189);
3. Erste Beratung des von der Bundesregierung eingebrachten Entwurfs eines Gesetzes über die Feststellung des Bundeshaushaltsplans für das Haushaltsjahr 2010 (Haushaltsgesetz 2010), Deutscher Bundestag, Stenografischer Bericht, 15. Sitzung, 20. Januar 2010, Plenarprotokoll 17/15 (cited as BT 2010–15);
4. Zweite Beratung des von der Bundesregierung eingebrachten Entwurfs eines Gesetzes über die Feststellung des Bundeshaushaltsplans für das Haushaltsjahr 2010 (Haushaltsgesetz 2010) Einzelplan 04 Bundeskanzleramt,

Deutscher Bundestag, Stenografischer Bericht, 30. Sitzung, 17. Marz 2010, Plenarprotokoll 17/30 (cited as BT 2010–30);

5. Erste Beratung des von der Bundesregierung eingebrachten Entwurfs eines Gesetzes über die Feststellung des Bundeshaushaltsplans für das Haushaltsjahr 2011 (Haushaltsgesetz 2011), Deutscher Bundestag, Stenografischer Bericht, 58. Sitzung, 15. September 2010, Plenarprotokoll 17/58 (cited as BT 2010–58);
6. Zweite Beratung des von der Bundesregierung eingebrachten Entwurfs eines Gesetzes über die Feststellung des Bundeshaushaltsplans für das Haushaltsjahr 2011 (Haushaltsgesetz 2011), Deutscher Bundestag, Stenografischer Bericht, 74. Sitzung, 24. November 2010, Plenarprotokoll 17/74 (cited as BT 2010–74);
7. Erste Beratung des von der Bundesregierung eingebrachten Entwurfs eines Gesetzes über die Feststellung des Bundeshaushaltsplans für das Haushaltsjahr 2012 (Haushaltsgesetz 2012); Unterrichtung durch die Bundesregierung: Finanzplan des Bundes 2011 bis 2015, Deutscher Bundestag, Stenografischer Bericht, 123. Sitzung, 7. September 2011, Plenarprotokoll 17/123 (cited as BT 2011–123);
8. Zweite Beratung des von der Bundesregierung eingebrachten Entwurfs eines Gesetzes über die Feststellung des Bundeshaushaltsplans für das Haushaltsjahr 2012 (Haushaltsgesetz 2012); Beratung der Beschlussempfehlung des Haushaltsausschusses zu der Unterrichtung durch die Bundesregierung: Finanzplan des Bundes 2011 bis 2015, Deutscher Bundestag, Stenografischer Bericht, 142. Sitzung, 23. November 2011, Plenarprotokoll 17/142 (cytowane jako BT 2011–142);
9. Erste Beratung des von der Bundesregierung eingebrachten Entwurfs eines Gesetzes über die Feststellung des Bundeshaushaltsplans für das Haushaltsjahr 2013 (Haushaltsgesetz 2013); Unterrichtung durch die Bundesregierung: Finanzplan des Bundes 2012 bis 2016, Deutscher Bundestag, Stenografischer Bericht, 191. Sitzung, 12 September 2012, Plenarprotokoll 17/191 (cited as BT 2012–191);
10. Zweite Beratung des von der Bundesregierung eingebrachten Entwurfs eines Gesetzes über die Feststellung des Bundeshaushaltsplans für das Haushaltsjahr 2013 (Haushaltsgesetz 2013); Beratung der Beschlussempfehlung des Haushaltsausschusses zu der Unterrichtung durch die Bundesregierung: Finanzplan des Bundes 2012 bis 2016, Deutscher Bundestag, Stenografischer Bericht, 207. Sitzung, 21. November 2012, Plenarprotokoll 17/207 (cited as BT 2012–207);
11. Erste Beratung des von der Bundesregierung eingebrachten Entwurfs eines Gesetzes über die Feststellung des Bundeshaushaltsplans für das Haushaltsjahr 2014 (Haushaltsgesetz 2014), Unterrichtung durch die

Bundesregierung: Finanzplan des Bundes 2013 bis 2017, Deutscher Bundestag, Stenografischer Bericht, 29. Sitzung, 9. April 2014, Plenarprotokoll 18/29 (cited as BT 2014–29);

12. Zweite Beratung des von der Bundesregierung eingebrachten Entwurfs eines Gesetzes über die Feststellung des Bundeshaushaltsplans für das Haushaltsjahr 2014 (Haushaltsgesetz 2014), Beratung der Beschlussempfehlung des Haushaltsausschusses zu der Unterrichtung durch die Bundesregierung: Finanzplan des Bundes 2013 bis 2017, Deutscher Bundestag, Stenografischer Bericht, 42. Sitzung, 25. Juni 2014, Plenarprotokoll 18/42 (cited as BT 2014–42);
13. Erste Beratung des von der Bundesregierung eingebrachten Entwurfs eines Gesetzes über die Feststellung des Bundeshaushaltsplans für das Haushaltsjahr 2015 (Haushaltsgesetz 2015), Unterrichtung durch die Bundesregierung: Finanzplan des Bundes 2014 bis 2018, Deutscher Bundestag, Stenografischer Bericht, 50. Sitzung, 10. September 2014, Plenarprotokoll 18/50 (cited as BT 2014–50);
14. Zweite Beratung des von der Bundesregierung eingebrachten Entwurfs eines Gesetzes über die Feststellung des Bundeshaushaltsplans für das Haushaltsjahr 2015 (Haushaltsgesetz 2015), Beratung der Beschlussempfehlung des Haushaltsausschusses zu der Unterrichtung durch die Bundesregierung: Finanzplan des Bundes 2014 bis 2018, Deutscher Bundestag, Stenografischer Bericht, 69. Sitzung, 26. November 2014, Plenarprotokoll 18/69 (cited as BT 2014–69);
15. Erste Beratung des von der Bundesregierung eingebrachten Entwurfs eines Gesetzes über die Feststellung des Bundeshaushaltsplans für das Haushaltsjahr 2016 (Haushaltsgesetz 2016), Unterrichtung durch die Bundesregierung: Finanzplan des Bundes 2015 bis 2019, Deutscher Bundestag, Stenografischer Bericht, 120. Sitzung, 9. September 2015, Plenarprotokoll 18/120 (cited as BT 2015–120);
16. Zweite Beratung des von der Bundesregierung eingebrachten Entwurfs eines Gesetzes über die Feststellung des Bundeshaushaltsplans für das Haushaltsjahr 2016 (Haushaltsgesetz 2016), Beratung der Beschlussempfehlung des Haushaltsausschusses zu der Unterrichtung durch die Bundesregierung: Finanzplan des Bundes 2015 bis 2019, Deutscher Bundestag, Stenografischer Bericht, 139. Sitzung, 25. November 2015, Plenarprotokoll 18/139 (cited as BT 2015–139);
17. Erste Beratung des von der Bundesregierung eingebrachten Entwurfs eines Gesetzes über die Feststellung des Bundeshaushaltsplans für das Haushaltsjahr 2017 (Haushaltsgesetz 2017), Unterrichtung durch die

Bundesregierung: Finanzplan des Bundes 2016 bis 2020, Deutscher Bundestag, Stenografischer Bericht, 186. Sitzung, 7. September 2016, Plenarprotokoll 18/186 (cited as BT 2016–186);

18. Zweite Beratung des von der Bundesregierung eingebrachten Entwurfs eines Gesetzes über die Feststellung des Bundeshaushaltsplans für das Haushaltsjahr 2017 (Haushaltsgesetz 2017), Beratung der Beschlussempfehlung des Haushaltsausschusses zu der Unterrichtung durch die Bundesregierung: Finanzplan des Bundes 2016 bis 2020, Deutscher Bundestag, Stenografischer Bericht, 202. Sitzung, 23. November 2016, Plenarprotokoll 18/202 (cited as BT 2016–202).

References

Alexander R. (2017): *Die Getriebenen – Merkel und die Flüchtlingspolitik: Report aus dem Innern der Macht*, München: Siedler Verlag.

Bilanz der Bankenrettung in Deutschland, Drucksache 19/4243, Bilanz der Landesbankenrettung in Deutschland Drucksache 19/4242.

Bonatti L., Fracasso A. (2013): The German Model and the European Crisis, *Journal of Common Market Studies*, 51(6), p. 10023–1039.

BVerfG, Urteil des Zweiten Senats vom 07. September 2011- 2 BvR 987/10 – Rn. (1–142), http://www.bverfg.de/e/rs20110907_2bvr098710.html.

BVerfG, Urteil des Zweiten Senats vom 12. September 2012- 2 BvR 1390/12 – Rn. (1–215), http://www.bverfg.de/e/rs20120912_2bvr139012.html.

Dyson K.H.F. (2014): *States, Debt, and Power: 'Saints' and 'Sinners' in European History and Integration*, Oxford: Oxford University Press.

Giegerich B., Terhalle M. (2017): The Munich Consensus and the Purpose of German Power, in: James Bindenagel/Matthias Herdegen/Karl Kaiser (eds.), *International Security in the 21st Century: Germany's International Responsibility*, Göttingen: Vandenhoeck & Ruprecht Gmbh & Co, p. 241 et seq.

Hellwig M. (2017): Deutschland und die Finanzkrise(n), *Wirtschaftsdienst* 97. Jahrgang, Heft 9 s. 606–607, https://archiv.wirtschaftsdienst.eu/jahr/2017/9/deutschland-und-die-finanzkrisen/

Małachowski W. (2010): Skutki kryzysu i działania antykryzysowe w gospodarce Niemiec, in: Joachim Osiński (ed.), *Państwa narodowe wobec kryzysu ekonomicznego*, Warsaw: SGH.

Maull H. (2015): Deutsche Außenpolitik – Verantwortung und Macht, *Zeitschrift für Außen- und Sicherheitspolitik*, 8, p. 213–237, quoted p. 227.

Pew Research Center, NATO Public Opinion: Wary of Russia, Leery of Action on Ukraine, 10 June 2015, http://www.pewresearch.org/wp-content/uploads/sites/2/2015/06/Pew-Research-Center-Russia-Ukraine-Report-FINAL-June-10-2015.pdf.

Pressekonferenz der Bundeskanzlerin und der Regierungschefinnen und Regierungschefs der Bundesländer, 18. Juni 2015, https://www.bundesregierung.de/breg-de/aktuelles/pressekonferenz-der-bundeskanzlerin-und-der-regierungschefinnen-und-regierungschefs-der-bundeslaender-846066.

Rede von Außenminister Frank-Walter Steinmeier anlässlich der 50. Münchner Sicherheitskonferenz, 01.02.2014, https://www.auswaertiges-amt.de/de/newsroom/140201-bm-muesiko/259554.

Rinke A. (2016): Migration, Sicherheit, Wirtschaft. Afrika wird zu einer Priorität der deutschen und europäischen Politik, *Internationale Politik*, 6, November/Dezember 2016, p. 8–16.

Rinke A. (2017): Deutschlands neue Nachbarn. Die Bundesregierung weitet ihren Blick auf den Krisenbogen um die EU, *Internationale Politik*, 4, Juli-August 2017, p. 42 – 48.

Schwarzer D. (2013): Germany's Role and Strategy in the Euro Area – Determining Factors and Scenarios, *The Polish Quarterly of International Affairs*, 2, s. 62 et seq.

Steinbrück P. (2011): Unterm Strich, *dtv München*, erweiterte Ausgabe 2011, p. 209 et seq.

Daniel Tilles

Immigration and public trust: Lessons for Poland from Brexit Britain

Abstract: The increase in prosperity in Poland and in other Eastern EU Member States and the impact of their demographic problems on the labor market have contributed to growing migration flows from the East and South of Europe. In recent years, Poland has been one of the largest recipients of immigrants in the entire EU, and during this period the country has been ruled by a party that presents itself as strongly opposed to and effectively preventing immigration. Despite this rhetoric, the government did indeed increase immigration but did so quietly. The author presents arguments confirming the thesis that such a solution is dangerous because it can undermine confidence in the political establishment and trigger a reaction directed at migrants. Poland should analyze the experience of Great Britain. This is where governments' similar approach - allowing large-scale immigration while avoiding public discussion or appearing to oppose it - has contributed to disrupting the political landscape and reinforcing extremes while fueling dislike of immigrants. One of the consequences was the vote to leave the European Union.

Keywords: immigration, Poland, Great Britain, public policies

Managing immigration has become one of the greatest challenges facing contemporary Europe, though it is usually perceived as an issue affecting primarily the wealthier western EU states. Indeed, for the newer members in the east of the bloc, emigration has long been the greatest challenge, as they grapple with brain drain and a difficult demographic situation. Where those countries are discussed with regard to immigration, it is usually in the context of their proclaimed efforts to prevent it, in particular the inflow of refugees following the 2015 migration crisis, as well as Muslim immigrants more broadly.

For example, a book published in 2018 on *The Impact of Migration on Poland* deals almost exclusively with outward migration. Where inward migration is discussed, it is mainly in the context of Poles returning from abroad. The single chapter on migration to Poland by non-Poles begins with the author saying it is 'a shorter chapter included for the sake of completeness'. Much of it deals with 'prospect' (i.e. potential) migration, Poland's longstanding ethnic minorities (who are not immigrants), or, again, with Poles returning from abroad.[1]

However, as Poland and other eastern member states have become wealthier, as their demographic problems have tightened labour markets, and as various push factors have increased migratory flows from Europe's east and south, they too have seen the number and diversity of arrivals increase. This is a process that has affected the largest of the eastern states, Poland, more than any other. Indeed, the country has in recent years been one of the biggest recipients of immigrants in the entire EU. This fact is often surprising to outsiders, and even to some Poles, especially given that the country has during this period been led by a government that presents itself as strongly opposed to immigration and as successful in preventing it. Yet in fact, despite this rhetoric, the government has actually encouraged these record levels of immigration. It has, however, done so quietly, while seeking public to maintain its anti-immigrant image.

This, it will be argued, is a dangerous combination, one that risks undermining public trust in the political establishment and creating a backlash against the immigrants themselves. In this regard, Poland can look to the experience of western European countries, and in particular the United Kingdom. There, a similar approach by governments to immigration over the last two decades – permitting it on a large scale while avoiding public discussion of it or claiming to be opposed to it – has helped disrupt the traditional political landscape, with a collapse of the middle ground and strengthening of the extremes, while also stoking resentment towards immigrants. One consequence of these trends was the vote to leave the European Union.

The Polish and British cases are not identical, of course – no two examples ever are. Each of the countries has very different historical experiences of migration as well as contrasting profiles of current migration. Britain has for decades received large numbers of arrivals from around the globe, and as a consequence is today one of Europe's most ethnically and religiously diverse societies. Poland, though it was one of Europe's most multi-ethnic and multi-religious states before World War Two, became as a consequence of that war one of its most homogeneous and received very few immigrants until recently. The two countries' politics, economies, societies and relationship with the EU also differ greatly.

Nevertheless, there are, as we shall see, useful parallels to be drawn between them when it comes to the question of migration and public trust, and lessons

1 A. White (2018): 'The impact of migration into Poland by non-Poles', in Anne White, Izabela Grabowska, Paweł Kaczmarczyk and Krystyna Slany, *The Impact of Migration on Poland: EU Mobility and Social Change*, London: UCL Press, p. 213.

that Poland can learn from the mistakes of the UK, where complacency or dishonesty from governments about immigration has had negative consequences.

An unprecedented wave of migration

In the postwar period up until 1989, 'immigration [to Poland] was virtually inexistent', notes Krystyna Iglicki. Following the fall of communism, the numbers of arrivals did gradually increase,[2] but immigration in the last few years has been unprecedented in the country's history in both nature and scale, and high even by international standards. The most recent available Eurostat data show that, in 2017, Poland issued more first residence permits to immigrants from outside the EU than any other country in the union. The figure of 683,228 was almost one-quarter of all permits issued in the EU that year[3] and was well over double the figure of 273,886 in Poland in 2013.[4] Likewise, the number of work permits issued to non-EU immigrants in Poland in 2017, almost a quarter of a million, was twice as high as the year before, four times more than in 2015, and over 20 times bigger than in 2006.[5]

The majority of these immigrants come from just one country, Ukraine. In 2017, 86 % of first residence permits and 82 % of the work permits went to Ukrainians. There are many more who come from Ukraine to work in jobs that require employers declarations rather than work permits, and also others working in the informal economy. Poland's central bank (NBP) estimates that in 2017 there were around 900,000 Ukrainians staying in the country, making them by far the biggest immigrant group.[6]

---

2 K. Iglicka (2014): 'Poland – a Country of Enduring Emigration', in: Felica Medved (ed.), *Proliferation of Migration Transition: Selected New EU Member States*, Brussels: European Liberal Forum, pp. 84, 86.

3 'First residence permits issued in the EU Member States remain above 3 million in 2017', 25 October 2018, *Eurostat*, https://ec.europa.eu/eurostat/documents/2995521/9333446/3-25102018-AP-EN.pdf/3fa5fa53-e076-4a5f-8bb5-a8075f639167.

4 F. Medved (2014): Synthesis and Reflections, in: Felica Medved (ed.), *Proliferation of Migration Transition: Selected New EU Member States*, European Liberal Forum, p. 249.

5 Zezwolenia na pracę cudcoziemców w Polsce w 2017 r., *Glówny Urząd Statystyczny*, 12 September 2018, http://stat.gov.pl/obszary-tematyczne/rynek-pracy/opracowania/zezwolenia-na-prace-cudzoziemcow-w-polsce-w-2017-r-,18,1.html; Iglicka, 'Poland – a Country of Enduring Emigration', p. 90.

6 I. Chmielewska, G. Dobroczek, A. Panuciak (2018): *Obywatele Ukrainy pracujący w Polsce – raport z badania: Badanie zrealizowane w 2017 r.*, Warsaw: Department Statystyki BNP, p. 4.

Again, this is not an entirely new situation. Since migration into Poland began to rise in the 1990s, the majority of arrivals have always been from Ukraine, encouraged by Poland's faster economic development as well as the geographical and linguistic proximity of the two countries. However, as with immigration overall, there has been a particularly rapid change in the last few years, with Ukrainians becoming more numerous, settled and visible than before, with their emigration accelerated by the push factor of instability and conflict in Ukraine since 2014.

For example, in the three years from 2011 to 2013, the number of employer declarations for hiring Ukrainian workers in Poland fell slightly, from 240,000 to 218,000. But in 2014 it jumped to 373,000 and by 2016 the figure was almost 1.3 million.[7] The latest data indicate that it reached 1.7 million in 2017,[8] and the 2018 figure may be higher still, given that the NBP estimates the number of Ukrainians in Poland rose from 900,000 to 1.3m in 2018.[9] (N.B. the number of employer declarations exceeds the estimated average number of Ukrainians in Poland because the same person can receive more than one declaration, and because they may only stay in the country temporarily.)

As well as the numbers, another change has been in the profile and visibility of Ukrainians in Poland. Whereas in the past, Ukrainian migrants tended to be older and less educated, often working in the agriculture, construction or domestic service, the recent wave has been made up on average by younger and better educated people, who are increasingly likely to work in public-facing sectors such as retail and hospitality. The NBP, for example, has compared pre- and post-2014 Ukrainian immigrants, finding that among the former the average age is 43 years and 31 % have completed higher education, while among the latter the average age is 33 years and 47 % have completed higher education. The proportion working in the hospitality or retail and wholesale trading sectors has risen from 12 % in the pre-2014 generation to 31 % among the more recent immigrants.[10] Another change has been a growth in Ukrainian students at Polish

---

7 *Ibid.*, p. 7.

8 http://orka2.sejm.gov.pl/INT8.nsf/klucz/658C47F2/%24FILE/i18648-o1.pdf.

9 Przez polski rynek pracy „przewija się" ok. 1,2 mln Ukraińców, *Business Insider Polska*, 11 March 2019, https://businessinsider.com.pl/wiadomosci/ukraincy-ilu-pracuje-w-polsce-dane-nbp/r1yf4pe

10 I. Chmielewska, G, Dobroczek, J. Puzynkiewicz (2016): *Obywatele Ukrainy pracujący w Polsce – raport z badania: Badanie zrealizowane w 2015 r.*, Warsaw: Department Statystyki BNP, pp. 4, 11, 17.

universities, whose number has almost quadrupled from under 10,000 in the 2012/13 academic year to almost 38,000 in 2017/18.[11] As a consequence of these changes, 80 % of Poles in one recent survey say they have come into contact with Ukrainians working in Poland, mostly commonly as shop workers.[12]

This mass Ukrainian migration is in itself an important story. It is likely to be the largest migration of people from one European country to another in recent times (certainly in such a short period). Yet it receives little attention in international media coverage or academic publications. To give a comparative example: in the three years after Poland joined the EU in 2004, the Polish population of the UK increased by around 350,000.[13] This was the biggest wave of migration in British history and received huge attention, not just in Britain and Poland but internationally too. By comparison, in the three years from 2014, an even larger number of Ukrainians have migrated to Poland, as we have seen, yet this gets very little coverage. Indeed, the profile of recent Ukrainian migrants in Poland is similar to that of the Poles who went to the UK after 2004, who tended to be younger and better educated than previous Polish immigrants, were likely to work in construction and hospitality, and were often over- or mis-qualified for their positions.[14]

It is also noteworthy that, in contrast to many western countries, where large waves of migration have created resentment, the mass arrival of Ukrainians has met with almost no hostility from Poles, who generally appreciate their economic contribution and seamless integration. The same survey cited above finds that a majority 52 % feel positively towards Ukrainian workers while only 12 % express negative sentiment.[15] Periodic attempts by far-right groups in Poland to

---

11 Studenci z Ukrainy. Dlaczego decydują się na studia w Polsce i jaka czeka ich przyszłość?, *Forbes*, 4 November 2018, https://www.forbes.pl/praca/ukrainscy-studenci-w-polsce-raport-kew/k2w36fd.

12 E. Rutkowska (2019): „Na Ukraińców jesteśmy (raczej) otwarci. Najmniej tolerancyjni okazują się jednak najmłodsi", *Dziennik Gazeta Prawna*, 11 March 2019, https://www.gazetaprawna.pl/artykuly/1402299,otwartosc-polakow-na-ukraincow-badanie.html.

13 M. Okólski, J. Salt (2015): Polish Emigration to the UK after 2004: Why Did So Many Come?, *Central and Eastern European migration Review*, vol. 3 no. 2, p. 21.

14 K. Burrell (2016): Migration to the UK from Poland: Continuity and Change in East-West European Mobility, in: Kathy Burrell (ed.), *Polish Migration to the UK in the "New" European Union After 2004*, London: Routledge, p. 30; Chmielewska, Dobroczek, Panuciak, *Obywatele Ukrainy pracujący w Polsce*, *op. cit.* p. 18.

15 E. Rutkowska, *op. cit.*

organise protests against Ukrainian immigrants have met with no success, with one in Wrocław in 2018 attracting only ten people.[16] This lack of tension and opposition is perhaps one reason why Ukrainian migration has received less attention than it should.

In addition to the Ukrainian majority, there have also been a growing number of migrants from outside Europe. The absolute figures are still comparatively small, but are growing rapidly – and, for reasons that will be outlined below, are likely to grow even further. Moreover, these immigrants have been more visible than their numbers suggest, given that they are concentrated in big cities and often engaged in public-facing professions, such as in the hospitality industry and transportation (particularly as ridesharing and food-delivery drivers). As Anne White notes, 'spatial concentration [of immigrants] … is not necessary for a minority to create the impression' that they are numerous. It is 'the sudden influx of more foreigners [that] … creates a strong impression[,] … particularly if the migrants are visible in [professions such as] catering'.[17]

Certainly there has been a sudden influx, in particular of migrants from South Asia. In 2017, over 13,000 work permits were issued in Poland for people from Nepal, India and Bangladesh combined, which is around four times higher than in the previous year.[18] The figure would be even higher were it not for a reported backlog of up to 25,000 people from those three countries who already have work offers in Poland but are waiting for a visa from the Polish embassy in New Delhi, whose staff and computer systems have struggled to keep up with demand.[19] In big cities in Poland, Asian workers have become increasingly visible, for example as Uber drivers, while they are also employed in Poland's rapidly expanding

16 Ukraińcy, won z Polski, Polska dla Polaków. ONR twierdzi, że nie nawołuje do nienawiści, *Gazeta Wyborcza*, 8 September 2018, http://wroclaw.wyborcza.pl/wroclaw/7,35771,23895553,ukraincy-won-z-polski-polska-dla-polakow-onr-twierdzi-ze.html. See also: Imigracja ze Wschodu, zagrożenie narodu. ONR protestował przeciwko polityce rządu PiS, *Dziennik.pl*, https://wiadomosci.dziennik.pl/wydarzenia/zdjecia/545253,1,onr-protest-imigracja-wschod-rzad-pis.html.

17 White, 'The impact of migration into Poland by non-Poles', *op. cit.*, p. 218.

18 Janusz. K. Kowalski and Adam Pawluć, „Nie tylko Ukraińcy. Pracodawcy coraz częściej sięgają po pracowników z egzotycznych krajów", *Dziennik Gazeta Prawna*, 22 February 2018, https://serwisy.gazetaprawna.pl/praca-i-kariera/artykuly/1106234,przybywa-pracownikow-z-egzotycznych-krajow.html.

19 25 tys. Hindusów, Nepalczyków i Banglijczyków chce pracować w Poslce, *Puls Biznesu*, 10 September 2018, https://www.pb.pl/25-tys-hindusow-nepalczykow-i-banglijczykow-chce-pracowac-w-polsce-939461.

corporate back-office sector. A study in 2018 found Indians to be the fourth-most-common foreign employees of business-services centres in Poland.[20]

That same study also showed that, among the top 10 nationalities of foreign employees at such centres, seven were other EU countries. Of those, all but one were western member states, which signifies another significant migratory trend into Poland. The government's Office for Foreigners records that the number of non-Polish EU citizens registering for temporary residence rose from around 27,000 in 2010 to over 70,000 in 2017. These arrivals are predominantly young, most commonly in their 20s, and mostly (around 70 %) male. The top five source countries are all in Western Europe. The largest number come from neighbouring Germany, but the biggest growth since 2010 has been among migrants from Italy and Spain, whose numbers increased by a factor of 4 to 5.[21]

The government's approach to immigration: for, and even against

What is particularly striking about this wave of immigration, which is unprecedentedly large and diverse for Poland, is that it has taken place under a government that is routinely described (including by itself) as 'anti-immigration'. This was an image forged in 2015, at the peak of Europe's migration crisis, when the Law and Justice (PiS) party, then in opposition, vociferously opposed the reception of asylum seekers, a position supported by a majority of the Polish public.[22] This was one of the factors that helped PiS come to power in elections that autumn, as it contrasted itself to the Civic Platform-led government of the time, which had agreed to the European Commission's plan to allocate member states with quotas for resettling asylum seekers.

Since then, the PiS government has continued to cultivate this image. It has very publicly refused to accept a single asylum seeker from Poland's quota, resulting in the European Commission taking legal action against it. And it has regularly criticised the consequences of mass migration in western European

---

20 *Business Services Sector in Poland 2018* (2018): Warsaw: Association of Business Service Leaders, p. 43, https://absl.pl/wp-content/uploads/2018/06/raport_absl_2018_EN_181120_epub.pdf.

21 Mapy i dane statystyczne imigrantów i służb migracyjnych Polski, migracje.gov.pl.

22 „CBOS zbadał stosunek Polaków do uchodźców. Tylko 5 proc. Chce ich przyjąć i pozwolić na osiedlenie się", *Gazeta Wyborcza*, 17 December 2015, http://wyborcza.pl/1,75398,19360117,cbos-zbadal-stosunek-polakow-do-uchodzcow-tylko-5-procent-chce.html.

countries. In 2017, the interior minister, Mariusz Błaszczak, warned that immigration had caused a 'bloody harvest' in Western Europe and promised that this would 'not be repeated' in Poland under the PiS government.[23] During its campaign in the 2017 local elections, PiS released its strongest anti-immigration message to date, publishing a video that presented an apocalyptic vision of what Poland would look like if the opposition were allowed to let refugees into the country.[24] At a campaign event ahead of the 2019 European elections, Jarosław Kaczyński, the chairman of PiS and Poland's *de facto* leader, warned of a 'cultural offensive' by 'Muslim civilisation' from which 'Europe must defend itself'.[25]

Yet what is striking is that, while cultivating this public image, senior government figures have at the same time been sending signals that they are comfortable with, and even supportive of, large-scale immigration, including from Muslim countries. But they have done so quietly, often when speaking to business or foreign audiences, and not directly to the Polish public.

In 2016, Mateusz Morawiecki, then the economy minister, told a small audience at the Economic Forum in Krynica that Poland needs to take 'intensive action' to counteract the declining size of its workforce and that he would therefore 'make a friendly invitation to several hundred thousand Ukrainians workers'.[26] Two years later, now as prime minister, Morawiecki again emphasised that Poland needs immigrants to fill gaps in the labour market.[27] Likewise, his minister for investment and development, Jerzy Kwieciński, says that 'our economy

---

23 „Błaszczak: Mamy do czynenia z „potężnym" kryzysem imigracyjnym", *Dziennik Gazeta Prawna*, 18 April 2017, https://www.gazetaprawna.pl/artykuly/1035638,blaszczak-kryzys-imigracyjny.html.

24 „PiS w spocie przypomina deklaracje PO o uchodźcach", *Rzeczpospolita*, 17 October 2018, https://www.rp.pl/Kraj/181019278-PiS-w-spocie-przypomina-deklaracje-PO-o-uchodzcach.html.

25 PiS wraca z tematem muzułmanskich imigrantów. Jarosław Kaczyński: Trzeba się bronić!, *Gazeta.pl*, 23 March 2019, http://wiadomosci.gazeta.pl/wiadomosci/7,114884,24577993,pis-wraca-z-tematem-muzulmanskich-imigrantow-jaroslaw-kaczynski.html.

26 M. Kolanko (2016): Morawiecki: Muimy uzupełniać ubytki na rynku pracy. Będę starał się, by nastąpiło zaproszenie kilkuset tysięcy pracowników z Ukrainy, *300 Polityka*, 7 September 2016, http://300polityka.pl/live/2016/09/07/morawiecki-musimy-uzupelniac-ubytki-na-rynku-pracy-bede-staral-sie-by-nastapilo-zaproszenie-kilkuset-tysiecy-pracownikow-z-ukrainy/.

27 Poland needs immigrants for its labor market: PM Morawiecki, *Poland In*, 2 July 2018, https://polandin.com/37906502/poland-needs-immigrants-for-its-labor-market-pm-morawiecki.

needs more and more foreign workers'.[28] The entrepreneurship and technology minister, Jadwiga Emilewicz, has also said that the government is 'ready to open its borders'.[29] Tellingly, the second and third of these quotes appeared in English-language media but seem not to have been reported in Polish, while the first and fourth received very little attention in Poland.

These words are being matched by concrete action. The government confirmed in 2018 that it was working on a 'new national migration policy' as part of its broader Strategy for Responsible Development. Among the aims is reportedly to make it easier for non-EU immigrants to settle and work in Poland, such as by expanding the list of countries with privileged access to the Polish labour market from the current six former Soviet states to also include Southeast Asian countries like Vietnam and the Philippines.[30] At the same time, the Polish government began direct negotiations with the Philippines in order to conclude an agreement facilitating the migration of Filipinos to Poland.[31] During a visit to Bangladesh in 2017, Poland's minister for family, labour and social welfare, Elżbieta Rafalska, agreed with the Bangladeshi government to establish a joint study group on migration. She highlighted Poland's recent high levels of immigration, and said that 'the trend is upward for absorption of more workers'.[32]

The reasons for this pro-immigration policy are clear. Poland has an ageing society, one of the world's lowest birth rates, and a large number of citizens

---

28 I. Francis (2018): Poland short of workers after exodus to Britain and Germany, *Sky News*, 29 April 2018, https://news.sky.com/story/poland-short-of-workers-after-exodus-to-britain-and-germany-11351969.

29 Konstytucja Biznesu do przeglądu w przyszłym roku. Rząd chce ściągnąć więcej pracowników z zagranicy, *Forbes*, 9 August 2018, https://www.forbes.pl/gospodarka/jadwiga-emilewicz-o-konstytucji-biznesu-i-imigracji-zarobkowej-do-polski/tjm1gxd.

30 G. Osiecki (2018): Rząd otwiera się na imigrantów. Cudzoziemcy pomogą nam załatać demograficzną dziurę, *Dziennik Gazeta Prawna*, 4 June 2018, https://serwisy.gazetaprawna.pl/praca-i-kariera/artykuly/1127723,zmiany-w-zatrudnianiu-cudzoziemcow-imigranci-bez-pozwolen-na-prace.html.

31 G. Osiecki, M. Chądzyński (2018): Nowa polityka migracyjna Polski. Rząd wprowadza ułatwienia w zatrudnianiu cudzoziemców, *Dziennik.pl*, 12 July 2018, https://gospodarka.dziennik.pl/praca/artykuly/577742,polityka-migracyjna-kryzys-praca-cudzoziemcy-filipiny.html; J. Kastner (2018): Poland cracks door open for Filipino workers, *Nikkei Asian Review*, 17 August 2018, https://asia.nikkei.com/Economy/Poland-cracks-door-open-for-Filipino-workers.

32 Bangladesh, Poland agree to work for safe migration, *Daily Sun*, 23 April 2017, http://www.daily-sun.com/printversion/details/221481/Bangladesh-Poland-agree-to-work-for-safe-migration-.

working abroad. Demographers forecast that the working-age population will fall from around 26 million people in 2015 to around 19 million by 2050 – a drop of almost 25 %.[33] The old-age dependency ratio is predicted to increase more than 30 percentage points during that period. That is the second highest rise in the European Union, with Poland also having the second-fastest increase in median age by 2050.[34] Combined with a booming economy, this has left unemployment at record lows,[35] with wages rising fast[36] and many employers struggling to find workers, leading businesses to demand that more migrants to be let in to ease these pressures. In August 2018, a group of business organisations and NGOs, including the Polish Chamber of Commerce and the Union of Entrepreneurs and Employers, publicly appealed to the government to make it easier for foreign workers to be employed.[37]

It is this lobbying that has encouraged the government to pursue the new, more open immigration strategy outlined above. Yet, at the same time, it has continued in public to claim to be opposed to immigration, in order to satisfy public demand. This balancing act is not sustainable, and could have dangerous consequences. The government has got away with it so far, but there are already signs of emerging tension.

---

33 A. Kiełczewska, P. Lewandowski (2017): Population ageing and the labour supply in Poland up to 2050, in: Piotr Lewandowski and Jan Rutkowski (eds.), *Population Ageing, Labour Market and Public Finance in Poland,* Warsaw: European Commission Representation in Poland, p. 12.

34 People in the EU – population projections, *Eurostat*, December 2017, https://ec.europa.eu/eurostat/statistics-explained/index.php?title=People_in_the_EU_-_population_projections.

35 D. Bartyzel (2017): Unemployment So Low It's Time for Poland to Worry About It, *Bloomberg*, 25 May 2017, https://www.bloomberg.com/news/articles/2017-05-24/unemployment-so-low-it-s-now-time-for-poland-to-worry-about-it.

36 UK workers experienced sharpest wage fall of any leading economy, TUC analysis finds, *Trades Union Congress*, 27 July 2016, https://www.tuc.org.uk/news/uk-workers-experienced-sharpest-wage-fall-any-leading-economy-tuc-analysis-finds; W. Ziomek (2018): Wzrost wynagrodzeń w 2019. Polska w czołówce, *Money.pl*, 2 December 2018, https://www.money.pl/gospodarka/wiadomosci/artykul/pensje-w-polsce-wzrost-plac,245,0,2423029.html.

37 P. Bednarz (2018): Potrzeba więcej ułatwień dla cudzoziemców. Pracowdawcy apelują o zmiany w prawie, *Business Insider Polska*, 22 August 2018, https://businessinsider.com.pl/finanse/zmiana-warunkow-zatrudniania-cudzoziemcow-apel-pracodawcow/vr771p1.

In particular, the nationalist right has been putting pressure on the government by trying to draw attention to immigration and raising concerns about how it could impact on Polish culture and society. One example of their success in doing so came in August 2018, when nationalist media angrily reported on a speech by a deputy minister of investment and development, Paweł Chorąży, in which he said that Poland must open up to migration if it wants to prosper.[38] Even though his words were little different from those of the other more senior ministers mentioned above, this time they started to gather attention (and also came shortly before important local elections).

In response, senior PiS figures vigorously denied they had any policy to permit large-scale immigration. The interior minister, Joachim Brudziński, said that 'on the issue of migration policy, I am not going to change [our] tough position by even one millimetre'. Chorąży's comments should be 'treated as academic digressions and not the position of the government', Brudziński reassured.[39] With the controversy not disappearing, Chorąży was then fired. A government spokeswoman explained that his 'comments on immigrants were extremely contrary to what the Polish government is doing'.[40] An anonymous source in the prime minister's chancellery said Morawiecki 'was furious' with the deputy minister and that there 'cannot be someone in the government who has such extremely different views from the government', which has a 'clear anti-immigration policy'.[41]

38 „Polska musi i nawet jeśli nie chce to powinna chcieć imigrantów" – wiceminister Paweł Chorąży o polityce integracyjnej, *Media Narodowe*, 1 September 2018, https://medianarodowe.com/polska-musi-i-nawet-jesli-nie-chce-to-powinna-chciec-imigrantow-wiceminister-pawel-chorazy-o-polityce-integracyjnej/.

39 I. Morawski (2018): Rząd przeciwny imigrantom otwiera dla nich szeroko drzwi, *Bankier.pl*, 10 September 2018, https://www.bankier.pl/wiadomosc/Rzad-przeciwny-imigrantom-otwiera-dla-nich-szeroko-drzwi-7613922.html.

40 Dymisja wiceminister Pawła Chorążego. Powód? Wypowiedź o imigrantach i repatriantach, *Newsweek*, 14 September 2018, https://www.newsweek.pl/polska/polityka/dymisja-wiceministra-pawla-chorazego-powodem-wypowiedz-o-imigrantach/fexhgh9.

41 M. Makowski (2018): Premier był wściekły. Morawiecki podjął decyzję o zdymisjowaniu ministra Chorążego. Zaważył wypowiedzi o imigrantach, *Wirtualna Polska*, 14 September 2018, https://opinie.wp.pl/news-wp-premier-byl-wsciekly-morawiecki-podjal-decyzje-o-zdymisjonowaniu-ministra-chorazego-zawazyly-wypowiedzi-o-imigrantach-6295185123436161a.

Learning from British failures

The Chorąży episode neatly encapsulates the bind the government finds itself in: trying to persuade its supporters (and perhaps itself) that it is opposed to immigration while at the same time accepting the economic arguments in favour of letting in larger numbers of foreign workers. This contradiction is simply not a sustainable long-term solution. At some stage, tensions will erupt among sections of the public that feel significant changes to their society have been made without (or even against) their consent. This is where the example of Britain is instructive. Many of the challenges the UK is has been facing in recent years, including Brexit, can be linked to anger over not only the fact that immigration has been taking place at an unprecedented rate, but also that many British people feel successive governments have deceived them about.

While the UK is seen as a country that has long experienced mass immigration, especially since the Second World War, it is important to remember that there has been a significant change over the last two decades. Up until the 1990s, annual net migration was relatively low, and indeed often negative. In the 30 years between 1964 and 1993, for example, twenty saw net emigration out of the UK. Net immigration into the UK was never higher than 58,000 in the remaining ten. This changed, however, in 1997, when the Labour Party came to power after 18 years of Conservative rule. It immediately oversaw a rise in immigration to the highest level in British history, reaching a net inflow of 273,000 by 2007 and averaging 214,000 during the party's 13 years in government.[42] This 'immigration policy will almost certainly be seen as [Labour's] primary legacy,' believes David Goodhart.[43]

Yet Labour allowed this unprecedented level of migration to take place without any real public discussion. In their 1997 election campaign, migration was hardly mentioned. The word only appears three times in the party's almost 18,000-word long election manifesto, and each of those was to emphasise the importance of 'having firm control over' it rather than any suggestion of increasing it.[44] The party's 2001 manifesto, despite being almost twice as long,

42 50 years of international migration to and from the UK, *Office for National Statistics*, 1 December 2016, https://www.ons.gov.uk/peoplepopulationandcommunity/populationandmigration/internationalmigration/articles/explore50yearsofinternationalmigrationtoandfromtheuk/2016-12-01.

43 D. Goodhart (2013): *The British Dream: Successes and Failures of Post-War Immigration*, London: Atlantic Books.

44 *New Labour: Because Britain Deserves Better*, 1997, http://www.labour-party.org.uk/manifestos/1997/1997-labour-manifesto.shtml.

did not mention migration at all.[45] Moreover, not only did Labour try to avoid talking about this issue, they actively tried to supress discussion, as they feared it would alienate their traditional white working-class support base. 'The deliberate policy of ministers … was to open up the UK to mass migration', wrote Andrew Neather, a former advisor to Labour Prime Minister Tony Blair. 'But ministers won't talk about it … [because] they probably realised the conservatism of their core voters: while ministers may have been passionately in favour of [immigration] … it wasn't necessarily a debate they wanted to be having in working men's clubs'.[46]

Yet this strategy was untenable. It was obvious to the public that mass immigration was taking place, and opposition to it was strong. A majority of the public was consistently saying in polls that 'there are too many immigrants' in the UK. The proportion of people who said immigration was the most important issue facing the country rose from just 3 % in the year Labour came to power to 44 % after a decade of their rule.[47] By the end of Labour's term, anti-immigration sentiment was stronger in the UK than any other big western country.[48] As Andrew Geddes and Peter Scholten note, the party's 'record on immigration was a key reason why it lost support' and, eventually, power.[49]

The Conservative government that replaced Labour in 2010 was arguably even more corrosive of public trust over immigration. For much of Labour's rule, the Conservatives had been raising concerns about immigration. In 2001 party leader William Hague famously accused Labour of turning Britain into a 'foreign land' and promised the public he would 'give you back your country'. At

---

45 *Ambitions for Britain*, 2001, http://labourmanifesto.com/2001/2001-labour-manifesto.shtml.

46 Don't listen to the whingers – London needs immigrants, *Evening Standard*, 23 October 2009, https://www.standard.co.uk/news/dont-listen-to-the-whingers-london-needs-immigrants-6786170.html.

47 UK Public Opinion toward Immigration: Overall Attitudes and Level of Concern, *Migration Observatory at the University of Oxford*, 7 June 2018, https://migrationobservatory.ox.ac.uk/resources/briefings/uk-public-opinion-toward-immigration-overall-attitudes-and-level-of-concern/.

48 *Transatlatnic Trends: Immigration*, http://www.gmfus.org/publications/transatlantic-trends-immigration-2010, p.5 See also, T. Vlandas (2016): Xenophibia Britannica? Anti-immigrant attitudes in the UK are among the strongest in Europe, *LSE Brexit Blog*, 21 October 2016, https://blogs.lse.ac.uk/brexit/2016/10/21/xenophobia-britannica-anti-immigrant-attitudes-in-the-uk-are-among-the-strongest-in-europe/.

49 A. Geddes, P. Scholten (2016): *The Politics of Migration and Immigration in Europe*, London: Sage, p. 29.

the 2005 election, the Tories ran an advertising campaign with the slogan 'It's not racist to impose limits on immigration'. Five years later, David Cameron made a campaign pledge that his government would cut net immigration from its then level of well over 200,000 a year to under 100,000. Yet once in power he actually oversaw a *rise* in the figure, up to a historical record of 332,000 in 2015.[50] By that year, the proportion of people saying immigration was the most important issue facing the country had increased to 56 %.[51]

This has had significant consequences for the Labour and Conservative parties themselves, for immigrants, and for Britain as a whole. Disillusionment among many voters, especially the white working class,[52] drove them away from the two main parties and led to growing support for anti-establishment and far-right movements.[53] The Eurosceptic, anti-immigration UK Independence Party (UKIP), for example, saw its share of the vote rise at every general election from 1997 to 2015, going from 0.34 % to 12.64 %. During this period the combined vote share of the two main parties, Labour and the Conservatives, fell to its lowest level for almost a century. In European elections, where votes for smaller parties are not discouraged by Britain's first-past-the-post parliamentary election system, the combined vote share of UKIP and the far-right British National Party (BNP) went from 8 % in 1999 to 28 % in 2014. In the latter election, UKIP obtained more votes than anyone else – the first time a party other than the Conservatives or Labour had won a British election for more than 100 years. Meanwhile, on the streets and in social media, a series of large far-right protest groups emerged – the English Defence League, Britain First and the Football

50 Net migration in the UK, *Migration Observatory at the University of Oxford*, 24 August 2018, https://migrationobservatory.ox.ac.uk/resources/briefings/long-term-international-migration-flows-to-and-from-the-uk/.

51 UK Public Opinion toward Immigration: Overall Attitudes and Level of Concern, *op. cit.*

52 E. Kaufmann (2018): *Whiteshift: Populism, Immigration and the Future of White* Majorities, London: Allen Lane, pp. 180, 182, 184–7; G. Evans, J. Mellon (2016): Working Class Votes and Conservative Losses: Solving the UKIP Puzzle, *Parliamentary Affairs*, volume 69, issue 2, pp. 464–479; P. Kellner (2011): Labour is not just the party of the working class, *YouGov*, 16 May 2011, https://yougov.co.uk/topics/politics/articles-reports/2011/05/16/labour-not-just-party-working-class.

53 R. Ford, M.J. Goodwin (2010): Angry White Men: Indivudual and Contextual Prdictors of Support for the British National Party, *Political Studies*, volume 58, issue 1, pp. 1–25; S.O. Becker (2018): Does Migration Cause Extreme Voting?, *CAGE Online Working Paper Series* 306; O. Bailey, L. Baston (2018): *For the Many?: Understanding and uniting Labour's core supporters*, London: Fabian Society, pp. 17, 18, 20.

Lads Alliance – who focus on concerns over immigration in general, and of Muslims in particular.

The culmination of these developments came in 2016, with the vote to leave the European Union. The motivations of those who voted for Brexit are varied, and the balance between them remains disputed among scholars and commentators, but it is clear that frustration with the political establishment in general, and over migration in particular, played a significant part. In opinion polls, Leave voters cite a desire to control immigration as the first or second most important reason for their decision.[54] The aftermath of the Brexit vote saw a wave of hate crimes against immigrants and ethnic and religious minorities, with Poles and Muslims a particular target.[55] Analysis by Matthew Goodwin and Caitlin Milazzo finds that 'increases in the rate of immigration at the local level and sentiments regarding control over immigration were key predictors of the vote for Brexit'.[56]

Brexit voters were disproportionately from the working class and poorer regions, and politicians have admitted that they did not pay enough attention to the impact migration had on such communities in terms of supressing wages and increasing competition for state resources such as housing and benefits.[57]

---

54 CSI Brexit 4: People's Stated Reasons for Voting Leave or Remain, *Centre for Social Investiggation*, 24 April 2018, http://csi.nuff.ox.ac.uk/wp-content/uploads/2018/05/Carl_Reasons_Voting.pdf; How the UK voted for Brexit, and why, *Lord Ashcroft Polls*, 4 February 2019, https://lordashcroftpolls.com/2019/02/how-the-uk-voted-on-brexit-and-why-a-refresher/.

55 Hate Crime, England and Wales 2017/18, *Home Office*, 16 October 2018, https://assets.publishing.service.gov.uk/government/uploads/system/uploads/attachment_data/file/748598/hate-crime-1718-hosb2018.pdf, p. 12; M. Holden (2016): UK vows action after racist attacks on Poles and Muslims in wake of Brexit, *Reuters*, 27 June 2016, https://www.reuters.com/article/us-britain-eu-poland-incidents-idUSKCN0ZD15G; D. Devine (2018): The UK Referendum on Membership of the European Union as a Trigger Event for Hate Crimes, working paper, 5 February 2018, *SSRN*, https://ssrn.com/abstract=3118190; F. Albornoz, J. Bradley, S. Sonderegge, The Brexit referendum and the rise in hate crime, working paper, 18 September 2018, *LSE*, http://cep.lse.ac.uk/seminarpapers/19-09-18-ALB_v2.pdf.

56 M. Goodwin, C. Milazzo (2017): Taking Back Control? Investigating the Role of Immigration in the 2016 Vote for Brexit, *The British Journal of Politics and International Relations*, volume 19, issue 3. See also: R. Eatwell, M. Goodwin (2018): *National Populism: The Revolt Against Liberal Democracy*, London: Pelican Books, pp. 35–6.

57 H. Warrell (2011): Balls admits Labour 'mistakes' on immigration, *Financial Times*, 26 September 2011. See also: W. Outhwaite (2019): Migration Crisis and Brexit, in: Cecilia Menjivar, Marie Ruiz and Immanuel Ness (eds.), *The Oxford Handbook of Migration Crises*, Oxford: Oxford University Press, p. 96.

Former Labour Home Secretary Jack Straw called the party's decision to open Britain's labour market to new members states in 2004 a 'spectacular mistake'.[58] The former Conservative Chancellor of the Exchequer George Osborne also admits that his government made 'mistakes' with regard to immigration: not the fact it allowed so many people in, but that it did so after previously making unrealistic promises to cut the numbers. This turned immigration into a 'lethal' issue that helped bring about the Brexit vote. Instead, the Tories should have sought to explain the 'value of immigration' to the public, he now admits.[59] Tim Shipman's behind-the-scenes account of the Brexit referendum reveals that Prime Minister David Cameron's office were desperate to avoid discussing immigration during the campaign because they knew it would be a vote-loser.[60]

And this brings us back to Poland. Like Labour, the current Polish government has sought to suppress open discussion about migration – by, for example, firing a minister who tried to do so. Even more dangerously, like the Tories it has pandered to anti-immigrant sentiment while at the same time allowing unprecedented mass immigration to take place. This is not to suggest that this could lead to a Polish exit from the European Union. Poland's circumstances are completely different from the UK. For one thing, Poles are among the most positive about EU membership among all member states, in contrast to the Brits' longstanding Euroscepticism. For another, almost all the migrants coming to Poland are from outside the EU, unlike in the UK, where since 2004 many have come from other member states. This meant that for many Brits leaving the EU was seen as a means to limit the inflow, whereas for Poland it would have relatively little impact on migration.

However, the Polish government's duplicitous immigration policy could, like in the UK, have three negative consequences. First, it could stoke anger towards and disillusionment with the political establishment. Second, it could lead to growing popularity for more extreme political parties and protest movements. And third, it could stir up hostility and aggression towards immigrants themselves. There have not been many signs of this so far, but that could change

58 A. Philipson (2013): Labour made a 'spectacular mistake' on immigration, admits Jack Straw, *The Telegraph*, 13 November 2013, https://www.telegraph.co.uk/news/uknews/immigration/10445585/Labour-made-a-spectacular-mistake-on-immigration-admits-Jack-Straw.html.

59 George Osborne 'regrets' mistakes that led to Brexit vote, *BBC News*, 31 October 2018, https://www.bbc.com/news/uk-politics-46039623.

60 T. Shipman (2016): *All Out War: The Full Story of How Brexit Sank Britain's Political Class*, London: William Collins, pp. 363–4.

if, for example, there is an economic downturn, stoking resentment towards immigrants competing for jobs and resources, or if the number of non-European immigrants increases.

The latter scenario is a strong likelihood. Changes to labour laws in Germany, Slovakia and the Czech Republic will make it easier for Ukrainians to work there. Companies from those countries are already increasing their efforts to compete with Polish firms for Ukrainian workers.[61] A recent report by the Centre for Eastern Studies also suggests that the supply of workers from Ukraine is slowing down.[62] This will all mean that Polish companies will increasingly look to Asia for workers, something media reports indicate is already happening.[63] As outlined above, it also appears to be something the government is willing to support.

To avoid some of the problems the UK has faced, it is therefore vital for the Polish government to speak more openly and honestly about immigration: about why they believe it is an economic necessity, how it can benefit the whole of society, and how it can be carried out in a safe, careful, properly managed way. Indeed, Poland has so far been a migration success story, with immigrants integrating well and contributing to the economy, while Poles themselves have generally welcomed them. This should be something the government is proud to speak about, rather than trying to hide it.

As Roger Eatwell notes with regard to Britain, public anger is not directed so much at immigrants themselves, but rather at 'governments which neither cared about nor listened to people' concerned about the economic and cultural impact of such rapid change. Indeed, he argues that very few want immigration banned or hold racist views; most understand and support the need for migration. The problem, says Eatwell, is 'a widespread failure of communication' by

---

61 Poland worried Ukrainian workers could choose Germany, *France24*, 9 January 2019, https://www.france24.com/en/20190109-poland-worried-ukrainian-workers-could-choose-germany; Czesi i Słowacy podkradają nam Ukraińców. To może być dobra wiadamość, *Money.pl*, 26 September 2018, https://www.money.pl/gospodarka/wiadomosci/artykul/czesi-i-slowacy-podkradaja-nam-ukraincow-to,118,0,2417014.html; Niemcy również szukają pracowników z Ukrainy do pracy przy produkcji samochodów, *Bankier.pl*, 17 December 2018, https://www.bankier.pl/moto/niemcy-rowniez-szukaja-pracownikow-z-ukrainy-do-pracy-przy-produkcji-samochodow-1942/.

62 M. Jaroszewicz (2018): *Migracje z Ukrainy do Polski: Stabilizacja Trendu*, Warsaw: Ośrodek Studiów Wschodnich, p. 5.

63 Polskie firmy zainteresowane pracownikami z Wietnamu, *Business Insider Polska*, 10 March 2019, https://businessinsider.com.pl/wiadomosci/pracownicy-z-wietnamu-w-polsce-zamiast-ukraincow/xfqyy4x.

government, with 'mainstream politicians typically loathe to speak openly about' immigration, which has fed the rise of political movements outside that mainstream. 'We need politicians to be braver, to lead and talk more openly about immigration policy[,] … to explain the labour needs of the economy.'[64]

Yet the Polish government shows no signs of learning from this example. Instead, it appears to hope that it can continue reaping the economic benefits of immigration while avoiding public discussion of it and continuing to insist it is opposed to it. It may, of course, be the case that the Polish public is not willing to accept large-scale immigration. Certainly, this conversation is made harder by the fact that the xenophobic rhetoric provoked by the refugee crisis, including from PiS itself, has turned 'migrants' and 'migration' into catch-all negative terms without differentiation between their various forms. So, although hostility was being expressed towards African and Middle Eastern asylum seekers and not immigrants per se (as the peaceful large-scale arrival of Ukrainians has shown), the idea of migration has now become so toxic that it is difficult to discuss constructively.

A recent international survey by the Pew Research Center found only 21 % of Poles agreeing that 'immigrants make our country stronger' while 50 % said instead that they are a 'burden on our country'. This made Poland one countries most negative about immigration among those surveyed.[65] However, when one rephrases the question to avoid the word 'immigrant' and to focus on a tangible example, the results are rather different. A poll commissioned by Polish newspaper *Dziennik Gazeta Prawna*, which was cited above, asked Poles how they feel about 'Ukrainians working in Poland', finding that 52 % expressed positive sentiment and only 12 % negative. Similarly, 45 % agreed that Ukrainians benefit the Polish economy while only 24 % disagree.[66]

Such disparities highlight that Poles, like Brits, may have concerns over immigration in abstract terms but can have positive feelings towards immigrants

64 R. Eatwell (2018): The rising tide of national populism: we need to talk seriously about immigration, *Open Democracy*, 3 November 2018, https://www.opendemocracy.net/en/opendemocracyuk/rising-tide-of-national-populism-we-need-to-talk-about-immigration/. See: also M. A. Schain, *Shifting Tides: Radica-Right Populism and Immigration Policy in Europe and the United States*, Washington, DC: Migration Policy Institute.

65 A. Gonzalez-Barrera, P. Connor, Around the World, More Say Immigrants are a Strength Than a Burden, *Pew Research Center*, 14 Marcy 2019, https://www.pewglobal.org/2019/03/14/around-the-world-more-say-immigrants-are-a-strength-than-a-burden/.

66 E. Rutkowska, Na Ukraińców jesteśmy (raczej) otwarci, *op. cit.*

themselves and appreciate their contribution. This emphasises why it is vital that politicians are brave enough to lead an open conversation about the type of immigration policy that the country needs, and let the public express their views on the kind that they want. Avoiding this conversation simply stores up problems for later and makes them more difficult to deal with when they do emerge. Poles will see society changing around them, and will feel this is taking place without their consent. As the example of Britain shows, this can have dangerous consequences for mainstream political parties, for immigrants themselves, and for the country as a whole.

References

25 tys. Hindusów, Nepalczyków i Banglijczyków chce pracować w Polsce, *Puls Biznesu*, 10 September 2018, https://www.pb.pl/25-tys-hindusow-nepalczykow-i-banglijczykow-chce-pracowac-w-polsce-939461.

50 years of international migration to and from the UK, Office for National Statistics, 1 December 2016, https://www.ons.gov.uk/peoplepopulationandcommunity/populationandmigration/internationalmigration/articles/explore50yearsofinternationalmigrationtoandfromtheuk/2016-12-01.

Albornoz F., Bradley J., Sonderegge S. (2018): The Brexit referendum and the rise in hate crime, working paper, 18 September 2018, LSE, http://cep.lse.ac.uk/seminarpapers/19-09-18-ALB_v2.pdf.

Ambitions for Britain, 2001, http://labourmanifesto.com/2001/2001-labour-manifesto.shtml.

Bailey O., Baston L. (2018): For the Many?: Understanding and Uniting Labour's Core Supporters, London: Fabian Society.

Bangladesh, Poland agree to work for safe migration, *Daily Sun*, 23 April 2017, http://www.daily-sun.com/printversion/details/221481/Bangladesh-Poland-agree-to-work-for-safe-migration-.

Bartyzel D., Unemployment So Low It's Time for Poland to Worry About It, *Bloomberg*, 25 May 2017, https://www.bloomberg.com/news/articles/2017-05-24/unemployment-so-low-it-s-now-time-for-poland-to-worry-about-it.

Becker S. (2018): Does Migration Cause Extreme Voting?, CAGE Online Working Paper Series 306.

Bednarz P. (2018): Potrzeba więcej ułatwień dla cudzoziemców. Pracowdawcy apelują o zmiany w prawie, *Business Insider Polska*, 22 August 2018, https://businessinsider.com.pl/finanse/zmiana-warunkow-zatrudniania-cudzoziemcow-apel-pracodawcow/vr771p1.

Błaszczak: Mamy do czynienia z „potężnym" kryzysem imigracyjnym, *Dziennik Gazeta Prawna*, 18 April 2017, https://www.gazetaprawna.pl/artykuly/1035638,blaszczak-kryzys-imigracyjny.html.

Burrell K. (2016): 'Migration to the UK from Poland: Continuity and Change in East-West European Mobility', in Kathy Burrell (ed.), Polish Migration to the UK in: *"New" European Union after 2004*, London: Routledge.

Business Services Sector in Poland 2018, Warsaw: Association of Business Service Leaders, 2018), https://absl.pl/wp-content/uploads/2018/06/raport_absl_2018_EN_181120_epub.pdf.

CBOS zbadał stosunek Polaków do uchodźców. Tylko 5 proc. Chce ich przyjąć i pozwolić na osiedlenie się, *Gazeta Wyborcza*, 17 December 2015, http://wyborcza.pl/1,75398,19360117,cbos-zbadal-stosunek-polakow-do-uchodzcow-tylko-5-procent-chce.html.

Chmielewska I., Dobroczek G., Panuciak A. (2018): Obywatele Ukrainy pracujący w Polsce – raport z badania: Badanie zrealizowane w 2017 r., Warszawa: Department Statystyki BNP.

Chmielewska I., Dobroczek G., Puzynkiewicz J. (2016): Obywatele Ukrainy pracujący w Polsce – raport z badania: Badanie zrealizowane w 2015 r., Warszawa: Department Statystyki BNP.

CSI Brexit 4: People's Stated Reasons for Voting Leave or Remain, Centre for Social Investiggation, 24 April 2018, http://csi.nuff.ox.ac.uk/wp-content/uploads/2018/05/Carl_Reasons_Voting.pdf.

Czesi i Słowacy podkradają nam Ukraińców. To może być dobra wiadomość, *Money.pl*, 26 September 2018, https://www.money.pl/gospodarka/wiadomosci/artykul/czesi-i-slowacy-podkradaja-nam-ukraincow-to,118,0,2417014.html.

Devine D. (2018): The UK Referendum on Membership of the European Union as a Trigger Event for Hate Crimes, working paper, 5 February 2018, SSRN, https://ssrn.com/abstract=3118190.

Don't listen to the whingers – London needs immigrants, *Evening Standard*, 23 October 2009, https://www.standard.co.uk/news/dont-listen-to-the-whingers-london-needs-immigrants-6786170.html.

Dymisja wiceminister Pawła Chorążego. Powód? Wypowiedź o imigrantach i repatriantach, *Newsweek*, 14 September 2018, https://www.newsweek.pl/polska/polityka/dymisja-wiceministra-pawla-chorazego-powodem-wypowiedz-o-imigrantach/fexhgh9.

Eatwell R., The rising tide of national populism: we need to talk seriously about immigration, *Open Democracy*, 3 November 2018, https://www.

opendemocracy.net/en/opendemocracyuk/rising-tide-of-national-populism-we-need-to-talk-about-immigration/.

Eatwell R., Goodwin M. (2018): National Populism: The Revolt against Liberal Democracy, London: Pelican Books.

Evans G., Mellon J. (2016): Working Class Votes and Conservative Losses: Solving the UKIP Puzzle, *Parliamentary Affairs*, volume 69, issue 2, pp. 464–479.

First residence permits issued in the EU Member States remain above 3 million in 2017, 25 October 2018, Eurostat, https://ec.europa.eu/eurostat/documents/2995521/9333446/3-25102018-AP-EN.pdf/3fa5fa53-e076-4a5f-8bb5-a8075f639167.

Ford R., Goodwin M. (2010): Angry White Men: Individual and Contextual Predictors of Support for the British National Party, *Political Studies*, volume 58, issue 1, pp. 1–25.

Francis I. (2018): Poland Short of Workers after Exodus to Britain and Germany, *Sky News*, 29 April 2018, https://news.sky.com/story/poland-short-of-workers-after-exodus-to-britain-and-germany-11351969.

Geddes A., Scholten P. (2016): The Politics of Migration and Immigration in Europe, London: Sage.

George Osborne 'regrets' mistakes that led to Brexit vote, *BBC News*, 31 October 2018, https://www.bbc.com/news/uk-politics-46039623.

Gonzalez-Barrera A., Connor P., Around the World, More Say Immigrants are a Strength Than a Burden, Pew Research Center, 14 March 2019, https://www.pewglobal.org/2019/03/14/around-the-world-more-say-immigrants-are-a-strength-than-a-burden/.

Goodhart D. (2013): The British Dream: Successes and Failures of Post-War Immigration, London: Atlantic Books.

Goodwin M., Milazzo C. (2017): Taking Back Control? Investigating the Role of Immigration in the 2016 Vote for Brexit, *The British Journal of Politics and International Relations*, volume 19, issue 3.

Hate Crime, England and Wales 2017/18, Home Office, 16 October 2018, https://assets.publishing.service.gov.uk/government/uploads/system/uploads/attachment_data/file/748598/hate-crime-1718-hosb2018.pdf.

Holden M., "UK vows action after racist attacks on Poles and Muslims in wake of Brexit", *Reuters*, 27 June 2016, https://www.reuters.com/article/us-britain-eu-poland-incidents-idUSKCN0ZD15G

How the UK voted for Brexit, and why, Lord Ashcroft Polls, 4 February 2019, https://lordashcroftpolls.com/2019/02/how-the-uk-voted-on-brexit-and-why-a-refresher/.

Iglicka K. (2014): 'Poland – a Country of Enduring Emigration', in: Felica Medved (ed.), Proliferation of Migration Transition: Selected New EU Member States, Brussels: European Liberal Forum.

Imigracja ze Wschodu, zagrożenie narodu. ONR protestował przeciwko polityce rządu PiS, *Dziennik.pl*, 18 March 2017, https://wiadomosci.dziennik.pl/wydarzenia/zdjecia/545253,1,onr-protest-imigracja-wschod-rzad-pis.html.

Jaroszewicz M. (2018): Migracje z Ukrainy do Polski: Stabilizacja Trendu, Warsaw: Ośrodek Studiów Wschodnich.

Kastner J. (2018): Poland Cracks Door Open for Filipino Workers, *Nikkei Asian Review*, 17 August 2018, https://asia.nikkei.com/Economy/Poland-cracks-door-open-for-Filipino-workers.

Kaufmann E. (2018): Whiteshift: Populism, Immigration and the Future of White Majorities, London: Allen Lane.

Kellner P. (2011): Labour Is Not Just the Party of the Working Class, *YouGov*, 16 May 2011, https://yougov.co.uk/topics/politics/articles-reports/2011/05/16/labour-not-just-party-working-class.

Kiełczewska A., Lewandowski P. (2017): 'Population Ageing and the Labour Supply in Poland up to 2050', in: Piotr Lewandowski and Jan Rutkowski (eds.), Population Ageing, Labour Market and Public Finance in Poland, Warsaw: European Commission Representation in Poland.

Kolanko M. (2016): Morawiecki: Musimy uzupełniać ubytki na rynku pracy. Będę starał się, by nastąpiło zaproszenie kilkuset tysięcy pracowników z Ukrainy, *300 Polityka*, 7 September 2016, http://300polityka.pl/live/2016/09/07/morawiecki-musimy-uzupelniac-ubytki-na-rynku-pracy-bede-staral-sie-by-nastapilo-zaproszenie-kilkuset-tysiecy-pracownikow-z-ukrainy/.

Konstytucja Biznesu do przeglądu w przyszłym roku. Rząd chce ściągnąć więcej pracowników z zagranicy, *Forbes*, 9 August 2018, https://www.forbes.pl/gospodarka/jadwiga-emilewicz-o-konstytucji-biznesu-i-imigracji-zarobkowej-do-polski/tjm1gxd.

Kowalski J.K., Pawluć A. (2018): Nie tylko Ukraińcy. Pracodawcy coraz częściej sięgają po pracowników z egzotycznych krajów, *Dziennik Gazeta Prawna*, 22 February 2018, https://serwisy.gazetaprawna.pl/praca-i-kariera/artykuly/1106234,przybywa-pracownikow-z-egzotycznych-krajow.html.

Makowski M. (2018): "Premier był wściekły". Morawiecki podjął decyzję o zdymisjonowaniu ministra Chorążego. Zaważył wypowiedzi o imigrantach, *Wirtualna Polska*, 14 September 2018, https://opinie.wp.pl/news-wp-premier-byl-wsciekly-morawiecki-podjal-decyzje-o-zdymisjonowaniu-ministra-chorazego-zawazyly-wypowiedzi-o-imigrantach-6295185123436161a.

Mapy i dane statystyczne imigrantów i służb migracyjnych Polski, migracje.gov.pl.

Medved F. (2014): 'Synthesis and Reflections', in Felica Medved (ed.), Proliferation of Migration Transition: Selected New EU Member States, Brussels: European Liberal Forum.

Morawski I. (2018): Rząd przeciwny imigrantom otwiera dla nich szeroko drzwi, *Bankier.pl*, 10 September 2018, https://www.bankier.pl/wiadomosc/Rzad-przeciwny-imigrantom-otwiera-dla-nich-szeroko-drzwi-7613922.html.

Net migration in the UK, Migration Observatory at the University of Oxford, 24 August 2018, https://migrationobservatory.ox.ac.uk/resources/briefings/long-term-international-migration-flows-to-and-from-the-uk/.

New Labour: Because Britain Deserves Better (1997): http://www.labour-party.org.uk/manifestos/1997/1997-labour-manifesto.shtml.

Niemcy również szukają pracowników z Ukrainy do pracy przy produkcji samochodów, *Bankier.pl*, 17 December 2018, https://www.bankier.pl/moto/niemcy-rowniez-szukaja-pracownikow-z-ukrainy-do-pracy-przy-produkcji-samochodow-1942/.

Okólski M., Salt J. (2015): Polish Emigration to the UK after 2004: Why Did So Many Come?, *Central and Eastern European Migration Review*, vol. 3 no. 2, 2015.

Osiecki G. (2018): Rząd otwiera się na imigrantów. Cudzoziemcy pomogą nam załatać demograficzną dziurę, *Dziennik Gazeta Prawna*, 4 June 2018, https://serwisy.gazetaprawna.pl/praca-i-kariera/artykuly/1127723,zmiany-w-zatrudnianiu-cudzoziemcow-imigranci-bez-pozwolen-na-prace.html.

Osiecki G., Chądzyński M. (2018): Nowa polityka migracyjna Polski. Rząd wprowadza ułatwienia w zatrudnianiu cudzoziemców, *Dziennik.pl*, 12 July 2018, https://gospodarka.dziennik.pl/praca/artykuly/577742,polityka-migracyjna-kryzys-praca-cudzoziemcy-filipiny.html.

Outhwaite W. (2019): 'Migration Crisis and 'Brexit'', in: Cecilia Menjivar, Marie Ruiz, Immanuel Ness (eds.), The Oxford Handbook of Migration Crises, Oxford: Oxford University Press.

People in the EU – population projections, Eurostat, December 2017, https://ec.europa.eu/eurostat/statistics-explained/index.php?title=People_in_the_EU_-_population_projections.

Philipson A. (2013): Labour made a 'spectacular mistake' on immigration, admits Jack Straw, *The Telegraph*, 13 November 2013, https://www.telegraph.co.uk/news/uknews/immigration/10445585/Labour-made-a-spectacular-mistake-on-immigration-admits-Jack-Straw.html.

PiS w spocie przypomina deklaracje PO o uchodźcach, *Rzeczpospolita*, 17 October 2018, https://www.rp.pl/

Kraj/181019278-PiS-w-spocie-przypomina-deklaracje-PO-o-uchodzcach.html.

PiS wraca z tematem muzułmańskich imigrantów. Jarosław Kaczyński: Trzeba się bronić!, *Gazeta.pl*, 23 March 2019, http://wiadomosci.gazeta.pl/wiadomosci/7,114884,24577993,pis-wraca-z-tematem-muzulmanskich-imigrantow-jaroslaw-kaczynski.html.

Poland needs immigrants for its labor market: PM Morawiecki, *Poland In*, 2 July 2018, https://polandin.com/37906502/poland-needs-immigrants-for-its-labor-market-pm-morawiecki.

Poland worried Ukrainian workers could choose Germany, *France24*, 9 January 2019, https://www.france24.com/en/20190109-poland-worried-ukrainian-workers-could-choose-germany.

Polska musi i nawet jeśli nie chce to powinna chcieć imigrantów – wiceminister Paweł Chorąży o polityce integracyjnej, *Media Narodowe*, 1 September 2018, https://medianarodowe.com/polska-musi-i-nawet-jesli-nie-chce-to-powinna-chciec-imigrantow-wiceminister-pawel-chorazy-o-polityce-integracyjnej/.

Polskie firmy zainteresowane pracownikami z Wietnamu, *Business Insider Polska*, 10 march 2019, https://businessinsider.com.pl/wiadomosci/pracownicy-z-wietnamu-w-polsce-zamiast-ukraincow/xfqyy4x.

Przez polski rynek pracy „przewija się" ok. 1,2 mln Ukraińców, *Business Insider Polska*, 11 March 2019, https://businessinsider.com.pl/wiadomosci/ukraincy-ilu-pracuje-w-polsce-dane-nbp/r1yf4pe

Rutkowska E. (2019): Na Ukraińców jesteśmy (raczej) otwarci. Najmniej tolerancyjni okazują się jednak najmłodsi, *Dziennik Gazeta Prawna*, 11 March 2019, https://www.gazetaprawna.pl/artykuly/1402299,otwartosc-polakow-na-ukraincow-badanie.html.

Schain M.A. (2018): Shifting Tides: Radica-Right Populism and Immigration Policy in Europe and the United States, Washington, DC: Migration Policy Institute.

Shipman T. (2016): All Out War: The Full Story of How Brexit Sank Britain's Political Class, London: William Collins.

Studenci z Ukrainy. Dlaczego decydują się na studia w Polsce i jaka czeka ich przyszłość?, *Forbes*, 4 November 2018, https://www.forbes.pl/praca/ukrainscy-studenci-w-polsce-raport-kew/k2w36fd.

Transatlatnic Trends: Immigration, 4 February 2011, http://www.gmfus.org/publications/transatlantic-trends-immigration-2010.

UK Public Opinion toward Immigration: Overall Attitudes and Level of Concern, Migration Observatory at the University of Oxford, 7 June 2018, https://migrationobservatory.ox.ac.uk/resources/briefings/

uk-public-opinion-toward-immigration-overall-attitudes-and-level-of-concern/.

UK workers experienced sharpest wage fall of any leading economy, TUC analysis finds, *Trades Union Congress*, 27 July 2016, https://www.tuc.org.uk/news/uk-workers-experienced-sharpest-wage-fall-any-leading-economy-tuc-analysis-finds.

Ukraińcy, won z Polski, Polska dla Polaków. ONR twierdzi, że nie nawołuje do nienawiści, *Gazeta Wyborcza*, 8 September 2018, http://wroclaw.wyborcza.pl/wroclaw/7,35771,23895553,ukraincy-won-z-polski-polska-dla-polakow-onr-twierdzi-ze.html.

Vlandas T. (2016): Xenophobia Britannica? Anti-immigrant attitudes in the UK are among the strongest in Europe, *LSE Brexit Blog*, 21 October 2016, https://blogs.lse.ac.uk/brexit/2016/10/21/xenophobia-britannica-anti-immigrant-attitudes-in-the-uk-are-among-the-strongest-in-europe/.

Warrell H. (2011): Balls admits Labour 'mistakes' on immigration, *Financial Times*, 26 September 2011.

White A. (2018): 'The impact of migration into Poland by non-Poles', in: Anne White, Izabela Grabowska, Paweł Kaczmarczyk and Krystyna Slany (eds.), The Impact of Migration on Poland: EU Mobility and Social Change, London: UCL Press.

Zezwolenia na pracę cudzoziemców w Polsce w 2017 r., Główny Urząd Statystyczny, 12 September 2018, http://stat.gov.pl/obszary-tematyczne/rynek-pracy/opracowania/zezwolenia-na-prace-cudzoziemcow-w-polsce-w-2017-r-,18,1.html.

Ziomek W. (2018): Wzrost wynagrodzeń w 2019. Polska w czołówce, *Money.pl*, 2 December 2018, https://www.money.pl/gospodarka/wiadomosci/artykul/pensje-w-polsce-wzrost-plac,245,0,2423029.html.

Marcin Darmas

Liberal democracy in the country of Jacobins

Abstract: The author begins this text about the condition of liberal democracy in France with a reflection on the ideal of the Republic and the conviction of the elites that France carries universal values and is a reference point. The sense of uniqueness and institutional dogmatism hinder growth make it impossible to implement important institutional reforms and make France unable to adapt to the requirements of globalisation processes. The inheritor of Roman political philosophy based on territorial unity and organisation through law is falling apart under the pressure of the broad migration and 'forgotten archipelagos' that refuse to accept the will of the centre – Paris. The latest yellow vests crisis shows how the 'logic of inheritors' (elites) clashes with the 'logic of the harmed and the humiliated', who have actually been forgotten by the state. However, a sacralised state replacing the Catholic Church, is no longer able to cope with the growing influence of Islam.

Keywords: France, Republic, liberal democracy, Macron, jacobins

On the eleventh of Germinal, in the fifth year of the French Republican Calendar, at six o'clock in the morning, members of the Committee of Public Safety and the Committee of General Security signed an arrest warrant: Georges Danton and his colleagues: Jean-François Delacroix, Camille Desmoulins, Pierre Philippeaux and Jean-Marie Hérault de Séchelles were accused of treason of the Republic. The originator of this idea was obviously Robespierre, who acted in accordance with the revolutionary logic that if Danton avoided the guillotine, heads of all members of both Committees would fall into a wicker basket. It is said that during the meeting on the day preceding the arrest of Danton, Saint-Just, confused for a while, threw his hat into the chimney.[1] Later, making use of Robespierre's notes, he started to draft the warrant that he read in front of the Convention late in the evening. In the long speech that had quite many characteristics of revolutionary speeches, Saint-Just referred to the French *genius* that nobody and nothing could stop, to his unblemished reputation on the international arena, to freedom, fraternity and equality – the values that are more honourable than friendship (Desmoulins was the best man on Robespierre's wedding and his favourite, and Danton was his friend), decency and truth (fabricated accusations of a royalistic plot). The thing more important than the life of

1 L. Madelin (1914): *Danton*, Paris: Hachette, p. 286.

a small number of revolutionaries was the cause (la cause) – the indivisible and eternal Republic that Saint-Just morally canonised. He even said with emphasis that 'the world has been empty since the Roman days'.[2]

These words were said at the end of the prosecution speech; apart for the rhetoric effect, they show the dual drama of the French Revolution. On the one hand, spiritual connection with Roman predecessors was groundlessly indicated and the historical cohesion of France was negated. This was because the revolution became the zero-point, and monarchy, the Church and aristocracy apparently did not exist at all according to this logic. On the other hand, the revolution was treated as an unquestionable dogma. The revolution could not be filled with uncomfortable incompleteness; the revolutionary logic had to be carried out in full, first through the terror of the guillotine and then by establishing highly centralised institutions that were resistant to changes. The narcotic intoxication with Jacobin thinking – something solid as a rock – has survived till today.

The republic as a dogma

In her brochure *A Few Notes about the French Republic*, Chantal Delsol aptly summarised this problem: 'Contrary to democracy, which is based on an anthropological vision – that is, something understood as reality – the republic is based on the ideal. In democracy, it is assumed (rightly or wrongly) that each adult individual is able to decide about his own fate and, consequently, about the common fate. The republic hopes that it will unite the society composed of various groups into a whole. This ideal of unity was well described by Cicero, who stated at the time of the split of the Roman Republic that seeing two peoples in one republic is like seeing two suns instead of one in the sky'.[3] There is no room here for quoting various theses aimed at finding an analogy between the French year 1989 and the Russian year 1917; this has been done dozens of times.[4] Nevertheless, it must be stressed that the French republican ideal slowly changed into a socialist – not to say communist – ideal. Delsol writes that both of them merge and often replace each other[5] After 1848, many working-class environments showed quite strong

2 *Le monde est vide depuis les Romains, Œuvres complètes de Saint-Just,* ed. Charles Vellay, Editions Eugène Factuelle, Paris 1908, vol. II, p. 331.

3 Ch. Delsol (2011): A few notes about the French Republic, in: *Idee republikańskie. Trzy idee,* [*Republican Ideas. Three Ideas*], ed. Wojciech Przybylski, Biblioteka Res Publiki Nowej, Warsaw, p. 17.

4 Such an attempt has recently been made by Tamara Kondratieva (2017): *Bolcheviks et jacobins. Itinéraire des analogies,* Paris: Éditions Payot.

5 Chantal Delsol, *op. cit.*, p. 19.

inclinations to red republicanism. When confronted with the practice of power, utopian republicanism lost its original virtues and became increasingly radical, concentrating power, putting the opposition, the Church, Girondists and aristocracy to the sword and leaving no space for the development of the middle classes.

Before becoming an institution, the republic is located in the circle of the moral ideal: the tradition of political philosophy will specify it as the 'morality of politics'.[6] Thus, being a moral ideal that has never been completely fulfilled, the republic gives rise to and sustains a certain myth, a sacred story showing an example and giving sense. In the days of the 1789 Revolution, the apologetics of the Roman Republic was stressed, which is reflected, for instance, by Saint-Just's prosecution speech. As Furet and Ozouf rightly noticed, the republican idea is also a kind of 'cultural dream': 'in a sense, it reveals the cult of the ancient and seems possible only in times when people were heroes or demigods'.[7]

Revolutionary France adopted an ideal and turned it into a regime. Moreover, there is a danger emerging from the nucleus of existence of the French Republic: the lack of understanding for the surrounding and changing world. This is one thing. The second thing is the assumption that the republic is the only possible way of existence of a political entity. There is a belief that France carries universal values in itself and that, in this way, it has become similar to ancient Athens, which Pericles called the 'teacher of Greece'. The Declaration of the Rights of Man and the Citizen was written in France, to a certain extent, for the whole world. The prologue to the recently published dialogue about institutions of the 5th Republic between the former Prime Minister Édouard Balladur and the journalist Alain Duhamel begins with the statement that 'the philosophy of the Enlightenment and the French Revolution left their mark on [France's – MD] entry into modernity and have become a model for all nations of the world'.[8] We can be outraged at the extremity of this approach. But the fact is that France feels to be, as we can see, a model for the entire globe, that this *sentiment* serves as a key component of its current identity. Consequently, France seems to be

---

6 B. Bourgeois (2000): *La raison moderne et le droit politique,* Paris: Vrin, p. 198.

7 *À certains égards, elles relève du culte des Anciens, et elle semble n'avoir été viable que dans ces temps où les hommes étaient des géants ou des demi-dieux,* M. Ozouf, F. Furet (1993): *Le siècle de l'avènement républicain,* Gallimard, Paris, p. 46.

8 *(…) la philosophie des Lumières, la Révolution française ont marqué son entrée dans le monde moderne, elle est devenue une référence pour tous les peuples,* É. Balladur, A. Duhamel (2017): *Grandeur, déclin et destin de la Ve République. Un dialogue,* Paris: Éditions de l'Observatoire, p. 7.

naturally regarded as a prevailing norm. And the institutions of the republic are the implementation of this norm. Other Western countries were able to adapt their institutions to social dynamics and international changes. France detests confrontation and hides behind its French uniqueness (*exception française*). It is worth remembering when we try to capture the distinctness of the criticism of liberal democracy formulated by French human science.

The permanent crisis

The French Revolution and the crisis resulting from it had a decisive impact on Kant's vision of *modernity*. The philosopher asked at that time: What is happening today? What is the difference between previous crises and the current crisis? What is the nature of the times in which we live and how do we participate in current events? Trying to answer these questions, Kant proposes a new way of perceiving *modernity*: it should be treated not as a historical period, but as an *issue*.[9] The current crisis of liberal democracy goes beyond the meaning of the term understood as *signum temporis* by Kant. *Our* crisis was not announced as the previous ones were, for example, in *Emile, or On Education*, where Rousseau writes about approaching states of crisis and the age of the Revolution.[10] *Our* crisis is a permanent state: 'our present is dominated entirely by *crisis* – to such an extent that it seems to be our soft underbelly, the essence of our times and our whole existence,' writes the political philosopher Myriam Revault d'Allones.[11] The extension of the scope of the concept leads to the obscuring of its meaning in everyday use. Much is said about the crisis of knowledge, the perception of reality, subjective experience, the social and political world. Thus, we should begin by making up for the neglections and return to the etymology of the Greek *krisis* (κρίσις). This word means 'the turning point of an uncertain process that allows us to make both a diagnosis and a forecast in our attempts to overcome crisis'. The Greeks used κρίσις both in Hippocratic medicine and in politics – Thucydides writes that the Peloponnesian War was the biggest crisis 'yet known in history, not only of the Hellenes, but of a large part of the barbarian world – I had almost

9 I. Kant (1784): Beantwortung der Frage: Was ist Aufklärung, *Berlinische Monatsschrift*, Berlin 1784, 2, pp. 481–494.

10 J.J. Rousseau (1979): *Emile, or On Education*, trans. Allan Bloom, New York: Basic Books, 1979.

11 *Notre présent est en effet envahi par la « crise », à tel point que celle-ci paraît le point névralgique, le point crucial de notre époque et de notre existence*, M. Revault d'Allonnes (2012): *Comment la crise vient à la philosophie*, Esprit, Mars-avril, pp. 108–117.

said of mankind'.[12] Theorising about tragedy, Aristotle defines crisis with the use of the term *peripeteia* (*περιπέτεια*), which means 'an unpredictable turn of events contrary to original expectations'.

In all of these cases, in all presented semantic registers of the term *crisis*, making a decision and settling the matter (in favour of one or another party) is of central importance. In modern debates on liberal democracy, it seems that decisions and settlements have been replaced with endless uncertainties concerning reasons, diagnosis and results. Revault d'Allones confirms this assumption in his essay entitled suggestively *Why We Do Not Like Democracy*, answering that this system has become 'for many of us a void, something insignificant and unreasonable, empty talk'.[13] The French philosopher agrees with analyses made by Claude Lefort, who ascertained the lack of the secure position of the rule of democracy in the transcendental sphere, which results in their continuous entanglement in self-legitimising debates.[14] Liberal democracy lacks certainty and points of reference, and conflicts do not cease: 'Devoid of guarantee and ultimate criteria, the democratic human being refers to a multitude of beliefs, opinions and judgements. This leads to the double temptation of generalised relativism (and, consequently, disappointment) or of seeking desperately for a society free of the uproar of divisions, as totalitarian phantasmagoria once proposed'.[15] Revault d'Allones writes that modern democratic existence is based on the process of desubstantialisation (*désubstantialisation*), isolation (*désincarnation*) and disconnection (*déliaison*) of the potential of power. The work of this French philosopher abounds in examples showing the transformation of the former policy based on coherence and authority into a state of permanent anxiety (*inquiétude*), ailments (*malaise*) and disillusionment (*déception*). In order to cope with the lack of strong legitimisation, liberal democracy uses two kinds of remedies. On

12 Thucydides, *History of the Peloponnesian War*, trans. Richard Crawley, http://www.documentacatholicaomnia.eu/03d/-460_400,_Thucydites,_History_Of_The_Peloponnesian_War,_EN.pdf

13 *Pour beaucoup d'entre nous, elle n'est aujourd'hui que vacuité, insignifiance, inconsistance et discours creux*, M. Revault d'Allones (2010): *Pourquoi nous n'aimons pas la démocratie*, Paris: Le Seuil, p. 7.

14 C. Lefort (1981): *L'invention démocratique*, Paris: Fayard.

15 *L'homme démocratique – privé de garanties et de critères ultimes – est ainsi renvoyé à la multiplicité des croyances, des opinions, des jugements. D'où la double tentation d'un relativisme généralisé (et donc d'une désaffection) ou de la recherche éperdue d'une société délivrée des affres de la division, comme le proposait en son temps la fantasmatique totalitaire*, M. Revault d'Allones, *op. cit.*, p. 9.

the one hand, it tries to universalise the ideology of liberal capitalism; on the other hand, it rehabilitates the discourse of "civilisation wars" and, therefore, looks for enemies, initiates interventions far from its borders in places where it considers democracy to be endangered in order to distract general attention from its own flaws and shortcomings.

The rehabilitation of trust

In his recently published book *A Good Government* (because of the ambiguity of the French word *gouvernance*, the title might as well be translated as *Good Rule*), Pierre Rosanvallon confirms to quite a significant extent the diagnosis of the disease of liberal democracy that was made both by Chantal Delsol and by Claude Lefort and Myriam Revault d'Allones. According to Delsol, only departure from the Jacobinian logic of the centralised state can alleviate the pain, and Revault d'Allonnes thinks that this can done by resigning from the economic paradigm (*paradigme économique*) that transforms the state into an enterprise. Claude Lefort shows how the legitimisation of liberal democracy quickly becomes outdated and, therefore, is questioned.

Rosanvallon arrives at quite similar conclusions: 'We can say that our governments are democratic, although we are not ruled democratically. This huge dissatisfaction stimulates present-day disillusionments and chaos'.[16] And he adds that creating the democracy of *trust (confiance)* and *assimilation (appropriation)* as soon as possible becomes a burning issue. In his opinion, societies must redefine their attitude to democracy, which has gradually become detached from them. It is necessary to implement a system that would allow citizens to 'practice directly the democratic functions that have been monopolised by the parliamentary regime so far'.[17] The explanation is simple: liberal democracy has trenched a moat between the political elites and the society. Rosanvallon puts the blame for this situation on the 'spectre of Caesarism' (*le spectre du césarisme*) that left an indelible mark on the presidential system of the Fifth Republic. It is time to fill up this trench by increasing the level of civic activity: hence the

16 *Nos régimes peuvent être dits démocratiques, mais nous ne sommes pas gouvernés démocratiquement. C'est le grand hiatus qui nourrit le désenchantement et le désarroi contemporains,* P. Rosanvallon (2015): *Le bon gouvernement,* Paris: Le Seuil, p. 9.

17 *... mis en œuvre [qui] permettrait aux citoyens d'exercer plus directement des fonctions démocratiques qui ont longtemps été accaparées par le seul pouvoir parlementaire, ibidem*, p. 22.

Frenchman's initiative presented on the pages of *The Parliament of the Invisible*.[18] In his opinion, it is necessary to shed a new light into the 'depths of society' onto those who feel abandoned, forgotten, misunderstood and who are "invisible" because they do not find recognition and have no tools to become organised and visible. This unshaped mass, which constitutes the lion's share of society, draws the strength of its contestation from disillusionment that leads to its gradual detachment from state institutions and media messages. This, in turn, gives rise to dispersed and undefined protest movements. Contrary to what might be thought, the "invisible" belong not only to pauperised classes; as Rosanvallon writes, this initiative refers to all social layers. The *Telling Life* project is to incline these people to depart from *invisibility* by means of the solidarity movement within the scope of global society. The *parliament* "granted" to the invisible is to create a platform that would allow people to express their opinions and needs.

As a remedy to the crisis of the representation, the French political scientist proposes that nations play the role of a triple guard. He identifies the "vigilant nation" (*peuple vigilant*), „veto nation" (*peuple veto*) and „nation-judge" (*peuple juge*). At the same time, Rosanvallon attacks politicians who fall very short of the types of ideal rulers: politics is for them neither a vocation in the Weberian sense (*politique par vocation*) nor the space of a man of trust (*l'homme de confiance*). In the first case, the Weberian politician by vocation, including a professional politician, was a response to the dilettante attitude of European officials and to affairs in which American politicians are involved. In the second case, the aim is to revive the model of *trustee* – a figure of essential importance for the characteristics of "good government".

Pierre Rosanvallon's recipe is simple. Before nations turn into a globalised mass of liberal democracies, it is necessary to shorten the distance between the rulers and the ruled and to recreate "straight talk" (*le parler vrai*) and political vocation.

When observing yellow-jacket protests, it is impossible to disagree with Rosanvallon's analysis. The French political system does not favour debates and the reduction of the *distance* between central power and small regional communities. Macron consistently frustrates the general discussion and prevents the use of the referendum – a mechanism that was introduced into the constitution by De Gaulle. There are two reasons for this: firstly, it would be very difficult to formulate a question that the Frenchmen would have to answer.

18 P. Rosanvallon (2014): *Le parlement des invisibles. Manifeste pour „raconter la vie"*, Paris: Le Seuil.

Secondly, the referendum might definitely put an end to Macron's presidency. Its democratic legitimacy is poor (support from 24 % in the first round of the election) and protests has only exposed this weakness. In these protests, the France of the Girondists and the France of the province has woken up. The yellow-jacket protest is actually the rebirth of two divisions: the Jacobins' option (centralisation) versus the Girondists' option (the sovereignty of individual provinces, decentralisation). It is also an amorphous class rebellion, the rage of the 'harmed and the humiliated', who feel lost in the globalisation logic against the *dominating* elites. Attempts to solve the social problem by President Macron resemble a dialogue of the deaf.

The writer's voice

Michel Houellebecq's prose can be regarded as the reflection of the current condition of the French society and the crisis of liberal democracy, particularly on the moral level. Although he describes the replacement of the elites of the Fifth Republic with Islamists in *Submission*,[19] it is a veiled and metaphoric message. Using Houellebecq's *vocabularium*, the Frenchmen were so desperate and *dispirited* that they voted for a big change – an *experiment* – in the latest presidential and parliamentary elections. The writer captured a certain mechanism of electoral behaviours that occurs increasingly often in modern liberal democracies. The French society is tired of old political elites – the aristocracy that it has watched for the last 30 years – and has replaced them. The tolerance threshold for *heirs* who fill up schools of administration and are later harnessed to work in Republican institutions has been exceeded. In this situation, the laws described by Pierre Bourdieu and Jean-Claude Passeron cease to apply.[20] Shortly before the student rebellions of 1968, these sociologists questioned the widespread opinions that university studies in France are a space of social mobility. The access of a larger number of young people to universities, mainly humanities and art faculties, was not tantamount to the real democratisation of the academic system. Social descent has always been a significant criterion in the explanation of school successes and failures. Students' protests at the end of the 1960s were more than a simple rebellion against the authorities; they resulted in asking a question about the social function being fulfilled by school and, consequently,

---

19 M. Houellebecq (2015): *Submission*, trans. Lorin Stein; Farrar, Straus and Giroux.

20 P. Bourdieu, J.-C. Passeron (1964): *Les Héritiers*, Paris: Les Éditions de Minuits; P. Bourdieu (1989): *La noblesse d'États. Grandes écoles et esprit de corps*, Paris: Les Éditions de Minuits.

society. In order to analyse the functioning of the current society and the role of school, Bourdieu introduced the concept of 'reproduction': it turned out that former protesters had become modern political elites. Roughly speaking, they come from affluent families, and their parents often attended the same schools of administration.

Liberal democracy in the French version questions this order and shows how unpredictable the choices of the electorate can be. As in Houellebecq's works, the French elites seem to say that they would elect the biggest *wastrel* in order to not let Le Pen win. Macron certainly does not resemble Houellebecq's wastrel – Mohammed Ben Abbes from *Submission*, but he is a big unknown – an electoral *experiment*. During his campaign, he skilfully manoeuvred between programs of traditional political families and did not care much about ideological belonging, emphasising the civil character of his movement. *Nota bene*, this occurred for the first time in the history of the Fifth Republic.

The central concept of Houellebecq's mutation is "metaphysical mutation". 'Once a metaphysical mutation has arisen, it tends to move inexorably toward its logical conclusion. Heedlessly, it sweeps away economic and political systems, ethical considerations and social structures'[21] and establishes a new order that prevents the individual from functioning as an active social subject. As Houellebecq writes, traditional social bonds based on emotions, small family, neighbourhood and self-government communities are being replaced with intellectual bonds parcelled out in impersonal cities according to the laws of the liberal market. Thus, faced with advancing changes, the individual ceases to be a subject and becomes an object – a cog in the liberal manufacture system based on metric differentiation. Of course, he does not lose the sense of his decision-making independence, as the manufacture system tries to provide him with conditions for attaining apparent happiness. The sense of 'non-controlled individualism' is constantly reinforced. This means that the individual still feeds himself with the form of "happiness" and "normality" imposed from above while believing in the freedom of choice in these categories. Persisting in this sheer lie, he participates in the self-enslavement process.

According to Houellebecq, narcotic intoxication with rationality is still prevalent in liberal democracies (Marcon in the speech inaugurating his presidency: 'France cannot turn its back on the Enlightenment …'). The French writer emphasises that rational decisions may bring results contrary to expectations. Moreover, rationality may lead to the revival of the original state of *war of*

21 M. Houellebecq (2000): *Atomised*, trans. Frank Wynne, London: Heinemann, p. 4.

everyone against all. It is characterised by permanent anxiety and the split that inevitably leads to a conflict.

Take, for example, the sexual sphere; according to Houellebecq, it has been subject to rational processes since the early 1950s and today it functions as a system of differentiation of people in the same way that money does. The above-mentioned rationalisation is a simple principle: it is based entirely on the numerical system of profits and losses. In the reality of consumer society, it is based on 'gaining maximum satisfaction for a specified price'. Thus, the factors that are purely functional and utilitarian for the customer and profitable for the producer and the seller really count here. In this arrangement, what is "advantageous" (or "profitable"), what is consequently "pleasant" and what is eventually "the most pleasant", becomes the most important thing for all social actors. This gradation leads to tragic anthropological consequences: 'To increase desire to the highest degree possible along with increasingly difficult fulfilment is the basic principle on which the civilisation of the West is based,' writes Houellebecq in *The Possibility of an Island.* He marks very precisely the moment of expiration of the traditional social model in France that initiated the stupefying drive towards self-destruction: 'On 14 December 1967 the government passed the Neuwirth Act on contraception at its first reading. … It was this which offered a whole section of society access to the sexual revolution, which, until then, had been reserved for professionals, artists and senior management – and some small businessmen. It is interesting to note that the "sexual revolution" is usually portrayed as a communal utopia, whereas in fact it was simply another stage in the rise of the individual. As the lovely phrase "hearth and home" suggests, the couple and the family were to be the last bastion of primitive communism in a liberal society. The sexual revolution was to destroy the last unit separating the individual from the market. The destruction continues to this day.'[22]

The legalisation of contraceptives subordinated such an intimate sphere of human existence as sexuality to the rules of the liberal economic market. This example shows us the incredible expansive power of the rational principle. The French writer also shows how diametrically the results of this rationality differ from original intentions. As Houellebecq mentioned, legalisation was supposed to make the 'dream of the community' come true; instead, however, it has stimulated individualism till today. Legalisation fails to integrate society – just the opposite: legalisation atomises, blows up and pluralises demands and desires endlessly. As Archbishop Życiński wrote, it 'casts the individual towards pluralism'. At

22 M. Houellebecq, *Atomised, op. cit.*, p. 135.

the same time, it turns the individual into an object. Demands become increasingly commercialised, too. This danger is present also in analyses of the author of Atomised; the human being becomes the object of commercialised demands.

Macron in the liberal domain

If we assume that one of the reasons of the current crisis of liberal democracy is the practising of *post-politics*, the election of Emmanuel Macron as President of the French Republic might lead us to hardly optimistic conclusions. Macron is the emanation of this *post-politics*.[23] The French presidential election was won by a man who was not associated with any party – a marketing product that turned the political movement and the Élysée Palace into a *start-up*. The charm of modernity in his person triumphed over tradition. Macron is an ideological chimera – partly a liberal, partly a socialist,[24] who sank the Socialist party and posed a serious threat to the existence of the Gaullist right wing. Although he is a poor speaker and a second-rate polemicist, he has won the trust of electors; he charmed them with his poster-happy marriage of a teacher and a secondary school pupil, triumphed in the role of a psychotherapist of masses who was not concerned about the disastrous level of territorial cohesion of the state and did not mention bombs ticking in the suburbs of Paris, Marseilles, Toulouse, Lille, Rennes, Strasbourg, Clermond-Ferrand. He succeeded thanks to his countless resources of optimism and vitality supported by pharmaceutical drugs (the Frenchmen remain the biggest consumers of psychotropic drugs in the European Union). Contrary to warning signs about the increase of Islamic movements (in 2004, the *Report on Symbols and Manifestations of Religious Belonging in Schools* was published,[25] in which the rising problem of new Muslim converts was shown without any doubt), the secular France won. Watching the discourse on Muslims, one cannot help but wonder at many contradictions and signs of hypocrisy.

---

23 P. Kusiak (2011): *Postpolityka. W poszukiwaniu istoty zjawiska* [*Post-politics. In Search of the Essence of the Phenomenon*], Colloqium Wydziału Nauk Humanistycznych i Społecznych, III/2011, p. 160. Paweł Kusiak defines *postpolitics* as the 'separation of power and politics. It is to serve as the result of transferring the competences of power from the level of national states to supranational bodies').

24 *Ibid.* Kusiak also refers to postpolitics as 'unideologised politics'.

25 *Les signes et manifestations d'appartenance religieuses dans les établissements scolaires*, Rapport présenté par Jean-Pierre Obin, Juin 2004, n. 2004–115, http://media.education.gouv.fr/file/02/6/6026.pdf (date of access: 10.05.2018).

In contradiction to other political systems – for example, federalism, which accepts multiculturalism – republicanism promotes integration. It must be surprising that the country where the Declaration of the Rights of Man and the Citizen does not react to signs of anti-Semitism and aggressive patriarchal culture among victims of history – persons coming from former colonies. In this case, psychologising replaces thinking for the Frenchmen. The elites want to speak about poverty and sexual emptiness that cause this situation than the different formation of children in mosques and Muslim families. Anti-Semitism is fought against on all fronts of the ideological battle, although actions being undertaken do not cover peripheral Paris. In his article published by *Le Monde* on 22 November 2001, Robert Rodeker was highly surprised that a country moved so much by the dismantling of communism could replace his own proletariat with Muslims.

It seems that the electoral process lasts unceasingly in the French version of liberal democracy. The Frenchmen were summoned to vote for the candidate of the Socialist Party in the general election twice – in the first and second round. The Republicans felt the hunger for democracy, too (two rounds again). This already means four. Then there was a breakneck campaign that lasted almost one year. A countless number of meetings, television and radio debates, forecasts and weekly polls. And later there were also elections to the National Assembly and the Senate. In 2017, the Frenchmen went to the ballot box eight times.

The media machine and Hollande's heritage

By exposing his presence continuously in the reality of the media, he created a new quality in present-day French politics. He brought about an endless plebiscite where he is the main subject. Each of his actions requires prior legitimisation of the established image. After the exhaustion of the potential of the given image on the time *continuum*, Macron replaces it with a new one, which is adapted to the current situation. It is impossible not to use Baudrillard's hyperbole: a politician casts off the dead skin (to the *cemetery of symbols*) and puts on a new one.[26] Thus, the modern politician has strictly defined fields of action: he must be able to present a good story that will appeal to the imagination of all citizens. In our media reality, it is the viewers who decide what is true, what is false, what is virtual and what is real. Reality has become a stage on which actors present their exceptional

26 J. Baudrillard (1993): *Symbolic Exchange and Death*, trans. Ian Grant, London: Sage Publications.

traits; following the path indicated by Christian Salmon, the audience decides which performance was more credible (not necessarily authentic) and closer to the truth in their opinion.[27] The researcher of the CNRS (Centre national de la recherche scientifique, National Research Centre) writes: 'in politics, there is no confrontation of programs and ideologies any more; what emerges there, is ghosts that convince us about their own existence … We participate in a process that occurs beyond language, in an unknown reality, no vocabulary has been created for its presentation yet'.[28]

Another function was fulfilled by ancient drama; as we remember, it was a didactic work and its significance was determined by its impact on spectators. If a theatre show could incline the recipient towards self-purification, this meant success. In present-day times, explains Salmon, the spectator is expected to impose a relevant stance upon the actor. The roles have reversed. In many respects, Macron's tale slightly resembles the one presented by Nicolas Sarkozy ten years earlier. It is, on the one hand, the narration of a golden boy who is not involved in political games, on the other hand, a providential man aware of his prerogatives who must reform France.

The election was influenced by the five numbers that reflected best Hollande's presidency and what the Frenchmen call French "impossibilism"[29]: the impossibility to abandon the 'welfare state', with the administration showing a Gargantuan appetite:

- economic growth: 1.5 %
- unemployment: 10 %
- 5.6 million civil servants,
- average per cent of fiscal collections: 45.6 %
- trade deficit: 48 billion EUR.

---

27 Ch. Salmon (2007): *Verbicide. Du bon usage des cerveaux humains disponibles*, Paris: Babel.

28 *La politique n'oppose plus des programmes et des idéologies, mais des fantômes qui cherchent à nous convaincre de leur réalité (…) Ce qui arrive se passe ailleurs à l'extérieur du langage, dans une réalité incognita, qui n'a pas encore forgé son vocabulaire*, Ch. Salmon, *op. cit.*, p. 11.

29 F.-O. Giesbert, *La tragédie du président. Scènes de la vie politique (1986–2006)*, Flammarion, Paris 2006.

De-Bolshevisation of France

The nature of reforms announced by Macron largely differs from his socialist background. During the celebrations of Victory Day on 8 May 2018, a World War II veteran addressed the President in an unusual and harsh tone: 'Please allow me to say that you should be firm towards all those political leftists who want to produce manure'.[30] Slightly confused, the President said: 'Do not worry and watch my actions carefully. I will not comment upon your words. Everyone has the right to speak, but … Order is necessary!'.[31]

Macron undertakes something that is called 'de-Bolshevisation', i.e., relieving of the public administration, by some French right-wing commentators and thinkers. According to this logic, French technocracy is a genuine daughter of communism.

The President of France presents his policy as a balance between protection and modernisation. Both the first and second element are to be introduced simultaneously. In the middle of the presidency, Marcel Gauchet notices that the second one definitely prevails.[32] Prime Minister Edouard Philippe represents the same line as President Macron does: 'These reforms are ambitious, balanced and fair. And France will still be a country of social rights'.[33] So much for declarations …

One of Macron's bigger reforms concerns the Labour Law Code. Its philosophy can be summarised as follows: to liquidate intermediaries between the employee and the employee, i.e., trade unions and labour courts. Pursuant to the new act, employers in small and medium-sized enterprises will have the right to dismiss an employee without negotiations with important trade unions. Macron

---

30 *Si je peux me permettre, soyez très ferme avec tous ces gauchos de la politique qui ne veulent que foutre la merde!*, on the basis of coverage in RTL Radio, http://www.rtl.fr/actu/politique/un-veteran-a-macron-soyez-tres-ferme-avec-tous-ces-gauchos-7793313155 (date of access: 10.05.2018).

31 *Ne vous inquiétez pas, regardez moi faire. Je ne commenterai pas ce que vous avez dit, mais… Il faut que tout le monde puisse s'exprimer mais… Il faut qu'il y ait un peu d'ordre*, on the basis of coverage in RTL Radio, http://www.rtl.fr/actu/politique/un-veteran-a-macron-soyez-tres-ferme-avec-tous-ces-gauchos-7793313155 (date of access: 10.05.2018).

32 http://premium.lefigaro.fr/vox/politique/2018/05/11/31001-20180511ARTFIG00014-marcel-gauchet-l-article-un-du-macronisme-c-est-l-europeisme.php (date of access: 15.05.2018).

33 https://www.sudouest.fr/2017/08/31/code-du-travail-edouard-philippe-defend-une-reforme-ambitieuse-equilibree-et-juste-3737167-710.php (date of access: 15.05.2018).

and Philippe's government also want to restrict the possibility of contesting personnel decisions to labour courts. In addition, severance pays for employees will be reduced (from six to three) in the case of two-year length of service. Incidentally, the language of the executive is characteristic here. The president and the prime minister speak about 'transformation' rather than 'reform' of the labour market. They use managerial rather than political language. This is because 'reform' has extremely pejorative connotations in France. The key word of this 'transformation' is *time*. The aim is to reduce as much as possible the stage of negotiations between the parties concerning the dismissal of an employee. Another key word is *trade unions*. The government wants to reduce the power of CGT and CFDT in enterprises. At the same time, changes are going to be introduced in lengths of services on the basis of the project of the Ministry of Labour led by Muriel Pénicaud, which are to make it easier for young people from the age group of 16–25 to enter the labour market and to compete.

The second reform, which is connected with state railways, is to be introduced on the basis of a ministerial decree. The president wants to act quickly and consults trade unions, but without debates in the National Assembly. This is because the SNCF carrier struggles with huge difficulties and is criticised by the European Union. *The future of rail transport* – a report submitted to Prime Minister Edouard Philippe on 15 February 2018 – leaves no doubt: the French railway is becoming unprofitable and, most importantly, dangerous for economy.[34] The author of the document – Jean-Cyril Spinetta – proposes a range of changes. Firstly, he suggests the liquidation of 45 % of unprofitable regional connections, which are used only in 2 %. Secondly, due to urges from Brussels, he proposes the fast opening of the French market to competitors by 2019. In addition, the government intends to liquidate the "exceptional" status of the railwayman's profession (140,000 employees are beneficiaries of permanent employment guarantee, are entitled to retire at the age of 50 and 55 years and to use charge-free medical services and an "automatic" career path). In return, the government will liquidate the debt of SNCF, which currently amounts to 46.6 billion EUR.

The third reform, prepared by the Minister of Treasury Gérald Darmanin, covers social grants and is to bring savings in the amount of 25 billion EUR. The general idea? Social welfare is too generous and paid out to an excessively wide group of recipients. In order to reduce the scope of beneficiaries, the budget

34 https://www.ecologique-solidaire.gouv.fr/sites/default/files/2018.02.15_Rapport-Avenir-du-transport-ferroviaire.pdf (date of access: 15.05.2018).

directorate proposes, for example, taking seniors' affluence into account in the calculation of personalised autonomous benefit (APA) or 'family transfers' in favour of students applying for APL (Aide personnalisée au logement, Personalised housing aid). When granting scholarships on the basis of social criteria, it would be necessary to 'reinforce the control of presence' of pupils using them. Delicately speaking, these are not the projects that would enable a "social breakthrough" about which the members of Parliament of the ruling majority speak.

While previous reforms were not seriously discussed by members of Parliament representing En Marche!, the reform of migration law made a few members of Parliament leave the party of the ruling president. Why is it controversial? Because of the toughening of this law. One of the primary and most controversial changes regarding the amendment of the act is the issue of detention of foreigners before their expulsion from the French Republic. Article 16 prolongs the period of detention of foreigners waiting for expulsion from 45 to 90 days. The government proposed 135 days. According to the left-wing opposition, including LFI (La France insoumise, Undefeated France), this article would lead to transformation of 'detention into real prison'. During the debate in the National Assembly, Danièle Obono – member of Parliament from LFI – said: 'We imprison the migrants that we consider to be criminals'. There are plans to keep children in detention centres, too. The act gives also the possibility to grant a four-year residence permit to persons applying for asylum; such a permit would facilitate the procedure for obtaining a permanent residence permit and prolong the existing period of residence.

Currently the pace of reforms proposed by Macron has considerably slowed down. This is obviously the aftermath of the yellow-jacket crisis. Called turgidly "national debate", social consultations being conducted by the government and the president have not resulted in the unblocking of the change policy so far. Moreover, as indicated above, they restrict the political legitimisation of Macron himself. In other words, they show that this legitimisation has been very weak since the beginning of his presidency.

Adapting France

To what? To modern times. 'France is an old country,' said Dominique de Villepin in the UN when objecting to the American intervention in Iraq after the September attacks. Modern times mean globalisation, and globalisation is liberalism. If this is so, Macron embodies this change almost perfectly. He is young, enterprising, devoid of complexes and likes referring to the language of economy and Anglo-Saxon pragmatism.

In his short essay *A New Government*,[35] published shortly after the presidential elections, Régis Debray describes the victory of Macron as the triumph of the neo-Protestant spirit. Its ingredients include: 1/ 'apotheosis of the market' (money as the rational rule of the social environment); 2/ 'diversity, pluralism and openness' (using the example of the United States, Debray shows the figure of 'pastor' dominating on the other side of the Atlantic: ambiguous, colourful and without state control); 3/ 'population transfer' (the Protestant is a world vagabond, pitches his tent wherever he wants and willingly accepts migrants, his fellow wanderers; he is flexible and can settle anywhere) 4/ 'distance' (Debray calls neo-Protestantism the 'madness of transparency', Catholicism is the cultivation of a remote *distance*, a secret, neo-Protestants open up and cultivate openness to emotions and directness). If Régis Debray stresses the importance of the cult of transparency (materialised in the act regarding the moralisation of political life – the first one voted down by the new government), he recognises a trace of neo-Protestantism in it and discovers American inspiration. Also other political actions taken by Macron met with favourable response in Protestant environments. Such was the case of his attitude to the acceptance of migrants and his support of Angela Merkel's actions. We know that a large part of the Protestant community is very sensitive to these subjects, which is proved, for instance, by the activity of Cimade – a non-governmental organisation with a Protestant origin.

Debray's idea is a stimulus for further considerations. Some structural characteristics of *Macronism* are really connected with Protestant culture. After all, the new president was a faithful follower of Paul Ricœur – a thinker openly declaring Protestant faith. We must also notice, like the philosopher Olivier Abel, that *Macronism* puts the individual in the centre. As *entrepreneurs*, all are encouraged to develop their skills and capabilities. Here we can see a parallel to Max Weber's idea of the relationship between Protestantism and the spirit of capitalism. We find here the praise of individual economic success, which seems completely justified in Protestant culture, whereas Catholic tradition approaches money with much more distance. Another thought that we can notice in Macron's victory is that individual success will improve the condition of the entire country.

The state – the French *Etat* – is a product of Catholic monarchy. As Debray writes, Macron attempts to dismantle the *Etat*: 'Within the scope of the national

35 R. Debray (2017): *Le nouveau pouvoir*, Paris: Cerf.

start-up, talented people move from private to public institutions, and their decisions on transfer are not free of abnegation. In this mental universe, the state is dirty, bureaucratic and old-fashioned. Civil society – the land does not lie, like the country in 1940 – is pure, dynamic and prestigious'.[36] Debray writes that people sitting in the benches of Edouard Philippe's government include founders of big enterprises (Infogammes and Robopolis), leaders of distribution and consulting companies and manufacturers of electronic composites. Debray adds that Macron clearly declares his intentions and the state will become a well-managed enterprise.

Nevertheless, the author of *A New Government* forgets that the current president of France makes use of prerogatives assigned to them by the Fifth Republic with truly monarchic freedom, so he is more than an administrator – he is a *superpresident* who says to employees-fellow citizens: 'do it yourself'.

The Islamic republic

The presidential campaign A.D. 2017 abounded in unexpected situations. Certain candidates were "wiped out" (maybe as a result of the impact of the toxic Internet domain of the Russian media, such as Russia Today). First, Alain Juppe's pride led to his downfall. Then the case of illegal employment of François Fillon's wife and sponsored suits saw the light of day. The ultimate downfall of Nicolas Sarkozy took place. Not to mention the abnegation of François Hollande, who gave farewell kisses of death to Benoît Hamon or Manuel Valls. Maybe he also endangered the existence of the Socialist Party.

One year before the election one could feel that everything has already been decided. The winner of the primary election on the right wing was supposed to compete with Marine le Pen – the candidate of the National Front. For the first time in the history of the Fifth Republic, they admitted competing for the second place openly and frankly. According to the philosopher Michel Onfray, Marine le Pen became a *product* of French politics so that it would be possible to defeat her.

Nothing was predictable, and the situation changed like in a kaleidoscope. However, one could be sure that Islam and terrorist threats would become important topics in this campaign. But this did not happen, too. That was strange if

---

36 Dans le cadre d'une start-up, le talent court du prive au public, ce qui ne va pas sans abnégation. Dans cet univers mental, l'Etat c'est sale, bureaucratique et ringard. La société civile – le terrain ne ment pas, comme la terre en 1940 – c'est propre, dynamique et prestigieux, R. Debray, *Le nouveau…*, *op. cit.*, p. 18.

we consider the sensitivity of this literary nation to dramatic events and literary comments. Here, I obviously mean *Submission* by Michel Houellebecq. I am not going to recall this novel here. It was published in Polish translation, and many reviews and comments on the latest best-seller of the author of *Atomised* have been made. It is, however, worth mentioning Boualem Sansal's novel entitled *2084*. The author of this book depicts an apocalyptic vision of the end of the Republic. It is a story about the vast Abistan empire, which took its name from the prophet Abi. It is a totalitarian regime where imprisonments, prohibitions and silent strangulations are commonplace. All people have to obey the rules of the religion of the god Yölah. Abistan's regime is based on amnesia and submission to one god. As in Orwell's works, personal thoughts are forbidden, and the omnipresent supervision system helps to discover the deviating ideas and actions of individuals. Officially unanimous people live in happiness and profess faith without asking unnecessary questions. Expressing doubts is forbidden. The dictatorial system is governed by perfectly codified rules and rituals. It functions without history. Only one man, the main protagonist – Ati, begins to have doubts. He learns about the existence of renegades living in ghettos, without the dictate of state religion. Sansal never uses the word 'Islam'. But this word does not even have to be used.

2084 describes an anti-utopia in Orwellian style. Of course, there is little chance that this scenario will really happen. It is true, however, that France is grappling with serious problems connected with its territorial cohesiveness. This is shown clearly by the migrant crisis in Majotta in 2017, not to mention the situation in the suburbs of big metropolises. As Pascal Bruckner says: 'France has found itself in the trap of political correctness, like the United States. Muslims are treated almost automatically as victims of the colonial past who require constant protection'.[37] And he adds: 'In many places of France, the applicable rules are a strange mixture of French law and Muslim Sharia law. This will be the most important task of the new president. … To regain control of the entire territory of France, because there are districts dominated by Muslims today. This is actually the last moment. I am really afraid that France is standing on the edge of the civil war'.[38]

37 P. Bruckner (2017): in: Marcin Darmas, Agaton Koziński, *Jarzmo wielkości Francji* [*Shackles of the Greatness of France*], Warsaw: Wydawnictwo Akademickie Dialog, p. 18.

38 M. Darmas, Agaton Koziński, *Jarzmo…*, *op. cit.*, p. 20.

Conclusion

Most reflections contained in De Gaulle's memoirs concern France, or actually what France is and, speaking in lofty words, what tasks it has to perform for the entire humanity. For the general, the land on the Loire and the Seine was destined – De Gaulle uses characteristic emphasis here – for extraordinary things. Its grandeur should cover the entire globe and inspire the world. Already in the first sentences of his memoirs, the founder of the Fifth Republic kicks off on a high note: 'My emotional side has a tendency to imagine France as a princess in a fairy tale or Madonna on frescos, dedicated to an exalted and exceptional destiny. I instinctively feel that the Providence created her either for full success, or for exemplary misfortunes. If, in spite of this, mediocrity is present in her actions, it strikes me as an absurd anomaly. However, the positive side of my intellect assures me that France is not herself as long as she is not in the first row'.[39]

These reflections show how difficult it is to exorcise and supersede such thinking in France. The sense of uniqueness and institutional dogmatism hinder growth, make it impossible to implement important institutional reforms and make France unable to adapt to the requirements of globalisation processes. The inheritor of Roman political philosophy based on territorial unity and organisation through law is falling apart under the pressure of the broad migration and 'forgotten archipelagos' that refuse to accept the will of the centre – Paris. The latest yellow-jacket crisis shows, as in a lens, how the 'logic of inheritors' clashes with the 'logic of the harmed and the humiliated', who have actually been forgotten by the state. *Etat sacré,* a sacralised state replacing the Catholic Church, is no longer able to cope under the pressure of galloping Islam.

And, finally, one more thing. Pascal Bruckner shows in *The Tyranny of Guilt: An Essay on Western Masochism*[40] how the distorted interpretation of original sin from the Enlightenment period becomes a poison that pollutes Western thinking. The "princess" of De Gaulle begins to be ashamed of herself, her colonial past and former errors; she stands in front of the mirror and disregards herself. We deal with a paralysing paradox here. On the one hand, the "princess" identifies with the dynastic heritage and would like to have a guarantee that her descendants will remain on the throne, and on the other hand, she resents her ancestors for having won their power with iron and having paid for it with their blood in the past.

39 Ch. de Gaulle (1955): *War Memoirs: Call to Honour, 1940–1942,* trans. Jonathan Griffin, London: Collins, vol. 1.

40 P. Bruckner, *The Tyranny of Guilt: An Essay on Western Masochism,* trans. Steven Rendall, Princeton University Press, 2010.

References

Balladur É., Duhamel A. (2017): *Grandeur, déclin et destin de la Ve République. Un dialogue*, Paris: Éditions de l'Observatoire.

Baudrillard J. (1993): *Symbolic Exchange and Death*, London: Sage Publications.

Bourdieu P. (1989): *La noblesse d'États. Grandes écoles et esprit de corps*, Paris: Les Éditions de Minuits.

Bourdieu P., Passeron J.-C. (1964): *Les Héritiers*, Paris: Les Éditions de Minuits.

Bourgeois B. (2000): *La raison moderne et le droit politique*, Paris: Vrin.

Bruckner P. (2010): *The Tyranny of Guilt: An Essay on Western Masochism*, Princeton: Princeton University Press, 2010.

Darmas M., Koziński A. (2017): *Jarzmo wielkości Francji [Shackles of the Greatness of France]*, Warsaw: Wydawnictwo Akademickie Dialog.

de Gaulle Ch. (1955): *War Memoirs: Call to Honour, 1940–1942*, London: Collins, vol. 1.

Debray R. (2017): *Le nouveau pouvoir*, Paris: Cerf, Paris 2017.

Delsol Ch. (2011): A few notes about the French Republic, in: *Idee republikańskie. Trzy idee, [Republican Ideas. Three Ideas]*, ed. Wojciech Przybylski, Warsaw: Biblioteka Res Publiki Nowej.

Giesbert F.-O. (2006): *La tragédie du président. Scènes de la vie politique (1986–2006)*, Paris: Flammarion.

Houellebecq M. (2000): *Atomised*, London: Heinemann.

Houellebecq M. (2015): *Submission*, New York: Farrar, Straus and Giroux.

Kant I. (1784): Beantwortung der Frage: Was ist Aufklärung, *Berlinische Monatsschrift*, Berlin, 2, pp. 481–494.

Kondratieva T. (2017): *Bolcheviks et jacobins. Itinéraire des analogies*, Paris: Éditions Payot.

Kusiak P. (2011): Postpolityka. W poszukiwaniu istoty zjawiska [Post-politics. In Search of the Essence of the Phenomenon], *Colloqium Wydziału Nauk Humanistycznych i Społecznych*, III/2011.

Le monde est vide depuis les Romains, Œuvres complètes de Saint-Just, ed. Charles Vellay, Editions Eugène Factuelle, Paris 1908, vol. II.

Lefort C. (1981): *L'invention démocratique*, Paris: Fayard.

Les signes et manifestations d'appartenance religieuses dans les établissements scolaires, Rapport présenté par Jean-Pierre Obin, Juin 2004, n. 2004–115, http://media.education.gouv.fr/file/02/6/6026.pdf (date of access: 10.05.2018).

Madelin L. (1914): *Danton*, Paris: Hachette.

Ne vous inquiétez pas, regardez moi faire. Je ne commenterai pas ce que vous avez dit, mais … Il faut que tout le monde puisse s'exprimer mais … Il faut qu'il y ait un peu d'ordre, on the basis of coverage in RTL Radio, http://www.rtl.fr/actu/politique/un-veteran-a-macron-soyez-tres-ferme-avec-tous-ces-gauchos-7793313155 (date of access: 10.05.2018).

Ozouf M., Furet F. (1993): *Le siècle de l'avènement républicain*, Paris: Gallimard.

Revault d'Allones M. (2010): *Pourquoi nous n'aimons pas la démocratie*, Paris: Le Seuil.

Revault d'Allonnes M. (2012): Comment la crise vient à la philosophie, *Esprit*, Mars-avril 2012, pp. 108–117.

Rosanvallon P. (2014): *Le parlement des invisibles. Manifeste pour „raconter la vie"*, Paris: Le Seuil.

Rosanvallon P. (2015): *Le bon gouvernement*, Paris: Le Seuil.

Rousseau J.J. (1979): *Emile, or On Education*, New York: Basic Books, 1979.

Salmon Ch. (2007): *Verbicide. Du bon usage des cerveaux humains disponibles*, Paris: Babel.

Si je peux me permettre, soyez très ferme avec tous ces gauchos de la politique qui ne veulent que foutre la merde!, on the basis of coverage in RTL Radio, http://www.rtl.fr/actu/politique/un-veteran-a-macron-soyez-tres-ferme-avec-tous-ces-gauchos-7793313155 (date of access: 10.05.2018).

Thucydides, *History of the Peloponnesian War*, http://www.documentacatholicaomnia.eu/03d/-460_-400,_Thucydites,_History_Of_The_Peloponnesian_War,_EN.pdf

Part III Poland Facing the Crises

Olaf Osica

Can states think? Political counsel in the times of crisis

Abstract: Nowadays, political decision-makers are becoming subordinated to the system they built for the needs of the campaign and based on constant media interaction with voters, for whom emotions and narrative coherence are the decisive criterion for supporting their policy. By rejecting knowledge as a source of decision making, they deprive themselves of the possibility of action that would allow them to manage the public sphere more effectively. The consequence of this is the disappearance of the political discourse based on knowledge in the public space, and thus the country's inability to think and act taking into account the public interest.Changing political communication is not possible, so the only way to break this negative trend is to build a framework of a new social contract, the essence of which would be to design the space between decision-makers, experts and society for creating, exchanging knowledge and managing it. This approach, above all, requires rebuilding trust between the world of experts, politicians and voters. This in turn means accepting the restrictions of each side, defining the role and constructing a catalog of good practices. This would, with the good will of the parties, give the cooperation a lasting and systemic character.

Keywords: political counsel, state, government, think-tank, social media

One of the greatest paradoxes in the operation of modern societies is the crisis of knowledge. Despite the open access to information, driven by the Internet and social media, societies seem to understand the world around them less and less. The information overload and the ensuing difficulty in interpreting complex social and political as well as economic issues contributes to people being closed within the so-called information bubbles, which are supposed to provide them with comfort.

In 2015, Public Policy Polling, an American opinion poll company, conducted a survey on a large sample of both Democrat and Republican voters, asking them whether they would support a military intervention in Agrabah. Almost a third of the Republican respondents answered positively, with 13 % opposing the idea. The inclinations of the Democrat voters turned out to be the opposite: 36 % opposing such intervention and 19 % in favour of it.[1]

---

1 As cited in: T. Nichols (2017): How America Lost Faith in Expertise And Why That's a Giant Problem, *Foreign Affairs*, March/April 2017. Internet access. Complete results

The location indicated in the survey, Agrabah, does not, in fact, exist. It is a fictitious country where the plot of 1992 Disney animated feature film "Aladdin" is set.

Liberal pundits interpreted the results of the survey as one more proof of aggressive tendencies among the Republicans. Their conservative counterparts refuted those accusations arguing, in turn, that it revealed the reflexive pacifism of the Democrats. "Experts in national security couldn't fail to notice that 43 percent of Republicans and 55 percent of Democrats polled had an actual, defined view on bombing a place in a cartoon."[2]

Nowadays, to know means as much as to identify oneself with one of the opposing social and political narratives. These are aimed to create in voters' minds coherent interpretations of events, thus *en passant* eliminating questions, doubts and the need to look for answers, all of which are constitutive elements for critical thought about the world, amounting to knowledge creation.

The contemporary crisis of knowledge is fuelled by several phenomena.

It started with the development of new technologies and the eruption of social media, which established new business models. Their essence lies in monetisation of user's every action in the net. The so-called profiling – consisting, simply put, in defining the preferences of each and every netizen according to their web searches – benefits companies, as it allows them to reach their customers with more precision. At the same time, it precludes the latter from accessing content considered incompatible with their profiles, and hence deemed bereft of advertising value.

That model rapidly found its way to political campaigns, which treat politics as commercial goods. Owing to that, the political message reached larger number of recipients, but inevitably became flattened so as to be able to elicit positive or negative emotional responses. It was no longer means of communication and dialogue, becoming instead a method to spur electorates.

The phenomenon of the so-called fake news, i.e. of mass dissemination of information whose sources are unknown or of distributing opinions whose popularity is driven by the social media algorithms, is both the effect of the manner societies communicate and a force ruining the reliability of any such communication.

---

of the research available on: https://www.publicpolicypolling.com/polls/trump-lead-grows-nationally-41-of-his-voters-want-to-bomb-country-from-aladdin-clinton-maintains-big-lead/

2 *Ibidem.*

Despite growing awareness of potential risks stemming from a social change engendered by the technological revolution, political communication became a hostage of the very same mechanism of Internet media as did services in the present-day economy. Knowledge and competence, rationality understood as decision-making according to reliable sources of information with a subsequent process of balancing arguments for and against a specific solution as well as thought given to the consequences of potential actions, all these gave way to campaigns based on imbuing emotions and reacting directly to events or shifts in electorate's moods.

However, the actual paradox lies in the fact that the success of emotion-driven electoral campaigns becomes problematic for those already in power. It renders efficient and wise governing virtually impossible, as the rules of public debate do not change with the announcement of election results. The difference between the period of the campaign and the time of being in the office is nowadays of strictly formal nature, i.e. it is stipulated by constitutional regulations. Nevertheless, in the practice of being in power, the entire political process is subjugated to the electoral *modus operandi*: it entails listening to social moods and their prompt satisfaction without regard for rationality of solutions, least of all for their long-term consequences.

Thus, we end up in a situation where policy-makers are no longer well-informed subjects creating policies, as they have instead turned into captives of a system which they had themselves constructed to meet the campaign requirements, relying on ceaseless media interaction with the voters, for whom emotions and narrative cohesion are the definite criteria for supporting any policies. Refusing to include knowledge as a source in their decision-making process, politicians deprive themselves of the ability to govern the public sphere more efficiently.

As a result of the above, knowledge-based political discourse peters out of the public space, further deepening the inability of the state to think and act in the public interest.

Due to the fact that a radical shift in political communication is unattainable, the only way to overcome this negative trend seems to be providing new foundation for social contract, one essentially entailing a space for decision-makers, experts and the society to create and exchange knowledge and to manage it.

Such approach requires most of all (re)building of trust between the worlds of experts, politicians and voters, which, in turn, involves accepting the limitations of each party, clearly defining its role and establishing a catalogue of best practices for it. Providing they demonstrate goodwill, it would enable such cooperation to become a lasting and systemic solution. Modelling it after the concept of knowledge economy, the foundation of modern day economies, the Western world is attempting to face the challenge of winning back the position of knowledge and import as the grounding for political activity.

The rise of knowledge institutions

Milieux of academics and experts are very much efficient and willing to criticise decisions made by politicians as ill-advised, based upon false premises and calculated to maximise electorate regardless of their consequences. And often they are quite right. One could cite, for instance, the Brexit campaign, during which not only were the negative aspects of leaving the EU ignored, but also blatant lies were used regarding facts and solid data.[3] Indeed, the remainers, too, benefitted from untrue information.

The cause of such approach is considered to be political populism "waging fake news and alternative facts", fostering divisions within societies by setting one groups against others. Michael Gove, Secretary of State for Justice in the Cameron Government and a Brexit supporter, openly admitted in one of interviews that he cared little about economists' opinions on the economic risks associated with Britain leaving the EU. "If you are talking about some of the independent economic authorities who've already weighed into the debate, they are people who have been wrong in the past. They are organisations, I'm afraid, that didn't predict the global crash in 2008 and the same organisations in many cases who said we should be inside the single currency. I am glad that all these organisations are not on my side. Margaret Thatcher said about economists, the great thing is that economists are fine but you mustn't inhale. I prefer to take the view of businesspeople who are actually generating jobs and creating wealth. The organisations that many people are citing in this debate are organisations that have been wrong in the past and I think they are wrong now."[4]

The criticism of political populism seldom involves the question of how it had come about that such kind of argumentation managed to seduce numerous groups of voters. It is neither exclusively, nor predominantly, the matter of modern technology allowing for the dissemination of questionable arguments using algorithms and funds, instead of their being legitimate and valuable

---

3 J. Stone (2017): Brexit lies: the demonstrably false claims of the EU referendum campaign, *Independent*, 17 December 2017.

4 EU referendum: Michael Gove questioned on Sky News, *Guardian*, https://www.theguardian.com/politics/blog/live/2016/jun/03/eu-referendum-michael-gove-questioned-on-sky-news

solutions. It is also the result of growing distrust towards experts and their analyses, distrust which had begun before the "fake news" era.

The process has been evolving, since it came about in the land of political counselling that the USA doubtless is. With time, the interest of governments in independent and neutral expert knowledge became a global trend, as indicated in the development of the so-called think tanks.

According to "Think Tanks and Civil Societies Program" (TTCSP) carried out by the University of Pennsylvania, responsible for compiling the Go to Global Think-Tank Index (www.gotothinktank.com), it is estimated that worldwide there are 6500 institutions of the kind. More than half of that number in the USA and Europe. Most are affiliated with universities. Insofar as the think-tank boom in the USA commenced in the 1980s, their number having doubled since (there were ca. 1800 of them in the US in 2017), with the European surge coming in the 1990s, Asia and Africa saw their dynamic development as late as in the noughties.

The reasons for the abundant growth of such institutions may be sought among variety of factors. Besides the informational and technological revolution, the harbinger of the fall of government and traditional media information monopoly, their development was also a reaction to the crisis of trust for politicians and the information they disclosed. Think tanks were supposed to defend citizens against political manipulation.

Another, often overlooked, factor was the inability of the university as institution to establish cooperation with the field of politics. The academic and political worlds, separated from each other with communicational barriers, conflicting expectations and belief in one's advantage over the other, all of these rendering cooperation difficult, especially regarding the socio-economic matters. Scholars drew strength from their conviction of having gained objective knowledge, whereas politicians enjoyed their social legitimation, enabling them to act irrespectively of the academic validity of their deeds.

The emergence of American think tanks was also accompanied by a major political strife: distrust of conservative communities towards liberal-dominated universities.

The idea behind think tanks, representing the academic realm in the world of politics, was to fill the gap between the university and politics by creating an interface through which the sides would be able to communicate. On one hand, knowledge was to undergo processing so that it would become accessible for laymen and could inform solution proposals. On the other, politicians were to submit their demands for research and expert opinions to serve as the basis for their decisions.

These interfaces – methods of operating and collaboration – assume various structures depending on the political culture. In the United States, think tanks have very distinct ideological profiles. In Germany, besides political foundations working as party think tanks founded by the parliament and besides institution financed by business, the state supports a series of research bodies unconnected to either business or politics, which take upon themselves the role of objective institutions, i.e. ones not involved in world-view disputes. In Central Europe, one can clearly see the pressure exerted upon academic institution so that they take more active part in providing solutions for the needs of politics. Political formations are unable to establish institutions that would combine scholarly reliability with a distinct ideological leaning.

In practice, though the extent varies depending on the latitude, the process led first to experts achieving autonomic status and a subsequent rise of their position; some of them left behind their original role of intermediaries and became independent players. Benefitting from trust confided in them, "the knowledge people" got deeply involved in public activity, at times assuming a *par excellence* political stance.

Crisis of expertise

Regardless of the *modus operandi* and the national specifics, the rise of institutions producing knowledge for the needs of politics reinforced the notion of academic research being in crisis or, more baldly put, of the death of expertise.[5] In the opinion of the parties involved, the reasons for the crisis are: the fall of the institution of university, the dominant position of social media and the societies being convinced that they do not require expert knowledge. However, the problem was not bound to get so much worse, had the world of the academia strived more to gain social interest and was open to criticism coming from the outside. As already mentioned, the emergence of the so-called think tanks was indeed an answer to the unwillingness of the academic world to deal with the challenges posed by real political issues.

The first reason behind the crisis of trust in the experts is the fact that the contemporary world of scholars and specialists, of universities, research institutes and think tanks did in fact undergo major commercialisation. "Many university faculties remind us of boutiques where Professors are expected to be a sort

5 T. Nichols (2015): Agonia wiedzy. Koniec ekspertów. Śmierć elit, https://wszystkoconajwazniejsze.pl/tom-nichols-agonia-wiedzy-koniec-ekspertow-smierc-elit/

of intellectual assistants. It makes an illusion of intellectual self-congratulation in children who should be educated instead of having their whims catered to."[6] Knowledge was transformed into another product and just like any other goods became an object of market mechanisms, in this case involving the ability to break through the white noise. The best communicated narrative triumphs, whereas the inability to produce a proper framework leaves creators of a given story outside the scope of public attention. That, in turn, often engenders the problem of the victory of form over substance, the latter becoming no more than an addition to the media coverage involving brief and alluring messages conforming to the prevailing trends.

Another aspect of the phenomenon is related to its funding. It is largely the result of the state's gradual withdrawal from financing science and a dominant expectation that it is only the market – students paying their tuition and companies funding research – that possesses the ability to objectively evaluate the value of the knowledge produced.

The model in which private funds are granted ever larger importance leads to distrust in the best case scenario and to a conflict of interest in the worst one. As noted by Prof. E. Group, the president of Leibniz Institut für Wirtschaftsforschung in Halle, financing of research chairs and institutes in Germany by corporations led to a situation when university recommendations are intertwined with elements of lobbying. "Would an economist whose position at the university is financed by a bank really recommend a bankruptcy of the bank instead of opting for using public money to come to its rescue?"[7] The issue also concerns fields such as public health, in which the medical community is accused of protecting not only the interest of the patient, but also of the pharmaceutical companies which finance doctor trainings.

Also with regard to expert opinions in the field of politics of international relations, an area seemingly unattractive for market manipulations, finding sponsors in external countries or companies becomes a major challenge. In the United States, the problem greatly concerns academic and expert communities which are privately funded in their entirety.[8] Even if the knowledge elaborated

6 *Ibidem.*

7 A. Cumurovic, R.E. Gropp (2017): Verbesserung von politischer Beratung und Wirtschaftspolitik, ZBW-Leibniz-Informationszentrum Wirtschaft, *Wirtschaftsdienst*, p. 244.

8 Cf. Foreign Powers Buy Influence at Think Tanks, *New York Times*, Sep. 6, 2015; https://www.nytimes.com/2014/09/07/us/politics/foreign-powers-buy-influence-at-think-tanks.html; It's time for think tanks and universities to take the democracy pledge, *Washington Post*, Jan. 16, 2019. https://www.washingtonpost.com/

there is lobbying-free, the source of money becomes an issue as a result of their withholding the information as to the sponsors of their research programmes.

Another cause of the crisis of trust in experts is the matter of responsibility. In the opinion of numerous politicians and voters the world of academics and experts is not rendered responsible for their mistakes, whereas societies have to learn them the hard way. Charges abound against economists, who proved unable to foresee the economic crisis of 2009, against political scientists, surprised by the so-called Arab spring in North Africa, against sociologists, who were predicting the failure of the supporters of Brexit in the UK referendum and of Donald Trump in the US presidential elections. It reinforces many in their belief that knowledge is of no importance in the process of policy-making. "Insofar as populist politicians used to go to much lengths to present their own expert opinions, nowadays they self-assuredly claim that expert knowledge is in fact devoid of all importance and societies had better rely on »people's common sense« or »alternative facts«."[9]

The third issue plaguing the realm of academic and expert institutions is their elitism, understood as operating in the milieux of political and economic elites and replicating solutions or promoting ideas that enjoy the most extensive media coverage and public interest at any given moment. It resulted in the emergence of "ideological bubble", in which there was no more room for thoughts not aligned with the dominating narratives, and – as such – closer to the real issues. It is no accident that European research institutes failed to develop a theory of European disintegration (at the scale and intellectual rigour comparable to the theories of integration), which could serve as a warning against malfunctioning of Union's institutional practice. The expert community seems similarly helpless when faced with the problem of predicting the consequences of the decline of the current form of transatlantic cooperation and NATO.

Finally, the pressure to be visible, recognisable as well as the ambition to influence the public debate resulted in an increasing inability of the knowledge-creating communities to promote coherent political actions and solutions taking into consideration actual social needs instead of particular ideological advantages. When, in 2002, the US Congress decided to reauthorise the Welfare Reform Act of 1996, "there was little agreement among the experts outside of government recommending changes to the 1996 law. Experts produced studies

---

opinions/2019/01/16/its-time-think-tanks-universities-take-democracy-pledge/?utm_term=.e9ead503b2ab

9 L. Brozus, O. Geden (2017): Experten, Politik und Populismus, ZBW-Leibniz-Informationszentrum Wirtschaft, *Wirtschaftsdienst*, p. 239.

advocating everything from expansions in child care subsidies and low-income housing vouchers to provisions that promote marriage and sexual abstinence. Along with little agreement among them on how to revise the law, there was also little restraint among experts in expressing their views."[10] Whereas in the past academic experts were accused of limiting themselves to providing analyses and descriptions of various issues instead of submitting concepts implementable in real life, present-day "ideological powerhouses" find it difficult to curb their ambitions and tend to recommend solutions with complete disregard for social and political constraints.

Against the backdrop of these growing problems, the world of political counsel found itself facing a major crisis. Robin Niblett, the director of the British Chatham House, one of the oldest think tanks in the world, argues that these institutions suffer from waning credibility and a lack transparency, particularly with regard to their funding, as well as from progressively losing touch with the reality.[11]

Knowledge as political decoration

The current state of affairs within the world of scholars and experts, however, reflects more than just the mistakes made by that community. Additionally, it is influenced by the shifts occurring on the political side of the issue. Although charges of ignoring knowledge are directed at populist politicians, who manipulate the public opinion in order to undermine the regulations of the liberal order, the conviction as to the irrelevance of knowledge and experts' opinions in political practice seems to bear marks of a cross-party consensus.

From the point of view of politics and public institutions, the massive increase in knowledge both in terms of the sheer number of publications, institutes, think tanks and individual experts, as well as in terms of the level of its difficulty and complexity raises major problems and challenges, at the same time activating defensive mechanisms.

Most of all, the growth of knowledge hubs threatens the autonomy of politics, which finds itself under pressure from scientific, i.e. implicitly objective, solutions to various issues; the essence of politics, however, entails forming the

---

10 A. Rich (2004): *Think tanks, public policy, and the politics of expertise*, Cambridge: Cambridge University Press, p. 3.

11 R. Niblett (2018): Rediscovering a sense of purpose: the challenge for western think-tanks, *International Affairs*, Volume 94 (6) – Nov. 1, 2018.

world according to ideas and making a choice between the desired and the possible, much more than implementing experts' panacea.

Consequently, what ensues is a process of "making expertise political" instead of "making politics scientific". It is a paradox, as the aim of the development in knowledge, declaratively supported also by politicians incl. the ones in power, is said to be grounding politics in as objective (neutral) criteria for decision making as possible. Instead, the opposite occurs.

As noted by the researchers from German Institute for International and Security Affairs (Stiftung Wissenschaft und Politik), a political counsel institution established by the German government, "we are dealing with the phenomenon of scientific knowledge being bent by the world of politics in a process determined not by supply on the part of science, but by demand on the part of politics."[12] And in a passage further on: "Expert's opinion compatible with the existing preferences of the political and administrative institutions is more likely to be taken into consideration. However, the knowledge undermining the stance assumed by political actors is often neglected, and so is knowledge potentially exposing the administrative apparatus to major operational challenges. The idea that scientific evidence should provide grounds for practical politics has turned into its opposite: it is politics that forms not only the way the research is received (its public reception), but also the process of its very development."[13]

That, in turn, leads to still more repercussions: the conviction that politically neutral knowledge does not exist and that every member of the community of experts must be somehow affiliated with the world of politics. Thus, her or his research and recommendations are as a matter of course perceived through the lens of the ongoing political strife. Such attitude promotes erosion of social trust in expert knowledge, hence depriving the state of an opportunity to reach decisions on the basis of research and analyses, their pre-determined reference point being the public interest, not political demand.

Obviously, everyone, including experts, must have some beliefs regarding the operation of the state, society and economy. However, having one's beliefs, an attribute of every thinking person, is a matter different altogether from providing arguments for making political decisions aligned with the predilections of the decision-makers, who benefits from the right of choosing a solution, granted to them. That right must be exercised within the framework of a strictly political

12 L. Brozus, O. Geden, *op. cit.*, p. 240.

13 *Ibidem.*

order and by people deemed legitimate to do it, i.e. elected politicians who would bear responsibility for their decisions with their voters.

And the final issue: one concerning the organisational culture of modern politics and state government. The fast pace of political life and the need of permanent exchange with the voters leave neither space nor time not only for thought, but also for the development of knowledge. Thus, the latter turns out to be no more than an obstruction in the process of efficient and, still more importantly, free of all nuances communication between politicians and the society. In such circumstances, gone are the opportunities of posing a problem, not to mention the stages of data collection, its analysis and, ultimately, presentation of potential solutions along with their consequences.

It is accompanied by: the process of rotation of partners for conversation on the side of politics as well as problems with accumulation of knowledge and managing it among institutions, including an utter lack of incentives for people attempting to introduce external knowledge management for the benefit of public institutions.

Knowledge and politics. Marriage of convenience

A series of political decisions in the present-day democracies is, therefore, made in a suboptimal manner, i.e. with a shortage of relevant data and without a cost-and-opportunity analysis. The latter applies mainly to actions that could be prepared in advance. Critical situation are by definition difficult to predict, thus one cannot prepare for those. In such moments, the whole responsibility is in the hands of the decision-makers. Their reaction is always a correlate of their experience, knowledge and maturity as well as their audacity in sorting the problem out.

However, when knowledge is no longer the basis for action in situations allowing for its inclusion the state loses its ability to think, becoming an object of activities, whose common denominator are makeshift reactions to the problems at hand. In that way, the probability of error of judgment and inadequate crisis response rises. What follows is a diminishing efficiency both in domestic and international politics.

Undemocratic states are not only less affected by the pressures of catering to social aspirations and emotions, but also able to manage knowledge with greater ease in order to politically dominate various fields. China, and Russia before that, provide great examples of the phenomenon.

Their political and economic positions stem not only from the weakening of the global liberal order established post-1945, but also largely from their own cost-and-opportunity analysis of social and economic models as well as from consistent implementation of adopted solutions. For China, the means of progress became appropriation and development of Western technologies, for Russia – creating infrastructure throughout Europe, precluding its clients' opportunities of diversifying their import of resources.

That does not mean that authoritarian regimes are bound to succeed, and democracies – to fail. Certainly, however, the former manage better with benefitting from resources of knowledge for the needs of their policies than liberal democracies established upon the assumption of political rationality, i.e. knowledge-based decision making.

The number of countries plagued by the issue also includes Poland. Political counsel understood as collaboration of the world of knowledge with the realm of politics, allowing for better decision-making, practically does not exists in the country. That fact is rendered even more intriguing, when we additionally consider that collaboration of politics with business has been developing for almost three decades now: the state is a client of many companies; the latter are paid for providing it with solutions. Thus, we have a model in which state institutions accept business counsel without investing in political counsel, which would enable it to define problems; at the same time the solutions for the state are provided by the economy. Such imbalance seems to pose a threat to sustainable development.

As oppose to the countries of Western Europe and the United States, the shallow nature of relationship between politics and knowledge in Poland is not a result of the crisis of the above-described model, instead stemming from the fact that it had never been properly developed in the first place. Despite a series of research institution being supported by the state, as well as several private organisations of the sort, Polish political expertise and Polish politics move along two parallel rail lines, which intersect occasionally, only to quickly drift apart again.

Such failure to establish a tradition of cooperation is both a problem and an opportunity.

It is a problem, because – as often mentioned – it does not enable political decision-makers in need of knowledge to understand the problems facing them, thus leaving them incapable of being more aware in their actions.

It is an opportunity, however, as it allows for basing such collaboration on proven solutions, at the same time avoiding mistakes committed by other countries.

Before we turn to the perspective of changing the current state of affairs, a question to answer should be: why – as opposed to the United States, Great Britain and Germany – the Polish model of political counsel has yet to be developed, i.e.

one amounting to more than occasional rather pedestrian interactions between experts and politicians.

There are many reasons for the above. Some of them have already been dealt with. Among others, one could mention the institutional weakness of the Polish political formations, making constant and professional analyses of the surrounding reality impossible. Not much has changed in that respect due to budgetary contributions for parties allocated especially for developing their own centres of expertise.

The lack of professional attitude stemming therefrom takes its toll in the form of severe inability to formulate and pose questions that the realm of politics needs to answer. All collaboration is therefore limited at best to informational services devoid of the components of recommendation and analysis of consequences of a given action, or, alternatively, to prompting solutions maladjusted to the political challenges at hand.

The inability to manage knowledge at the level of political institutions has its origins also in the apparent lack of interest in solutions that cannot be used in the ongoing political competition. Finally, the process of politicisation of knowledge described above engenders a tendency to similarly politicise its creators, which works as a disincentive to collaboration.

At the same time, the main shortcoming on the part of experts is their academic attitude, understood as inability to communicate with the world of politics in an efficient manner. There are no models of collaboration; no methods of conveying knowledge or of analysing it have been elaborated so that it could constitute an added value. The phenomenon is further exacerbated by a far-reaching fragmentation (specialisation) of expertise, which is flawed with its ineptitude to think in terms of the whole of state's policy. The latter often proves frustrating for politicians, who have to take into account the realities and potentialities of action regarding the entire state, and not mere fragments of it.

The issue of failure to communicate is often suppressed, a phenomenon benefitting from a common notion of disapproval for the manner that politics works. However, defying modern democracy as a system prone to "alternative facts" is altogether different from misapprehension of the rules of political activity engendered by the cooperation patterns. The former is a subjective matter, the latter a manifest lack of professionalism.

The disillusionment with politics on the part of experts' milieux results also from a deeper phenomenon. Numerous representatives of science, though they are rather unlikely to be direct about it, do in fact expect to actively influence political decisions, instead of merely providing knowledge as basis for decisions made by politicians. If, therefore, the resolutions taken by the latter contradict what they have counselled, it arouses experts' sense of frustration and their sense of not being heard out. There must also be a mistake on the side of politicians, who manifest disregard for feedback, which should not only constitute an element of political culture, but also a method of learning from mutual mistakes.

That the division of roles must be clear remains an immutable fact: it is the politician who decides and who must take responsibility for it. Advisor is depended upon to provide reliable knowledge, but cannot lay claim to resolving issues, as he does not take responsibility for political decisions.

Knowledge politics

It is not an easy feat to find actors in the realm of large business and economy who have not heard of "knowledge economy". The concept, brought to general use thanks to i.a. Peter Drucker, an originator of a series of notions in managing companies and a guru of the corporate world, posits, simply put, that globalisation and emergence of information societies results not only in an opportunity, but in fact in a necessity to approach economy in a qualitatively novel manner. Besides material goods, an ever greater importance is ascribed to intangible goods, the creation of which is largely determined by human knowledge.

According to an OECD definition, knowledge society is "an expression coined to describe trends in advanced economies towards greater dependence on knowledge, information and high skill levels, and the increasing need for ready access to all of these by the business and public sectors."

Knowledge-based economy constitutes, therefore, a qualitative shift not only in thinking about production and economic potential, but most of all of the framework of modern business: it now deals with creating and accumulating knowledge and managing it in such a way so as to gain competitive advantage over others. Such approach resulted in a massive increase in the interest for business counsel and consulting, the golden age of which commenced in 1945 and has lasted ever since, while the profession of a business consultant still proves one of the most interesting occupations.

It is both rather intriguing and, concurrently, symptomatic that there is no similar notion present in the world of politics, even though the latter deals essentially with elaboration of intangible goods, i.e. concepts, and ideas making operation of societies and states efficient. Business counselling has been ascribed a code in the Polish Classification of Economic Activities [PKD] (section M, division 70) and has been deftly described and defined at the level of both required education and services it provides. Political counselling on the other hand not only does not have its PKD code, but also functions as an equivalent of services regarding political communication and public relations.

The differences in attitudes and expectations between the worlds of knowledge and politics serve only to further validate the notion of no added value to be achieved by way of mutual cooperation. Therefore, the only form of counsel sanctioned by the realm of politics is political marketing. However, the elaboration of a political message is very different form political action, which must require a thorough knowledge of both problems and the methods of solving them.

Nevertheless, the identification of the so-called spin doctors with political advisors has become common. If we enter the phrase "political counsel" into a search engine, we are provided with a series of links to study programmes in the field of marketing and advertisement.

> Graduates of Public and Political Consulting course – we can read on a website of one of universities – are qualified to work in public institutions, offices of MPs, political organisations, local government bodies, especially in the field of elaboration and realisation of social and political campaigns as well as designing media campaigns. They can also find employment in public relations agencies, as well as work as spokespersons, public opinion analysts, political image advisors, managers and employees of campaign headquarters. They may be dealing with political coaching or work in the training industry.[14]

Positioning political counselling in the context of media and campaign activities is a proof of far-reaching misunderstanding of both the role and the duties of the advisory profession. It can also serve as an indication of the source of crisis of Polish politics, in which the knowledge of good government gave way to the knowledge of winning the elections. The phenomenon seems additionally interesting, as it finds no direct reflection on the business side of things, even though politics is commonly thought to be corrupted by transference of business logic into the public sphere.

Meanwhile, the role of an efficient counsellor in large corporations, one able to establish new contacts or prove successful in negotiations, is far from identical with the role of a counsellor possessing the knowledge necessary to fulfil submitted orders. Marketing and advertisement serve to sell the things crafted by way of applying immense knowledge and skill, never the other way around.

---

14 Wydział Nauk Społecznych, Uniwersytet Śląski, Doradztwo polityczne i publiczne, http://www.wns.us.edu.pl/pl/2-uncategorised/17-doradztwo-polityczne-i-publiczne (transl. to English by MS).

If knowledge economy not is only a self-explanatory notion, but also – as it seems – a commonly accepted phenomenon, why cannot it be applied also within the realm of politics? Considering the fact that the crisis of liberal-democratic order is largely due to the growing social imbalance resulting from the manner of accumulation and division of goods and the dominating role of financial markets and global corporations, it seems more than likely that the subsequent phase of globalisation will unfold to a larger extent according to the rules of political rather than economic thought.

The return of the state as a wise regulator of the markets and economy proves today one of the conditions for the survival of liberal order. There can be no wisdom, however, where there is no knowledge. Knowledge politics seems, therefore, to be a necessary element of restoring the balance between public and market interests. The latter has valued knowledge as a key resource enabling it to prevail over the political sphere for quite some time now.

Pillars of the new contract

The challenges posed by the development of Poland, stemming from the ever larger complexity of global political and economic processes, require a progress in self-awareness of public institutions. For over three decades, the Polish economy and society have benefitted from a massive political prosperity: abolished barriers, inflow of assets and a dominating role of social and economic notions of the West. Such "liberal cocoon" allowed for real transference of many functions to supranational institutions, first and foremost to the European Union, which serves as a political and regulatory interface with the world of global institutions.

The waning importance of Europe worldwide, the spreading of new technologies at a pace far exceeding their regulation, as well as the return to protectionism on the part of key global players, particularly China and the US, all force us to exert some intellectual effort. Unable to co-create the rules and principles of the new global order, the Polish society and economy will be reduced to the role of its passive recipients. It does not have to prove detrimental in all fields, but it may preclude some from developing.

Much like the notion of knowledge economy, its political counterpart should be based upon four pillars.

The first pillar comprises education and trainings. Despite a mass of graduates of political sciences and related disciplines, only a small number of them has the skills potentially useful when cooperating with the world of real politics. It seems to result from the structure of education. Courses and lectures emphasise the knowledge of history, institutions and legal regulations; they focus in a much lesser degree, if at all, on the issues of the actual *modus operandi* of public institutions. The knowledge that political institutions exist is far from identical with the set of skill enabling one to take a conscious part in the political processes. It is true both of studies of domestic public institutions and of international organisations. In other words, academic knowledge gained by countless students of political sciences, international relations and sociology courses is limited to theories, concepts and laws, whereas matters regarding procedural issues, the practical operation and the manner of implementing solutions remain outside the educational scope.

The same holds true for the knowledge of methods of cooperation with political decision-makers, of defining and analysing problems and of preparing recommendations. Whereas in the world of professional business, politics and international institutions we are dealing with common patterns, organisational codes and, at times excessively described, processes of informing and making decisions and managing problems, the Polish realm of counsel does not have at its disposal any standards making its activity coherent. In such circumstances, professionalisation proves unattainable.

The second pillar is the method of communicating and transferring information. It is not an issue regarding technology, which is of secondary importance here, but of the ability to establish efficient dialogue by way of understanding the needs of the decision-makers. It concerns both the manner of presenting matters, defining problems as well as creating patterns of constant communication on the basis of written materials or conversations. As in well-organised information service, deftly described by Tadeusz Kotarbiński, cooperation of experts and politicians requires rapidity, fidelity, required precision, clarity and definiteness.[15]

The third pillar is constituted by economic incentives and institutional circumstances. Knowledge-based development not only requires financial support, as any other activity, but also legal and institutional solutions fostering the emergence of planes of conversation. What is required is an interface enabling the state to efficiently acquire knowledge from within various fields in order to subsequently format it in such a way so that it could serve as a basis for political action. In practice, it would involve the necessity to formally appreciate all the various bodies within public administration and institutions as well as political formations that deal with analysis and strategy. They must not only be

15 T. Kotarbiński (1982): *Traktat o dobrej robocie*, Wrocław-Warszawa-Kraków-Gdańsk-Łódź: Zakład Narodowy im. Ossolińskich, p. 205.

supervised by the decision-makers themselves, but also possess the ability to aggregate knowledge coming both from within and without them.

Cooperation with external experts should rely on common standards for all public institutions and transparence in inviting for collaboration, its range, the format of the knowledge transferred as well as remuneration for it. The currently prevailing model of ordering expert opinions seems unable to introduce added value and apparently ignores the realities of modern political life in which time, conciseness of message and the ability to exchange opinions are of key importance.

On the part of counselling institutions and experts, common regulations as to the transparency of financing their activity and avoidance of conflict of interest have to be established.

The fourth pillar concerns the ability of centres of analysis and research, expert teams to develop themselves, i.e. to be innovative. That sort of innovation is nothing else than competition in the field of new solutions, ideas and methods of improving public institutions in order for the state to be willing and able to know and understand more. Regardless of their formal situation – whether within or outside the administration – they must have the opportunity to establish public and private intellectual partnerships reaching further than their current dispositions, as well as have their own right to decide on the selection of subjects and issues to tackle. For there is an inherent risk that many public institutions, tasked with generating knowledge required by the state, will rather resonate political discussions than initiate them. Therefore the process of defining goals for research institutions by policy-makers is equally important as their openness to the ideas reaching beyond the day to day political interest.

***

> Government and expertise rely on each other, especially in a democracy. The technological and economic progress that ensures the well-being of a population requires a division of labor, which in turn leads to the creation of professions. Professionalism encourages experts to do their best to serve their clients, respect their own knowledge boundaries, and demand that their boundaries be respected by others, as part of an overall service to the ultimate client: society itself.[16]

The worlds of contemporary economy and politics cannot exist without one another. The notion, prevalent for many years, that the sole duty of politics is to create conditions for economic growth is now proving much more complicated. The civilisational costs of rapid development of markets and technologies

16 Tom Nichols, *op. cit.*

force a new approach to politics. The latter is to foster balance between economic interests of corporations and public interests of citizens. The state as an arbitrator, weighting against each other the pros and cons of solutions within, say, energy economics, education or labour market must have at its disposal the knowledge allowing it to perform such role. Although politics will never escape social emotions, particular interests of various sectors and the pressures of technological trends, these should be objects of a deeper reflection. Knowledge cannot guarantee that the decisions made will be free of mistakes, nor that they will win support during elections. However, it is the element enabling also political activity to learn from its mistakes, ensure continuity of competence and expertise as well as to define its social commitments in a manner more informed.

References

Brozus L., Geden O. (2017): Experten, Politik und Populismus, ZBW-Leibniz-Informationszentrum Wirtschaft, *Wirtschaftsdienst*.

Cumurovic A., Gropp R.E. (2017): Verbesserung von politischer Beratung und Wirtschaftspolitik, ZBW-Leibniz-Informationszentrum Wirtschaft, *Wirtschaftsdienst*.

Kotarbiński T. (1982): *Traktat o dobrej robocie*, Wrocław-Warszawa-Kraków-Gdańsk-Łódź: Zakład Narodowy im. Ossolińskich.

Niblett R. (2018): Rediscovering a sense of purpose: the challenge for western think-tanks, *International Affairs*, Volume 94 (6) – 1 November.

Nichols T. (2017): How America Lost Faith in Expertise and Why That's a Giant Problem, *Foreign Affairs*, March/April.

Rich A. (2004): *Think tanks, public policy, and the politics of expertise*, Cambridge: Cambridge University Press.

Stone J. (2017): Brexit lies: the demonstrably false claims of the EU referendum campaign, *Independent*, 17 December.

Artur Wołek

Politicisation and the sudden end of the consensus. The European migrant crisis in 2015 vs. Polish immigration policy

Abstract: The events of 2015 left a mark on the attitude of Poles to the problem of migration, and perhaps on the attitude of Poles towards global phenomena. The aim of the author in this case study is to reconstruct the facts and activities of governments of Ewa Kopacz, and then of Law and Justice. A combination of three factors influenced the reactions of Polish politicians to the migration crisis. These were: definition of Polish immigration policy as primarily security-related activities, pressure exerted by Poland's European partners and violent politicization of immigration policy during the 2015 election campaigns. In order to fully explain the administration's activities during the crisis, the author reconstructs the most important events of the crisis itself and the government's policy in this regard, then presents the genealogy of Polish immigration policy. In the third part, he analyses the impact mechanisms of constitutive features of Polish migration policy on the decisions of Polish governments during the migration crisis, and at the end he discusses the medium and long-term consequences of the decisions for the Polish migration policy.

Keywords: immigration, migration crisis, public policies, security, political campaign

The European migrant crisis in 2015 did not affect Poland to a degree comparable to Germany, Austria or Hungary. Poland was not a part of the maps of 1.1 million Syrians, Afghans and Iraqis moving from southern Europe, or rather the global South, towards the rich and stable North. Polish border guards, the police, heads of provinces and local governments did not have to face the challenges that were experienced by their German and earlier Greek and Hungarian colleagues. Nevertheless, the events of 2015 have left a permanent mark on the attitude of Poles to the migration issue or, maybe even more broadly, to the attitude of Poles, including Polish politicians, to the global phenomena in which we do not participate at first glance, but which require the reaction of the Polish state.

The subject-matter of the following case study is not the migration crisis itself or the reaction of Polish authorities to the crisis. This issue has been analysed many time and the reconstruction of basic events does not arouse much controversy.[1] In this analysis, the reconstruction of facts is aimed at explaining and

1 See, e.g., K. Pędziwiatr, A. Legut (2017): Polskie rządy wobec unijnej strategii na rzecz przeciwdziałania kryzysowi migracyjnemu [The attitude of Polish governments to the

answering the question why the government of Ewa Kopacz and then the Law and Justice (PiS) party took certain actions. In social sciences, going beyond the description is always risky, but it seems that we can say with a high degree of certainty that the reactions of two Polish governments to the European migrant crisis in 2015 were influenced by a combination of three factors. They included the earlier definition of Polish immigration policy mainly as a security action, the pressure exerted by European partners of Poland and the intense politicisation of immigration policy in the course of electoral campaigns in 2015.[2]

For the purpose of full explanation of actions of Polish governments during the crisis, we will first reconstruct the most important events making up the crisis and governmental policy in this respect and then we will present the genealogy of Polish immigration policy in order to highlight its features that had the most significant impact on the election of Polish politicians in 2015. In the third part, we will analyse mechanisms of impact of constitutive features of Polish migrant policy on decisions of Polish governments in the situation of the European migrant crisis. Finally, I will discuss medium- or maybe also short-term consequences of decisions made at that time for the Polish migrant policy.

The attitude of Poland to the European migrant crisis

The need to change the European migrant policy towards its stronger harmonisation has been indicated for several years.[3] During the term of the

EU strategy for the prevention of migration crisis], in: K. Wojtaszczyk, J. Szymańska (ed.), *Uchodźcy w Europie. Uwarunkowania, istota, następstwa* [*Refugees in Europe. Circumstances, essence, consequences*], Warsaw: Instytut Europeistyki UW, pp. 608–621; A. Adamczyk (2016): Polska wobec kryzysu imigracyjnego [The attitude of Poland to the immigration crisis], in: A. Adamczyk, A. Sakson, C. Trosiak (ed.), *Polityczne i społeczne aspekty wielokulturowości. Migracje i mniejszości* [*Political and social aspects of multiculturalism. Migrations and minorities*], Poznań: Wydawnictwo UAM, pp. 99–120; A. Nyzio (2017): The Second Revival? The Visegrad Group and the European migrant crisis in 2015–2017, *Politeja*, no. 5(50), pp. 47–99.

2 The term 'migration crisis' is used most frequently with regard to the events of 2015. The subject-matter of this paper is the immigration policy that is a part of migration policy and a broader social policy trying to solve issues concerning migrations [immigration, emigration, integration of foreigners, etc.).

3 See J. Brzozowski (2011): Polityka migracyjna Unii Europejskiej: stan obecny i perspektywy [Migration policy of the European Union: current situation and perspectives], *Studia Europejskie*, no. 3, pp. 56–71.

European Commission headed by José Barroso (2010–2014), this proposal was brought up by the Swedish Commissioner for Internal Affairs Cecilia Malmström, which is understandable since the Swedish Minister for Migration and Asylum Policy Tobias Billström (earlier he and the Commissioner were ministers in Fredrik Reinfeldt's government) noticed already in October 2012 that '9 out of 27 EU countries accept 90 % of refugees arriving in Europe every year' and this situation would require 'a more coherent approach'. Two years later, he said that these countries 'are beginning to have enough of this'.[4] The reform of the migrant policy became also one of the more important topics of the "electoral campaign" of Jean-Claude Juncker as a candidate for the new chairman of the Commission, but it began to be elaborated more intensely only as a result of the rapid increase in the number of migrants, mainly from Syria – a country suffering from war and the humanitarian catastrophe. Whereas around 5,500 persons arrived in the European Union across the Mediterranean Sea in January 2015, this number rose to over 220,000 migrants per month in October of the same year.[5] This intensive influx 'showed not only the ineffectiveness of tools used until then within the Community European asylum policy, but also the lack of European coherence and strong divisions within the EU', as Pędziwiatr and Legut notice.[6]

The first summit of the European Council in March 2015, on which the issue of migrants still played a relatively marginal role, ended in non-controversial conclusions on the increase of support for the Operation Triton being conducted by Frontex on the Mediterranean Sea and the reiteration of the earlier decision that the long-term solution of the issue of migrants must be based on closer co-operation with the countries of origin and transit, including support in the protection of borders and the management of migrations. The subsequent summit of the Council (23 April 2015) was held in the shadow of the disaster of a ship carrying migrants from Libya to Italy, in which over 800 persons died. During that summit, a decision was made to triple the resources for the Operation Triton, to intensify anti-smuggling actions, and the need for closer co-operation with Turkey and Libya as countries from which largest groups of migrants reach Europe was stressed once again. On that occasion, a proposal was

4 Quoted after C. Hasselbach (2013): Still no sign of a common asylum policy in the EU, *DW*, 10.01.2013, https://p.dw.com/p/17Hhi.

5 Data of the Office of the United Nations High Commissioner for Refugees, see: https://www.unhcr.org/news/press/2015/12/567918556/million-refugees-migrants-flee-europe-2015.html.

6 K. Pędziwiatr, A. Legut, *op. cit.*, p. 611.

made for the first time to reinforce the internal solidarity and responsibility of the EU through a 'voluntary pilot project on resettlement across the EU, offering places to persons qualifying for protection'.[7]

This idea was developed by the European Commission, which had worked on a European Agenda on Migration since March 2015. In the document published on 13 May 2015, the Commission not only proposed a 'temporary distribution scheme for persons in clear need of international protection to ensure a fair and balanced participation of all Member States to this common effort,' but also announce the preparation of a permanent 'mandatory and automatically-triggered relocation system'.[8]

Faced with an intense influx of migrants to a few countries of the southern flank of the EU ("first-line countries"), the European Commission clearly chose relocation as a basic tool for handling the European migrant crisis. This was particularly puzzling because previous relocation experiences were not particularly encouraging. The EU Pilot Project on Intra-EU Relocation from Malta covering refugees who had arrived in Malta in the years 2010–2013 (EUREMA I and II) brought poor results. Not only slightly more than 300 migrant acceptance offers were acquired, but also refugees from Malta were effectively resettled mainly to countries that accept many migrants, anyway (France, Germany, Great Britain). The new countries of the EU without the tradition of acceptance of refugees (Poland, Romania, Bulgaria, Slovakia) fulfilled their commitments only to a small extent, although they had been assumed fully voluntarily.[9] It seems that the EC has drawn one essential conclusion from the pilot program: if relocation is to be effective, it has to be compulsory for member states.

In addition, in order to mitigate the pressure of illegal migration, the Commission announced an agenda on resettlements of refugees staying in camps in third countries to all EU states. This agenda was also supposed to function on the basis of a common obligatory eye that would take into consideration the gross national product, the number of population, the unemployment rate

---

7 *Special meeting of the European Council*, 23/04/2015, https://www.consilium.europa.eu/en/meetings/european-council/2015/04/23/.

8 *Communication from the Commission to the European Parliament, the Council, the European Economic and Social Committee and the Committee of the Regions. A European agenda on migration*, https://ec.europa.eu/home-affairs/sites/homeaffairs/files/what-we-do/policies/european-agenda-migration/background-information/docs/communication_on_the_european_agenda_on_migration_en.pdf.

9 See: http://www.resettlement.eu/page/intra-eu-relocation.

and the number of persons who applied for an asylum in the past and resettled refugees.[10]

It is worth stressing that the Commission was strongly supported by the European Parliament when insisting on the introduction of the obligatory immigrant separation mechanism. Already at the beginning of April 2015, the presidium of the faction of EPP – the biggest one in the Parliament – supported the 'binding mechanism of solidarity' based on the allocation of quotas, and at the end of April 2015 the Parliament adopted a similar resolution by a majority of 2/3 of votes. There was, however, a clear division among MPs in this matter; only 10 % of Polish members of the EP voted for the resolution, with less than half of members from Hungary and Czech Republic supporting it.[11] Rafał Trzaskowski, the Polish Deputy Minister for Foreign Affairs responsible for European affairs, said firmly: 'the division of responsibility must be based on the principle of voluntariness ... It is difficult to imagine any quotas and the imposition of such obligations on Member States ... This issue must be left to Member States ....'[12]

On the subsequent summit of the European Council on 25–26 June 2015, a decision was made on the 'temporary and exceptional' relocation of 40,000 persons 'requiring obviously international protection' from first-line countries (Italy and Greece) within 2 years. The relocation was quasi-voluntary: Member States were to report their readiness to accept a certain number of migrants, but the limit of expectations was to be determined by the quota mechanism established by the Commission. In order to prevent a spontaneous repeated relocation, it was also envisaged that persons participating in the program would be obliged to stay in the country of settlement for 5 years. In addition, the Council confirmed the decision to resettle 20,000 refugees staying in third countries to all EU members also on the basis of the established quota-based distribution mechanism.[13] The mechanism adopted on the June meeting was effective to a limited extent. In July 2015, slightly more than 32,000 immigrants were consensually separated and it was agreed that others would be allocated till the end of the year. However, Hungary and Austria refused to participate in the program, arguing

10 Cf. K. Pędziwiatr, A. Legut, *op. cit.*, p. 613.

11 See A. Nyzio, *op. cit.*, p. 54.

12 Quoted after Polish Radio IAR, *Unia Europejska szuka rozwiązania problemu imigrantów. Chce niszczyć łodzie i zwiększyć patrole*, [*The European Union seeks solution to the immigration issue. It wants to destroy boats and increase patrols*], https://www.polskieradio.pl/5/3/Artykul/1427091,Unia-Europejska-szuka-rozwiazania-problemu-imigrantow-Chce-niszczyc-lodzie-i-zwiekszyc-patrole.

13 See K. Pędziwiatr, A. Legut, *op. cit.*, pp. 613–614.

that they were already overburdened with immigrants. Moreover, as a result of the rising wave of refugees on the southern borders of the EU in July 2015, the quota that was divided with such difficulty turned out to be a drop in the ocean.

At the end of August 2015, Germany suspended the application of the principle that refugees are obliged to apply for asylum in the first EU state (Dublin Convention) that they entered and began to accept all refugees from Syria. At the beginning of September 2015, they opened the border for the migrants who had entered Hungary and tried to get through to Bavaria via Austria. In the face of the rising crisis, Chancellor Angela Merkel recognised the solution proposed by the Commission as the only one that was readily available and increased diplomatic pressures on the acceptance of one common binding European mechanism for the solution of the European migrant crisis.[14] As a result of this, the European Commission presented a new package of proposals aimed at tackling the crisis on 9 September 2015.

In these proposals, it not only returned to the idea of compulsory emergency separation of migrants – in this case, 120,000 people – but also tried to introduce a permanent mechanism of obligatory relocation for all Member States based on economic growth indexes and the number of accepted migrants. The Commission declared financial support for countries accepting resettled immigrants, but at the same time, it actually announced penalties for states that would temporarily (only this option was allowed) refuse to participate in the program. The proposal of the Commission met with approval from the European Parliament already on 17 September 2015, but opposition from Central European states (and also Finland) was much stronger this time. In the voting of the Parliament, only 11 out of 106 members of the EP from the Visegrad Group countries voted for the proposal of the EC.[15] Supported by Romania, its leaders openly declared that they would vote against the proposal of the Commission in spite of huge diplomatic pressure. Eventually, the procedure of qualified majority voting was applied during the extraordinary session of the European Council for Justice and Internal Affairs scheduled for 22 September. Devoid of the blocking minority (Finland abstained), Central European states were outvoted and put under an obligation to accept altogether almost 1/4 of immigrants being resettled.

During this key session of the Council, Minister of Interior Teresa Piotrowska voted for the proposal of the Commission, which was a complete change of the

14 A profound report on these events is presented by R. Alexander, *Angela Merkel and the Migration Crisis. Day by day* (published in Polish as: *Angela Merkel i kryzys migracyjny. Dzień po dniu*, Warsaw: Teologia Polityczna, 2017].

15 A. Nyzio, *op. cit.*, p. 77.

Polish attitude expressed until then and the abandonment of arrangements concerning the common strategy of Visegrad Group countries. Previously, despite the reactivity of its policy, Poland consistently stuck to the idea that solidarity in the EU's actions could not be compulsory. At the same time, Prime Minister Ewa Kopacz clearly opened the way to diplomacy aimed at including Poland in the voluntary immigrant relocation program by speaking in the Polish Sejm in May 2015: 'We do not escape from solidarity with refugees, but we must evaluate our logistic capabilities and take the different language of these people into account. We must declare responsibly to what extent we are prepared for this. We want to be reliable and truthful in our offer'.[16]

Thus, Kopacz's government adopted the apparently safe framework for the creation of common European immigration policy proposed by the Commission and strongly supported by first-line countries (particularly Italy and Greece) and, from a certain moment, by Germany.[17] It was based on the slogan of solidarity – not with refugees, but with EU states that could not cope with the increasing wave of immigrants. In return for the acceptance of relatively small groups of refugees (according to July findings, 2,000 refugees were accepted within two years), the adoption of such policy allowed Poland to expect support in issues of key importance for Poland and of rather secondary importance for first-line countries, such as sanctions against Russia. At the same time, Poland still could firmly stick to the principle of voluntariness, because solidarity had assumed voluntariness in European discourse until then.

Thus, Poland expressed various objections concerning the implementation of the European migration agenda by the Commission: it protested against opening the issues regulated by the Dublin convention system, stressed the need to distinguish between economic migrants and refugees and to intensify actions supporting refugees outside EU border on the one hand and protect the external border of the EU more effectively, including the reinforcement of Frontex, on the other hand. However, the essence of the Polish position was resistance towards any kind of obligatory distribution key and the highlighting of a broader dimension of European solidarity, including the lack of geographic balance in proposals

---

16 *Premier Ewa Kopacz o przyjmowaniu uchodźców: Będę zabiegała o to, by dobrowolność w tej kwestii nadal obowiązywała* [*Prime Minister Ewa Kopacz on the acceptance of refugees: I will make efforts to maintain voluntariness in this matter*], https://www.premier.gov.pl/wydarzenia/aktualnosci/premier-ewa-kopacz-o-przyjmowaniu-uchodzcow-bede-zabiegala-o-to-by.html.

17 J. Bielecki (2015): Niemcy uczą solidarności [Germans teach solidarity], *Rzeczpospolita*, 21.07.2015, https://www.rp.pl/Uchodzcy/307209766-Niemcy-ucza-solidarnosci.html.

of the Commission, which focused on the southern flank of the EU while failing to include a broader scope of actions aimed at counteracting illegal immigration (e.g., the protection of the eastern border of the EU by Poland).

In this context, the sudden turn of the policy of Kopacz's government in September 2015 and failure to notice its potential politically disastrous results is less surprising. Minister Trzaskowski stated that since 'we had no blocking majority …, we decided that it would be better to negotiate our conditions … If we had expressed an open protest, we would have had no impact on decisions. Our efforts led to the recognition of our conditions'.[18] Undoubtedly, the propaganda dimension of these declarations was very significant, but it seems that the politicians of the PO really thought that the quality of what was happening did not differ from the previous series of failures and successes in Polish European policy – in other words, *business as usual*. The September decision was not only a one-off act and, contrary to original intentions of the Commission, did not introduce any permanent relocation mechanisms and assumed the control of migrants participating in the program in terms of security; taking the results of such control into account, it was also possible to refuse the acceptance of certain persons.

Paradoxically, ministers from PO were right in categories of European policy. Although, for the first time in migration issues, the rule of majority voting was used and the protesting Central European states were formally forced to participate in the relocation program, this decision has not had any significant consequences so far. Although its legality, questioned by the Visegrad Group states, was confirmed by the Court of Justice of the EU, this decision has remained ineffective to a large extent. Until May 2016, less than 1 % of the assumed quota of refugees was relocated.[19] Only the countries that did not object to the relocation fulfilled their obligations, although to a very limited extent, whereas Central European countries either did that on a purely symbolic scale (Czech Republic,

18 Rafał Trzaskowski: Polska przyjmie 4,5 tysiąca uchodźców [Rafał Trzaskowski: Poland will accept 4,500 refugees], https://fakty.interia.pl/raporty/raport-imigranci-z-afryki/informacje/news-rafal-trzaskowski-polska-przyjmie-4-5-tysiaca-uchodzcow,nId,1890520.

19 Communication from the Commission to the European Parliament, the European Council and the Council, Brussels 8.05.2016, http://ec.europa.eu/dgs/home-affairs/what-we-do/policies/european-agenda-migration/proposal-implementation-package/docs/20160518/communication_third_report_on_relocation_and_resettlement_en.pdf.

Slovakia) or did nothing (Poland). The final blow to compulsory relocations was struck by France, which declared in February 2016 that it was not able to accept new refugees under the relocation program after the fulfilment of the obligation assumed in September 2015.[20]

European migrant policy went in a different direction from the autumn of 2015. In the first place, support was enlarged for immigrants' countries of origin, particularly in Africa, and countries of transit. The negotiations with Turkey, which was a key country in this respect, lasted till March 2016 and resulted in an arrangement that has weakened the wave of migrants flowing into Europe via this country so far. Turkey agreed to accept all migrants that would reach Greece via Turkey, in return for which persons subject to international protection would be taken directly from refugee camps in Turkey. At the same time, support in the amount of 6 billion EUR was promised to Turkey, talks about the liberalisation of the visa regime for the citizens of Turkey were to be accelerated and negotiations on the accession of this country to the EU were to be unfrozen. Although the bloody suppression of the coup d'etat by President Recep Erdogan in July 2016 suspended the last two processes, Turkey still seems to constitute an effective barrier for migrants heading for Europe. Particularly because the EU adopted more intense actions aimed at the protection of the external border of the EU (the reinforcement of Frontex, the expansion of electronic migrant identification systems).

However, the consent of Ewa Kopacz's government to compulsory quotas of resettled migrants had far-fetched consequences in terms of internal policy. It led to a change of the entire paradigm of Polish migration policy: the marginal depoliticised policy shaped mainly by experts was transformed into a significant element of the political agenda that would have a significant impact on the result of the election. The recreation of the framework for the conduct of Polish migrant policy after 1989 and the changes that followed in 2015 will help us understand why Kopacz's government pursued the aforementioned strategy in 2015 and capture the mechanism that led to its disaster and the change of the paradigm of Polish migrant policy.

---

20 Kryzys migracyjny. Premier Francji przeciwny stałym kwotom relokacji uchodźców [Migration crisis. French Prime Minister objects to steady refugee resettlement quotas], *Polish Radio*, 14.02.2016, https://www.polskieradio.pl/5/3/Artykul/1582292,Kryzys-migracyjny-Premier-Francji-przeciwny-stalym-kwotom-relokacji-uchodzcow.

The genealogy and framework of Polish migrant policy

Until 2015, Polish immigration policy was formed in an evolutionary and rather consensual manner, certainly far from the first pages of newspapers. Its development is well described,[21] so it is worth focusing here on permanent elements of Polish immigration policy – on its semantic framework that determines not only its goals and methods, but also defines its nature and public problems being solved. The framework that had a significant impact on decisions made by Ewa Kopacz's government.[22]

The first of these elements is the fact that the framework of immigration policy formation is dominated entirely by the perspective of security. Poland began to create its immigration policy after 1989 at the time when the securitisation of this issue took place in the entire Europe, which 'created intersubjectively a sense of existential threat (with immigration) so important that it had political consequences'.[23] A large group of electors and politicians began to state that the issue of immigration must be 'controlled' or 'tackled' somehow, and regulations concerning migration began to be included within the institutional framework

---

21 See particularly S. Łodziński, M. Szonert (2017): „Niepolityczna polityka"? Kształtowanie się polityki migracyjnej w Polsce w latach 1989–2016 ["Non-political policy"? The formation of migration policy in Poland in the years 1989–2016], *Studia Migracyjne – Przegląd Polonijny*, no. 2, pp. 39–66; A. Kicinger (2009): Beyond the Focus on Europeanisation: Polish migration policy 1989–2004, *Journal of Ethnic and Migration Studies*, no. 1, pp. 79–95; A. Górny et al. (ed.) (2010): *Transformacja nieoczywista. Polska jako kraj imigracji* [*Non-obvious transformation. Poland as a country of immigration*], Warsaw: Wydawnictwo Uniwersytetu Warszawskiego; A. Weinar (2006): *Europeizacja polskiej polityki wobec cudzoziemców* 1990–2003 [*The Europeanisation of Polish policy towards foreigners 1990–2003*], Warsaw: Wydawnictwo Naukowe Scholar.

22 For the concept of framework in public policies, see: M. Pawlak (2017): Polityki publiczne wobec migracji [Public migration policies], in: J. Kwaśniewski (ed.), *Nauki o polityce publicznej. Monografia dyscypliny* [*Public policy sciences. The monograph of the field*], pp. 288–310; J.L. True et al. (2007): Punctuated-Equilibrium Theory Explaining Stability and Change in Public Policymaking, in: P. Sabatier (ed.), *Theories of the Policy Process*, Cambridge: Westview Press, pp. 176–188; P. Cairney (2012): *Understanding Public Policy: Theories and issues*, Houndmills: Plagrave, pp. 185–187; P. Hall (1993): Policy Paradigms: Social Learning and the State: The case of economic policymaking in Britain, *Comparative Politics*, no. 3, pp. 275–296.

23 B. Buzan et al. (1998): *Security: A New Framework for Analysis*, Boulder: Lynne Rienner Publishers, Boulder, p. 25.

of the security policy.[24] This was rather a matter of secondary importance for Poland, but our common perception of the border as a physical barrier against external dangers in the course of the Europeanisation of Polish public policies taking place in the 1990s did not meet with any counterbalance.

Therefore, since the early 1990s, the "default" framework of Polish immigration policy has been security and the prevention of the threat created potentially by foreigners arriving from the East. The entire normative skeletal system of Polish immigration policy that was built in the 1990s and ultimately resulted in the Foreigners Act (which entered into force in 1997) actually boils down to the determination of rules of entry, stay, settlement and expulsion of unwanted foreigners. The team led by Rafał Matyja, which examined governmental strategic documents referring to Polish migrant policy that had been created at the beginning of the current decade, notices the essential durability of this mindset:

> … the most interesting thing seems to be the sphere of tacit assumptions of migrant policy or hidden fears that accompany it. … These assumptions refer mainly to fears of immigration as a source of threat of public security (terrorism, ethnic and racial tensions, hardly controllable crime, the creation of national ghettos similar to those existing in states with a long immigration tradition); the character of new immigration societies, the level of their control by organised crime structures, special services of native countries, etc.; conflict on the labour market between immigrants and Polish citizens (the decrease of salaries and wages, illegal employment without costs of its legalisation); fears of negative social reactions (xenophobic attitude, the dislike for immigrants, political movements motivated by anti-immigrant slogans).[25]

24 For more about the concept of securitisation, see: J. Huysmans (2000): The European Union and the Securitization of Migration, *Journal of Common Market Studies*, no. 5, pp. 751–777; A. Buonfino (2004): Between Unity and Plurality: The Politicization and Securitization of the Discourse of Immigration in Europe, *New Political Science*, no. 26(1), pp. 23–49; H. Stritzel (2007): Towards a Theory of Securitization: Copenhagen and Beyond, *European Journal of International Relations*, no. 3, pp. 357–383; R. Buraczyński (2015): Sekurytyzacja polskiej polityki migracyjnej a sytuacja przygranicznych regionów Polski Wschodniej [The securitisation of Polish migration policy vs. the situation of border regions of Eastern Poland], *Studia Migracyjne – Przegląd Polonijny*, no. 1, pp. 85–110; Ł. Fijałkowski (2012): Teoria sekurytyzacji i konstruowanie bezpieczeństwa [The theory of securitisation and the construction of security], *Przegląd Strategiczny*, no. 1., p. 155.

25 R. Matyja, K. Pędziwiatr, A. Siewierska-Chmaj (2015): *Polska polityka migracyjna* [*Polish migration policy*], Warsaw: Wydawnictwo Uniwersytetu Warszawskiego, p. 40.

The key role of security in immigration policy has never been questioned by important political actors; it aroused controversy rather in the context of international obligations of Poland regarding help for refugees.

This is because the second perspective that influenced the formation of Polish immigration policy was Europeanisation. Kicinger and Koryś notice that 'many institutions and tools created on the West in response to the phenomenon of immigration were transferred to Poland during the EU harmonisation process. This led to a paradox: attempts were made to create a migrant policy before it became really necessary, if this need should be measured by the number of immigrants',[26] and Duszczyk and Lesińska even state that EU institutions gave the 'key impulse for the development of migrant policy'.[27]

The Europeanisation process has been deeply analysed with regard to immigrant integration policy; although formally the latter is not subject to harmonisation within the EU, it was imitatively transferred to the Polish reality from the strategy of the European Fund for the Integration of Third-Country Nationals supported by the European Commission.[28] Thus, when planning Polish integration policy at the beginning of the current decade, the Ministry of Labour and Social Policy created direct copies of tools promoted by the Fund. As in the entire Europeanisation process, the existence of funds for the integration of immigrants available to Poland under certain conditions was quite important. However, another significant factor was certainly the fact that the civil servants of the Ministry of Labour and Social Policy preparing Polish integration policy took part in works of the network of national integration contact points and certainly felt the normative pressure of their European colleagues.

The events of September 2015 prove the exaggeration of Weinar's statement that after 2003 'Poland as a member state gradually ceded the sovereignty of decisions in this respect [i.e., migrant policy] to European communities, and

26 A. Kicinger, I. Koryś (2011): The Case of Poland, in: G. Zincone, R. Penninx, M. Borkert (ed.), *Migration Policymaking in Europe. The Dynamics of Actors and Contexts in Past and Present*, Amsterdam: Amsterdam University Press, Amsterdam, p. 347.

27 M. Duszczyk, M. Lesińska, Europeizacja polskiej polityki migracyjnej i jej efekty [The Europeanisation of Polish migration policy and its results], in: A. Górny et al. (ed.), *op. cit.*, p. 75.

28 See M. Pawlak (2013): Imitacja w tworzeniu polskiej polityki integracji cudzoziemców [Imitation in the creation of Polish foreigner integration policy], Studia Migracyjne – Przegląd Polonijny, no. 39(3), pp. 97–121.

the further search of the model was limited by pan-European solutions',[29] but mechanisms of institutional transfer, imitation, adaptation and learning played undoubtedly the leading role in the formation of the entire Polish immigration policy. Again, this did not cause much controversy, because the matters of asylum seekers, who began to be perceived as the main subject-matter of immigration policy were on the margin of Polish public affairs.

This was because Polish immigration policy – and this was its third permanent feature before 2015 – was created beyond the political arena, within a group of civil servants, experts and activists of non-governmental organisations (NGOs) and without the participation of politicians or journalists representing public opinion. During the 7th term of office of the Sejm, when the most important strategic governmental documents about Polish migrant policy, this term appears in reports on the works of the Parliament twice (until the end of 2014). At the same time, the 'course of legislative works did not reveal any significant substantive differences' in issues making up the immigration policy.[30]

On a quite common scale, particularly in migration studies, it is assumed that the exclusion of an issue from public debate makes it easier to prepare a reasonable public policy, because knowledge is used for informing decision-makers and reinforcing the results of work of the organisation rather than legitimising decisions only symbolically.[31] It seems that this belief concerns particularly the issue of immigration, because European societies most often have an unfriendly attitude to it, and politicians acting under their pressure are inclined to adopt an irrational symbolic policy.

In the case of Poland, however, depoliticisation had two rather unexpected consequences. The most obvious one is the lack of preparation of public opinion for a discussion on the issue of immigration and, consequently, the spontaneous extreme politicisation of the immigration policy that is referred to below. However, already the earlier creation of this policy within a confined group of "professionals" – experts and civil servants – led to the formation of two worlds that do not always meet: formally applicable strategic decisions and practical immigration policy. All strategic documents adopted by the government in the last decade referred to migration issues, usually regarding the protection of the

29 A. Weinar (2005): *Polityka migracyjna Polski 1990–2003. Próba podsumowania* [*The migration policy of Poland 1990–2003, A summary attempt*], Warsaw: Centrum Stosunków Międzynarodowych, p. 1.

30 R. Matyja, K. Pędziwiatr, A. Siewierska-Chmaj, *op. cit.*, p. 88, 91.

31 See C. Boswell (2009): *The Political Uses of Expert Knowledge: Immigration Policy and Social Research*, Cambridge: Cambridge University Press.

state against threats resulting from migration processes (e.g., the sectoral document *Polish migrant policy – the current situation and proposed actions* in 2012, but also the long-term country development strategy *Poland 2030. The third wave of modernity*, or *The strategy of development of Human Capital 2020* – both from 2013). However, those documents were also believed to indicate the need for limited immigration that would compensate for the shortage of manpower resulting from the low birth rate and the emigration of around 2 million Poles after 2004. Thus, Polish immigration policy was based on two pillars: on the one hand, the provision of security through strict control of immigration, and, on the other hand, recompensing for shortages on the labour market through selective support of immigration (most often time-limited immigration) of selected groups of employees.

This was reflected in the institutional dimension of the creation and implementation of migration policy. Here the main entity is the Ministry of Interior, which – along with its subordinate units: the Border Guard and the Office for Foreigners – is responsible for all matters concerning the access of foreigners to the territory of the Republic of Poland, the legalisation of their stay and for asylum policy, including the running of reception centres for asylum seekers. Against this background, the Ministry of Labour and Social Policy, which is responsible for the essential part of the immigrant integration policy and the admission of immigrants to the Polish labour market, has the small institutional potential of implementation of these policies. The best testimony of the marginal role of immigration policy for the activity of the Ministry of Labour and Social Policy is the lack of an organisational unit co-ordinating activities in this respect (the competencies of the minister are performed by two large departments dealing with the labour market and with social welfare and integration).

Two sources seem to indicate quite well how the implementation of immigration policy looked in practice in the critical area of integrated policy that was handled by the Ministry of Labour and Social Policy to a prevailing extent. The first source is MIPEX – a synthetic index used for comparing the conditions of immigrant integration in 38 countries, including 28 EU states. Using 167 indicators from eight policy areas (labour market mobility, family reunion, education, health, political participation, permanent residence, access to nationality, anti-discrimination), MIPEX measures to what extent the authorities of each state provide suitable conditions for the acquisition of the position of an integrated member of society by immigrants. In 2010, Poland ranked 37th (36 points out of 100), and in 2014, it ranked 32nd (41 points out of 100). The factor regarded as particularly low was the access of immigrants to education, health care and – in spite of significant improvement since 2010 – to the labour market.[32]

The same phenomena are analysed in the report of the Supreme Audit Office after the verification of the social welfare system for refugees in the period of 2012–2014.[33] In the view of the Supreme Audit Office, the Polish social welfare system does not guarantee the integration of immigrants with the society, nor does it create suitable conditions for them to become independent. A large part of persons participating in Individual Integration Programs uses social welfare after their end. The inspectors of the SAO notice a number of reasons for this. In the first place, Individual Integration Programs are systemically ostensible; they are not individualised, do not contain individualised tasks and do not cover the effective learning of Polish or social skills. In fact, they are reduced to the payment of benefits. This results mainly from the fact that funds from the state budget assigned to county family support centres implementing refugee integration programs covered only costs of payment of money benefits and health insurance during participation in the program. Thus, actions aimed at the integration of refugees would have to be implemented within the scope of ordinary social welfare tasks, which is not very likely due to their specific nature, cost-intensiveness and marginal role for a majority of counties.[34]

The SAO highlights the lack of co-ordination of integrative policy not only in the vertical sense (implementations), but also in the horizontal sense. This is due to the absence of mechanisms enforcing co-operation between the administration subject to the Ministry of Interior and Administration that is responsible for the pre-integration of persons awaiting the consideration of the application for refugee status and the refugee integration policy for which the Ministry of Labour and Social Policy is responsible. Consequently, the period of waiting for the decision of the Office for Foreigners that takes many months and, in 40 %

32 Migrant Integration Policy Index 2015, http://mipex.eu/poland.

33 Supreme Audit Office, *Pomoc społeczna dla uchodźców. Informacja o wynikach kontroli* [*Social services for refugees. Information about the results of the audit*], 159/2015/P/14/049/KPS, Warsaw, October 2015.

34 Cf. E. Piechowska (2015): *Obecność uchodźców w małych gminach. Doświadczenia Góry Kalwarii i Podkowy Leśnej w integracji uchodźców i edukacji ich dzieci* [*The presence of refugees in small communes. The experiences of Góra Kalwaria and Podkowa Leśna in the integration of refugees and the education of their children*], Warsaw, http://interwencjaprawna.pl/wp-content/uploads/obecnosc-uchodzcow-w-malych-gminach.pdf.

of cases, violates the statutory requirement to consider an application within 6 months, is usually wasted from the perspective of the refugee's integration.

Observations of this kind lead some researchers specialising in Polish immigration policy to conclude that we deal with deliberate, though not necessarily planned administrative actions – a sort of hidden agenda. With the belief that actions aimed at the integration of immigrants are a method of encouraging foreigners to settle in Poland, which 'is not a goal of Polish migrant policy [because] settlement migration is not a desirable phenomenon from the perspective of the state'.[35]

We cannot exclude attitudes like this, particularly because of – as other studies suggest – "pro-state discourse" prevailing among civil servants and ministerial experts dealing with migrations. In this discourse, the immigrant is treated like a problem that must be tackled by means of institutions and law in the defence of the citizen's interests.[36] However, dynamic changes on the Polish labour market, which is gradually opening up to foreigners, gathered pace in the period of 2007–2011, so we should rather seek other explanations of the reasons of formation of the Polish version of policy gap between strategies and the practice of immigration policy.

In the years 2006–2011, there was a change in the very restrictive rules of legal employment of foreigners in Poland. It became possible to employ citizens of Eastern Partnership states and Russia on the basis of the employer's statement submitted to the labour office – initially as a pilot solution and subsequently pursuant to the 2011 Act. In 2009, the laborious two-level procedure for obtaining a work permit was liquidated, the period of its validity was prolonged to three years and the rule that each loss of work by a foreigner puts him under an obligation to leave Poland immediately was no longer applicable. The fact that the right to stay

35 M. Lesińska (2010): Polityka integracyjna [Integrative policy], in: A. Górny et al. (ed.), *Transformacja nieoczywista. Polska jako kraj imigracji [Non-obvious transformation. Poland as a country of immigration]*, Warsaw: Wydawnictwo Uniwersytetu Warszawskiego, pp. 103–106.

36 A. Grzymała-Kazłowska (2007): *Konstruowanie „innego". Wizerunki imigrantów w Polsce [Constructing the "other". Images of immigrants in Poland]*, Warsaw: Wydawnictwo Uniwersytetu Warszawskiego, pp. 113–120; parallel conclusions are presented by K. Skowrońska (2017): Niejednoznaczna władza, wspólne normy i niedopowiedziane cele: Działanie Wydziału Spraw Cudzoziemców Mazowieckiego Urzędu Wojewódzkiego jako studium przypadku pola organizacyjnego polityki migracyjnej w Polsce [Ambivalent power, common norms and vague goals: Actions of the Foreigners Affairs Department of the Masovian Provincial Office as a case study of the organisational field of migrant policy in Poland], *Studia Polityczne*, no. 45(2), pp. 217–239.

in the Republic of Poland is strictly connected with legal employment led also to the actual liberalisation of the rules of granting a temporary residence permit and later also a permanent residence permit. As a result of this, Poland became a country with the highest number of issued temporary residence permits in the entire EU in 2017, at the time of economic prosperity (683,000 – almost 22 % of all permits issued in the EU).[37] All of this, however, takes place in conditions of the formally unchanged, very restrictive policy of granting residence permits in the Republic of Poland.

It is, therefore, not surprising that researchers specialising in Polish migrant policy find it 'difficult to evaluate the status and the model adopted in Poland'. While 'political documents suggest that the government is strongly interested in the increase of immigration, statutory provisions continue to create many limitations that may prevent decisions on arrival or return to Poland'.[38] Matyja and his team put this fact down to the 'inability of the clerical factor to introduce a large organisational change … that would be a consequence of the essential change of the vision [of immigration policy] where the burden would be shifted on the needs of the labour market'.[39]

In my view, however, we can propose another explanation of these discrepancies between formal regulations, strategic documents and the practice of Polish immigration policy. The framework of migrant policy created in the early 1990s turned out to be very permanent and resistant to changes of social reality. Their inadequacy could be seen already in the second half of the 1990s, when the phenomenon of illegal engagement of seasonal employees from the East emerged on a large scale. It did not meet with any reaction of the Polish state – it was neither counteracted or legalised. Kicinger may be right when saying that Polish politicians stuck to restrictive solutions for fear that a more liberal policy allowing

37 Eurostat, *Residence permits statistics*, https://ec.europa.eu/eurostat/statistics-explained/index.php/Residence_permits_statistics#First_residence_permits:_an_overview.

38 M. Duszczyk (2014): Ewolucja polskiej polityki migracyjnej w zakresie migracji zarobkowych po 1989 r. [The evolution of Polish migrant policy with regard to economic migrations after 1989], *Studia Biura Analiz Sejmowych Kancelarii Sejmu*, no. 4 (40); see also M. Duszczyk (2012): *Polska polityka imigracyjna a rynek pracy* [*Polish immigration policy vs. the labour market*], Warsaw: Oficyna Wydawnicza Aspra; P. Kaźmierkiewicz (2007): Otwarcie polskiego rynku pracy dla migrantów ekonomicznych – potrzeby i proponowane rozwiązania [The opening of the Polish labour market for economic migrants – needs and proposed solutions], in: W. Klaus (ed.), *Migranci na polskim rynku pracy. Rzeczywistość, problemy, wyzwania* [*Migrants on the Polish labour market. Reality, problems, challenges*], Warsaw: Stowarzyszenie Interwencji Prawnej.

39 R. Matyja, K. Pędziwiatr, A. Siewierska-Chmaj, *op. cit.*, p. 88.

foreigners to work legally during the period of high unemployment would be negatively interpreted by public opinion; at the same time, they realised that economy was in need of cheap manpower from abroad.[40] From the perspective adopted here, it is more important that the illegal mass employment of foreigners was commonly believed not to jeopardise security. Thus, if the basic framework of reference of migration policy is security, the employees from Eastern Europe who do not jeopardise it are not a part of the same problem, are outside the framework of migration policy and constitute a part of the labour market policy. The same way of thinking was used ten years ago, when the rules of foreigners' access to the Polish labour market began to be formally liberalised. The fact that the modification of these rules results in the change of the real impact of migration policy and that a few hundred thousand Ukrainians had settled in Poland quite suddenly was not noticed because it was commonly believed not to affect security.

Obviously, this dual approach – very restrictive towards asylum seekers and 'extremely liberal towards temporary economic immigrants'[41] – was possible only thanks to the political insignificance of these two issues. Until 2015, none of the political entrepreneurs saw the possibility of capitalising on this inconsistency, the consensus of politicians defined migration policy as a part of security policy and entrusted its fulfilment to professionals: civil servants and experts.

Decision-making mechanisms during the crisis

Due to the lack of confirmed sources about the course of negotiations regarding the obligatory relocation of migrants, it is assumed quite commonly that pressures were so strong that 'Germans managed to break Poles', although the author of these words notices that the resistance of Kopacz's government was not very strong.[42] Without negating these hypotheses, I would like to show how the aforementioned framework of understanding of Polish immigration

40 A. Kicinger (2005): Between Polish Interests and the EU Influence: Polish migration policy development 1989–2004, *CEFMR Working Paper*, no. 9, p. 22.

41 M. Lesińska, M. Duszczyk (2018): Polityka migracyjna [Migrant policy], in: M. Lesińska, M. Okólski (ed.), *25 wykładów o migracjach* [*25 lectures on migrations*], Warsaw: WN Scholar, p. 262.

42 R. Alexander (2018): Angela Merkel nie rozumiała Polski. Wygrana PiS-u zaskoczyła Niemców. Wywiad przeprowadził Michał Kokot [Angela Merkel did not understand Poland. The victory of PiS surprised Germans. An interview by Michał Kokot], *Gazeta Wyborcza. Magazyn Świąteczny*, 3.11.2018; cf. also R. Alexander, *op. cit.*, pp. 110–112.

policy allowed Ewa Kopacz's government to reach the conclusion that political meanders in response to pressures from European partners would pass unnoticed and eventually would cause little controversy, as no extraordinary things were happening.

The key fact was that both the European Commission and Kopacz's government took security positions and perceived migrants as a threat to security. Therefore, they believed that this problem would have to be tackled by means of tools used for coping with threats to public order.

One week before the crucial voting in Brussels, during the Sejm debate over the government's information 'about the European migrant crisis and its repercussions for Poland', which was held on the initiative of the opposition, Minister Teresa Piotrowska used the jargon of a policeman, or even a border guard in her speech:

> The control of the inflow of persons to Poland through the southern sections of our border is exercised in accordance with the following assumptions. Firstly, planning the number of officers for the performance of tasks on the basis of the continuous assessment and analysis of risk. Secondly, using offensive operational & reconnaissance methods if any illegal crossing of the border is found. … In practice, the Border Guard, which in most of the cases detains illegal immigrants or takes them over from the Police and other services that detained them, performs mainly such tasks as determining foreigners' identity, accepting (or refusing to accept) their requests for protection in the territory of Poland, informing them about the legal consequences of this procedure and referring them to relevant reception centres. … In the case of persons staying illegally in Poland, actions are being taken to force them to leave the territory of our country.[43]

One week later, justifying the change of the government's attitude, Deputy Minister of Interior Piotr Stachańczyk also referred to the issue of security, saying that the 'agreement fulfils all conditions that Poland was concerned about. It lays very strong emphasis on the need to control borders, ensures the division of incoming persons into illegal migrants and refugees, and guarantees that those subject to relocation will be checked as identified as real refugees already in the first country of arrival'.[44]

---

43 Statements on sessions of the Sejm, session no. 100 on 16.09.2015 (1st day of the session). Minister of Interior Teresa Piotrowska, http://sejm.gov.pl/Sejm7.nsf/wypowiedz.xsp?posiedzenie=100&dzien=1&wyp=004.

44 Trzaskowski: jest decyzja o liczbach, wszystkie postulaty Polski uwzględnione [Trzaskowski: there is a decision on figures, all proposals of Poland taken into consideration], https://wiadomosci.wp.pl/trzaskowski-jest-decyzja-o-liczbach-wszystkie-postulaty-polski-uwzglednione-6027684816446081a.

Such a strategy of legitimisation of the government's actions was presumably an answer to anticipated social fears; at the same time, however, it created a space of dialogue with the opposition. Today it is hard to believe, but in the aforementioned debate the government deserved Jarosław Kaczyński's praise for its 'announcements of building the Fortress Europe and the Fortress Poland'. Later Kaczyński only criticised the government, but mainly for succumbing to foreign pressure, as a result of which 'we will no longer be hosts in our own country'. Finally he advocated 'giving help [to refugees], but using a safe financial method'.[45]

It seems that the government and PiS competed on 'who will provide better security to Poles in case of crisis' for the entire electoral campaign for the Parliament until the end of September. As a part of this game, Prime Minister tried to refer to the previously valid consensual approach to migrant policy and to present the issue of adopting a stance towards the migrant crisis as a cross-party national cause [in which] we must be unanimous'.[46] Therefore, at the beginning of September, she invited opposition politicians to consultations, but she met with a flat refusal: 'It is Prime Minister Ewa Kopacz who currently bears responsibility for what is happening in Poland, including foreigners' affairs,' said Beata Szydło, PiS's official candidate for prime minister.[47] Thus, over a few weeks, immigration policy was politicised very strongly and became the object of electoral competition and a tool of fighting for power. This process is symbolically described by two press headlines divided only by ten days: 'PO and PiS speak with one voice about immigrants. Decisions only after the election' and 'Polish politicians use refugees in the campaign'.[48]

---

45 Statements on sessions of the Sejm, session no. 100 on 16.09.2015 (1st day of the session). Member of Parliament Jarosław Kaczyński, http://sejm.gov.pl/Sejm7.nsf/wypowiedz.xsp?posiedzenie=100&dzien=1&wyp=007.

46 Premier Ewa Kopacz w TVP Info: W sprawie uchodźców musimy być jednomyślni, [Prime Minister Ewa Kopacz in TVP Info: We must be unanimous on the subject of refugees], https://www.premier.gov.pl/wydarzenia/aktualnosci/premier-ewa-kopacz-w-tvp-info-w-sprawie-uchodzcow-musimy-byc-jednomyslni.html.

47 Szydło: to premier Kopacz bierze odpowiedzialność za sprawy uchodźców [Szydło: Prime Minister Kopacz is responsible for refugees' affairs], https://wiadomosci.onet.pl/kraj/szydlo-to-premier-kopacz-bierze-odpowiedzialnosc-za-sprawy-uchodzcow/d2p0s3.

48 G. Osiecki (2015): PO i PIS jednym głosem w sprawie imigrantów. Decyzje dopiero po wyborach [PO and PiS speak with one voice about immigrants. Decisions only after elections], *Dziennik Gazeta Prawna*, 01.09.2015, https://www.gazetaprawna.pl/artykuly/891340,po-i-pis-jednym-glosem-w-sprawie-imigrantow-decyzje-dopiero-po-wyborach.html; R. Grochal, A. Kondzińska (2015): Polscy politycy grają uchodźcami w kampanii. Szydło: Niemcy chcą szantażować Europę [Polish politicians

The victory of PiS in the political game of 'providing security to Poles' can be seen not only in the result of the election of 25 October 2015, but in the radical change of Poles' attitude to migrants. In one of CBOS's regular surveys concerning the attitude to refugees in May 2015, 72 % of respondents declared that Poland should accept refugees from countries affected by armed conflicts, whereas only 21 % were of the opposite opinion. However, when asked specifically about refugees from the Middle East and Africa, 53 % of respondents stated that they should not be given shelter, as compared to 33 % of favourable answers (46 % in the case of Ukrainians). In the same survey, 66 % of respondents agreed with the statement that the presence of foreigners enriches cultural diversity and makes people more open towards others, and only 13 % were of the opposite opinion. As we know from other studies, in comparison to the 1990s, the social distance towards foreigners measured by questions about the attitude to the immigrant as a neighbour (9 % were against) or a son/daughter-in-law (23 % were against) decreased during the last decade.

In the second half of 2015, there was a sharp increase of negative answers to the question concerning the acceptance of refugees from war-affected countries: they reached 38 % in August, 43 % in October and 53 % in December. In the spring of 2016, this rate rose to 61 % and later dropped to around 50 % for a longer period.[49]

---

use refugees as an argument in the campaign. Szydło: Germans want to blackmail Europe], *Gazeta Wyborcza*, 10.09.2015, http://wyborcza.pl/1,75398,18746167,polscy-politycy-graja-uchodzcami-w-kampanii-szydlo-niemcy.html.

49 Centrum Badania Opinii Społecznej [Centre for Public Opinion Research], *Polacy wobec problemu uchodźctwa. Komunikat z badań* [*The attitude of Poles to the issue of refugees. A study report*], CBOS, Warsaw, June 2015; Centrum Badania Opinii Społecznej, *Stosunek do uchodźców w kontekście kryzysu imigracyjnego w Europie. Komunikat z badań* [*The attitude to refugees in the context of the immigration crisis in Europe. A study report*], CBOS, Warsaw, September 2015; Centrum Badania Opinii Społecznej, *O uchodźcach w przededniu unijnego szczytu poświęconego kryzysowi imigracyjnemu. Komunikat z badań* [*About refugees on the eve of the EU summit concerning the immigration crisis. A study report*], CBOS, Warsaw, October 2015; Centrum Badania Opinii Społecznej, *Polacy o uchodźcach – w internecie i w „realu". Komunikat z badań* [*Poles about refugees – on the Internet and in real life. A study report*], CBOS, Warsaw, November 2015; see G. Dutka (2017): Polacy w obliczu współczesnych procesów i problemów migracyjnych. Poczucie zagrożenia i jego społeczno-demograficzne uwarunkowania na podstawie analizy wyników badań sondażowych [Poles in the face of contemporary migration processes and problems. A sense of threat and its social-demographic conditions on the basis of the analysis of results of surveys], *Opuscula Sociologica*, no. 4(22), pp. 67–80.

We can draw two conclusions from the lack of coherence in Poles' opinions about immigration and foreigners and from the pace of changes in their attitude to the acceptance of refugees. Firstly, in May 2015 this issue was of completely marginal importance to a majority of citizens and opinions on that subject were influenced most probably by the question asked by the pollster. Secondly, Poles were subject to the influence of numerous media coverages that suddenly made the issue of refugees important. It seems that the way of reading these messages was largely determined by PiS's intensive campaign started at the end of September 2015.

PiS brought about such a radical change of social attitudes by referring to the discourse used in Poland after 1989 only on the margin of the public sphere. The best-known case of introducing this language is Jarosław Kaczyński's statement at the electoral meeting in Maków Mazowiecki on 12 October. During that meeting, wondering whether there were any agreements concerning the admittance of 100,000 (sic!) Muslims to Poland, the leader of PiS mused on the health consequences of immigration: 'There are already symptoms of diseases that have been absent in Europe for a long time: cholera on the Greek island, dysentery in Vienna, various kinds of parasites, the protozoa that are not dangerous in these people's bodies but may be dangerous here. This is not an appeal to discriminate anyone, but checking is necessary'. When asked to comment upon this statement, President Andrzej Duda demanded that the government 'answer the question whether it is prepared for various circumstances in connection with this [consent to relocation], that is, whether Poles are adequately protected today, for example in epidemiological respect'.[50]

Without engaging in digressions how consciously PiS referred to racist discourse,[51] we can certainly state that the issue of refugees was deliberately demonised in order to provoke an emotional reaction and validate the issue that had been ignored by a vast majority of Poles only a few weeks before. Thus, we can say that PiS made a strategic enactment of the new discourse on migration

50 For Kaczyński's statement, see https://video.wp.pl/i,kaczynski-o-imigrantach-sa-juz-objawy-cholery-pierwotniaki-pasozyty,mid,1801147,cid,4051,klip.html?ticaid=11cbf2; Andrzej Duda in the "Kawa na ławę" programme, https://www.tvn24.pl/raporty/andrzej-duda-w-kawie-na-lawe,1019.

51 Prezydent Duda i „choroba uchodźców" na nagłówkach światowych mediów. „Skojarzenia z retoryką nazistowską" [President Duda and "refugee disease" make the headlines of the international media. Associations with the Nazi rhetoric], http://wyborcza.pl/1,75477,19044509,duda-i-chorobyuchodzcow-na-naglowkach-swiatowych-mediow.html.

policy.[52] While at the beginning of September 2015 it played the old game with the government about who was more credible in providing security, the subject-matter of the political dispute at the end of the month was no longer the effectiveness of the government, but existential threat from wild Muslim hoards. A good illustration of this new discourse is the cover of the issue of the PiS-controlled *W Sieci* weekly of 21 September 2015, with Prime Minister Ewa Kopacz in a burqa decorated with sticks of dynamite. This cover announced the main text of the issue: 'Ewa Kopacz will give us hell upon Berlin's order'. Over the Prime Minister's head we can see the calm face of Kaczyński, who declares: 'First our loved ones, then the nation and later others'.[53] When PiS came to power, expressions of this kind occurred less frequently, but were maintained by the social media that supported 'the camp of good change' and used for mobilising PiS's electorate.

Thus, Kopacz's government failed to notice the politicisation of immigration quickly enough; in any case, it was not able to prevent such politicisation. Moreover, in trying to maintain the consensus around immigration as a security issue that must be left to specialists, it left PiS a space for the redefinition of this policy as an existential, non-marginal issue that arouses emotions and mobilises people to act.

In my belief, this resulted also from the fact that the government formed its positive communication of the issue of refugees only by referring to Poland's responsibility towards Europe. This can be understood if we remember that Polish migration policy was formed largely as a part of the Europeanisation process even before Poland's accession to the EU.

We can quote opinions of leading politicians of PO appealing for confirmation of 'the credibility of Poland in the European Union', because 'Europe and our European partners expect this solidarity from us'. After all, 'We, Poles, may be in a difficult situation at any moment because of the dynamic situation in Eastern Europe and in eastern Ukraine. We will expect help and solidarity with Poland when we need it'. Obviously, they appealed for sympathy for refugees and asked rhetorical questions: 'Can we afford a gesture of solidarity towards those who are really escaping from their own country only because they are afraid of losing their health or life?', but such questions always appeared on the margin

52 Cf. M. Krzyżanowski (2018): Discursive Shifts in Ethno-Nationalist Politics: On Politicization and Mediatization of the "Refugee Crisis" in Poland, *Journal of Immigrant & Refugee Studies*, no. 1–2, pp. 76–96.

53 See: https://www.wsieciprawdy.pl/nowe-wsieci-kopacz-urzadzi-nam-pieklo-pnews-2433.html.

of opinions of Prime Minister Kopacz or Minister of Foreign Affairs Grzegorz Schetyna.[54]

Besides, Schetyna clearly located migrant policy in the field of European policy: 'Today we have a great opportunity, and this debate should also support that goal, to show that we are a mature and responsible member of the Union that helps solve problems instead of creating them. We have heard so many times in this room that Poland should pursue a more active policy within the European Union. Today, standing aside or turning our back on the current crisis is definitely below our ambitions to play an important role in the Community and to influence its current policy. (Applause) Poland is able to conduct an ambitious and brave policy also with regard to refugees, asylum, immigration'.[55]

The statements of PO's politicians contain virtually no references to Christian or human values that would oblige us to help the needy; there was no attempt to combine the inflow of immigrants with the demand for manpower in the aging Polish society affected by mass emigration. Thus, the fact that Minister Piotrowska is a religious teacher by education may have played a certain role in "breaking" her in Brussels; maybe even arguments referring to values appeared as an element of pressure from German politicians, as Alexander states, but not a trace of them has remained in the public discussion. The strategy of Kopacz's government was maintained within the framework of Polish migration policy that had been created for it in the previous two decades: the professional provision of security to Poles and coping with challenges set for us by Europe. By politicising migrant policy, PiS radically changed its framework: the issue of security must not be left to public order experts, when the existential threat from barbaric hoards exists, and Europe is their ally, because it tries to solve its problems at the expense of Poland, imposing its hazardous decisions brutally on us. This is how we could describe the framework in which Polish migrant policy has existed since the autumn of 2015.

54 Statements on sessions of the Sejm, session no. 100 on 16.09.2015 (1st day of the session). Prime Minister Ewa Kopacz, http://sejm.gov.pl/Sejm7.nsf/wypowiedz.xsp?posiedzenie=100&dzien=1&wyp=002.

55 Statements on sessions of the Sejm, session no. 100 on 16.09.2015 (1st day of the session). Minister of Foreign Affairs Grzegorz Schetyna, http://sejm.gov.pl/Sejm7.nsf/wypowiedz.xsp?posiedzenie=100&dzien=1&wyp=003.

Conclusion: consequences of changes in 2015 for Polish migrant policy

Established in November 2015, PiS's government became, to a large extent, the hostage of the new framework of Polish migrant policy created by this party. We can presume that there was a plan to calm down the hot emotions of the electoral campaign in the first period. The civil servants of the Ministry of Interior and Administration began to implement the July and September decisions of the Council: a draft ordinance of the Council of Ministers on the relocation of foreigners was prepared, criteria of qualification of migrants for relocation to Poland were created, and Polish officers joined activities aimed at checking qualified refugees in respect of security.[56]

However, as a result of the November 2015 attacks in Paris and presumably also the reactions that they caused in the political and media base of the "camp of good change", Szydło's government adopted a position claiming that 'the decisions of the EU Council on the relocation of refugees and immigrants to all EU states that have been criticised by us still have the status of applicable EU law. However, after the tragic incidents in Paris, we do not see the political possibility of their implementation'.[57] In addition, as a part of propaganda fight against critics of this decision, Prime Minister Szydło announced in the European Parliament that 'Poland has accepted around 1 million refugees from Ukraine'.[58]

Refraining from the evaluation of such policy, we must notice that the total subordination of the issue of immigration to current political needs of the ruling party actually excludes the conduct of a rational public policy in this respect.

---

56 Chancellery of the Prime Minister, *Wykaz prac legislacyjnych i programowych Rady Ministrów. Projekt rozporządzenia RM w sprawie relokacji cudzoziemców* [*A list of legislative and program works of the Council of Ministers. A draft ordinance of the Council of Ministers on the resettlement of foreigners*], https://bip.kprm.gov.pl/kpr/form/r2199,Projekt-rozporzadzenia-Rady-Ministrow-w-sprawie-relokacji-cudzoziemcow-w-roku-20.html.

57 Zamach w Paryżu. Przyszły minister ds. europejskich: "Nie wykonamy decyzji o przyjęciu uchodźców" [Paris attacks. Future Minister for European Affairs: We will not implement the decision on the acceptance of refugees], *Gazeta Wyborcza*, 14.11.2015, http://wyborcza.pl/1,75398,19186929,zamach-w-paryzu-przyszly-minister-ds-europejskich-przeciw.html.

58 Szydło: 'Poland has accepted one million refugees from the Ukraine'. And what do the figures show?, http://wiadomosci.gazeta.pl/wiadomosci/1,114871,19504967,milion-uchodzcow-z-ukrainy-liczby-mowia-zupelnie-co-innego.html.

Until 2015, Polish migrant policy was shaped in total isolation from the world of politics; therefore, its politicisation meant a collapse of the framework that had been created for the previous 20 years. After 2015, the work of civil servants and experts in this field lost its sense, since each day may bring a politician's statement that would destroy their efforts so far.

This was experienced by Deputy Minister for Development and Investment Paweł Chorąży, who was the head of the team preparing new *Social-economic priorities of migrant policy*. In March 2018, the Council of Ministers adopted the priorities that radically contradicted the framework of migrant policy established by PiS, and implementation documents were to be elaborated till the summer of 2018. In September 2018, the Deputy Minister was dismissed for his public statement that actually did not go beyond the position adopted by the government. The Deputy Minister said that the 'inflow of immigrants to our country must increase so that economic growth could continue' and added that Poland should accept immigrants because they contribute to the creation of the 'prosperity of states that have achieved success'.[59] By adopting its attitude, the government actually went much, much further – which we must notice – than PO's governments in strategies adopted by them. Not only did it state that the 'inflow of foreigner to Poland will play an increasingly important role … and immigration is not only a circulatory and seasonal phenomenon'; it also announced the creation of tools aimed at 'attracting employees and entrepreneurs from abroad … The most important projects include the support of employers looking for employees abroad and foreigners looking for information about work in Poland, as well as the creation of a system of incentives for taking up work and settlement in Poland for Poles living abroad and foreigners with desired qualifications'.[60]

---

59 D. Szymański (2018): Paweł Chorąży zdymisjonowany. Wiceminister "zagalopował się" w słowach o imigrantach [Paweł Chorąży dismissed. Deputy Prime Minister went too far in his words about immigrants], *Business Insider*, 14.09.2018, https://businessinsider.com.pl/wiadomosci/wiceminister-inwestycji-i-rozwoju-pawel-chorazy-zdymisjonowany/z75j6b4; M. Makowski (2018): News WP: "Premier był wściekły". Morawiecki podjął decyzję o zdymisjonowaniu ministra Chorążego. Zaważyły wypowiedzi o imigrantach [WP News: 'Prime Minister was angry'. Morawiecki decided to dismiss Minister Chorąży for his statements about immigrants], 14.09.2018, https://opinie.wp.pl/news-wp-premier-byl-wsciekly-morawiecki-podjal-decyzje-o-zdymisjonowaniu-ministra-chorazego-zawazyly-wypowiedzi-o-imigrantach-6295185123436161a.

60 Ministry of Investment and Economic Development, *Nowe priorytety rządowej polityki migracyjnej* [*New priorities of governmental migrant policy*], 29.03.2018, https://www.miir.gov.pl/strony/aktualnosci/nowe-priorytety-rzadowej-polityki-migracyjnej;

The events described above indicate the permanency of some of the aforementioned features of Polish migrant policy. The first permanent feature is the apparent character of program or strategical documents adopted by the government, which are actually not normative at all. The actual policy is either reactive, or programmed by an unexplicated, deeply rooted cognitive framework. However, whereas during PO's rule migration policy was on the margin of politics and this discrepancy was visible only for interested observers, the politicisation of this issue in PiS's times led to a violent yet short row when a ministerial civil servant treated the government's declaration seriously.

The second permanent feature of Polish migrant policy, which explains how the adoption of *Social-economic priorities of migrant policy* by Mateusz Morawiecki's government was possible at all, is the placement of the compensatory economic immigration outside the field of immigration policy: since economic immigrants do not pose a threat to security and are beneficial for Poland, they are not immigrants (=refugees). The demonisation of refugees by the media of the "camp of good change" seems to stimulate this way of thinking.

The case of Minister Chorąży shows the dysfunctionality of such framework of migrant policy: if any politician associates economic immigrants with refugees, the prepared tools in the field of public policies can be thrown away. The threat is potentially larger here. One day – e.g., because of political entrepreneurs or as a result of economic collapse – public opinion may decide one day that Ukrainians working in Poland are immigrants and extend the attitude to refugees maintained by the media of the "camp of good change" for the last few years to Ukrainians. Considering the number of Ukrainian immigrants in Poland, this would create the risk of a social conflict on a huge scale.

Thus, the change that occurred in Polish migrant policy due to the wrong assessment of the situation by Ewa Kopacz's government and the politicisation of the issue of migrants by PiS postpones for an indefinite time the creation of a migrant policy adapted to the labour market needs that would reinforce the competitiveness of Polish economy and build a foreigner integration model that would help avoid the problems being experienced by a part of Western European countries.[61]

---

zob. M. Wysocki (2018): Nowe priorytety! Chcemy więcej imigrantów [New priorities! We want more immigrants], 29.03.2018, http://wgospodarce.pl/informacje/48080-nowe-priorytety-chcemy-wiecej-imigrantow.

61 Cf. R. Matyja, K. Pędziwiatr, A. Siewierska-Chmaj, *op. cit.*, p. 87.

References

Adamczyk A. (2016): Polska wobec kryzysu imigracyjnego [The attitude of Poland to the immigration crisis], in: A. Adamczyk, A. Sakson, C. Trosiak (ed.), *Polityczne i społeczne aspekty wielokulturowości. Migracje i mniejszości [Political and Social Aspects of Multiculturalism. Migrations and Minorities]*, Poznań: Wydawnictwo UAM, pp. 99–120.

Alexander R. (2017): *Angela Merkel and the Migration Crisis. Day by day* (published in Polish as: *Angela Merkel i kryzys migracyjny. Dzień po dniu*), Warsaw: Teologia Polityczna.

Alexander R. (2018): Angela Merkel nie rozumiała Polski. Wygrana PiS-u zaskoczyła Niemców. Wywiad przeprowadził Michał Kokot [Angela Merkel did not understand Poland. The victory of PiS surprised Germans. An interview by Michał Kokot], *Gazeta Wyborcza. Magazyn Świąteczny*, 3.11.2018.

Bielecki J. (2015): Niemcy uczą solidarności [Germans teach solidarity], *Rzeczpospolita*, 21.07.2015, https://www.rp.pl/Uchodzcy/307209766-Niemcy-ucza-solidarnosci.html.

Boswell C. (2009): *The Political Uses of Expert Knowledge: Immigration Policy and Social Research*, Cambridge: Cambridge University Press.

Brzozowski J. (2011): Polityka migracyjna Unii Europejskiej: stan obecny i perspektywy [Migration policy of the European Union: current situation and perspectives], *Studia Europejskie*, no. 3, pp. 56–71.

Buonfino A. (2004): Between Unity and Plurality: The Politicization and Securitization of the Discourse of Immigration in Europe, *New Political Science*, no. 26(1), pp. 23–49.

Buraczyński R. (2015): Sekurytyzacja polskiej polityki migracyjnej a sytuacja przygranicznych regionów Polski Wschodniej [The securitisation of Polish migration policy vs. the situation of border regions of Eastern Poland], *Studia Migracyjne – Przegląd Polonijny*, no. 1, pp. 85–110.

Buzan B. et al. (1998): *Security: A New Framework for Analysis*, Boulder: Lynne Rienner Publishers.

Cairney P. (2012): *Understanding Public Policy: Theories and Issues*, Basingstoke: Palgrave.

Centrum Badania Opinii Społecznej [Centre for Public Opinion Research], Polacy wobec problemu uchodźctwa. Komunikat z badań [The attitude of Poles to the issue of refugees. A study report], CBOS, Warsaw, June 2015.

Centrum Badania Opinii Społecznej, O uchodźcach w przededniu unijnego szczytu poświęconego kryzysowi imigracyjnemu. Komunikat z badań

[About refugees on the eve of the EU summit concerning the immigration crisis. A study report], CBOS, Warsaw, October 2015.

Centrum Badania Opinii Społecznej, Polacy o uchodźcach – w internecie i w „realu". Komunikat z badań [Poles about refugees – on the Internet and in real life. A study report], CBOS, Warsaw, November 2015.

Centrum Badania Opinii Społecznej, Stosunek do uchodźców w kontekście kryzysu imigracyjnego w Europie. Komunikat z badań [The attitude to refugees in the context of the immigration crisis in Europe. A study report], CBOS, Warsaw, September 2015.

Chancellery of the Prime Minister, Wykaz prac legislacyjnych i programowych Rady Ministrów. Projekt rozporządzenia RM w sprawie relokacji cudzoziemców [A list of legislative and program works of the Council of Ministers. A draft ordinance of the Council of Ministers on the resettlement of foreigners], 16.10.2018,https://bip.kprm.gov.pl/kpr/form/r2199,Projekt-rozporzadzenia-Rady-Ministrow-w-sprawie-relokacji-cudzoziemcow-w-roku-20.html.

Communication from the Commission to the European Parliament, the Council, the European Economic and Social Committee and the Committee of the Regions. A European agenda on migration, 13.05.2015, https://ec.europa.eu/home-affairs/sites/homeaffairs/files/what-we-do/policies/european-agenda-migration/background-information/docs/communication_on_the_european_agenda_on_migration_en.pdf.

Communication from the Commission to the European Parliament, the European Council and the Council, Brussels, 8.05.2016, http://ec.europa.eu/dgs/home-affairs/what-we-do/policies/european-agenda-migration/ proposal-implementation-package/docs/20160518/communication_third_report_on_relocation_and_resettlement_en.pdf.

Data of the Office of the United Nations High Commissioner for Refugees, 22 December 2015, see: https://www.unhcr.org/news/press/2015/12/567918556/million-refugees-migrants-flee-europe-2015.html.

Duszczyk M. (2012): *Polska polityka imigracyjna a rynek pracy* [*Polish Immigration Policy vs. the Labour Market*], Warszawa: Oficyna Wydawnicza Aspra.

Duszczyk M. (2014): Ewolucja polskiej polityki migracyjnej w zakresie migracji zarobkowych po 1989 r. [The evolution of Polish migrant policy with regard to economic migrations after 1989], *Studia Biura Analiz Sejmowych Kancelarii Sejmu*, no. 4(40).

Dutka G. (2017): Polacy w obliczu współczesnych procesów i problemów migracyjnych. Poczucie zagrożenia i jego społeczno-demograficzne uwarunkowania na podstawie analizy wyników badań sondażowych [Poles in the face of contemporary migration processes and problems. A sense of threat and its social-demographic conditions on the basis of the analysis of results of surveys], *Opuscula Sociologica*, no. 4(22), pp. 67–80.

Eurostat, Residence permits statistics, https://ec.europa.eu/eurostat/statistics-explained/index.php/Residence_permits_statistics#First_residence_permits:_an_overview.

Fijałkowski Ł. (2012): Teoria sekurytyzacji i konstruowanie bezpieczeństwa [The theory of securitisation and the construction of security], *Przegląd Strategiczny*, no. 1, p. 155.

Górny A. et al. (2010): *Transformacja nieoczywista. Polska jako kraj imigracji* [*Non-obvious Transformation. Poland as a Country of Immigration*], Warsaw: Wydawnictwa Uniwersytetu Warszawskiego.

Grochal R., Kondzińska A. (2015): Polscy politycy grają uchodźcami w kampanii. Szydło: Niemcy chcą szantażować Europę [Polish politicians use refugees as an argument in the campaign. Szydło: Germans want to blackmail Europe], *Gazeta Wyborcza*, 10.09.2015, http://wyborcza.pl/1,75398,18746167,polscy-politycy-graja-uchodzcami-w-kampanii-szydlo-niemcy.html.

Grzymała-Kazłowska A. (2007): *Konstruowanie „innego". Wizerunki imigrantów w Polsce* [*Constructing the "Other". Images of Immigrants in Poland*], Wydawnictwo Uniwersytetu Warszawskiego.

Hall P. (1993): Policy paradigms: social learning and the state: the case of economic policymaking in Britain, *Comparative Politics*, no. 3, pp. 275–296.

Hasselbach C. (2013): *Still no sign of a common asylum policy in the EU*, DW 10.01.2013, https://p.dw.com/p/17Hhi.

Huysmans J. (2000): The European Union and the securitization of migration, *Journal of Common Market Studies*, no. 5, pp. 751–777.

Kaźmierkiewicz P. (2007): Otwarcie polskiego rynku pracy dla migrantów ekonomicznych – potrzeby i proponowane rozwiązania [The opening of the Polish labour market for economic migrants – needs and proposed solutions], in: W. Klaus (ed.), *Migranci na polskim rynku pracy. Rzeczywistość, problemy, wyzwania* [*Migrants on the Polish Labour Market. Reality, Problems, Challenges*], Wasraw: Stowarzyszenie Interwencji Prawnej.

Kicinger A. (2005): Between Polish Interests and the EU Influence: Polish migration policy development 1989–2004, *CEFMR Working Paper*, no. 9.

Kicinger A. (2009): Beyond the Focus on Europeanisation: Polish migration policy 1989–2004, *Journal of Ethnic and Migration Studies*, no. 1, pp. 79–95.

Kicinger A., Koryś I. (2011): The case of Poland, in: G. Zincone, R. Penninx, M. Borkert (ed.), *Migration Policymaking in Europe. The Dynamics of Actors and Contexts in Past and Present*, Amsterdam: Amsterdam University Press.

Kryzys migracyjny. Premier Francji przeciwny stałym kwotom relokacji uchodźców [Migration crisis. French Prime Minister objects to steady refugee resettlement quotas], Polish Radio, 14.02.2016, https://www.polskieradio.pl/5/3/Artykul/1582292,Kryzys-migracyjny-Premier-Francji-przeciwny-stalym-kwotom-relokacji-uchodzcow.

Krzyżanowski M. (2018): Discursive shifts in ethno-nationalist politics: on politicization and mediatization of the "refugee crisis" in Poland, *Journal of Immigrant & Refugee Studies*, no. 1–2, pp. 76–96.

Lesińska M. (2010): *Polityka integracyjna* [*Integrative policy*], in: A. Górny et al. (ed.), *Transformacja nieoczywista. Polska jako kraj imigracji* [*Non-obvious Transformation. Poland as a Country of Immigration*], Warszawa: Wydawnictwo Uniwersytetu Warszawskiego.

Lesińska M., Duszczyk M. (2018): *Polityka migracyjna* [*Migrant policy*], in: M. Lesińska, M. Okólski (ed.), *25 wykładów o migracjach* [*25 Lectures on Migrations*], Warsaw: WN Scholar.

Łodziński S., Szonert M. (2017): „Niepolityczna polityka"? Kształtowanie się polityki migracyjnej w Polsce w latach 1989–2016 ["Non-political policy"? The formation of migration policy in Poland in the years 1989–2016], *Studia Migracyjne – Przegląd Polonijny*, no. 2, pp. 39–66.

Makowski M. (2018): News WP: "Premier był wściekły". Morawiecki podjął decyzję o zdymisjonowaniu ministra Chorążego. Zaważyły wypowiedzi o imigrantach [WP News: 'Prime Minister was angry'. Morawiecki decided to dismiss Minister Chorąży for his statements about immigrants], 14.09.2018, https://opinie.wp.pl/news-wp-premier-byl-wsciekly-morawiecki-podjal-decyzje-o-zdymisjonowaniu-ministra-chorazego-zawazyly-wypowiedzi-o-imigrantach-6295185123436161a.

Matyja R., Pędziwiatr K., Siewierska-Chmaj A., *Polska polityka migracyjna* [*Polish Migration Policy*], Warsaw: Wydawnictwo Uniwersytetu Warszawskiego.

Migrant Integration Policy Index 2015, http://mipex.eu/poland.

Ministry of Investment and Economic Development, Nowe priorytety rządowej polityki migracyjnej [New priorities of governmental migrant policy], 29.03.2018, https://www.miir.gov.pl/strony/aktualnosci/nowe-priorytety-rzadowej-polityki-migracyjnej.

Nyzio A. (2017): The Second Revival? The Visegrad Group and the European migrant crisis in 2015–2017, *Politeja*, no. 5(50), pp. 47–99.

Osiecki G. (2015): PO i PIS jednym głosem w sprawie imigrantów. Decyzje dopiero po wyborach [PO and PiS speak with one voice about immigrants. Decisions only after elections], *Dziennik Gazeta Prawna*, 01.09.2015, https://www.gazetaprawna.pl/artykuly/891340,po-i-pis-jednym-glosem-w-sprawie-imigrantow-decyzje-dopiero-po-wyborach.html.

Pawlak M. (2013): Imitacja w tworzeniu polskiej polityki integracji cudzoziemców [Imitation in the creation of Polish foreigner integration policy], *Studia Migracyjne – Przegląd Polonijny*, no. 39(3), pp. 97–121.

Pawlak M. (2017): *Polityki publiczne wobec migracji* [*Public migration policies*], [in:] J. Kwaśniewski (ed.), *Nauki o polityce publicznej. Monografia dyscypliny* [*Public Policy Sciences. The Monograph of the Field*], pp. 288–310.

Pędziwiatr K., Legut A. (2017): Polskie rządy wobec unijnej strategii na rzecz przeciwdziałania kryzysowi migracyjnemu [The attitude of Polish governments to the EU strategy for the prevention of migration crisis], in: K. Wojtaszczyk, J. Szymańska (ed.), *Uchodźcy w Europie. Uwarunkowania, istota, następstwa* [*Refugees in Europe. Circumstances, Essence, Consequences*], Warsaw: Instytut Europeistyki UW, pp. 608–621.

Piechowska E. (2015): *Obecność uchodźców w małych gminach. Doświadczenia Góry Kalwarii i Podkowy Leśnej w integracji uchodźców i edukacji ich dzieci* [*The Presence of Refugees in Small Communes. The Experiences of Góra Kalwaria and Podkowa Leśna in the Integration of Refugees and the Education of Their Children*], Warsaw, 30.09.2016, http://interwencjaprawna.pl/wp-content/uploads/obecnosc-uchodzcow-w-malych-gminach.pdf.

Polish Radio IAR, Unia Europejska szuka rozwiązania problemu imigrantów. Chce niszczyć łodzie i zwiększyć patrole [The European Union seeks solution to the immigration issue. It wants to destroy boats and increase patrols], 22.04.2015, https://www.polskieradio.pl/5/3/Artykul/1427091,Unia-Europejska-szuka-rozwiazania-problemu-imigrantow-Chce-niszczyc-lodzie-i-zwiekszyc-patrole.

Premier Ewa Kopacz o przyjmowaniu uchodźców: Będę zabiegała o to, by dobrowolność w tej kwestii nadal obowiązywała [Prime Minister Ewa Kopacz on the acceptance of refugees: I will make efforts to maintain voluntariness in this matter], 15.05.2015, https://www.premier.gov.pl/wydarzenia/aktualnosci/premier-ewa-kopacz-o-przyjmowaniu-uchodzcow-bede-zabiegala-o-to-by.html.

Premier Ewa Kopacz w TVP Info: W sprawie uchodźców musimy być jednomyślni, [Prime Minister Ewa Kopacz in TVP Info: We must be unanimous on the subject of refugees], 8.09.2015, https://www.premier.gov.pl/wydarzenia/aktualnosci/premier-ewa-kopacz-w-tvp-info-w-sprawie-uchodzcow-musimy-byc-jednomyslni.html.

Prezydent Duda i „choroba uchodźców" na nagłówkach światowych mediów. „Skojarzenia z retoryką nazistowską" [President Duda and "refugee disease" make the headlines of the international media. Associations with the Nazi rhetoric], 19.10.2015, http://wyborcza.pl/1,75399,19044509,duda-i-choroby-uchodzcow-na-naglowkach-swiatowych-mediow.html.

Rafał Trzaskowski: Polska przyjmie 4,5 tysiąca uchodźców [Rafał Trzaskowski: Poland will accept 4,500 refugees], 22.09.2015, https://fakty.interia.pl/raporty/raport-imigranci-z-afryki/informacje/news-rafal-trzaskowski-polska-przyjmie-4-5-tysiaca-uchodzcow,nId,1890520.

Skowrońska K. (2017): Niejednoznaczna władza, wspólne normy i niedopowiedziane cele: Działanie Wydziału Spraw Cudzoziemców Mazowieckiego Urzędu Wojewódzkiego jako studium przypadku pola organizacyjnego polityki migracyjnej w Polsce [Ambivalent power, common norms and vague goals: Actions of the Foreigners Affairs Department of the Masovian Provincial Office as a case study of the organisational field of migrant policy in Poland], *Studia Polityczne*, no. 45(2), pp. 217–239.

Special meeting of the European Council, 23/04/2015, https://www.consilium.europa.eu/en/meetings/european-council/2015/04/23/.

Statements on sessions of the Sejm, session no. 100 on 16.09.2015 (1st day of the session). Minister of Interior Teresa Piotrowska, 16.09.2015, http://sejm.gov.pl/Sejm7.nsf/wypowiedz.xsp?posiedzenie=100&dzien=1&wyp=004.

Statements on sessions of the Sejm, session no. 100 on 16.09.2015 (1st day of the session). Member of Parliament Jarosław Kaczyński, 16.09.2015, http://sejm.gov.pl/Sejm7.nsf/wypowiedz.xsp?posiedzenie=100&dzien=1&wyp=007.

Statements on sessions of the Sejm, session no. 100 on 16.09.2015 (1st day of the session). Prime Minister Ewa Kopacz, 16.09.2015, http://sejm.gov.pl/Sejm7.nsf/wypowiedz.xsp?posiedzenie=100&dzien=1&wyp=002.

Statements on sessions of the Sejm, session no. 100 on 16.09.2015 (1st day of the session). Minister of Foreign Affairs Grzegorz Schetyna, 16.09.2015, http://sejm.gov.pl/Sejm7.nsf/wypowiedz.xsp?posiedzenie=100&dzien=1&wyp=003.

Stritzel H. (2007): Towards a theory of securitization: Copenhagen and beyond, *European Journal of International Relations*, no. 3, pp. 357–383.

Supreme Audit Office (2015): *Pomoc społeczna dla uchodźców. Informacja o wynikach kontroli* [*Social Services for Refugees. Information about the Results of the Audit*], 159/2015/P/14/049/KPS, Warsaw, October 2015.

Szydło: 'Poland has accepted one million refugees from the Ukraine'. And what do the figures show?, 20.01.2016, http://wiadomosci.gazeta.pl/wiadomosci/1

,114871,19504967,milion-uchodzcow-z-ukrainy-liczby-mowia-zupelnie-co-innego.html.

Szydło: to premier Kopacz bierze odpowiedzialność za sprawy uchodźców [Szydło: Prime Minister Kopacz is responsible for refugees' affairs], 9.09.2015, https://wiadomosci.onet.pl/kraj/szydlo-to-premier-kopacz-bierze-odpowiedzialnosc-za-sprawy-uchodzcow/d2p0s3.

Szymański D. (2018): Paweł Chorąży zdymisjonowany. Wiceminister "zagalopował się" w słowach o imigrantach [Paweł Chorąży dismissed. Deputy Prime Minister went too far in his words about immigrants], "Business Insider", 14.09.2018, https://businessinsider.com.pl/wiadomosci/wiceminister-inwestycji-i-rozwoju-pawel-chorazy-zdymisjonowany/z75j6b4.

True J.L. et al. (2007): Punctuated-equilibrium theory explaining stability and change in public policymaking, in: P. Sabatier (ed.), *Theories of the Policy Process*, Cambridge, MA: Westview Press, pp. 176–1188.

Trzaskowski: jest decyzja o liczbach, wszystkie postulaty Polski uwzględnione [Trzaskowski: there is a decision on figures, all proposals of Poland taken into consideration], 22.09.2015, https://wiadomosci.wp.pl/trzaskowski-jest-decyzja-o-liczbach-wszystkie-postulaty-polski-uwzglednione-6027684816446081a.

Weinar A. (2005): *Polityka migracyjna Polski 1990–2003. Próba podsumowania* [*The Migration Policy of Poland 1990–2003, A Summary Attempt*], Warsaw: Centrum Stosunków Międzynarodowych.

Weinar A. (2006): *Europeizacja polskiej polityki wobec cudzoziemców* 1990–2003 [*The Europeanisation of Polish Policy Towards Foreigners 1990–2003*], Warsaw: Wydawnictwo Naukowe Scholar.

Wysocki M. (2018): *Nowe priorytety! Chcemy więcej imigrantów* [*New priorities! We want more immigrants*], 29.03.2018, http://wgospodarce.pl/informacje/48080-nowe-priorytety-chcemy-wiecej-imigrantow.

Zamach w Paryżu. Przyszły minister ds. europejskich: "Nie wykonamy decyzji o przyjęciu uchodźców" [Paris attacks. Future Minister for European Affairs: We will not implement the decision on the acceptance of refugees], *Gazeta Wyborcza*, 14.11.2015, http://wyborcza.pl/1,75398,19186929,zamach-w-paryzu-przyszly-minister-ds-europejskich-przeciw.html.

Marek Cichocki

Conflict over the rule of law between the Polish government and the European Commission as an example of a multifaceted crisis in the EU

Abstract: The conflict between the Polish government and the European Commission regarding the rule of law should be treated as an example of a multidimensional crisis in the European Union, which requires a comprehensive approach. In this analysis, the author draws attention to the international dimension, showing a high degree of mutual horizontal relationships between courts and legal circles that seek to become independent of national contexts. The author also shows the evolution of the concept of the rule of law in the EU which is narrowed down to a purely legalistic approach. He also refers to the institutional context of the dispute which shows the creation of new competences and centralization of existing ones by the EU institutions as a result of the deepening crisis of the European integration. Finally, the author tries to identify the sources of actual concerns of the Member States regarding the changes introduced in the Polish judiciary and show how the arguments adopted by the Polish side deviate from them.

Keywords: rule of law, Poland, European Commission, national state, courts

At the start, I think it is appropriate to point out that the objective of this analysis is not to assess the changes in constitutional judiciary and in the Polish justice system, which have been introduced since December 2015 by the Law and Justice (Prawo i Sprawiedliwość, PiS) government – neither their content, nor impact. I am also not going to deal with the analysis of the internal political conflict that has erupted due to these changes, involving the government, the political opposition and the judiciary. These are topics worthy of a separate study.[1]

In my analysis, I am going to focus on the issue of the conflict between the Polish government and EU institutions, mainly the European Commission, which broke out due to the changes in the judiciary. For the purpose of this study, this case will be treated as a multifaceted and multidimensional crisis in relations between a Member State and the European Union on the basis of

---

1 To date, only the early changes regarding the functioning of the Constitutional Tribunal were presented as a separate study in the form of a book: L. Mażewski (2017): *Wiele hałasu o nic? Konflikt wokół Trybunału Konstytucyjnego w latach 2015–2016 w perspektywie rozważań modelowych*, Radzymin: von Borowiecky.

respect for the rule of law. I would like to analyse the various aspects of this crisis, which concerns at least several important issues that I would like to raise, and at the same time I wonder to what extent the Polish side was aware of them and how it reacted to them. First, I would like to consider how the justice system and constitutional judiciary, which can be essentially considered to be national competences, work today in the area of European integration and, more broadly, in the area of international relations. Second, I want to deliberate on the evolution of the very idea of the rule of law, which took place over the course of recent decades and its political significance within the Western world today. Third, I want to analyse the institutional context of the dispute over the rule of law in the EU and the impact of the current conflict between Poland and the European Commission on that context. Finally, I want to take into consideration the difficulties in explaining the sources and motives of the changes in the Polish judiciary and presenting arguments that could effectively function in the international area of the EU.

I believe that these issues contribute to the current crisis situation concerning the rule of law in Poland in relations with EU institutions, although the list is not fully exhaustive. In order to assess the impact of this conflict, it seems very important to trace the extent to which the authors of the changes in the Polish justice system were aware of the existence of these issues, as well as to discuss their reactions. Is it possible to formulate a list of problems that should have been taken into account in building the political strategy of the state in order to resolve the conflict on this basis?

Judiciary in the international network

It may be argued that the authors of the post-2015 changes to the Polish judiciary were initially completely unaware of the nature of the system of existing links between the domestic judiciary and the external system in Europe and in the EU. This is why they approached the justice system in the traditional way, treating it as one of the elements of the internal system of the state, while not being fully aware of the extent of international relations and dependencies connected with it. The international reaction to the changes in the Polish judiciary introduced by the Law and Justice government, the reaction of the EU and other institutions, as well as international associations in Europe, came as a surprise to the ruling party, while revealing the existence of relations that were mostly unknown in Poland to that point. It needs to be said, however, that ignorance in this respect was not only characteristic of political decision-makers, but also concerned, to a large extent, the main stakeholders in the changes in the judiciary – Polish judges.

What I am referring to here are the growing phenomena of internationalism, interdependence, as well as the system of international governance, of which the judiciary is one of the most interesting and, at the same time, worrying examples. By its very nature, this example serves as a very good illustration of the growing tension between the strength of international relations and the traditional sovereignty of a democratic state. Undoubtedly, justice and law-making are key areas, where this tension is visible.

As Dani Rodrik shows, the system of global governance has always stood in opposition to the "tyranny" of the nation state, creating mechanisms to ensure its own independence and primacy, thus provoking criticism from those who have asked about its representativeness and accountability towards democratic governments and societies.[2] Given that, the EU and the European integration process are often presented as a completely unique kind of experimental system of international governance.[3] It is intended to express a general tendency and even to set directions for deeper interdependence in the modern world, in which the traditional structures of the nation state, including the traditional judiciary, are slowly losing their former significance. Accordingly, in her book *A New World Order*, Anne-Marie Slaughter comes to the conclusion that it is this obvious tendency that diminishes the significance of international politics as a space of hierarchical relations and actions of nation states, since it becomes more and more focused on the tightening and more complex networks of mutual sectoral and horizontal dependencies. According to Slaughter, the traditional concept of a unitary state, governed hierarchically, is increasingly giving way to the reality of a disaggregated state, in which a growing role is played by horizontal transnational connections, connecting relevant institutions, centres, milieus and structures from different countries, thus forming a single system of international, supranational governments.

A particular attention should be paid to increasingly strong horizontal links in the areas of business, regulation centres, in legislation and in the field of judiciary, especially with regards to cooperation of courts and legal milieus.[4] The

2 D.Rodrik (2012): *The Globalization Paradox*, New York: W. W. Norton & Company, pp. 207–220.

3 Ch. F. Sabel, J. Zeitlin (2008): Learning from Difference: The New Architecture of Experimental Governance in the EU, *European Law Journal*, vol. 14, no. 3, May 2008, pp. 271–327.

4 A-M. Slaughter (2004): *A New World Order*, Princeton: Princeton University Press, pp. 12–15.

author devotes a separate chapter to the latter issue in her book, in which she presents the various aspects of the growing horizontal interdependence of courts and judges in Europe and on a global scale.[5] This phenomenon differs from hierarchical legal ties, which are traditionally believed to be the result of the increasing influence of international law and its institutions, such as the International Court of Justice, on states in the 19th and 20th centuries, the role of which is to settle disputes between states and to interpret the rules of said law. The case of horizontal interdependence is a rather new phenomenon, where judges from different states and different courts begin to perceive themselves as independent actors in the transnational space that Slaughter refers to as "a common judicial enterprise," which comprises various forms of mutual communication, interaction, exchange of views and experiences, taking over practices and setting standards. These processes can be followed on the example of a developing and growing cooperation between constitutional courts in the field of constitutional law norms and their jurisprudence (with a special role of the Venice Commission), in the field of protection of universal human rights (with a prominent role of the European Court of Human Rights) and, increasingly in the EU, direct relations between national courts and the European Court of Justice as the final authority.

However, it is worth noting that in some cases, this network exchange is not at all horizontal and mutual, since there are clearly defined roles of the "donor" and the "recipient" of standards, practices and interpretations; hence it has a clearly hierarchical nature. This is particularly evident in the case of political issues and the division into Western and Central and Eastern Europe and the so-called third countries, where there is often a unilateral transfer of interpretations, standards and practices, using laws and concepts such as "rule of law" and "democratisation" (Venice Commission).[6] However, this phenomenon is not at all indisputable and gives rise to justified controversies. The horizontal interdependence of judges and courts is not based solely on cooperation and exchange – it also creates structures and legal awareness, which increasingly distances itself from states and institutions of democratic societies, claiming full autonomy. This reinforces the phenomenon of the internal stratification of states, which lose the ability to influence the resulting transnational area of law and judicial cooperation.

---

5 *Ibid.*, Chapter: „Judges: Constructing a Global Legal System", pp. 65–103.

6 *Ibid.*, p. 72–73.

On the one hand, this falls in line with the theory and practice of so-called monitory democracy,[7] the subordination of national democracies to international standards and institutions, and corresponds to the ideas of the independent role of law and the courts, shared by many judges and lawyers. On the other hand, however, it is a source of a growing political conflict regarding a concept that is often referred to as international constitutionalism – including the belief that the EU is a normative empire and represents all of European civilisation – as opposed to constitutional nationalism, or democratic, sovereign nation state.[8]

The lack of awareness of the existence of such links between the judiciary and judicial and legal milieus in the international space has become one of the main weaknesses of the Polish government's policy in resolving the conflict with the European Commission regarding the rule of law. It could be stated that by proposing changes in the Polish justice system, the Law and Justice government has wandered into a minefield that it had no idea existed.

Rule of law as an issue beyond the institutional dimension

Statutory changes, which have been introduced since December 2015 concerning the functioning of the Constitutional Tribunal, common courts, the Supreme Court and the National Council of the Judiciary (NCJ), have since become the subject of a conflict between the Polish government and the European Commission. The escalation of the conflict surrounding the statutory changes introduced in the area of the functioning of the judiciary has led the Commission to launch procedures against Poland and to the threat of implementing the provisions of Article 7 of the TEU. This meant that the government in Warsaw was officially accused of violating one of the fundamental principles of the functioning of the European Union enshrined in the treaties – the rule of law. Such a situation was unprecedented. Due to the lack of the required majority in the Council of the European Union, the procedure initiated against Poland was not brought to an end – the formal voting of the states. Instead, the Commission has decided to refer the case to the Court of Justice of the European Union.

The issue of the rule of law – a fundamental principle which, since the Copenhagen Declaration of 1973, has been recognised as one of the fundamental values that constitute European integration – is at the heart of the conflict

---

7 J. Keane (2009): *The Life and Death of Democracy*, New York: Norton & Company, pp. xxvii, 689–690.

8 F. Furedi (2018): *Populism and the European Cultural Wars*, London, New York: Routledge, pp. 71–74.

between Warsaw and Brussels. It could therefore be assumed in advance that there would be a need to clarify how the rule of law was to be understood. The problem of enforcing the fundamental values of the EU enshrined in Article 2 of the TEU in Member States has always been essentially due to the general nature of these values. By their very nature, they could only serve as guidelines, which should be clarified by means of various interpretations and experiences. The rule of law is no different in this regard – it should be regarded as an unquestionable rule and thus not subject to negotiation or discussion, but on the other hand, there can be different understandings of how it is to be implemented. While the Commission launching a procedure against Poland was a political problem, the question of how the principle of the rule of law, enshrined in the Treaty, should be properly understood is not only a crucial legal question, but above all an important intellectual and philosophical challenge with enormous political potential. In fact, it is even a question of the relationship between politics and law. Therefore, contrary to the position taken in the conflict by the Commission and those EU Member States' governments which seek to punish Warsaw, the way of understanding the principle of the rule of law in Europe is not at all an undisputed or obvious. In fact, it is quite the contrary – a subject of significant controversy over ideas, different experiences and different practices. These differences are already expressed in the very different meanings and traditions that we attribute to concepts used in different languages to describe one and the same principle – the rule of law, *praworządność, Rechtsstaat.*

The Commission's position on compliance with the principle of the rule of law, as well as stances of other European institutions, such as the Venice Commission, confirm not the undisputed nature of this principle, but rather the dominance of its one-sided interpretation, which stems from the phenomenon of legalism described by Judith Shklar back in the 1960s.[9] She claims that the West has always sought its own identification and identity, referring to the category of the rule of law, when confronted with the outside world – in the cold war with the post-Soviet states, the countries of the entire former Eastern Bloc, the countries of the former European colonisation, the so-called third world or simply with non-European countries in the world. It also readily contrasted them with what it referred to as "Eastern absolutism" – China, Islam or, in a broad sense, the Orient. According to Shklar, subsequent attempts to make the rule of law a heart of the Western tradition have gone hand in hand with the increasingly

9 J. Shklar (1986): *Legalism. Law, Morals and Political Trials*, Cambridge: Harvard University Press, pp. 3–27.

narrow definition of this category under the influence of the growing importance of legalism. In her opinion, in recent decades legalism has become the dominant political ideology in the West, which is particularly connected with the evolution of Western post–World War II liberalism, although the author also sees elements of conservative liberalism (Hayek). In her opinion, as a political ideology, legalism leads to a radical separation of law from politics (which, among other things, is reflected in the orthodox understanding of the division of power as a separation of powers within the constitutional order) and from all moral categories. As a result, the sense of the rule of law is completely distorted by the ideology of legalism, which means that it is – above all – linked to the category of order and the *status quo*, contrasted in practice with the categories of freedom and justice, leading to the denial of fundamental European values. Shklar states that it is striking that supporters of the ideology of legalism use the category of the rule of law, to refer to the need to fight against arbitrary power, without seeing the threat of real tyranny in their own stance.

Shklar's arguments are often presented in the debates of philosophers of law and politics; however, they are rarely brought up by university law professors, judges or lawyers, for whom legalism has become a kind of "internalised professional ideology."

In its conflict with Poland, the European Commission has adopted a completely legalistic understanding of the rule of law as one of the fundamental values enshrined in the TEU. Thus, this conflict led to an excellent precedent for a serious debate in the EU on the consequences of such a one-sided interpretation of European values. It will create an opportunity to take a stand in the European debate by presenting arguments to the contrary, seeking allies in criticising legalism in the EU and thus influencing public opinion. The conflict between Poland and the European Commission could focus the much-needed debate on the understanding of the rule of law. This, however, did not happen.

The awareness of the fact that changes in the Polish judiciary are not only a political but also an intellectual challenge that will have a European dimension, was probably not too widespread beyond a very narrow circle of people, such as the leader of Law and Justice himself, a few Polish MEPs and a couple intellectuals associated with the right wing in Poland.[10] The chaotic nature of the

10 J. Kaczyński (2010): *Czy Polska jest państwem prawa.* Lecture at the Jagiellonian University, "Pressje", Teka XXIV Klubu Jagiellońskiego; see also: K. Mazur (2016): *Jarosław Kaczyński – ostatni rewolucjonista III RP*, Jagiellonian Club, January 2016, https://klubjagiellonski.pl/2016/01/18/jaroslaw-kaczynski-ostatni-rewolucjonista-iii-rp/ [retrieved on: 6.05.2019].

conflict surrounding the Constitutional Tribunal and the, often reactive, nature of the changes introduced in the judiciary, certainly did not contribute to building a serious intellectual base for the changes themselves and for the Ministry of Justice, and later the Ministry of Foreign Affairs, to conduct thoughtful actions in response to the procedure launched by the European Commission against Poland.

The only example of a real attempt to carry out an intellectually deeper analysis of the issue of the conflict over the rule of law was probably the establishment of the Expert Group on the Constitutional Tribunal Issues in 2016 by the Speaker of the Sejm. The Group comprised a number of professors of law and political sciences, as well as one retired judge of the Supreme Court. In July 2016, the Group presented a comprehensive report,[11] the aim of which was a thorough analysis and evaluation of the opinion issued by the European Commission for Democracy through Law (the so-called Venice Commission) in March 2016. Despite the fact that the report concerned only the first, early stage of the conflict regarding the rule of law between Warsaw and Brussels –the December amendment of the Act on the Constitutional Tribunal of June 2015 – and could not cover all issues related to changes in the functioning of the Supreme Court (SC), common courts and the NCJ, it contains a number of very important assessments and theses concerning the fundamental problem of a different approach to systemic problems and legalistic interpretation of the rule of law. The Group's analysis was based primarily on the text of the Venice Commission's opinion, but also on draft acts on the Constitutional Tribunal submitted by political parties to the parliament and a draft prepared by the Constitutional Tribunal's judges themselves in 2011–2013.

The authors of the report point to a contradiction between two different approaches to the problem of the rule of law and the role of the Constitutional Tribunal, one of which exposes the sovereignty of the political nation, the other – the sovereignty of its legal system. In their opinion, this difference is reflected in the Polish constitutional tradition, especially in the March and April Constitutions, enacted in the interbellum. Simultaneously, the very same difference exists between the proposals of the political parties concerning the Act on the Constitutional Tribunal and the opinion of the Venice Commission and the draft of the Constitutional Tribunal judges: "While the first emphasise the

11 http://www.sejm.gov.pl/media8.nsf/files/ASEA-ADRKBW/%24File/Raport%20Zespo%C5%82u%20Ekspert%C3%B3w%20do%20spraw%20Problematyki%20Trybuna%C5%82u%20Konstytucyjnego.pdf [retrieved on: 6.05.2019].

discourse of representative democracy, similar to the language of the Polish March Constitution, the opinion of the Venice Commission and the draft Act on the Constitutional Tribunal, which was prepared by its judges in 2011–2013, is rather dominated by the language of constitutional democracy, in the vein of discourse treating the Constitution as a source of legitimacy for every public authority, both parliament and its chambers, as well as courts and tribunals."[12] Subsequently, the authors of the report state: "In the latter view, the role of the 'sovereign' or the 'political nation', as indicated in the Constitution of the Republic of Poland of 1997, often mentioned in public debate in Poland, grows weaker and wanes, replaced by the Constitution itself, as an independent source of legitimacy. Given such an understanding, the legal state becomes superior in relation to a "sovereign entity," bound by the contents present in the legal system, which is governed by the Constitutional Tribunal."[13] Meanwhile, the language of Article 2 of the Polish Constitution is clear and unambiguous: "The Republic of Poland shall be a democratic state ruled by law and implementing the principles of social justice," which places the emphasis on both democratic control, as well as the rule of law, thus preventing a strictly legalistic approach to the rule of law. The Polish Constitution does not include language such as "liberal democracy" or "constitutional democracy," to which the Venice Commission explicitly refers in item 133 of its opinion and for which the rule of law is to be a fundamental characteristic. The authors of the report also refer to the issue of the separation of powers, which in their opinion must be co-operative in nature and must not lead to an institutional lockdown of activities on the part of one of the powers in relation to the other powers: "The Constitution of the Republic of Poland establishes a balance in the separation of powers, since it distinguishes three types of powers, each of which operates on the basis of the superior authority of the Nation, while at the same time conferring appropriate competencies on each body that acts as a given power. The Parliament has been entrusted with the prerogative of law-making, while the Constitutional Tribunal has been clearly given the tasks of a judicial authority, which should not encroach on the competencies of the Parliament with its jurisprudence, since it could result in systemic changes – the establishment of a judicial-constitutional jurisdiction state."[14]

Reading the Group's report from the standpoint of the further evolution of the conflict between Warsaw and Brussels on the rule of law, it is hard to shake off

12 Report of the Expert Group on the Constitutional Tribunal Issues, pp. 5.
13 *Ibid.*, pp. 5–6.
14 *Ibid.*, pp. 9.

the impression that it is an example of a very important, respectable and unnecessary job. The activities of the Group did not lead to any follow-up activities, nor did they become a basis for the creation of a well-thought-out communication strategy of the Polish government in contacts with other EU Member States or EU institutions. This example serves as a good illustration of the inability of the state administration and political structures to take advantage of its intellectuals in crisis situations. Meanwhile, in many places, the report accurately identifies the problems that have emerged as a result of the conflict over the rule of law. This accuracy is well illustrated by Paul Blokker's analysis of the causes and context of the constitutional and democratic crisis in Central and Eastern Europe[15] even before the dispute between Warsaw and Brussels arose.

Blokker's analysis enables us to understand that the ongoing conflict over the rule of law in Poland is an element of a broader phenomenon and a longer process that is taking place in Europe. Blokker points out the fact that in the whole of Central and Eastern Europe, the process of democratic political change took place according to the model of constitutional democracy adopted from the outside world, which meant above all a formalistic, elitist and technocratic understanding of what democracy should be in practice. This, however, determined the understanding of the separation of powers, the rule of law and the privileged position of the judiciary over politics, as well as the general understanding of what the constitution is and the very idea of constitutionalism. According to Blokker, this model of constitutionalism perfectly matched the views prevailing in the West – that democracy in Central and Eastern Europe should be introduced through law, institutions and legal procedures, thus being a "judicial democracy" or a "democracy by judiciary."[16] This was prompted not only by the conviction that the region was incapable of democratic independence, but also – as mentioned earlier and described by Shklar – by the political ideology of legalism, enforced with particular meticulousness in the case of the transitioning countries of Central and Eastern Europe. Consequently, this meant taking a narrow view of the constitutional order, which could no longer be regarded as a political process involving citizens and their representative institutions. Instead, it has become the domain of constitutional justice, its laws, procedures and acts.

---

15 P. Blokker (2014): *New Democracies in Crisis? A comparative constitutional study of the Czech Republic, Hungary, Poland, Romania and Slovakia*, London, New York: Routledge, pp. 3–6, 16–40.

16 K. L.Scheppele (2005): Democracy by Judiciary. Or, Why Courts Cn Be More Democratic than Parliaments, in: A. Czarnota, M. Krygier, W. Sadurski, *Rethinking the Rule of Law after Communism*, Budapest: CEU Press, pp. 25–60.

This legalistic approach to constitutional democracy and the idea of "democracy by judiciary" is closely tied to the phenomenon of the emergence of ever stronger international, horizontal judicial structures and legal environments, which strive to become independent from national political contexts, described in the first part of this analysis. Blokker criticises such a legalistic approach to constitutionalism and is unequivocally in favour of re-establishing civil constitutionalism.

Institutional dimension of the crisis

The issue of compliance with the rule of law did not appear at the level of EU institutions with the formation of the Law and Justice government in Poland after the parliamentary elections in autumn of 2015, nor did it appear after the first changes introduced by this government regarding the functioning of the Constitutional Tribunal. The rule of law is enshrined among the fundamental values observed by the countries taking part in the European integration since the first declaration on European identity – the so-called Copenhagen Declaration of 1973. The Treaty of Nice and enshrining a list of fundamental values – including the rule of law – in the EU Treaties also gave rise to a political discourse within the Union on enforcing compliance with these values. The debate also featured a debate on the introduction of the Charter of Fundamental Rights.

The way in which the Union can enforce compliance with the values enshrined in the Treaties, was clarified in Article 7 of the Treaty of Lisbon, which contains a procedure in the Council, because it is the Council that is supposed to react to the actions of a given Member State inconsistent with the principles set out in Article 2 of the Treaty. In 2012, the issue of the enforcement of common principles was raised again as a real political and institutional problem in connection with Victor Orban's takeover of power in Hungary, the acquisition of a constitutional majority by his party and the commencement of reforms of the Hungarian constitutional system. January 2012, saw debate on the situation in Hungary held by the European Parliament, organised in response to the European Commission's statement, according to which many of the legal changes made by Orban's government could be regarded as incompatible with the EU values.[17] In March 2013, several EU Member States: Denmark, Finland, Germany and the Netherlands sent a letter to the President of the European Commission in which they stated the need to effectively defend European values such as democracy, the rule of law and human rights and called for a new mechanism to be developed in this

---

17 For more details on this debate, see: F. Furedi (2018): *Populism and the European Culture Wars*, London, New York: Routledge 2018, pp. 11–15.

respect. At the same time, the Commission presented its assessment of Member States' judicial systems – the EU Justice Scoreboard – and highlighted the essential link between respect for the rule of law and the functioning of the EU single market. In response to a call by Member States to establish systemic solutions to address the issue of EU values, at the Justice and Home Affairs Council in June 2013, in March 2014 the European Commission adopted its own special mechanism for monitoring Member States' compliance with the rule of law, in addition to the solutions already provided for in Article 7 of the Treaty on European Union.[18] This additional mechanism enabled the Commission to unilaterally make the decision whether there was a threat to the rule of law in a Member State and whether it should respond on behalf of the EU as a whole. Such a decision would then result in a "dialogue" between the Commission and the Member State concerned and to enable the Commission to make recommendations for the necessary remedial action within a set period of time. Should the Member State decide not to comply with the recommendations, the Commission could launch the procedure provided for in Article 7 of the Treaty in the Council.

The adoption of a special new oversight mechanism pertaining to the rule of law by the Commission in 2014 was thus linked to the institutional and political discussion that has been going on in the EU since 2012, regarding the changes to the judicial system and the constitutional system introduced by Victor Orban in Hungary.

This case also had a broader context, namely, the institutional changes pertaining to the competencies and the balance of power between EU institutions and Member States in response to deepening internal crises, particularly in the euro area. After 2010, the crisis situation triggered a dynamic of institutional changes in the EU, which was characterised by an unprecedented level of acceptance for the centralisation of EU competences in specific areas at the expense of national competences – such as establishment of new EU oversight mechanisms, including in the areas of budgetary policy and crisis management. This was accompanied by a growing politicisation of EU institutions, which did not necessarily mean their greater legitimacy. However, it often manifested itself as a visible, greater influence on Community institutions on the part of stronger states in the EU.[19] The Commission's decision of March 2014 was therefore a typical

18 Communication from the Commision to the European Parliament and the Council. A new EU Framework to strengthen the Rule of Law COM/2014/0158.

19 R. Higgs (1987) described the mechanism of strengthening the competences of central institutions in response to the crisis on the basis of the American example in detail in: *Crisis and Leviathan*, Oxford: Oxford University Press, pp. 57 et seq. For the phenomenon of politicisation as a result of a crisis, see: L. van Middelaar (2016): The

example of taking advantage of a crisis situation by gaining new supervisory and oversight competences, but it also indirectly offered new opportunities for some EU countries to influence other countries through EU institutions, bypassing traditional political negotiations and trade-offs as part of the usual intergovernmental way of reaching compromises in the Council. Thus, with regard to compliance with the fundamental principles of the European Union enshrined in Article 2 of the Treaty, it weakened the intergovernmental nature of the resolution of disputes between States provided for in Article 7.

These precise reasons led to the negative assessment of the new Commission procedure by the Council's legal services,[20] which considered that the new mechanism leads in fact to the creation of new competencies for itself by the Commission, with no legal basis in the Treaty on European Union. Thus, the mechanism was deemed incompatible with the general principle of the EU that it exercises only those competences which have been conferred to it by the Member States. The only procedure describing the institutional way for enforcing Member States' compliance with the EU values described in Article 2 of the Treaty is Article 7, which refers only to the Council's competencies. If, therefore, the procedure proposed by the Commission were to be applied to any of the Member States, it would in fact be a procedure outside the existing framework established by the treaties. Despite this unequivocal criticism, the Commission's new procedure established in 2014 was first launched against Poland in 2016 as a result of the Commission's statement that the rule of law was threatened by changes in the judicial system introduced by the Law and Justice government.

In the light of the entire process of institutional changes and the surrounding controversies, it was clear from the outset that the Polish government's conflict with the Commission over the rule of law could, as a precedent, have far-reaching institutional consequences for the EU as a whole. It is because this dispute has led to a creation of a new mechanism for oversight and control over the Member States' compliance with common values by the EU institutions. In this context, it is impossible not to ask the question about the extent of the Polish government's – or rather the Polish Ministry of Foreign Affairs and the Ministry of Justice – awareness of the importance of institutional implications at the time of getting into conflict with the Commission. With this in mind, were they prepared to develop appropriate legal and political action strategies

---

Return of Politics – The European Union after the crises in the eurozone and Ukraine, *JCMS 2016* Volume 54, Number 3, pp. 495–507.

20 Opinion of the Legal Service, Council of the European Union, 10296/14, Brussels, 27 May 2014.

that would allow them to exploit the serious doubts about the legitimacy of the actions taken by the Commission to their advantage? By entering into a dispute with the Commission, Poland certainly had a great chance to exert a significant impact on the dynamics of institutional and political changes in the EU. In retrospect, we can come to the unfortunate conclusion that the awareness of the institutional context of the dispute with the Commission was low on the Polish side, and that Poland's actual impact on the institutional dynamics of the Union through the dispute over the rule of law was rather unconscious, unintended and rather unfavourable, and that it was an impact that deepened the centralisation of supervision and oversight over the Member States.

It seems that the strategy of the Polish government was based on the conviction that the conflict should be resolved relatively quickly by political methods within the Council. Reality proven that this objective was rather difficult to achieve. Additionally, especially at the very outset of the conflict, there was a clear hesitation on the part of the Polish government regarding the form of reaction to the Commission's actions towards Poland. It seems that it was in this initial phase that Warsaw made the fundamental mistake of *de facto* entering into the dialogue procedure established by the Commission. Rather than trying to establish the country's position through gestures of goodwill and openness, the validity of the procedure used by the Commission should have been called into question immediately, particularly given the fact that it raised serious concerns throughout the EU from the outset. It was therefore possible to break away from the passive role in which the Commission could authoritatively shape arguments confirming that the Polish Government was introducing changes in the Polish judiciary without a proper legal basis, acting outside the boundaries of the law, and reverse the allegation at procedural level by posing a formal question – to what extent does the Commission itself act without a legal basis and in breach of the limits of the law provided for in the Treaties, when applying an additional procedure in order to verify compliance with the rule of law in Poland?[21] In other words, instead of entering a "dialogue", Poland should enter into a procedural dispute with the Commission, which would probably lead to a conclusion in the EU Court of Justice after a long time. It is probable that in its decision, the Court would have had to accept objections regarding the legal

21 The issue of legal and political implications of the procedure adopted by the Commission was analysed in detail by P. Oliver, J. Stefanelli (2016): Strengthening the Rule of Law in the EU: The Council's Inaction, *JCMS* 2016, Volume 54, Number 5, pp. 1075–1084, indicating in particular the effect of the inaction of the Council, which, according to Article 7 of the EU Treaty, should be the main institutional actor.

basis for the Commission's actions, or at least point out the non-binding nature of the Commission's actions towards the Member State. In any case, by calling into question the Commission's procedure, the Polish side had the opportunity to present its own interpretation of the situation and shift the focus of the conflict from the assessment of changes in the judiciary in Poland to the problem of internal procedures in the EU and interinstitutional relations. As a result, the first stage of the conflict would lead to the decision of the Court concerning not the changes introduced by the Polish government, but the legitimacy of the Commission's actions. This would give the Polish government the much-needed extra time to prepare a good strategy explaining the motives for the changes and to present its own position to other EU Member States in the Council, without the overbearing presence of the Commission as a supervising teacher.

Despite the fact that the above issue was raised in an expert debate in Poland,[22] it remains a mystery why the Polish government did not decide to enter into a procedural dispute with the Commission. Apparently it was assumed that the Commission's actions would be quickly exhausted and concluded by a political decision of the Council by the Member States, as it was not possible to reach an unanimous support for sanctions against Poland due to the stance of Hungary, nor was there ever a clear majority of countries prepared to take action against Poland under Article 7.

However, the events took place in a different direction, less favourable for Poland. In particular, the strong political motives for the Council's inaction have been underestimated, as a result of which the Council has refrained from taking a decision on the Commission's actions towards Poland. The Council has deliberately left the Commission some breathing room regarding this issue. This is a dangerous precedent, as it indicates that the procedure for oversight over the rule of law may, in the case of Poland, turn into a permanent situation without a conclusion, which will continue to have a negative impact on Poland's political standing in the EU. At this stage of the dispute, it is difficult to imagine what would be the decisions of the Polish government that would satisfy the Commission and would enable it to conclude the procedure. Despite the criticism the Commission's ineffective action regarding the conflict with Poland, it has strengthened its institutional role as the main actor in the political process on the EU side and managed to defend its procedure. In the worst-case scenario, this procedure may be considered ineffective, but not illegitimate or illegal,

22 S. Dębski (2018): Poland & Political Crisis of the European Union, https://poland.pl/politics/opinions/poland-political-crisis-european-union/ [retrieved on: 26.04.2019].

which may result in subsequent attempts at improving it. The Polish side has also failed to maintain the political nature of the conflict over the rule of law, what would be resolved by the Council. As a result, the Polish case is now the subject of a decision of the CJEU which – what is worse – will consider the contents of the Polish government's decisions changing the judiciary, which is in total opposition to the argument still being raised by the Polish side that the organisation of the judiciary is an exclusive competence of the Member States.

Strategy for building arguments

One of the more important aspects of the conflict with the European Commission over the rule of law was the way in which the Polish government tried to explain the motives and objectives of the changes in the judiciary introduced in the country to the EU institutions and Member States. This issue should not be ever treated as one-dimensional – from the outset it was not just a situation in which the Polish Government explained the reasoning for the changes to other Member States and to the bodies of EU institutions to dispel doubts as to whether there really was a breach of fundamental EU principles in this area. The problem was certainly exacerbated by the very nature of the changes, some of which were clearly reactive and resulted primarily from the dynamics of the internal political dispute. This was certainly a serious problem in terms of claiming the objectivity of the causes and goals, as well as presenting a clear, rational and acceptable message explaining what the judicial reform programme was all about.

However, the internal context in the EU, the previously described political and institutional dynamics surrounding the crisis, especially the obvious desire for the Commission, as well as its individual representatives, to gain political power as a result of the conflict with Poland, was also important. The unequivocally negative attitude of some EU countries towards the political situation in Hungary after 2012 and in Poland after 2015, often based on stereotypes or prejudices, should also not be underestimated here. The active participation of the Polish parliamentary opposition, as well as judges and lawyers in perpetuating these prejudices and criticising the changes in the judiciary in the EU and international forums was also not without its significance.

The actions undertaken by international structures of legal communities interested in taking advantage of the conflict with Poland to further their own agenda, as well as to increase the independence of the horizontal network of international connections in the field of judiciary and law-making, regardless of the contexts of national policy and its institutions, should also be kept in mind.

To sum up, the Polish government had to face not only internal contradictions and sometimes simple errors made in the process of reforming the judiciary, but also the actions of many actors – both domestic and foreign – at various levels of the EU arena, whose aim was to undermine the credibility of the Polish side. In such a situation, an effective message from the Polish government, explaining the motives and objectives of the changes, was quickly gaining political importance.

A comprehensive presentation of the position of the Polish government, describing the reasons for the changes introduced in the judiciary, was presented in March 2018 with the publication of the so-called *White Paper on the Reform of the Polish Judiciary* – two years after Poland started the conflict with the European Commission regarding the issue of the rule of law.[23] The publication of this document coincided with the Commission transitioning to the next stage of the procedure launched against Poland – submitting the issue of threat to the rule of law in Poland to the Council. The aim of this document was therefore to systematically present the arguments of the Polish government to representatives of the other Member States. As its authors state in the introduction to the *White Paper*: "Our government invites you to read it and would welcome any comments or questions you may consider relevant. It is our intention to explain our reforms as best as possible so as to leave no doubt that they are fully in line with European standards."

While explaining the reasoning of the changes, the authors focus on three types of arguments: First – the way the Polish justice system functions, primarily on the issue of excessive length of the proceedings and the impact of ineffective operation of the justice system on the abysmal trust towards judges and courts among the society. Second – the issue of a failure to account for the communist past among the judges. Third – the lack of a sufficient democratic accountability of the judiciary within the framework of constitutional cooperation between the three powers, resulting in various forms of corruption. The distribution of motives and thus the weight of the all three arguments is noteworthy. While the first issue branches out into nine separate problems, the second one comprises fifteen and the third one comprises eight problems. While explaining the reasoning for the implemented changes, the focus in this document is clearly on the problem of the failure to account for the communist past among the judges in Poland.

---

23 https://www.premier.gov.pl/wydarzenia/aktualnosci/rzad-przedstawia-biala-ksiege-w-sprawie-reform-polskiego-wymiaru.html [retrieved on: 26.04.2019].

Regardless of whether such causes and objectives of the reform corresponded to the actual social expectations in Poland, it is worth considering whether such an argument could be credible and convincing for the purpose of the debate on the European and international forum. It seems that the head of the Polish government, Prime Minister Mateusz Morawiecki, was convinced that it will be enough. In many of his foreign interviews, speeches and discussions, he consistently emphasised the issue of the accountability for the communist past as one of the most important reasons for the changes introduced in the Polish judiciary. In this context, the Prime Minister provided examples of the judicial reform and verification of judges in Germany as part of the denazification after 1945 and after reunification in 1991, as well as in France under the rule of de Gaulle. In his statements, the Polish Prime Minister brings up the lack of decommunisation of the Polish justice system after 1989, which should convince the Polish partners in the EU of the legitimacy of the implemented changes. Could such a communication strategy have had the intended effect?

The argument relating to the necessary catching up of the abandoned decommunisation process in the Polish judiciary, regardless of individual cases of judges in Poland, is not consistent with the actual reasons for the weakness of the Polish judiciary in the Republic of Poland. According to Adam Czarnota, the main reasons for the unsatisfactory operation of the Polish justice system lie primarily in the poor functioning of the judges' autonomy and self-regulation, which is conducive to pathological situations, as well as in the legal culture of judges inherited from the Polish People's Republic, further reinforced by the system of legal education and the functioning of courts.[24] I do not want to get into more detail on the extent to which the communication strategy adopted by the government to inform about the reasons for the changes in the judiciary corresponded with the actual reasons for the weakness of the Polish judiciary. The matter is not entirely without significance to the credibility and, therefore, the effectiveness of the government's arguments extended towards its European partners, not to mention the internal debate. It is worth noting that, according to Czarnota – who is well-aware of the consequences of the lack of

24 A. Czarnota (2019): Rule of lawyers or rule of law? On constitutional crisis and rule of law in Poland, in: ed. B. Iancu & E. Tanasescu, *Governance and constitutionalism*, London, New York: Routledge 2019, pp. 51–63. Relatively similar conclusions were drawn a few years before the outbreak of the dispute over changes in the Polish justice system by F. Zoll (2008) in the analysis Polen als Rechtsstaat. Der schwierige Nachlass der Regierung Kaczyński und sein Einfluss auf die Rechtsstaatlichkeit Polens, *Polen-Analysen* Nr. 38/2008 Deutsches Polen Institut.

decommunisation in the justice system – in the final days of the Polish People's Republic, there were around 4,000 judges in the justice system, while today there are 10,000 of them.

The fundamental problem with the government's arguments and communication strategy seems to lie elsewhere. By raising the issue of making up for the sorely lacking decommunisation in the justice system, the Polish Prime Minister seems to appeal – above all – to the distant historical experiences of his European counterparts, as well as to their elementary sense of justice – understood in moral terms. Meanwhile, the motivation of some EU countries behind supporting the Commission launching a procedure against Poland in response to the alleged breach of the rule of law is different and specific. If we set aside all rhetoric relating to "defending the European values" against the threat of the so-called illiberal democracy, two basic motives play a central role in the Member States' policy towards Poland and the issue of the rule of law. Firstly, the analysis of the record of Poland's hearing in the Council on the 26th of June 2018,[25] quickly shows that some Member States raise the issue of fear of the legal consequences of introducing changes in the justice system in Poland, such as an extraordinary complaint. During the hearing, this issue was pointed out many times as the most worrying and questionable one. This clearly shows that for many Member States, the issue of the rule of law is not primarily linked to an axiological or moral set of European values – as Frans Timmermans, the main political actor in the conflict with Poland, most often presents this issue – but to very specific interests relating to investment and property within the common market. If we therefore set aside all the rhetoric using moral and historical notions, it becomes apparent that many people in the Union see the rule of law not as a moral issue, but as an issue of interests and the preservation of legal guarantees for entities operating in the common market. Therefore, it seems that the essence of the problem is the fear that the Polish government may want to use the changes in the judiciary to obtain instruments of political pressure that will allow it to change the conditions of functioning of economic entities from other Member States on the Polish market, or even to eliminate the privileged position of some of them, which may be the result of earlier solutions implemented in the post-1989 transition period.

The second motive is also linked to the common market and also refers more to the sphere of interests, rather than values. It is about linking the rule of law to

25 Report of the hearing held by the Council on 26 June 2018, Council of the European Union, Brussels 8 August 2018, 10906/18.

European funds, which, according to the net contributing countries, is a necessity when – in the case of Hungary or the Czech Republic – there is a suspicion of political corruption associated with the redistribution of EU funds.

It therefore seems that building a coherent communication strategy aimed at informing other Member States about the reasons for the changes in the Polish judiciary has been long overdue, allowing the Commission to consolidate its own point of view on the case among many Member States. First of all, the main part of this strategy – the failure to account for the communist past – resulted from internal Polish politics and internal political debate. In other words, it was not a deliberate result of the diagnosis of the fears of the governments of other Member States regarding the effects of changes introduced in the Polish justice system.

Conclusions

The conflict between the Polish Government and the European Commission over the rule of law should be treated as an example of the multifaceted crisis in the Union, which required a comprehensive approach, since this was the case of dealing with many different aspects of a conflict situation. This analysis points out the international dimension of the situation, presenting a high degree of mutual, horizontal links between courts and legal milieus, which focus on becoming independent from national, democratic contexts. The evolution of the very concept of the rule of law in the EU, which is consistently narrowed down to a purely legalistic approach, was also presented and highlighted. I also referred to the institutional context of the dispute, which shows the creation of new competences and the centralisation of existing ones by EU institutions as a result of the deepening crisis in the functioning of European integration.

Finally, I tried to identify the sources of the Member States' actual fears about the changes introduced in the Polish judiciary, and to show how the arguments and communication strategy adopted by Poland fails to address them properly. In fact, each of these aspects would require the Polish government to treat them as separate issues and use a different set of instruments and solutions, but first and foremost, it would also require awareness of the diversity of the context of the dispute with the Commission concerning the rule of law. It concerns both deeper reflection on the very concept of the rule of law, which would require a readiness to initiate a meaningful debate on the subject, influences the dynamics of institutional changes within the EU. This, in turn, would require developing a strategy, as well as impact the way of communicating precise arguments, aimed at dispelling and neutralising real fears on the part of the Member States. It seems that the awareness of all of these aspects emerged late and not without resistance, which did not allow Poland to leave the passive role of the "accused" even once throughout the entire conflict. Another significant issue in this situation was also the lack of a single crisis management centre, which would allow for the development, coordination and evaluation of actions on the Polish side.

It is not possible to carry out a reliable and solid assessment of the effects of the changes introduced in the Polish justice system today, since there has been a very emotional conflict regarding this subject in Poland for quite some time now. However, the assessment of the external reaction concerning the situation of Poland in the EU simply cannot be positive. Poland has failed to present convincing arguments that would defend the country and alleviate the fears of other Member States, while allowing prejudices and stereotypes towards Poland to be deepened in the EU. The conflict did not lead to initiating any serious debate on the very nature of the rule of law in the EU, and its impact on the institutional dynamics of the EU should be seen as a failure from a Polish perspective.

References

Blokker P. (2014): *New Democracies in Crisis? A comparative constitutional study of the Czech Republic, Hungary, Poland, Romania and Slovakia*, London, New York: Routledge.

Communication from the Commission to the European Parliament and the Council. A new EU Framework to strengthen the Rule of Law, 2014, COM/2014/0158.

Czarnota A. (2019): Rule of lawyers or rule of law? On constitutional crisis and rule of law in Poland, in: B. Iancu, E. Tanasescu (eds.): *Governance and Constitutionalism*, London, New York: Routledge, pp. 51–63.

Dębski S. (2018): Poland & Political Crisis of the European Union, https://poland.pl/politics/opinions/poland-political-crisis-european-union/ [retrieved on: 26.04.2019].

Furedi F. (2018): *Populism and the European Cultural Wars*, London, New York: Routledge.

Higgs R. (1987): *Crisis and Leviathan*, Oxford: Oxford University Press.

Kaczyński J. (2010): Czy Polska jest państwem prawa. Lecture at the Jagiellonian University, "Pressje", Teka XXIV Klubu Jagiellońskiego.

Kancelaria Premiera, Rząd przedstawia Białą Księgę w sprawie reform polskiego wymiaru sprawiedliwości, https://www.premier.gov.pl/wydarzenia/aktualnosci/rzad-przedstawia-biala-ksiege-w-sprawie-reform-polskiego-wymiaru.html [retrieved on: 26.04.2019].

Keane J. (2009): *The Life and Death of Democracy*, New York: W. W. Norton & Company, 2009.

Mażewski L. (2017): *Wiele hałasu o nic? Konflikt wokół Trybunału Konstytucyjnego w latach 2015–2016 w perspektywie rozważań modelowych*, Radzymin: von Borowiecky.

Mazur K. (2016): Jarosław Kaczyński – ostatni rewolucjonista III RP, Jagiellonian Club, https://klubjagiellonski.pl/2016/01/18/jaroslaw-kaczynski-ostatni-rewolucjonista-iii-rp/ [retrieved on: 6.05.2019].

Oliver P., Stefanelli J. (2016): Strengthening the Rule of Law in the EU: The Council's Inaction, *JCMS*, Volume 54. Number 5, pp. 1075–1084.

Opinion of the Legal Service, Council of the European Union, 10296/14, Brussels, 27 May 2014.

Raport Zespołu Ekspertów do spraw Problematyki Trybunału Konstytucyjnego z dnia 15 lipca 2016 r. [Report of the Expert Group on the Constitutional Tribunal Issues], http://www.sejm.gov.pl/media8.nsf/files/ASEA-ADRKBW/%24File/Raport%20Zespo%C5%82u%20Ekspert%C3%B3w%20do%20spraw%20Problematyki%20Trybuna%C5%82u%20Konstytucyjnego.pdf [retrieved on: 6.05.2019].

Report of the hearing held by the Council on 26 June 2018, Council of the European Union, Brussels, 8 August 2018, 10906/18.

Rodrik D. (2012): The Globalization Paradox, New York: W. W. Norton & Company.

Sabel Ch.F., Zeitlin J. (2008): Learning from Difference: The New Architecture of Experimental Governance in the EU, *European Law Journal*, Volume 14. Number 3, pp. 271–327.

Scheppele K.L. (2005): Democracy by judiciary. Or, why courts can be more democratic than parliaments, in: A. Czarnota, M. Krygier, W. Sadurski (eds.): *Rethinking the Rule of Law after Communism*, Budapest: CEU Press, pp. 25–60.

Shklar J. (1986): *Legalism. Law, Morals and Political Trials*, Cambridge: Harvard University Press, 1986.

Slaughter A.-M. (2004): *A New World Order*, Princeton: Princeton University Press.

van Middelaar L. (2016): The Return of Politics – The European Union after the crises in the eurozone and Ukraine, *JCMS*, Volume 54. Number 3, pp. 495–507.

Zoll F. (2008): *Polen als Rechtsstaat. Der schwierige Nachlass der Regierung Kaczyński und sein Einfluss auf die Rechtsstaatlichkeit Polens*, Polen-Analysen Nr. 38/2008, Darmstadt: Deutsches Polen Institut.

Tomasz Grzegorz Grosse

Polish political parties towards the European Union and its crises

Abstract: This study is an analysis of the programs of major political parties in Poland in 2015-2019 towards the European integration. The aim of the study is to present views on selected topics about the future of the EU in the context of its crises (mainly in the eurozone and the migration one) as well as the possibilities of overcoming them. In the first part, the author focuses on a synthetic presentation of Polish European doctrine in a historical perspective. Then he presents the views of the government (and its party support). Finally, the views of the largest opposition parties, especially those that got to parliament in 2015, are shown. The aim is to attempt to show which views of the opposition are consistent with the position of the government or are convergent with Polish doctrine in European politics. Finally, the author analyses what matters are controversial, and thus goes beyond the consensus of political forces in relation to European policy.

Keywords: political parties, Eurozone crisis, migration crisis, Polish European doctrine

Introduction

This study provides an analysis of programmes concerning European integration of the main political parties in Poland in the period 2015–2019. This period begins with elections to the Polish Parliament in 2015, which resulted in a change of the ruling government – from the coalition of Civic Platform (Platforma Obywatelska, PO) and Polish People's Party (Polskie Stronnictwo Ludowe, PSL) to the United Right – a coalition led by the Law and Justice (Prawo i Sprawiedliwość, PiS). The analysed period ends with the elections to the European Parliament (EP) in 2019.

The aim of the study is to present views on selected topics concerning the future of the European Union in the context of its crises (mainly in the euro area and the refugee crisis), as well as the possibilities of overcoming them. The question of the role of the state in the EU, and thus the vision of the preferred political model of the Union, is of great importance. European values comprise an important aspect of this study, including on the one hand, the role of the state in the EU and, on the other hand, in the context of Polish internal disputes, as well as Polish disputes with European institutions regarding the rule of law. What is more, this study also concerns the issue of euro area reforms, as well as prospects for membership in the Economic and Monetary Union (EMU). Another issue covered by the study is response to the migration crisis, as well as views concerning the internal market. Furthermore, I will analyse opinions and views on deepening cooperation within the framework of the defence policy (CSDP[1]) and a vision for the future of EU foreign policy (CFSP[2]). In this context, I will analyse, on the one hand, the attitude towards transatlantic relations and, on the other, the Russian threat. I will also take into account other geopolitical aspects, such as the parties' approach to EU enlargement.

In the first part I will focus on a synthetic presentation of Polish doctrine regarding European politics in a historical perspective, followed by the summary of the views of the government (and the ruling parties). Like I mentioned earlier, in the 2015–2019 period, the government was supported by the United Right coalition. Finally, the article will present a summary of the views of the largest opposition parties, especially those that were elected to the Polish parliament in 2015. The aim is to try and present which views of the opposition parties are consistent with those of the government, as well as with Polish doctrine regarding European politics – this will ensure their further strengthening in the international arena and should not change, even if the upcoming elections result in the change of a government. These issues are therefore part of a cross-party political consensus in the European arena and are strongly supported by public opinion. The study also poses a question regarding controversial issues, which go beyond the consensus of political players in relation to European policy.

Doctrine

Polish doctrine regarding European politics is difficult to concisely sum up, not least due to the relatively short-lived participation in integration processes, but also due to the differences in the approach towards the EU between the main political players – the Eurosceptic and pro-European approaches, often emphasised and highlighted in the literature.[3] Nevertheless, one may be tempted to outline a certain common perspective and a continuity of actions in European politics. All subsequent Polish governments after 2004 stressed the need for "a strong Poland in strong Europe," which means that they were oriented towards serving the national interests, while supporting the extension of integration. They also rejected the idea of building federations within the EU and criticised

1 The Common Security and Defence Policy.

2 The Common Foreign and Security Policy.

3 M.A. Vachudova (2008): Tempered by the EU? Political parties and party systems before and after accession, *Journal of European Public Policy*, 15:6, pp. 861–879.

the tendency for a permanent division into a "two-speed Europe" – the euro area and the rest of the EU. Around 2012, the doctrine regarding EMU membership also seems to have emerged. Becoming a part of the euro area hinged on overcoming the crisis, reforming the monetary union and appropriate strengthening of the Polish economy, so as not to share the fate of the southern countries, which entered into the EMU.[4] During the migration crisis, politicians from the major parties insisted on the protection of the EU's external borders. They generally distanced themselves or directly opposed permanent mechanisms for relocating refugees or immigrants. Polish doctrine consistently advocates for the expansion of the four freedoms in the internal market and opposes protectionist tendencies in this area. The successive Polish governments supported the development of the EU's foreign and defence policy, under the proviso that it would not constitute a competition or a threat to NATO and transatlantic relations. The EU's foreign policy postulated the development of cooperation with the eastern EU Member States, supported by the membership of Ukraine and the Balkan states in the EU, as well as demanding that Russia respect international law and the sovereignty of other states.

Views of the government

In accordance with the prevalent doctrine regarding European politics in Poland, Law and Justice rejected the development of integration towards a federation. The party's programme stresses that the EU should remain a community of sovereign and equal nations. A strong, efficient and sovereign state serves as the foundation for both national democracy and the interests of the national political community. Law and Justice pointed out that in Europe, democracy can be found primarily in the Member States, which is why it is so important to respect both the subjectivity of all countries, as well as the voice of national parliaments in decisions made at the EU level. The party intended to increase the participation of these parliaments in the future EU system.

The protection of the subjectivity of the Polish state meant opposition to the growing power of the largest member states in integration processes, which is why the main principle of Prime Minister Beata Szydło in terms of European

4 Ch. Schweiger (2014): Poland, Variable Geometry and the Enlarged European Union, *Europe-Asia Studies*, vol. 66, no 3, pp. 405–410.

politics was: "equal with the equal, free with the free."[5] This means that Law and Justice wanted equality of all Member States in the EU and getting rid of double standards in the approach to larger and smaller countries within the Union.[6] It also intended to break with the policy of patronage concerning the strongest countries, accusing their predecessors of using such an approach. According to this party's programme, Polish European policy should be informed by Polish national interests, instead of expectations of the most influential partners.[7] On the other hand, Law and Justice politicians were opposed to further centralisation of powers in the EU and thus wanted to slow down the progress of integration.[8] They believed that the competences of EU institutions should not be extended without amending the treaties. "The European Commission is neither a super-government nor the European Parliament is a super-parliament," which is why any and all "competences not conferred on the Union by the Treaties should be the responsibility of the Member States."[9] At the same time, Law and Justice expressed concern, seeing the increase of disciplinary supervision of the Member States by EU institutions and forcing them to uphold the EU law.[10]

Law and Justice did not want to rush joining the euro area.[11] The government kept a "pragmatic distance from the euro," supporting the necessary reforms of the EMU, while opposing divisions within the internal market and within the European Union itself (namely, the concept of two-speed Europe).[12] In particular,

5 *Przemówienie Premier Beaty Szydło na XV Forum Polityki Zagranicznej*, 9.11.2017, http://www.minsk.msz.gov.pl/pl/aktualnosci/xv_forum_polityki_zagranicznej [retrieved on: 27.04.2018].

6 *Program PiS 2014*, http://pis.org.pl/dokumenty [retrieved on: 27.04.2018], p. 158; *Deklaracja Europejska PiS*, item 9, http://pis.org.pl/dokumenty [retrieved on: 27.04.2019].

7 *Program PiS 2014*, *op. cit.*, p. 154.

8 Z. Krasnodębski (2015): Co dla Polski oznaczają zmiany w Unii Europejskiej?, in: *Myśląc: Polska*, Programme Convention of Law and Justice and the United Right, Katowice, 3–5 July 2015, pp. 80–81.

9 *Informacja Ministra Spraw Zagranicznych Jacka Czaputowicza o zadaniach polskiej polityki zagranicznej w 2018 roku*, Sejm of the Republic of Poland, 21 March 2018, http://www.msz.gov.pl/pl/aktualnosci/wiadomosci/minister_jacek_czaputowicz_o_priorytetach_polskiej_dyplomacji_w_2018_roku [retrieved on: 27.04.2018].

10 *Program PiS 2014*, *op. cit.*

11 *Program PiS 2014*, *op. cit.*

12 Konrad Szymański: Strefa euro nie odjeżdża Polsce, *Rzeczpospolita*, 22.05.2017, http://www.rp.pl/Unia-Europejska/305219925-Konrad-Szymanski-Strefa-euro-nie-odjezdza-Polsce.html [retrieved on: 27.04.2018].

the party did not consent to the establishing of separate political institutions for the euro area, such as a parliament, government or finance minister, and finally to establishing a separate budget for the EMU.[13] Nevertheless, the government approved the shaping of cooperation in Central Europe, including the deepening of cooperation within the Visegrad Group and the Three Seas Initiative.[14] The main objective of these activities was to counteract the Franco-German dominance in the EU, as well as the prevalence of Western European interests over those of Central Europe.

The government did not agree to the imposed refugee relocation quotas. It was also against the centralisation of the migration policy in Brussels, instead proposing to strengthen the EU's external borders and to intensify humanitarian and development policy activities beyond the Union's borders.[15]

According to the Polish doctrine regarding European politics, Law and Justice demanded the respect and further expansion of the four freedoms on the internal market, guaranteed by the treaty, as well as opposed all protectionist actions, including those stemming from the amendment of the directive on posted workers, which restricted the freedom of movement of labour within the European Union.[16] The Minister for European Affairs in the Ministry of Foreign Affairs was of the opinion that "social standards cannot be imposed in the Union from top down, because the Member States not only radically differ in their wealth, but also in terms of their economic model."[17] The government opposed the introduction of new European taxes, as well as tax harmonisation within the EU. It voted against the majority vote on these issues in the EU, pointing out that taxation is a sovereign competence of national authorities, especially democratically elected parliaments. In addition, the government was critical of the EU's increasingly ambitious climate policy, including the elimination of coal-based energy.[18]

---

13 Z. Krasnodębski, "Co dla Polski oznaczają zmiany w Unii Europejskiej?", *op. cit.*

14 *Program PiS 2014, op. cit.*

15 *Informacja Ministra Spraw Zagranicznych Jacka Czaputowicza o zadaniach polskiej polityki zagranicznej w 2018 roku, op. cit.*; Konrad Szymański: Strefa euro nie odjeżdża Polsce, *op. cit.*

16 *Informacja Ministra Spraw Zagranicznych Jacka Czaputowicza o zadaniach polskiej polityki zagranicznej w 2018 roku, op. cit.*

17 Długa droga do odrodzenia Unii, an interview with Konrad Szymański, *Rzeczpospolita*, 14 March 2019, p. A9.

18 J. Szyszko (2015): Globalna polityka klimatyczna, in: „Myśląc: *Polska*, Programme Convention of Law and Justice and the United Right, Katowice, 3–5 July 2015, pp. 33–36.

The government party approved progress concerning the EU's defence policy, although it clearly stressed that it could not compete with NATO, be its copy or pose a threat to the Treaty and to transatlantic relations. The Minister for European Affairs pointed out "the need to build European defence in agreement with NATO, which prevents duplicating structures and military investments."[19] In addition, Law and Justice advocated for equal opportunities for all Member States to tap into the European Defence Fund, standing in opposition to favouring the largest corporations and research centres in Western Europe. The party also supported further enlargement of the EU to include the Balkan states and Ukraine,[20] as well as sought to develop the Eastern Partnership and transatlantic relations. It demanded that all EU Member States should adopt a joint approach towards the Russian Federation, in particular towards its aggressive policy towards the West. Many of the views of Law and Justice, particularly regarding the EU's foreign and defence policy, seem to be in line with the European doctrine of Polish diplomacy.

Views of the opposition

The largest opposition party, the Civic Platform, has for years supported the further progress of European integration. To name some examples, the party supported the strengthening of the European Commission (EC) as an institution that in principle contributes to the protection of the interests of smaller Member States. Radosław Sikorski, former Minister of Foreign Affairs, supported the idea of reducing the number of commissioners, as well as merging the positions of President of the European Council and the President of the European Commission.[21] Some of his statements could indicate his support towards federation, for example in relation to the support for a pan-European list of candidates in EP elections. Civic Platform recognised the need to support the EU globally. According to Grzegorz Schetyna, head of Civic Platform: "today only the European Union can compete against global powers, no single country is able to do it."[22] Schetyna supported the progress of integration, including the strengthening of existing EU institutions, but opposed excessive bureaucratisation of the EU, and

19 Długa droga do odrodzenia Unii, *op. cit.*

20 *Program PiS 2014*, *op. cit.*, p. 159.

21 Przemówienie ministra spraw zagranicznych Radosława Sikorskiego wygłoszone w Berlinie 28 listopada *2011*, TVN24.pl, https://www.tvn24.pl/polska-a-przyszlosc-unii-europejskiej,192356,s.html [retrieved on: 27.04.2018].

22 G. Schetyna, Europo, wracamy!, *Gazeta Wyborcza*, 14 March 2019, p. 12.

thus had a rather distanced approach to the centralisation of power in Brussels. "I have some doubts, however, whether the right step to solve the problems is to further expand the number of agencies, of which the Union already has more than 20. The agencies contribute to the expansion of European bureaucracy, which is hardly perceived as good by Europeans."[23] Civic Platform advocated for the enlargement of the EU to include more states in order to counteract the influence of the eastern powers – primarily China and Russia – on the EU's neighbours. However, an increase in the number of Union members would in all likelihood lead to difficulties in the management of Union policies. Hence, it can be concluded that Civic Platform valued the geopolitical objectives pertaining to the enlargement of the Community more than the improvement of governance in the EU, all the more so since it also approached the centralisation of power in Brussels with a certain distance.

According to Schetyna, the Polish state should regain its political influence in the EU, and as a result, take better care of the interests of Poles. He believed that this could be achieved thanks to the active and responsible European policy, as well as by improving the image of Poland in the eyes of its partners. "The Polish government has completely marginalised Polish activity and significance in the EU. This is why, the fundamental goal of any sensible Polish politician should be, first and foremost, Poland regaining its significance in the EU."[24] This was a concept of a state involved in EU politics, as well as based on responsible discourse and image. Undoubtedly, the key issue for this image was the question of Poland's compliance with European values, as well as greater openness towards the proposals of EU leaders – namely France and Germany – compared to rather distrustful conservative government. At the same time, an element that moved Poland closer to the centre of Europe was the decision to oppose and counteract the phenomenon of a two-speed Europe, which could potentially lead to the marginalisation of Poland in the event of staying outside the euro area for good.

This was the approach of the largest opposition party and the leader of the liberal camp towards the strength of the Polish state with regard to joining the mainstream of the progress of integration. The progress of integration did not constitute a threat to the state and its sovereignty (contrary to the views held by conservative parties), but rather an opportunity, under the proviso of participation in the mainstream of European politics. "If the Polish issues are discussed at the main table, we will be able to find the majority support for all

23 G. Schetyna, Europo, wracamy!, *op. cit.*
24 G. Schetyna, Europo, wracamy!, *op. cit.*

of them."[25] However, Civic Platform recognised the need for some protection of national autonomy from an excessive centralisation tendency seen in Brussels. "In accordance with the principle of subsidiarity, we will ensure that decisions in the Union are taken at the lowest possible level – as close as possible to the people concerned."[26] Sikorski also believed that a number of competences should remain under the control of individual Member States, especially with regard to "national identity, religion, lifestyle, public morals and tax rates."[27] This refers to the conservative approach to political issues represented by Law and Justice.

Even at the beginning of the crisis of the EMU, the Civic Platform government was in favour of adopting the euro as quickly as possible. However, seeing the impact of the growing problems in the monetary union, in 2012 he claimed that joining the euro zone will hinge on ending the crisis, reforming the EMU and properly preparing the Polish economy for membership in the monetary union. At the same time, the government led by Civic Platform tried to make sure that Poland participated in all initiatives taken by the Member States belonging to the EMU, such as the Fiscal Pact or the Banking Union, a tactic, which was dubbed "keeping our foot in the door."[28] With Poland being governed by Law and Justice, Civic Platform continued its earlier agenda while supporting the introduction of further EMU reforms. Nevertheless, in 2018, the head of Civic Platform pointed out that Poland should prepare for the adoption of the common currency, and at the same time, attempts should be made to convince Poles to this project.[29] By stating that, the party has softened its position towards the EMU, recognising that the crisis has been resolved and that the preparations for membership in the monetary union need to be restarted. This change in approach referred to a large extent to the process of polarisation on the Polish political scene, which increasingly translated into emphasising the pro-European stance of Civic Platform. It

25 *Przyszłość Polski – Wielki Wybór*, 04 April 2019, https://platforma.org/aktualnosci/przyszlosc-polski-wielki-wybor [retrieved on: 27.03.2019].

26 *Przyszłość Polski – Wielki Wybór*, op. cit.

27 *Przemówienie ministra spraw zagranicznych Radosława Sikorskiego…*, op. cit.

28 Tusk obiecuje, że przed wejściem do eurolandu odbędą się konsultacje. Danuta Huebner już mówi, że nie możemy „stać okrakiem nad barykadą", *wPolityce.pl*, 20 December 2012, https://wpolityce.pl/polityka/147055-tusk-obiecuje-ze-przed-wejsciem-do-eurolandu-odbeda-sie-konsultacje-danuta-huebner-juz-mowi-ze-nie-mozemy-stac-okrakiem-nad-barykada [retrieved on: 27.04.2018].

29 Schetyna: Przyjęcie euro nie musi oznaczać wzrostu cen, *Rzeczpospolita*, 27.02.2018, http://www.rp.pl/Platforma-Obywatelska/302279962-Schetyna-Przyjecie-euro-nie-musi-oznaczac-wzrostu-cen.html [retrieved on: 27.04.2018].

can be said with high probability, that the most important motive for the sudden change in Civic Platform's stance was the fear of deepening the phenomenon of a two-speed Europe – marginalisation of Poland in relation to the European centre located in the euro area.

In 2015, the Civic Platform government backed the EU regulation imposing the refugee relocation quotas in the EU. Influenced by public opinion and lost elections, the party changed its stance on this issue to a more hard-line one, recognising that the relocation of refugees must take place on a voluntary basis and that EU policy must focus on the control of the EU's external borders.[30] At the same time, the head of Civic Platform promised that he would not accept illegal migrants in the event of winning the elections.[31] Thus, the stance of the main opposition party became closer to that espoused by the ruling Law and Justice. Civic Platform has made this decision knowing the voters' opinion, who were against accepting refugees and immigrants, particularly those from outside Europe.[32]

In accordance with Polish doctrine regarding European politics, the largest opposition party declared its willingness to expand the four freedoms in the internal market. Schetyna criticised the French President for "pushing through bureaucratic solutions to raise labour costs in Central European countries, including Poland, weakening their competitiveness as a result. (…) To be effective, the European Union must remain an area of freedom for people, labour, investment and services."[33]

Referring to the Polish doctrine regarding European politics, Civic Platform supported the maximisation of the inflow of EU funds to Poland. "We are going to defend the European funds for our regions, cities and villages and ensure the increased participation of local authorities in their distribution."[34] In 2018, the head of Civic Platform also objected to linking the disbursement of European funds to the rule of law, which was in line with the position of the Law and

30 Platforma Obywatelska, http://www.platforma.org/aktualnosc/45497/projekty-platformy-polska-europa-swiat-polskaobywatelska [retrieved on: 27.04.2018].

31 Schetyna potwierdza: Nie będziemy przyjmować nielegalnych migrantów, *Newsweek*, 10.05.2017, http://www.newsweek.pl/polska/schetyna-nie-bedziemy-przyjmowac-migrantow-po-o-uchodzcach,artykuly,409922,1.html [retrieved on: 27.04.2018].

32 Stosunek Polaków i Czechów do przyjmowania uchodźców, *CBOS*, no. 87/2018, July 2018.

33 G. Schetyna, Europo, wracamy!, *op. cit.*

34 *Przyszłość Polski – Wielki Wybór*, *op. cit.*

Justice government.[35] Civic Platform also recalled an initiative of its own government (ruling in Poland in 2007–2015) regarding the energy union, in particular joint European purchases of oil and gas from external producers.

With regard to the EU's foreign and defence policies, the earlier agenda was carried out without an interruption – this means advocating for further integration within the framework of these policies, while maintaining good transatlantic relations. Schetyna proposed "extending the Union's defence capabilities, including the budget, coordination of European production for its defence, as well as military solutions to ensure the capability to carry out EU missions."[36] At the same time, he called for the European Union to: "take a stronger initiative towards NATO regarding their future cooperation. The EU should aim at reaffirming transatlantic ties and strengthening the operational links between the military capabilities of both organisations."[37] Civic Platform also called for a consistent European stance on the aggressive policy of the Russian Federation. The party also backed further development of the EU's Eastern policy and the emphasis on counter-terrorism within the framework of the CSDP.[38] Moreover, in line with the European politics doctrine, Civic Platform also postulated encouraging partners from the EU to expand the Community. "Let us accept the Balkan countries when they are ready. Moreover, let us respect the European aspirations of the Eastern Partnership countries, especially the strategic Ukraine, crucial both for Poland and the EU."[39]

Regarding these issues, the opposition parties echoed the stance of the Law and Justice government. At the end of 2018, however, new accents appeared in the statements of the Civic Platform politicians. Criticism of the US administration led by President Donald Trump became increasingly evident, with objections regarding deepening Poland's bilateral military relations with the US by the government (including criticism of the Fort Trump project, the aim of which was to

35 Schetyna: Rządy PiS przeminą, budżet UE zostanie, 27.02.2018, http://fakty.interia.pl/polska/news-schetyna-rzady-pis-przemina-budzet-ue-zostanie,nId,2550855#utm_source=paste&utm_medium=paste&utm_campaign=chrome [retrieved on: 27.04.2018].

36 G. Schetyna, Europo, wracamy!, *op. cit.*

37 G. Schetyna, Europo, wracamy!, *op. cit.*

38 Platforma Obywatelska, http://www.platforma.org/aktualnosc/45497/projekty-platformy-polska-europa-swiat-polskaobywatelska [retrieved on: 27.04.2018].

39 G. Schetyna, Europo, wracamy!, *op. cit.*

increase the presence of US troops in Poland).[40] The politicians representing Civic Platform more and more often pointed out the need for Polish diplomacy to support the development of the EU defence policy, with regards to complementing and strengthening NATO's potential, as well as building European geopolitical autonomy in terms of EU's relations with the world's major powers. By doing so, the representatives of the Polish opposition have clearly moved closer to the agenda previously known from Paris and Berlin, all while distancing themselves from the strongly pro-American stance of the Law and Justice government.

The agenda of another opposition party – .Modern [.Nowoczesna] tend to be much more pro-European, although due to its declining electoral support in 2018 its influence on the policy of the authorities was rather marginal. .Modern strongly backed all pro-integration initiatives debated in the EU, as well as advocated for the adoption of the euro as quickly as possible.[41] The party also believed that Poland should accept refugees and immigrants, as well as supported all EU initiatives in this respect. Referring to Polish doctrine regarding European politics, .Modern advocated for promoting the four freedoms on the internal market.[42] In a similar spirit, the party supported furthering the EU's foreign and defence policy. It is also worth noting that an alliance was formed among the parties of the liberal opposition, named the European Coalition, which was joined not only by Civic Platform and .Modern, but also by the Polish People's Party, the Democratic Left Alliance and the Greens, in order to run as a single entity for the elections to the European Parliament (2019).

On the other hand, Kukiz'15 is an opposition party that presented a more Euro-sceptic stance than the Law and Justice government, which resulted in stiffening the government agenda in many parts of its European policy. In systemic matters, Kukiz'15 advocated for a "Europe of sovereign nations" and decried the "imperialist tendencies of Germany and France" – the tendency for both countries to dominate the EU,[43] Poland's policy should therefore aim at diminishing the

---

40 Politycy komentują prezydencką wizytę w USA, *Onet.pl*, 19 September 2018, https://wiadomosci.onet.pl/kraj/andrzej-duda-w-usa-komentarze-politykow/5mph8zr [retrieved on: 27.12.2018].

41 *Tekst wystąpienia Ryszarda Petru w sejmowej dyskusji o polskiej polityce zagranicznej*, https://nowoczesna.org/tekst-wystapienia-ryszarda-petru-w-sejmowej-dyskusji-o-polskiej-polityce-zagranicznej/ [retrieved on: 27.05.2018].

42 *„Nowoczesna Polska dla każdego". Program Nowoczesnej*, 2016, https://nowoczesna.org/nowoczesna-polska-dla-kazdego-program-partii/ [retrieved on: 27.05.2018].

43 *Paweł Kukiz o Unii Europejskiej*, http://web.archive.org/web/20190601212258/http://ruchkukiza.pl/pawel-kukiz-o-unii-europejskiej/ [retrieved on: 27.05.2018].

role of the bureaucracy in Brussels, as well as defending the national democracy, thereby reducing the power of EU institutions over Member States.[44] The party was quick to dismiss the possibility of Poland's accession to the EMU, which was declared a "failed experiment." Kukiz'15 thus proposed a controlled disbanding of the EMU as the only possible scenario that could benefit Europe. The party also strongly opposed the EU's plans to relocate refugees and immigrants. They supported the internal market, while at the same time calling for curbing the protectionist tendencies in Western Europe and proposing deregulation of the EU law. At the same time, their politicians opposed preferential treatment of foreign investors in Poland at the expense of the rights of domestic entrepreneurs or consumers. They were also in favour of Poland withdrawing from the EU energy and climate agreements, since according to them, it leads to the destruction of Polish industry and energy price hikes.

Conflict over the judicial reform

At the turn of 2017 and 2018, a violent conflict broke out between the government and part of the opposition over internal reforms, in particular changes in the justice system. These changes were also criticised by the European institutions, as well as by some Member States and presented as a violation of one of the key values of the EU – the rule of law. The dispute with the opposition also concerned the role of Poland in the EU, in this case perceived in the context of prestige and impact on decision-making. It was increasingly important for the deepening polarisation of the political scene in Poland concerning the area of European integration. Among Polish parties – including those constituting the opposition – a strong division into national and Euro-sceptic groups as well as liberal and pro-European movements emerged.

During the debates regarding the reform of the justice system, two different visions of European integration became apparent – one of them pursued by the conservative government, while the other was supported by the liberal opposition. Government representatives have repeatedly declared that they do not want Poland to leave the EU, although at the same time they called for a change in the current political practice of the Union. For the government, the intervention of the European institutions (both the Commission and the Court of Justice of the European Union – CJEU) is a violation of the laws enshrined in the treaties, which reserves judicial reforms to the exclusive competence of the

44 *Strategia Zmiany. Program Kukiz'15*, / http://web.archive.org/web/20190601211716/ http://ruchkukiza.pl/klub-poselski/strategia-zmiany/ [retrieved on: 27.05.2018].

Member States.[45] What is more, the criticism of the Polish reform was perceived as too far-reaching interference in Poland's internal affairs, meddling with both Polish sovereignty and Polish democracy. People supporting such a position clearly voiced their concerns in defence of the competencies of the Member States from EU's interference, especially beyond the scope of European treaties. Therefore, the opposition's efforts to find support abroad were treated as an act of treason, both by representatives of the government party and by some opposition politicians (such as Kukiz'15).[46] On the other hand, the representatives of the liberal opposition believed that external political interference – both by some Member States and by the European institutions – was justified by the processes of European integration, which results in countries losing their full sovereignty, which is then "shared" with other Member States and EU institutions. Thus, the EU institutions were not treated as "external," but as part of the political system.

Due to that conflict, the two visions of further European integration – liberal and conservative – clashed with each other. According to Law and Justice, European integration should be based on the autonomy and subjectivity of nation states, and true democracy is possible only at a national level. This means that other states should respect the agenda of the government elected by local populace. At the same time, external interference distorts the rights of voters and thus restricts national democracy. The liberal and cosmopolitan vision of integration, represented by pro-European opposition, envisions the EU Member States giving up more and more powers in favour of European institutions, which implies that political deliberations and elections held in Member States may be influenced by the media and politicians from other countries or officials representing EU institutions.

As I have already mentioned, the political division in Poland went along the fault line of values. The agenda of one side was based on liberal standards and the positive attitude towards integration stemming from them. The other side called

---

45 Szef MSZ podsumował działania resortu. Czaputowicz: Rząd podejmuje wysiłki w celu realizacji zobowiązań wyborczych, *wPolityce.pl*, 7 December 2018, https://wpolityce.pl/polityka/424568-szef-msz-podsumowal-dzialania-resortu [retrieved on: 27.12.2018]; Eurokraci w kropce. Czaputowicz: Gdy nowelizacja ustawy o SN wejdzie w życie, nie będzie podstawy do utrzymywania skargi w TSUE, *wPolityce.pl*, 10 December 2018, https://wpolityce.pl/polityka/424999-eurokraci-w-kropce-niebawem-nie-bedzie-podstawy-do-skargi [retrieved on: 27.12.2018].

46 Mocne słowa Jakubiaka: Wizyta Schetyny u Angeli Merkel to Targowica, *Do Rzeczy*, 25 September 2018, https://dorzeczy.pl/78208/Mocne-slowa-Jakubiaka-Wizyta-Schetyny-u-Angeli-Merkel-to-Targowica.html [retrieved on: 27.12.2018].

upon the conservative and national values, which resulted in distrust of EU's competence creep. Thus, it is no wonder that the conflict revolved mostly around European values. For the liberal opposition, the problem was that the government violated these values, especially the rule of law. "The EU was founded and is developing as a community of values, with human rights, democracy, rule of law and solidarity at the forefront. It is a shame that the Polish government has been violating these values since 2015. We will ensure that these standards, especially the equal rights of women and men, people with disabilities and minorities, are strongly enforced."[47] On the other hand, conservative parties and organisations believed that the EU institutions have been increasingly encroaching on the autonomy of Member States, including their failure to respect the national identity, as well as their fundamental political and constitutional structures (Article 4 of TEU), violated the principle of conferral enshrined in the Treaty (which means that EU institutions may not exceed the competences conferred upon them by the Member States in the Treaties), the principles of subsidiarity and proportionality (Article 5 of TEU)[48] and even democracy – one of the core values of the EU (Article 2 of TEU), as they have interfered too much in the order and decisions of democratic communities at the national level. Conservative parties find the EU's departure from Christian and pro-family values, as well as the top-down imposition of liberal standards without respecting national traditions or the views of voters to be impalatable.[49] That is why Law and Justice proposed that the Union should return to its roots – to the values shared by the founding fathers.

The liberal opposition accused the government of seeking a way to carry out a Polexit – Poland's exit from the EU. These concerns were particularly grave during the 2018 local and regional self-government elections, when the problem of compliance of the Polish constitution with the judgements of the CJEU arose. It is worth recalling here, that for many years there has been a dispute within the EU as to whether the principle of primacy of European law includes national

47 *Przyszłość Polski – Wielki Wybór*, *op. cit.*

48 Subsidiarity means that the central government should in principle be supportive, but without interfering with governance, which can be carried out at lower levels. When applying this principle, it is paramount to leave as much freedom for making decisions and governing as possible at lower levels of democratic communities, for example the local government. Proportionality means that higher-level administrative intervention does not go beyond what is strictly necessary. Cf. T.G. Grosse (2019): "Unia subsydiarna", Report for the Jagiellonian Club, Krakow, 2019.

49 *Program PiS 2014*, *op. cit.*, p. 12–13; *Deklaracja Europejska PiS*, *op. cit.*, items 1 and 2.

constitutions.[50] Many national constitutional tribunals believe that it does not. The principle of primacy was to be enshrined in the Constitutional Treaty, but as a result of its failure, it was withdrawn from the Treaty of Lisbon. The only element of it still left is a declaration added to the Treaty, which states the status quo – the principle of primacy is not explicitly enshrined in the Treaty, but results from the case-law of the CJEU.[51] Thus, the constitutional dispute taking place in Poland does not have to lead to a Polexit. If this were the case, the same threat would apply to several other countries, including Germany – they also believe that their constitution is not subject to the principle of primacy. What is more, even the Polish Constitutional Tribunal (in 2005 and 2010, when the Law and Justice party was not in power) recognised the supremacy of the Polish Constitution. In the opinion of the Tribunal, "the transfer of competences to the EU does not entitle the organisation to establish new legal acts or make decisions that would stand in opposition to the Polish Constitution," which is the "primary source of law in Poland."[52] The 2018 dispute proves that the government parties were ready to defend the autonomy of the Polish state and the constitutional order against the competence creep of EU institutions. For the liberal opposition, however, this context was of secondary importance if the protection of the national constitutional order were to increase the risk of a Polexit.

Politicians of the liberal opposition focused on the compatibility of Polish policy in the EU with the proposals for European reforms put forward by the EU institutions and the largest Member States. The improvement of the image of Poland in the European Community was of paramount importance. This necessitated a greater willingness to compromise on external proposals. According to the arguments raised by the opposition politicians, only the improvement of Poland's image guarantees a greater influence on the course of European reforms.[53] On the other hand, government politicians found the assessment of proposals for changes taking place in the EU from the point of view of national interests, as well blocking proposals which are not perceived as beneficial for

50 A. Vauchez (2015): *Brokering Europe: Euro-Lawyers and the Making of a Transnational Polity*, Cambridge: Cambridge University Press.

51 *Declaration no. 17 concerning primacy, Treaty of Lisbon amending the Treaty on European Union and the Treaty establishing the European Community, signed at Lisbon, 13 December 2007*, OJ C 306, 17.12.2007.

52 *Judgement of the Constitutional Tribunal of 24 November 2010*, K32/09.

53 Schetyna: PiS zniszczyło międzynarodowy wizerunek Polski, *Dziennik Gazeta Prawna*, 24.02.2018, https://www.gazetaprawna.pl/artykuly/1106895,schetyna-na-radzie-krajowej-po.html [retrieved on: 27.12.2018]

Polish society as crucial. Such an attitude may, and sometimes must, result with damaging the image of Polish government abroad. Defending national interests, especially those that won the majority in the elections, is the fundamental task of a democratic government. The head of Law and Justice claimed that his party "was authorised by the voters to defend the interests of Poland, and not to suck up to anyone in the EU or to take care of someone else's interests."[54] Thus, for conservatives, respect for democracy and national interests defined at the time of the elections was of fundamental importance, while image issues were far less important.

Conclusions

1) The agenda of the United Right government in 2015–2019 was in many aspects consistent with the stance of previous government coalitions and Polish doctrine regarding European politics. It was also in line with the opposition agenda with respect to several areas, particularly those where the public opinion was clearly formed (such as in the case of migration). The convergence of stances was also visible in the reluctance to expand European bureaucracy, in relation to the promotion of a liberal approach to the internal market, as well as in relation to the defence of EU funds for Poland (within the framework of cohesion, agricultural and innovation policy). Many similarities were observed in the area of geopolitical agenda. The largest parties expressed their fear towards the Russian threat, supported EU enlargement to the east and the Western Balkans, and preferred to maintain strong transatlantic relations. Representatives of the largest parties also supported the development of EU security and defence policies, but only under the proviso that this does not weaken the alliance with the USA and the role of NATO in the defence of Europe. This created a broad field of national consensus in relation to the Polish doctrine regarding European politics. It should be noted, however, that the Law and Justice government showed more reluctance towards many of the reforms debated within the EU, compared to its predecessors and the liberal opposition. This concerned, among other things, the expansion of the EU's defence policy.

54 "Wywiad z Jarosławem Kaczyńskim", 25.05.2016, Prawo i Sprawiedliwość, http://pis.org.pl/aktualnosci/zostalismy-upowaznieni-przez-wyborcow-do-obrony-interesow-polski [retrieved on: 27.12.2018].

2) The opposition was divided with respect to several areas of the agenda. For example, in the case of migration, some representatives of the opposition, including some liberal groups, fell in line with the government stance, while other opposition politicians called for greater openness to immigrants and supported the centralisation of competences in this respect at the EU level (for example .Modern). Liberal parties were in favour of membership in the euro area, while others, just as the ruling party, were against it (Kukiz'15). The largest division within the opposition, reflecting the entire political scene, concerned, on the one hand, liberal and pro-European groups, and on the other hand, national and Euro-sceptic ones.
3) The conflict between the government and the liberal opposition around the judicial reform has contributed to the deepening of the political division in Poland, which has increasingly concerned European affairs. The polarisation of agendas diluted the consensus among the political players towards the EU in Poland. The dispute over the reform of the justice system has led to the radicalisation of agendas and stances, both in the case of liberal, as well as right-wing parties. For some right-wing voters, the agenda of Law and Justice seemed to be excessively pro-European, which meant that new parties emerged, demanding Poland's exit from the EU.[55] The liberal side of the spectrum also saw the emergence of new parties, whose agendas were much more radical than that of Civil Platform (.Modern, Spring [Wiosna]).
4) In the period covered by this study, two slightly different concepts of Poland within the EU emerged, both among the government parties and the liberal opposition. National sovereignty was of fundamental importance for Law and Justice, as manifested by limiting the competence creep on the part of the European Commission and the CJEU, recognising the primacy of Polish Constitution over EU law, as well as unwillingness to accept any interference in Polish politics from EU institutions or other Member States. The defensive attitude towards these external entities was aimed at strengthening the Polish state. On the other hand, politicians of Civic Platform did not see the issue of a threat to state sovereignty. They believed that Polish power lied in the

55 Janusz Korwin-Mikke's Freedom Party and the National Movement formed a coalition before the 2019 EP elections and supported Poland's departure from the EU. Other Euro-sceptic parties on the right side of the Polish political spectrum include the True Europe Movement [Ruch Prawdziwa Europa] (supported by Fr. T. Rydzyk) and politicians of A. Macierewicz's faction within the Law and Justice party. Cf. A. Macierewicz (2018): Cena patriotyzmu, *Wiara, Patriotyzm i Sztuka*, no. 12 (98), 20 December 2018–23 January 2019.

greater activity within the EU, participation in the European decision-making centre and improvement of Poland's image among the international community. The liberal opposition was also more open to proposals for the progress of European integration presented by Berlin and Paris, as well as by the EU institutions.

5) Both sides of the political conflict in Poland exhibited different approaches to European crises and the role of nation states and EU institutions in overcoming them. For the government, crises have been dealt with inadequately and ineffectively by the European institutions. For this reason, Poland did not want to agree to the membership in the EMU, and it is also why European ideas for the centralisation of governance in terms of migration policy were criticised. Thus, the government chose the autonomy of state in monetary policy. It also demanded that national competences in the field of migration policy should be retained, accepting only general coordination and support of national policies by EU institutions and from the EU budget. On the other hand, the politicians of the liberal opposition did not put much attention in the experience of the economic crisis in the EMU, backing this project primarily because of the desire to move closer to the EU decision-making centre and to minimise the risk of a Polexit. They more or less endorsed the increase of EU competences in the field of migration policy in order to overcome the migration crisis. However, for electoral reasons, they did not advertise that stance publicly.

References

Cebul K. (2018): *Miejsce i rola Polski w Unii Europejskiej w świetle debat parlamentarnych w Sejmie RP w latach 2004–2011*, Warsaw: Wydawnictwo Naukowe UKSW, Warsaw.

Czachór Z. (2014): "Polska w Unii Europejskiej: między uniwersalizmem a partykularyzmem", [in:] *Polska w procesie integracji europejskiej: dekada doświadczeń (2004–2014)*, K.A. Wojtaszczyk, M. Mizerska-Wrotkowska, W. Jakubowski (eds.), Warsaw: WDiNP UW.

Grosse T.G. (2015): Czy „zróżnicowana integracja" może prowadzić do federacji w Europie?, *Przegląd Zachodni*, no. 1 (354), pp. 21–36.

Grosse T.G. (2017): "»Jeśli kochasz Europę …«. Rozważania o strategii Niemiec wobec problemów integracji europejskiej", [in:] *Polska – Niemcy – Unia Europejska. Razem czy osobno*? Z. Czachór, T. Marcinkowski (eds.), Warsaw: Dom Wydawniczy Elipsa, pp. 29–41.

Grosse T.G. (2018): Polska, Francja i Niemcy wobec Unii. Europejskie wizje w Trójkącie Weimarskim, Report, *Nowa Konfederacja*, 05.11.2018, https://nowakonfederacja.pl/raport/polska-francja-i-niemcy-wobec-unii-europejskie-wizje-w-trojkacie-weimarskim/ [retrieved on: 27/12/2018].

Grosse T.G. (2019): Unia subsydiarna, Kraków: Report for the Jagiellonian Club.

Guerra S. (2012): "Poles In the EU: Prior to and After Accession", [in:] *New neighbours – on the diversity of migrants' political involvement*, A. Dziewulska, A.M. Ostrowska (eds.), Warsaw: Centre for Europe.

Haughton T. (ed.) (2011): *Party politics in Central and Eastern Europe. Does EU membership matter*?, London: Routledge.

Informacja Ministra Spraw Zagranicznych Jacka Czaputowicza o zadaniach polskiej polityki zagranicznej w 2018 roku, Sejm of the Republic of Poland, 21 March 2018, http://www.msz.gov.pl/pl/aktualnosci/wiadomosci/minister_jacek_czaputowicz_o_priorytetach_polskiej_dyplomacji_w_2018_roku [retrieved on: 27.04.2018].

Konrad Szymański: Strefa euro nie odjeżdża Polsce, *Rzeczpospolita*, 22.05.2017, http://www.rp.pl/Unia-Europejska/305219925-Konrad-Szymanski-Strefa-euro-nie-odjezdza-Polsce.html [retrieved on: 27.04.2018].

Kowalczyk K. (2014): Typologia polskich partii politycznych według kryterium programowego, *Środkowoeuropejskie Studia Polityczne*, no. 1.

Krasnodębski Z. (2015): Co dla Polski oznaczają zmiany w Unii Europejskiej?, [in:] *Myśląc: Polska*, Programme Convention of Law and Justice and the United Right, Katowice, 3–5 July 2015, pp. 80–81.

Lindstrom N. (2015): *The Politics of Europeanization and Post-Socialist Transformations*, Palgrave Basingstoke.

Marciniak E., Godlewski T. (2016): Jakościowy portret „elektoratu zmiany" w wyborach parlamentarnych 2015 roku – podobieństwa i różnice, *e-Politicon*, no. XVII, Spring.

Nowoczesna Polska dla każdego. Program Nowoczesnej, 2016, https://nowoczesna.org/nowoczesna-polska-dla-kazdego-program-partii/ [retrieved on: 27.05.2018].

Pacześniak A. (2015): Eurosceptycyzm polskich partii politycznych – ile w tym przekonania, a ile pragmatyzmu?, *Politeja*, no. 2(33).

Paweł Kukiz o Unii Europejskiej, http://ruchkukiza.pl/pawel-kukiz-o-unii-europejskiej/ [retrieved on: 27.05.2018].

Platforma Obywatelska, http://www.platforma.org/aktualnosc/45497/projekty-platformy-polska-europa-swiat-polskaobywatelska [retrieved on: 27.04.2018].

Pollack M. (1994): Creeping Competence: The Expanding Agenda of the European Community, *Journal of Public Policy*, vol. 14, pp. 95–145.

Program PiS 2014, http://pis.org.pl/dokumenty [retrieved on: 27.04.2018].

Przemówienie ministra spraw zagranicznych Radosława Sikorskiego wygłoszone w Berlinie 28 listopada 2011, TVN24.pl, https://www.tvn24.pl/polska-a-przyszlosc-unii-europejskiej,192356,s.html [retrieved on: 27.04.2018].

Przemówienie Premier Beaty Szydło na XV Forum Polityki Zagranicznej, 9.11.2017, http://www.minsk.msz.gov.pl/pl/aktualnosci/xv_forum_polityki_zagranicznej [retrieved on: 27.04.2018].

Schetyna potwierdza: Nie będziemy przyjmować nielegalnych migrantów, *Newsweek*, 10.05.2017, http://www.newsweek.pl/polska/schetyna-nie-bedziemy-przyjmowac-migrantow-po-o-uchodzcach,artykuly,409922,1.html [retrieved on: 27.04.2018].

Schetyna: PiS zniszczyło międzynarodowy wizerunek Polski, *Dziennik Gazeta Prawna*, 24.02.2018, https://www.gazetaprawna.pl/artykuly/1106895,schetyna-na-radzie-krajowej-po.html [retrieved on: 27.12.2018].

Schweiger Ch. (2014): Poland, Variable Geometry and the Enlarged European Union, *Europe-Asia Studies*, vol. 66, no 3, pp. 394–420.

Stosunek Polaków i Czechów do przyjmowania uchodźców, *CBOS*, no. 87/2018, July 2018.

Strategia Zmiany. Program Kukiz'15, http://web.archive.org/web/20190601211716/http://ruchkukiza.pl/klub-poselski/strategia-zmiany/ [retrieved on: 27.05.2018].

Styczyńska N. (2018): *Więcej czy mniej Europy*? Krakow: Wydawnictwo Uniwersytetu Jagiellońskiego.

Szyszko J. (2015): Globalna polityka klimatyczna, in: *Myśląc*: Polska, Programme Convention of Law and Justice and the United Right, Katowice, 3–5 July 2015, pp. 33–36.

Tekst wystąpienia Ryszarda Petru w sejmowej dyskusji o polskiej polityce zagranicznej, https://nowoczesna.org/tekst-wystapienia-ryszarda-petru-w-sejmowej-dyskusji-o-polskiej-polityce-zagranicznej/ [retrieved on: 27.05.2018].

Vachudova M.A. (2008): Tempered by the EU? Political parties and party systems before and after accession, *Journal of European Public Policy*, 15:6, pp. 861–879.

Vauchez A. (2015): *Brokering Europe: Euro-Lawyers and the Making of a Transnational Polity*, Cambridge: Cambridge University Press.

Weatherill S. (2004): Competence Creep and Competence Control, *Yearbook of European Law*, vol. 23, issue 1, pp. 1–55.

Wywiad z Jarosławem Kaczyńskim, 25.05.2016, Prawo i Sprawiedliwość, http://pis.org.pl/aktualnosci/zostalismy-upowaznieni-przez-wyborcow-do-obrony-interesow-polski [retrieved on: 27.12.2018].

Żuk G. (2013): *Europe in Polish Public Discourse*, Frankfurt: Peter Lang.

Marcin Kędzierski

Public policy in the age of the Crisis of the West – conclusions for Poland

Abstract: The purpose of this study is to summarize the considerations presented by authors of this publication to present a preliminary analysis of the conclusions drawn from them for public policy or, in a narrower sense, for public management in Poland. The author divides the argument into three main parts. In the first, there was conducted a critical analysis of the most important theoretical and empirical theses regarding the global Western Crisis and the models of the logic of hierarchy related to the formation of international order. The second part will be devoted to the analysis of the most important Polish strategic document, i.e. the Strategy for Responsible Development (SRD). Finally, the third part will constitute a summary along with a description of the ability to carry out the long-term development strategy described in the SRD in the perspective of the Crisis of the West.

Keywords: summary, Crisis of the West, Strategy for Responsible Development, Polish administration

Introduction

The aim of this study is to summarise considerations presented by individual authors – both “metapolitical” considerations rooted in the broadly understood political philosophy and empirical considerations expressed in the form of case studies. However, it is not a question of attempting a synthesis of the aforementioned text, but rather making a preliminary analysis of conclusions arising out of them for public policy, or – within a narrower scope – for public management in Poland.

Having the aforementioned goal in mind, we will divide this research into three main parts. In the first part, we will carry out a critical analysis, on the one hand, of the most important (in the author’s opinion) theoretical and empirical arguments concerning the global Crisis of the West[1] and the possibilities of solving it that have been presented in the entire volume and, on the other hand, the so-called models of the logic of hierarchy connected with the formation of

1 In this chapter, the term ‘West’ will be treated *sensu largo* as a community of states characterised by liberal democracy and market economy. And the capitalised term ‘Crisis’ shall mean the crisis of the West in its broad sense.

international order. This analysis is supposed to bring about an attempt to make a synthesis that will comprehensively describe the specifics of the modern international order that is currently *in statu nascendi*.

The second part will be devoted to an analysis of the most important Polish strategic document – the Strategy for Responsible Development (SRD). It will be carried out from the perspective of challenges diagnosed in this publication that arise out of the emerging new international order. It will cover the verification of the coherence of the description of "megatrends" indicated in the SRD, with challenges presented in the first part of this chapter.

Finally, the third part will constitute a summary along with a description of the ability to carry out the long-term development strategy described in the SRD in the perspective of the Crisis of the West. In this part, we will focus particularly on limitations affecting the ability to conduct rational public policy in the future.

The crisis of the West vs. the new international order

The authors of all studies agree that we witness the deep Crisis that affects the broadly understood West. This argument is not particularly controversial – it has been present in world literature at least for a few years. However, there are differences as to the reasons for this Crisis and its potential consequences. In this text, Olaf Osica correctly identified the four crises that are regarded separately or equally as sources of the global Crisis in international public discourse:

1) the crisis of American leadership resulting from the rebellion against the USA as the "liberal Leviathan" after 1945 and the growing objection against globalisation and free trade flow;
2) the civilisational crisis resulting from the self-destruction of Western identity brought about by liberal ideas, which has become diluted in the world of universalistic ideas and has lost the ability to defend its own narration and, consequently, interests;
3) the crisis of the middle class in Western Europe, which became deprived of state support as a result of the disassembly of public services;
4) the crisis in the field of political economy resulting from mutual discrepancies between globalisation, democracy and sovereignty, as a result of which states cannot pursue the fulfilment of all of the three ideas at the same time.[2]

The aforementioned list of reasons for the outbreak of the Crisis could be extended with an additional group of very significant phenomena, such as:

2 See the chapter by Olaf Osica in this book, pp. 39–57.

5) climatic changes resulting from growing global political tensions that directly or indirectly affect the situation of states belonging to the Western world (e.g., the migrant crisis, the Arabian Spring, the Syrian war, etc.);
6) demographic changes consisting in the increase of the population of the global South and the ageing of Western societies, which results in serious dilemmas for socio-economic systems of developed states;
7) technological changes, including the emergence of the Internet, which result, e.g., in the dispersion of power and the higher "brittleness" of political systems.

The above list certainly does not exhaust all sources of the Crisis, which – at least because of its complexity – must have been caused by a series of factors having diverse impacts in various periods. However, whereas the outbreak of the global financial crisis and, consequently, the global economic crisis in 2008 is quite commonly regarded as the symbolic beginning of the Crisis of the West, Rodrik's trilemma described in the fourth item, called also the paradox of globalisation, is worth special attention. It is worth stressing that the paradox indicated by Rodrik was the focus of interest of a few authors of this book. Presenting a simplified view of the paradox of globalisation, we must say that a state may retain its sovereignty on condition that it restricts its participation in globalisation processes or internal rules of liberal democracy. Likewise, societies may decide to participate in globalisation according to democratic rules, but this must take place *de facto* outside the structures of the sovereign state.[3] The key problem, however, lies in the fact that the international order based on liberal democracy and the globalisation of economic process that came into being in the post–Cold War era relied fundamentally on the possibility of fulfilment of all of the three aforementioned values: openness, sovereignty, and liberal democracy.

In this context, it is worth noticing the process of evolution of liberal democracy that is described by Marek Cichocki in his text. He points out the fact that liberal democracy has been redefined towards "monitored democracy" in the last few years. As Cichocki writes, as opposed by the traditional form of representative democracy, which was connected mainly with the state and the community of citizens and was based on the public opinion/system of political parties, monitored democracy 'is based on the functioning of the entire network mechanism of non-parliamentary and non-state government control centres (international institutions, organisations and agenda, civil societies, media, courts

3 See: D. Rodrik (2011): *One Economics, Many Recipes: Globalization, Institution, and Economic Growth*, Warsaw: Wydawnictwo Krytyki Politycznej.

and tribunals) acting for the protection of democratic standards, public interest, responsibility and control".[4]

The problem lies in the fact that monitored democracy essentially changes the way of functioning of the sovereign post-Westphalian state that is one of the elements of Rodrik's trilemma. It introduces the logic of equal orders of power that is exercised not only by political actors or intergovernmental institutions that could still be regarded as quasi-state institutions within the meaning of sovereignty, interdependence or international law sovereignty (e.g., international tribunals), but also by non-state entities that are not subject to the jurisdiction of the political power of the state or one of the intergovernmental organisations. We can count among them global corporations, rating agencies, international non-governmental organisations, international religious movements, etc. The evolution of liberal democracy was not accompanied by the process of formation of a hierarchical structure of power on the global level, which meant in practice some form of global government having democratic legitimacy, as it difficult to treat the UN or even G8/G20 as such an entity. The lack of efficient global government, or even the lack of prospects for the creation of such global power having broad legitimacy in the foreseeable future, proves the brittleness of monitored democracy in a certain sense. Consequently, the aforementioned evolution of liberal democracy resulted in the situation in which Rodrik's trilemma may be reduced *de facto* to the dilemma of globalisation vs. the sovereign state, because the "old" representative liberal democracy seems to be dying in our eyes, and its new "diluted" form falls short of the expectations of Western societies. The reduced form of Rodrik's dilemma is also reflected by the new axis of the political dispute and the global division into globalistic and localistic movements.[5] Although the choice of globalisation means the sacrifice of sovereignty and the choice of the sovereign state means the sacrifice of openness, liberal democracy becomes a victim of both "globalism" and "localism", which was forecasted, among others, by Benjamin Barber as early as the middle of the 1990s.[6] He went even further in his diagnosis by suggesting that even the self-propelling dialectic dispute between globalism and localism would have an adverse impact on liberal democracy.

4 See the chapter by Marek Cichocki in this book, pp. 13–37.

5 M. Kuź (2015): Globaliści vs. lokaliści [Globalists vs. Localists], *Nowa Konfederacja*, 3(57)/2015, https://nowakonfederacja.pl/globalisci-vs-lokalisci/ [access date: 01.05.2019].

6 See: B. Barber (1995): *Jihad vs. McWorld*, New York: Times Books, 1995.

Having this in mind, we must ask whether it is possible to defend liberal democracy. On the basis of the research done so far, we can distinguish two hypothetical paths. One of them assumes the construction of global legitimacy for some form of monitored democracy, whereas the other one assumes the return to traditional representative democracy rooted in the structures of the national state that is not "entangled" in the network-based international structure of power. In spite of its attractiveness for localistic political movements, this second solution is unlikely, mainly due to the progressive globalisation of economic processes and the information revolution that can be subjected to political control by the national state to a decreasingly small extent. Moreover, we can predict with a high degree of likelihood that the direction of development of both of these phenomena (globalisation and information revolution) will not change radically in the next few years, and it will be possible to impede these processes on a national scale only by means of solutions that … contradict the ideas of liberal democracy (censorship, the limitation of access, etc.). In this sense, as opposed to Rodrik's conception, the departure from globalisation does not have to lead to the maintenance of liberal democracy, but to the development par excellence of a new form of authoritarianism or non-liberal (aliberal) democracy that has been pushed through by Viktor Orbán.[7]

Admittedly, we can argue, like Osica does in his text, that the 'further functionality of the liberal order in Europe, but at the expense of decreased global ambitions and concentration on internal socio-economic problems'.[8] Such a perspective can be regarded as very interesting and intellectually inspiring, but, nevertheless, it is questionable even in the context of peripheralisation of the Old Continent. It seems that, regardless of the shifting of Europe from the centre towards global peripheries, a large part of European economic and political elites having an influence on the shape of political decisions and accustomed to a certain status will not be interested in a considerable decrease of global aspirations, which can be seen, for instance, in the policy being pursued by the President of France Emmanuel Macron since 2017.[9]

The first path is much more interesting. As national states and their ability to conduct effective policy seem to become weaker, the best proof of which is the international practice of tax avoidance, we can imagine the consent of societies to the transfer of the increasing number of competences to the transnational

7 See: https://budapestbeacon.com/full-text-of-viktor-orbans-speech-at-baile-tusnad-tusnadfurdo-of-26-july-2014/ [access date: 01.05.2019].

8 See the chapter by Olaf Osica in this book, pp. 39–57.

9 See the chapter by Marcin Darmas in this book, pp. 163–184.

level. Assuming that rational citizens of national states will tend to recognise more clearly, on the one hand, the weakness of national states in rivalry with new non-state centres of power and, on the other hand, to see the individual benefits of globalisation (both elements are significant here), the *sui generis* formation of the global government could seem to be a question of time. In a sense, such way of thinking was not a separate case until 2008 – it was expressed, for instance, by the Lisbon Treaty, which increased the number of cases decided by a qualified majority in a voting by 44.[10] However, the problem lies in the fact that, although national states have not tackled the challenges of globalisation in a definitely better way in the last few years, their active monetary and financial policy after 2008 helped to make it through the global financial crisis unscathed in social perception. It seems that this belief was the reason for the restoration of confidence in the Union/intergovernmental method in the EU.[11]

However, irrespective of the return of faith in the causal power of national states (which is not tantamount to the restoration of full causal power), Western societies are losing the sense of individual benefits of globalisation. This phenomenon affects particularly the middle class in the West; as opposed to inhabitants of less affluent states and the wealthiest persons, it was not an economic beneficiary of globalisation.[12] In 2030, according to forecasts, the global share of expenses of the Western middle class will decrease to around 30 % and will rise to almost 60 % in Asia (in 2009, this share accounted for 64 % and 23 %).[13] Adding the fact mentioned, among others, by Osica that we have witnessed the disassembly of the welfare state offering public services in the last several years,[14] we deal with

---

10 See: J.J. Węc (2011): *Traktat lizboński. Polityczne aspekty reformy ustrojowej Unii Europejskiej w latach 2007–2009*, [*The Lisbon Treaty. Political Aspects of the Political & Social Reform of the European Union in the Years 2007–2009*], Kraków: Wydawnictwo Znak, pp. 153–154 and 168.

11 T.G. Grosse (2016): Podsumowanie. W kierunku teorii dezintegracji regionalnej [Summary. Towards the Theory of Regional Disintegration], in: T.G. Grosse (ed.), *Polityki europejskie w dobie kryzysu* [*European Policies In the Age of Crisis*], Warsaw: Wydawnictwo Naukowe Scholar, pp. 282–286.

12 See: B. Milanovic (2012): *Global Income Inequality by the Numbers: in History and Now. An Overview*, Policy Research working paper; no. WPS 6259. Washington, DC: World Bank. http://documents.worldbank.org/curated/en/959251468176687085/pdf/wps6259.pdf [access date: 01.05.2019].

13 See: H. Karas (2010): *The Emerging Middle Class in Developing Countries*, The Brookings Institution 2010 https://www.oecd.org/development/pgd/44798225.pdf [access date: 01.05.2019].

14 See the chapter by Olaf Osica in this book, pp. 39–57.

the situation in which the impoverished middle class devoid of state support, which is the social foundation of liberal democracy, begins to shrink, which will most probably ruin the idea of global political power. This may happen particularly because the share of the middle class in the global population will radically decrease for two reasons. Firstly, the population is increasing dynamically; after World War II, when the framework of the liberal international order was emerging, the population amounted to 3 billion people. In 2050, it will reach around 10 billion. Secondly, as Thomas Piketty and some other authors indicate, successive industrial revolutions and the globalisation lead to growing income inequalities,[15] which will most probably increase even further as a result of the fourth industrial revolution and the advent of technologies based on artificial intelligence. It is difficult to suspect the emergence of an entity having sufficient financial and, even more importantly, technological potential that would gather a global political movement of the "poor" capable of establishing a government that could effectively balance the interests of global "holders".

So, why should we regard this first "global" path as more interesting? This results from the fact that, in spite of strong national identities returning in the Western world – which is reflected by Donald Trump's victory, the Brexit or successes of parties such as the National Rally in France or the League in Italy – we can also observe the growing feeling of helplessness and the lack of causal power; however, they slowly begin to be accompanied by changes fitting into the trend of network neo-mediaevalism.[16] It assumes the need to reduce the areas controlled by the state and allow equal orders of power to function. Importantly, they do not have to respect all liberal principles – it is only necessary to stick to certain strictly determined borders. Thus, it seems reasonable to ask to what extent the trend of social neo-mediaevalism can be regarded as compatible and reconcilable with liberal democracy. The answer of representatives of this direction of thinking will be as follows: although these trends are not concurrent, the limitation of certain postulates of liberalism will paradoxically allow us to retain some of its most important achievements. As Grzegorz Lewicki – one of the representatives of this view in Poland – indicates: 'The European Union may last if only it realises that neo-liberalism … is not the only possible remedy to the ailments of this world. A better long-term prescription will be neo-mediaevalism – the approval

15 T. Piketty (2014): *Capital in the Twenty-First Century*, transl. Arthur Goldhammer, Harvard University Press.

16 See, e.g., H. Bull (1977): *The Anarchical Society. A Study of Order in World Politics*, Columbia University Press, New York; J. Zielonka (2008): *Europa jako imperium [Europe as an Empire]*, Warsaw: Polski Instytut Spraw Międzynarodowych.

of varied and personalised organisational, political and ideological solutions taken straight from the Middle Ages. Paradoxically, some liberal ideas may be saved if we realise this on time and sacrifice part of neo-liberal solutions on the altar of history. If, however, we go on denying this, sticking to neo-liberalism and multiculturalism in their current shape and putting Islam and Christianity to blame, liberalism in Europe will certainly come to an end'.[17] To sum up, the trend of network neo-mediaevalism may be a prescription for overcoming the crisis of liberal democracy, even though it may be a shock therapy for the latter.

On the margin of the discussion about the Crisis of the West and the available methods of solving it, we should note the problem of dispersion of power in the age of technological development and information revolution. Because of the dissemination of information technologies, a growing number of interest groups is able to impact the political process effectively. However, as politics covers more and more complex issues that an average citizen knows little about, the space for the generation of fake news co-creating public debate is increasing. But irrespective of whether the expansion of the circle of participants of the debate affects its quality, the ability of rulers to create political decision "sovereignly" is certainly becoming limited, both in the external and internal dimension. As Artur Wołek correctly noted in the previously presented case study, 'the reaction of two Polish governments to the migrant crisis in 2015 was caused by a combination of three factors: the previous identification of Polish immigrant policy mainly as activities in the field of security, the pressure exerted by European partners of our country and the rapid politicisation of immigrant policy in the course of electoral campaigns of 2015'.[18] Consequently, governments more and more often become hostages of existing narrations and various stakeholders.

The above consideration concerning the crisis of liberal democracy and prospects of overcoming it should lead us to the question about the structure of the (new) international order that is still (or has been until quite recently) based on liberal democracy. On the basis of the classical theory of international relations, Olaf Osica distinguishes three possible scenarios of formation of such an order that must assume hierarchical order by definition ("three models of the logic of hierarchies"):

---

17 G. Lewicki (2017): *Unia Europejska jak Cesarstwo Rzymskie. Nadchodzi nowe średniowiecze [The European Union as the Roman Empire. The New Middle Ages Are Coming],* https://klubjagiellonski.pl/2017/11/04/unia-europejska-jak-cesarstwo-rzymskie-nadchodzi-nowe-sredniowiecze/ [access date: 01.05.2019].

18 See the chapter by Artur Wołek in this book, pp. 207–240.

Tab. 1: Typology of the main phenomena of network neo-mediaevalism

Sphere	Source	Characteristics
Policy	Technical progress promoting international actors	Decentralisation of power – instead of one centre, there are many nodal points that must be built up with a control system for the purpose of effective rule; the anarchisation of policy through masking of existing nodal points, the need for their continuous mapping
Society and religion	Vital disorientation – the need for coherent interpretation of reality, i.e., the need for authorities that build harmonious interpretation on the basis of border concepts adopted by the social group concerned	"Shock of the future" (Toffler), "complex risk" (Beck), looking for authorities structuring reality on behalf of individuals (demand for suppliers of spiritual trust); the emergence of civil religious communities pursuing the ideal of service, communitarianism
Culture and economics	Impossibility of adaptation of masses to the dynamics of globalisation changes – the need for a guardian	New paternalism – readiness to give up a large part of individualism in return for economic security (*guanxi* – dependent community networks) and physical security (protection against organised crime); the return of discourse accepting the existence of social hierarchy
Philosophy	Impossibility of denying border concepts (transcendentals) and logic concepts due to their practical importance	Defence of border concepts in philosophy by elites in opposition to postmodernism and other kinds of scepticism
Demographics	Cultivation of individualism and individual self-fulfilment model	Long-term extinction of part of the population with freethinking view with a simultaneous increase of the part of the population brought up in the patriarchal system
	Technical progress and fascination with its potential	Blurring of the borders between products of technology and art; inspiration with technology

Source: G. Lewicki (2010): Sieciowa teoria nowego średniowiecza [The Network Theory of the New Middle Ages], in: Kraków: „Pressje" teka 20, p. 93.

1) balancing of interests of states (the realistic approach);
2) the rule of some people over others, i.e., domination (the approach based on the theory of dependence);
3) the agreement between states (the liberal approach).[19]

In spite of the widespread view in public space that the modern international order is based on agreement and co-operation, it is difficult to verify such a hypothesis in an unambiguous manner. Although the situation of balancing of states' interests did not occur from the collapse of the Soviet Union until the emergence of China as a competitor for the hegemonic position, because the USA had no equal competitor in the last decade of the 20th century and the first decade of the 21st century, but doubts arise in the case of the other two logics. Was the policy of American administration under Clinton, Bush and Obama based more on the liberal logic of agreement or on the Wallersteinian concept of dependence? The same goes for policies inside the EU – are we able to determine to what extent the Federal Republic of Germany has followed the liberal logic of a Europeanised civil power, and to what extent it has pursued the logic of dominance (e.g. within the Eurozone[20]) or the logic of interest balancing (e.g., in relations with France and Great Britain in the pre-crisis period) since its reunification in 1990?

Taking this into account, the "liberality" of the fading international order was discretionary to some extent. Although undoubtedly there have been many proofs of the dominance of the logic of co-operation and agreement in the last thirty years, such as the progress of European integration and the establishment of the Economic and Monetary Union or the concept of co-operative security, even in these cases we can recognise the pursuit of interest of dominant states – i.e., Germany in the case of the Eurozone, and the USA in the case of co-operative security. At the same time, this did not mean the absence of benefits for smaller states in connection with the aforementioned processes. The best example is Poland, whose unprecedented development in the last 30 years could be attributed to dependence on German economy benefiting from the joint currency on the one hand and on the NATO's guarantee of security on the other hand, although it is worth adding here that the above dependencies had their own price – respectively, the lack of sufficient investments in research and development and delays in the modernisation of the Polish army. However, as Osica rightly suggests, we must not forget that the post–Cold War period was

19 See the chapter by Olaf Osica in this book, pp. 39–57.
20 See the chapter by Ryszarda Formuszewicz in this book, pp. 101–135.

not a "golden era" for everybody – it is enough to look at what happened in the Balkans or on the border territories of the former Soviet Union (Caucasus, Transnistria).[21]

For this reason, although the choice of a specific "model of the logic of hierarchies" in the creation of the new international order has an unquestionable impact on the position of individual states, particularly middle-sized and small states, it does not determine this position entirely. It is assumed that the realistic logic of the balance of powers (the "concert of powers") and the logic of dominance will be less favourable for smaller players in the long term than the logic of agreement and co-operation, particularly if they make an attempt to build a specific kind of political subjectivity. On the other hand, we can imagine the situation when a smaller state can benefit from the fact of remaining in a hegemonic system – both a unipolar and multipolar system, which is proved best by the situation of such states as South Korea and Israel, which have experienced a civilisational leap during the Cold War period. This means that, from the perspective of the national interest of states such as Poland, it is impossible to determine clearly preferences for any of the aforementioned logics *ex ante*.

Also, we must not forget that even the choice of the liberal model of the logic of hierarchies is only slightly dependent on smaller actors of international relations, even if they have a theoretically larger impact on the formation of the global order within its framework. Going further, even if we assume a certain impact of smaller states on the shape of the aforementioned order, because of the growing degree of dependence of foreign policy on the existing narrations and specifics of internal policy, the abilities of governments to co-create the order in a rational and adaptive manner are even more strongly limited. These observations have very practical consequences for the conduct of public policy, particularly in combination with conclusions arising from reflections on possible directions of evolution of liberal democracy. This issue will be considered in the last part of this chapter.

Strategy for responsible development vs. the crisis of the West

The main document determining goals and rules of conducting the long-term development policy in Poland is the Strategy for Responsible Development (SRD) adopted by the Council of Ministers on 14 February 2017. SRD is a very large and comprehensive document that combines the qualities of a strategy and an operational program. As the authors write in the introduction:

21 See the chapter by Olaf Osica in this book, pp. 39–57.

> The strategy is an instrument to manage main development processes in Poland, defining a new model of development. It combines a strategic and operational dimension by delineating necessary activities and implementation instruments – flagship products and strategic products ensuring its implementation. In addition, it establishes a co-ordination and implementation system by assigning roles to public entities and methods of co-operation with the world of business and science and with society.[22]

The awareness of the need for agile management adequate to the following changes, which is defined by the then Deputy Prime Minister Mateusz Morawiecki as 'economic pragmatism', fits into global trends of public policy that tries to respond to challenges arising from the Crisis of the West. In the summary of the aforementioned introduction, he writes that 'finding the proper balance between democracy and capitalism, between the market and society, is the challenge that many societies of Western Europe, or more broadly the Western world, face nowadays'.[23]

As for references to the global order, the introduction contains only the implied criticism of the Washington Consensus – a set of rules determining the international economic and development policy since the late 1980s that applied *de facto* till the global financial crisis in 2008.

> The foundation on which the Polish capital and welfare would be built was a set of rules of the Washington Consensus that assumed, among others, deregulation, privatisation, the liberalisation of trade and the free flow of capital. A similar path was taken by other economies of our region. However, these solutions did not take into account the characteristics of the post-communist reality – the weakness of state institutions, the unreformed justice system, the low level of savings and the disturbed ownership structure in industries of key importance for the formation of the new economic order. The dogma that the best industrial policy is the lack of industrial policy also prevailed. In the field of social policies, the specific rule of Darwinism was dominant, which left all communities and professional groups on the margin of public life. This approach involved high social costs that were uncritically regarded as a necessary element of reforms. For over a quarter of the century, Polish economic policy was not less or more neo-liberal. It was simply provisional.[24]

However, the presentation of the criticism of the liberal order in such a veiled manner should not be surprising, taking into account the unprecedented success of Polish economy – GDP/capita measured by purchasing power has risen from 29 % in 1989 to almost 70 % of the European average. This means that, within less than 30 years, Poland managed to return to the level that, according to reports

22 *Strategy for Responsible Development*, Ministerstwo Rozwoju, Warsaw 2017, p. 6.
23 *Ibidem*, p. 4.
24 *Ibidem*, p. 2.

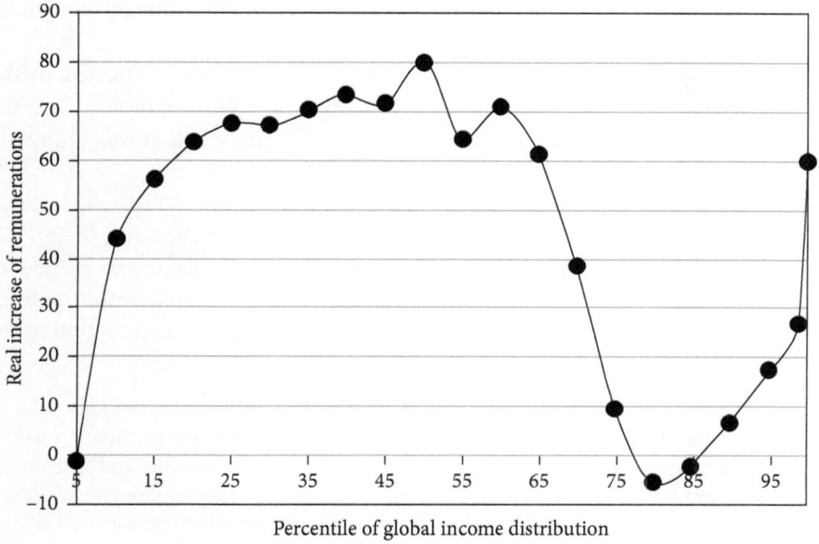

Chart 1: Change of real income between 1988 and 2008 for various percentiles of global income distribution (measured in international dollars from 2005). Source: Milanovic, B., *Global Income Inequality* ..., p. 15.

of economic historians, was recorded at the end of the era of Jagiellonians' rule for the last time.[25] Recalling Milanovic's elephant chart, Poland ranked at the top of the "hump" in the period under analysis, as opposed to the middle class of Western societies, whose situation has worsened not only in a relative, but sometimes also absolute sense as a result of globalisation processes, etc.

Except the introduction, the content of the SRD also contains references to the global Western Crisis in its broad sense. The authors of the strategy recognise the crisis of the European integration process as the most important challenge resulting from the current international political situation. Interestingly, they seek its causes not only in the migrant crisis, the prolonging crisis of the

25 See: M. Piątkowski (2013): *Poland's new golden age: shifting from Europe's periphery to its center*, Policy Research working paper, no. WPS 6639. Washington, DC: World Bank. http://documents.worldbank.org/curated/en/285611468107064618/Polands-new-golden-age-shifting-from-Europes-periphery-to-its-center [access date: 01.05.2019].

Eurozone or the Brexit, but also in the 'weakness of the political system in making decisions that meet citizens' expectations'.[26]

Tab. 2 presents a list of short-term and long-term factors indicated in the SRD that may affect the development potential of Polish economy. The list encompasses mainly threats indicated in the SWOT analysis that was indirectly carried out in the Strategy.

Excluding potential threats related to the signature of the TTIP, which never materialised, the vast majority of challenges indicated in the SRD in 2017 is analogous to challenges described in world literature and collected by authors of individual chapters. There is only one exception – the perspective resulting from Rodrik's trilemma is virtually absent from the Strategy. In the introduction to the SRD, Mateusz Morawiecki writes:

> The state has a fundamental role to play in the initiation and implementation of the change of the model of socio-economic development. … The care of modernisation and economic subjectivity is the measure of the best traditions of authorities and societies of the free world. These values do not contradict the openness of economies within the scope of global economic processes. Just the opposite – the activity of modern and efficient state institutions is an added value for the increase, expansion and competitiveness of local economic entities. The last financial and economic crisis has proved beyond all doubt that the creation of competitive edges in times of instability is the advantage of states that have implemented their own cross-section strategies of foreign expansion, development of individual sectors or innovativeness consistently for years.[27]

In the above fragment, we can see strong faith, at least on the declarative level, in the causal power of the sovereign state that 'does not contradict the openness of economies' (globalisation), at the same time being 'the measure of the best traditions of authorities and societies of the free world' (liberal democracy). It seems that the political reality of the last few years undermines this faith – it is enough to look at the ongoing dispute about the rule of law in Poland between the government in Warsaw and European institutions. Irrespective of the political dimension of this conflict, both on the internal level (the government vs. the opposition) and the external level (the struggle for competencies between the European Commission and the Council, as well as the struggle between various factions in the EC), the dispute about the rule of law affects the fundamental problem indicated by Rodrik. In order to regain the causal power of the state and the ability to have an active impact on economic policy and other matters, the Polish government must sooner or later question the rules of monitored

26 *Strategy for Responsible Development…*, p. 18.
27 *Ibidem*, p. 2.

Tab. 2: The most important external factors that may affect the development potential of Poland in the short term and in the long term

Short-term factors	Long-term factors (megatrends)
– weakening of the dynamics of development of global economy, particularly the aggravation of problems of the most important economic partners of Poland (the worsening of the state of public finance, the low economic growth rate and structural problems, persistent unemployment among young people, the influx of immigrants, the threat of terrorism, growing euroscepticism);	– the deepening concentration of capital and the related growing of social inequalities accompanied by the impoverishment of the middle class, which results in the intensification of populistic tendencies and objection to globalisation; this may lead to the weakening/decline of international economic co-operation and the destabilisation of social and economic systems (weaker coherence of the social tissue and the intensification of global migrations);
– weakening of the economic growth rate in China in conditions of increasing internal imbalance and the change of the model of development;	– demographic trends that enforce not only the transformation of the labour market, but also a change in the structure of economy and the development of its individual parts or the stagnation of other parts;
– the lower increase rate in the USA than before the crisis and, on the other hand, the prospect of stricter monetary policy and the related reinforcement of the dollar, which may result in the outflow of capital from economies of developing countries;	– automation, robotisation and computerisation of economic processes that pose a threat both to the labour market and – in the case of computerisation – internal and external security;
– the imbalance on the raw material markets and the price competition of their exporters creating the risk of economic destabilisation and lower innovativeness;	– the lower level of labour consumption of modern economies, which creates the need to elaborate mechanisms of sharing labour; at the same time, the increasing demand for steady access to information creates a potential security risk;
– armed conflicts and the lack of political & economic stability, including in countries in border territories of the EU (e.g., Ukraine, Syria), that result, e.g., in an increased influx of immigrants;	– the need to include the impact of business activity on the natural environment and the adaptation of production techniques and technologies, as well as the intensification of results of climate changes;

(*continued on next page*)

Tab. 2: (continued)

Short-term factors	**Long-term factors (megatrends)**
– tendencies to integrate more strongly within the European and Monetary Union, which may result in the closer co-ordination of economic policies, which means also a broader scale of interactions between individual economies (both in the positive and negative sense) on the one hand, and divisions in the EU on the other hand; – negative consequences of the Brexit that may cover the functioning of the common market, the method of economic management in the EU, and the size and destination of funds from the EU budget; – changes of the model of functioning of the European budget, including the possibility of changes in the European cohesion policy and the Common Agricultural Policy that may result in a decrease of European funds granted to Poland; – entry into force of the Transatlantic Trade and Investment Partnership (TTIP) and the Comprehensive Economic and Trade Agreement between the European Union and Canada (CETA), which might bring negative consequences for agriculture and the chemical industry or excessively reinforce the position of foreign investors;	– limited water, raw product and energy resources posing a threat to the safety and quality of life and the development prospects of sectors relying on these resources;

Source: Strategy for Responsible Development ..., pp. 19–23.

democracy or surrender to it (or make a radical revision of these rules – this, however, is very unlikely). It seems that the conflict around the introduction of tax on large-format stores is a perfect example of this phenomenon. Even the aforementioned Viktor Orbán, who expresses the will to follow the path of non-liberal (aliberal) democracy, was actually forced to resign from a few issues of key importance to him, although he appears to be much more assertive (again at least on the declarative level). As opposed to the Prime Minister of Hungary, the Law and Justice (PiS) government makes more or less successful attempts to maintain the balance in negotiations with European institutions by referring constantly to compliance with values and rules of liberal democracy. An example of this attitude is the elaboration of the White Book on changes in the Polish justice system, where their similarity to the liberal world order is proved. Anyway, the message of the campaign of the Law and Justice (PiS) before the elections for the European Parliament in 2019 seems to strengthen the illusory belief in the analogousness of the rules of openness and sovereignty and (monitored) liberal democracy. Although the adoption of such a perspective may be justified for tactical reasons, it can be criticised not only for its lack of cohesion, but primarily for the lack of visible results. Further proceedings before the EU's Court of Justice, concluded with decisions implemented ultimately by the Polish government, will probably increase the social legitimacy not only of the narration of the supporters of monitored democracy, but mainly the supporters of Poland's exit from the EU.

The same goes for the migrant policy being pursued by the PiS government – being fiercely opposed to the refugee relocation mechanism and conducting actions aimed at opening the Polish labour market to foreigners at the same time will have similar consequences. It is worth noting, however, that this problem is caused by the complexity of this phenomenon rather than the lack of awareness of the challenges of modern times among political decision-makers – the content of the SRD proves, in a sense, that the level of this awareness is quite high. Similar difficulties are faced by governments of other countries; until now, no convincing solutions have been presented that would offer a chance to "overcome" Rodrik's dilemma. In other words, the entire Western world is looking for an answer to the question considered in the first part of this chapter: how to lead liberal democracy out of the crisis, how to save the liberal global order and is this possible at all? This problem is particularly important from the perspective of middle-sized countries such as Poland, which have no direct impact on the shape of the international order and on the rules/values on which the dominant political system is based.

Conclusions for public policy in Poland

The following conclusions constitute a summary of reflections contained in this chapter and should not be treated as conclusions resulting from all texts included in this volume. For the clarity of reasoning, the conclusions will be presented in items in a synthetic manner.

1) For a vast number of reasons, liberal democracy that has assumed the form of monitored democracy is undergoing a deep crisis that has weakened it to a considerable degree. The weakness of liberal democracy that is deepening as a result of progressive economic globalisation and technological revolution processes will result in the reduction of Rodrik's trilemma ("openness – sovereignty – liberal democracy") to the dilemma between the openness policy ("globalism") and the sovereignty policy ("localism"). Irrespective of whether we deal with the choice of globalistic or localistic policy, liberal democracy will be the victim of the dialectic dispute between these two visions.
2) In spite of having regained causal power, e.g., due to their active policy in the post-crisis era, national states have not regained the real competitive edge over other internationally active non-state entities in the last few years. Moreover, the foreign policy of states, regardless of their size/potential, is gradually becoming a hostage of internal policy, thus making it more difficult for these states to fulfil their *raison d'etat*. At the same time, the vision of creating the global government or any other form of global public management with general legitimacy seems very unlikely contrary to earlier opinions.
3) In the next few years, in view of the relative weakening of the national state and the lack of possibility of transferring political power to the global level, we should expect an increase of anarchy in international relations, which may (but does not have to) lead to the formation of a new hierarchy in the form of a new international order. Consequently, in spite of the growing importance of the dispute between the USA and China for international relations, the new order does not have to be caused directly by the resolution of the conflict between Washington and Beijing due to the multitude of entities and interactions occurring between them. At the same time, the emergence of the new order may be accompanied by turbulent events (wars, revolutions). However, it is worth stressing that the currently functioning international order does not guarantee global peace and is not fully liberal – it bears some similarity to the dependence model (centre vs. peripheries).
4) The evolutionary overcoming of the crisis of liberal democracy and the rescuing of the liberal international order seems to be possible through the introduction of the rules of network neo-mediaevalism, which would mean, e.g., the restriction of the number of areas being the focus of interest of monitored democracy and, at the same time, the determination of boundary conditions of functioning of individual entities in international space. Such a solution could also help weaken the rising internal tensions that are present in many contemporary states, even though, as in the case of creation of the global government, the choice of such a model still seems unlikely.

5) The development potential of middle-sized states that cannot fulfil the role of hegemonic powers/concert powers is determined not only by the model of international order itself, but also by its broadly understood structure. As a result of this, we cannot determine clearly which model of hierarchy is definitely better – its optimality is largely dependent on the broader political, economic and social context.[28]
6) Middle-sized states, such as Poland, have a very limited possibility of influencing the rules/values of liberal democracy and the structure of the international order,[29] which forces them to use even more adequate agile management that is able to respond to changes of the international environment that are beyond their control. One of the proofs showing the relative weakness of this influence are de facto Poland's unsuccessful efforts to reinforce the liberal international order and the rule of sovereign equality that have been undertaken on the forum of the UN Security Council within Poland's two-year term of office in this body since January 2018. This also means that conclusions arising from the Crisis of the West are essentially insignificant for public policy in Poland because the scope of significant political choices made by Polish decision-makers is actually strongly limited. Importantly, this limitation is caused both by the character of monitored democracy that has prevailed in the last several years and by the circumstances of the globalisation process. This remark is important particularly with regard to the growing tension of the political dispute in our country.
7) Labelled as 'good change policy', Polish policy after 2015 is characterised by moving between the "sovereignty" narration and "openness" actions. However, the strive for larger sovereignty – in other words, assertiveness on the international arena – must sooner or later lead to a conflict with entities representing the logic of monitored democracy. The resolution of this conflict will depend not only on actions to be undertaken by both parties or on

---

28 In this context, very interesting observations are made by Bartłomiej Sienkiewicz (in his interview to Krzysztof Mazur https://klubjagiellonski.pl/2018/06/15/sienkiewicz-nasi-przodkowie-skazali-polske-na-peryferyjnosc/ and Maciej Grodzicki in his interview to Grzegorz Sroczyński (http://next.gazeta.pl/next/7,151003,24652456,czy-polska-przetrwa-kolejna-fale-globalizacji-nadchodzi-szok.html) [access date: 04.05.2019].

29 The speech delivered by Donald Tusk at the University of Warsaw on 3 May 2019 can also be regarded as proof of this lack of influence: https://oko.press/pelny-tekst-tusk-nie-dajcie-sobie-wmowic-ze-mamy-myslec-w-sposob-jednakowy-ze-mamy-nie-przeszkadzac-i-popierac/).

a specific context, but also on the general condition of the national state and monitored democracy.

8) In light of the Crisis of the West, the emergence of a new order and, at the same time, the lack of real impact on the course of processes taking place in the international environment, the main task of every Polish government is to conduct policy in such a way that it would be possible to make flexible turns while benefiting from the advantages of the current international order. The problem is, however, that combining the "openness" narrative with "sovereign" policy may prove very difficult or even impossible in practice – both because of external (objection from international institutions) and internal limitations (objections from new political identity movements). At the same time, in the author's opinion, there is no need to revise the Strategy for Responsible Development. The suggested solution would rather be to resign from actions limiting room for manoeuvre for public policy in the future. This remark refers both to foreign policy (e.g., the excessively strong pro-American option in foreign policy) and to internal policy (e.g., the extension of the Family 500+ program).

References

Barber, B. (1997): *Dżihad kontra McŚwiat*, Warsaw: Wydawnictwo Literackie MUZA SA.

Bull, H. (1977): *The Anarchical Society. A Study of Order in World Politics*, New York: Columbia University Press, New York.

Grosse, T.G. (2016): Podsumowanie. W kierunku teorii dezintegracjii regionalnej, in: T.G. Grosse (ed.), *Polityki europejskie w dobie kryzysu*, Warsaw: Wydawnictwo Naukowe Scholar.

Karas, H. (2010): *The Emerging Middle Class in Developing Countries*, The Brookings Institution 2010, https://www.oecd.org/development/pgd/44798225.pdf [access date: 01.05.2019].

Kuź, M. (2015): Globaliści vs. lokaliści, *Nowa Konfederacja*, 3 (57)/2015, https://nowakonfederacja.pl/globalisci-vs-lokalisci/ [access date: 01.05.2019].

Lewicki, G. (2010): *Sieciowa teoria nowego średniowiecza*, in: Kraków: „Pressje" teka 20.

Lewicki, G. (2017): *Unia Europejska jak Cesarstwo Rzymskie. Nadchodzi nowe średniowiecze*, https://klubjagiellonski.pl/2017/11/04/unia-europejska-jak-cesarstwo-rzymskie-nadchodzi-nowe-sredniowiecze/ [access date: 01.05.2019].

Mazur, K. (2018): *Nasi przodkowie skazali nas na peryferyjność*, wywiad z Bartłomiejem Sienkiewiczem, https://klubjagiellonski.pl/2018/06/15/sienkiewicz-nasi-przodkowie-skazali-polske-na-peryferyjnosc/ [access date: 04.05.2019].

Milanovic, B. (2012): *Global Income Inequality by the Numbers: in History and Now. An Overview*, Policy Research working paper; no. WPS 6259, World Bank, Washington DC, http://documents.worldbank.org/curated/en/959251468176687085/pdf/wps6259.pdf [access date: 01.05.2019].

Piątkowski, M. (2013): *Poland's New Golden Age: Shifting from Europe's Periphery to Its Center*, Policy Research working paper; no. WPS 6639. World Bank, Washington DC, http://documents.worldbank.org/curated/en/285611468107064618/Polands-new-golden-age-shifting-from-Europes-periphery-to-its-center [access date: 01.05.2019].

Piketty, T. (2015): *Kapitał w XXI wieku*, Warsaw: Wydawnictwo Krytyki Politycznej.

Rodrik, D. (2011): *Jedna ekonomia – wiele recept. Globalizacja, instytucje i wzrost gospodarczy*, Warsaw: Wydawnictwo Krytyki Politycznej.

Sroczyński, G. (2019): *Czy Polska przetrwa kolejną falę globalizacji?*, interview to Maciej Grodzicki http://next.gazeta.pl/next/7,151003,24652456,czy-polska-przetrwa-kolejna-fale-globalizacji-nadchodzi-szok.html [access date: 04.05.2019].

Strategia na rzecz Odpowiedzialnego Rozwoju, Warsaw: Ministerstwo Rozwoju, 2017.

Tusk, D. (2019): *Nadzieja i odpowiedzialność. O konstytucji, Europie i wolnych wyborach*, Wystąpienie przewodniczącego Rady Europejskiej Donalda Tuska na Uniwersytecie Warszawskim w rocznicę Konstytucji 3 maja, https://oko.press/pelny-tekst-tusk-nie-dajcie-sobie-wmowic-ze-mamy-myslec-w-sposob-jednakowy-ze-mamy-nie-przeszkadzac-i-popierac/ [access date: 04.05.2019].

Węc, J.J. (2011): *Traktat lizboński. Polityczne aspekty reformy ustrojowej Unii Europejskiej w latach 2007–2009*, Kraków: Wydawnictwo Znak.

Zielonka, J. (2008): *Europa jako imperium*, Warsaw: Polski Instytut Spraw Międzynarodowych.

Biographical notes

Marek Cichocki
Research director of the Natolin European Centre and editor-in-chief of the periodical "New Europe. Natolin Review". Professor at the Collegium Civitas. Former advisor to the President of the Republic of Poland in the field of the Constitutional Treaty and Sherpa for the negotiations of the Lisbon Treaty. He specialises in the subject of German affairs, European integration and history of political thought. Author of numerous publications on the above-mentioned topics.

Marcin Darmas
Doctor, sociologist, journalist. Assistant professor at the Institute of Sociology University of Warsaw. He collaborates with Political Theology, the Znak monthly and Fronda LUX. Author of books: "Jarzmo wielkości Francji" (2017) and "Obywatel rycerz. Zarys socjologii filmu" (2014) and publications about France.

Ryszarda Formuszewicz
A graduate of law at Adam Mickiewicz University in Poznań and comparative law at University of Bonn, Germany. Currently Senior Fellow at the Centre for Eastern Studies in Warsaw (Department for Germany and Northern Europe). She worked at Institute for Western Affairs (1999–2009), Polish Institute of International Affairs (2009–2014) and National Security Bureau (Department of Strategic Analyses). In 2016–2017 she was a delegated project coordinator for Genshagen Foundation. Her areas of expertise include Germany's foreign and EU policies.

Tomasz Grzegorz Grosse
Sociologist, political scientist and historian. He is a professor at the University of Warsaw. He specialises in the analysis of economic policies in the EU and the Member States, as well as in public management, geo-economics, Europeanisation, EU theoretical thoughts. He recently published: "Post-crises Europe" (The Polish Institute of International Affairs) "Searching geo-economics in Europe" (Polish Academy of Science, 2014) and edited: "European Union Policies at the Time of Crisis" (Scholar 2016).

Marcin Kędzierski
Economist, graduate of international relations at the University of Economics in Krakow and doctoral studies at the Department of Public Economy and Public

Administration UEK, collaborator of the Tertio Millennio Institute (2008–2009), since 2011 an assistant at the Department of European Studies at UEK, currently an adjunct there. In the years 2009–2012, he was a member of the Management Board for financial matters, and in the period 2012–2015 he was the President of the Jagiellonian Club.

Olaf Osica

Manager of the think-tank sector, advisor and consultant of companies and public institutions in the field of international policy analysis. In 2011–2015 the director and currently chairman of the Board of the Center for Eastern Studies in Warsaw. Doctor of social and political sciences of the European University Institute in Florence. He was awarded a scholarship of the US Department of State, the Ministry of Foreign Affairs of France and GFPS-Poland.

Daniel Tilles

Assistant professor of history at the Pedagogical University of Krakow and editor-in-chief of *Notes from Poland*, an English-language news service. He completed his doctorate at Royal Holloway, University of London and his research focuses on political extremism (especially fascism and the far right), migration and Jewish history. His most recent book is *British Fascism Antisemitism and Jewish Responses, 1932–40* (Bloomsbury, 2015). As a commentator on current affairs he has written for, among others, *Foreign Policy, Politico Europe* and *Haaretz.*

Artur Wołek

Professor of administration and public policies at the Jesuit University Ignatianum in Krakow, associate of the Center for Political Thought in Krakow, previously worked at the Institute of Political Studies of the Polish Academy of Sciences and the Warsaw School of Economics. He co-founded the Faculty of Political Studies at WSB-NLU in Nowy Sącz and served as dean there. He was a visiting lecturer in Bratislava, Riga and Olomouc, among others. He specialises in the issues of constitutionalism and public management, particularly in Central Europe. In the 1990s he cooperated with Michał Kulesza in the 1998 local government reform. He was the director of the Windsor Group Foundation, the speech-writer of the President of Krakow and the editor of the "Conservative Quarterly".

List of Figures

List of Tables

Studies in European Integration, State and Society

Edited by Magdalena Góra, Zdzisław Mach and Katarzyna Zielińska

Vol. 1 Józef Niżnik: Democracy versus Solidarity in the EU Discourse. 2012.

Vol. 2 Grzegorz Żuk: Europe in Polish Public Discourse. 2013.

Vol. 3 Zdzisław Mach (ed.): Local Community, Power and European Integration. 2017.

Vol. 4 Janusz Węc: Germany's Position on the System Reform of the European Union in 2002–2016. 2018.

Vol. 5 Krzysztof Kowalski / Łucja Piekarska-Duraj / Barbara Törnquist-Plewa (eds.): Narrating Otherness in Poland and Sweden. European Heritage as a Discourse of Inclusion and Exclusion. 2019.

Vol. 6 Marek Aleksander Cichocki / Tomasz Grzegorz Grosse (eds.): The Many Faces of Crisis. An Analysis of Crisis Management from an Economic and Political Perspective. 2019.

Vol. 7 Marek Aleksander Cichocki (ed.): Contemporary States and the Crisis of the Western Order. 2020.

www.peterlang.com

www.ingramcontent.com/pod-product-compliance
Ingram Content Group UK Ltd.
Pitfield, Milton Keynes, MK11 3LW, UK
UKHW041825100926
8556IPUK00002B/32